TOKYO GHOUL:re

東京喰種

6

SUI ISHIDA

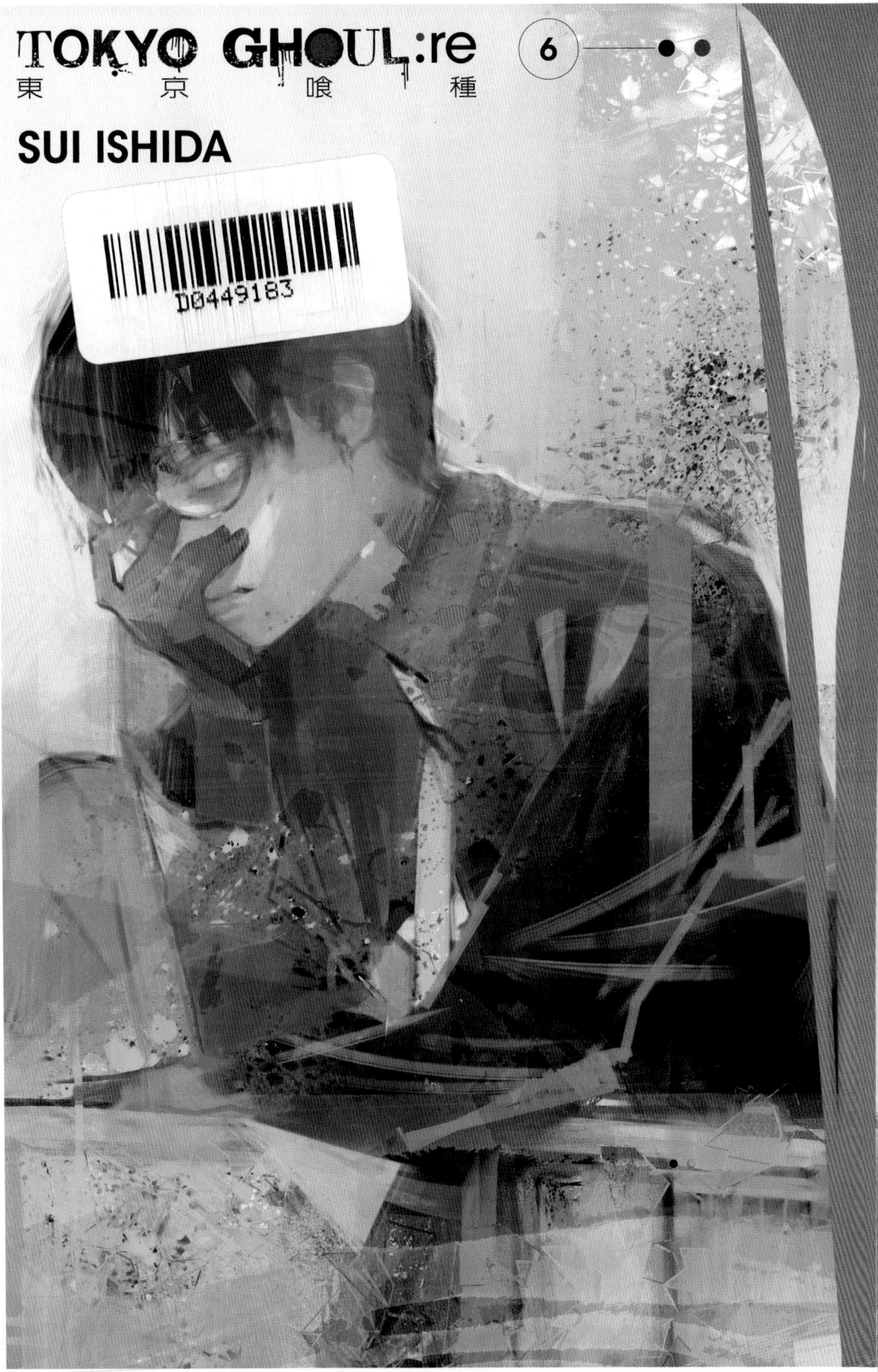

TOKYO GHOUL:re 6

東 京 喰 種

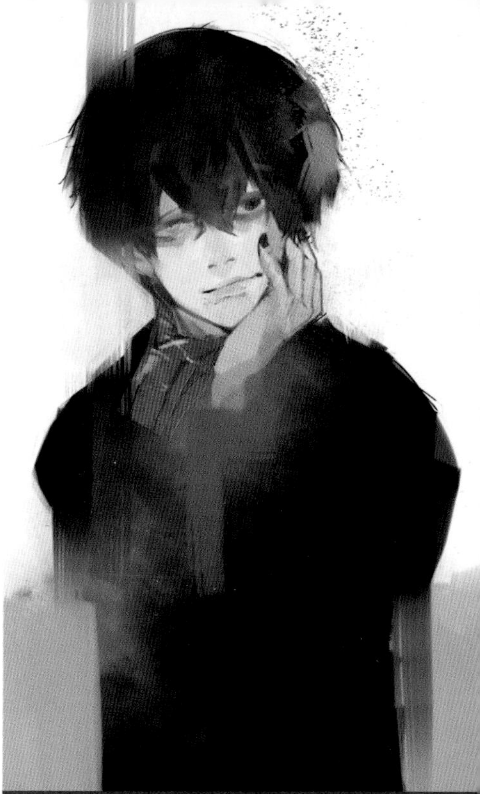

CONTENTS

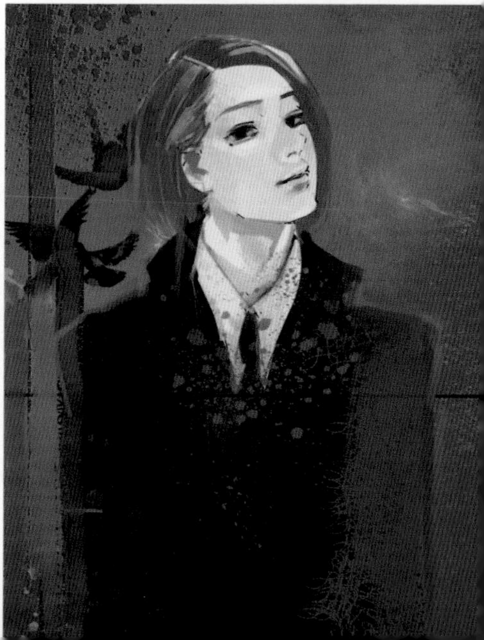

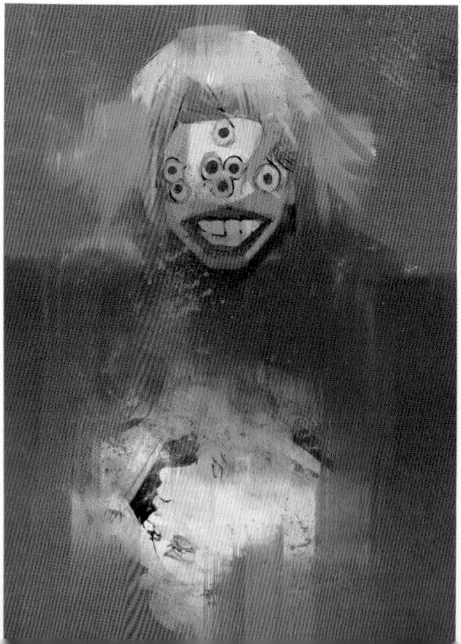

CCG Ghoul Investigators

Tokyo Ghoul :re

The CCG is the only organization in the world that investigates and solves Ghoul-related crimes. Founded by the Washu Family, the CCG developed and evolved Quinques, a type of weapon derived from Ghouls' Kagune. Quinx, an advanced, next-generation technology where humans are implanted with Quinques, is currently under development.

Mado Squad

Qs (Quinx) Investigators implanted with Quinques. They all live together in a house called the **Chateau** along with Investigator Sasaki.

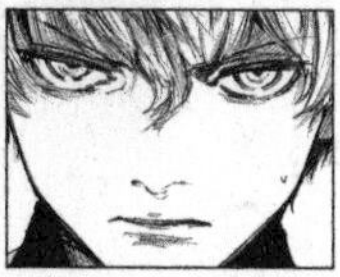

● Haise Sasaki
佐々木琲世
Rank 1 Investigator
Mentor to the Quinx Squad. Despite being half-Ghoul, he is passionate about guiding the Quinxes. He has no memory of his past. And whose voice sometimes echoes in his head...?!

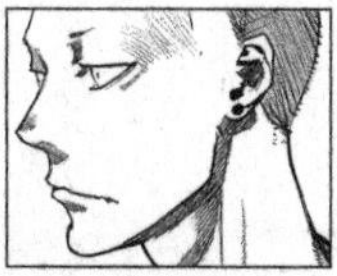

● Ginshi Shirazu
不知吟士
Rank 2 Investigator
Current Quinx Squad Leader. Agreed to the Quinx procedure for mainly financial reasons. Despite his thuggish appearance, he has a very caring side. Struggling to use his Quinque.

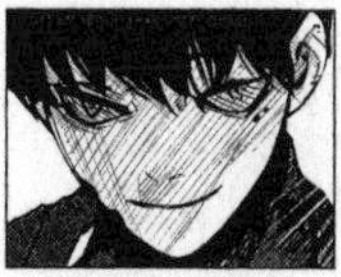

● Kuki Urie
瓜江久生
Rank 1 Investigator
Former Quinx Squad Leader. The squad's most talented fighter. His special investigator father was killed by a Ghoul and Urie seeks to avenge him. Has a strong rivalry towards Takeomi Kuroiwa.

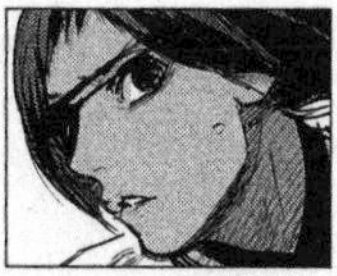

● Toru Mutsuki
六月 透
Rank 1 Investigator
Both his parents were killed by a Ghoul. Assigned female at birth, he transitioned after undergoing the Quinx procedure. Promoted for his actions during Operation Auction Sweep.

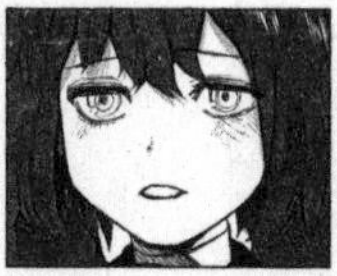

● Saiko Yonebayashi
米林才子
Rank 2 Investigator
Little aptitude as an investigator, but was by far the most suitable candidate for the Quinx Procedure. She is very bad at time management. A sucker for games and snacks. Self-proclaimed "fairy of the Chateau."

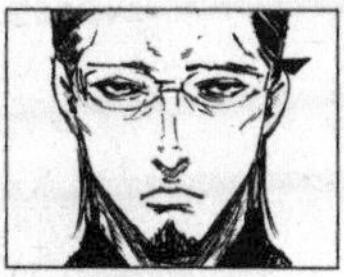

● Matsuri Washu
和修 政
Special Investitgator
Yoshitoki's son. A Washu supremacist and skeptical of the Quinxes. Brought down the Rosewald family in Germany.

S1 Squad

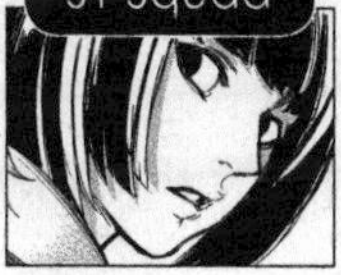

● Kori Ui
宇井 郡
Special Investigator
Promising investigator formerly with Arima Squad. Became a special investigator at a young age, but has a stubborn side. Considers Haise a threat.

Fura Squad

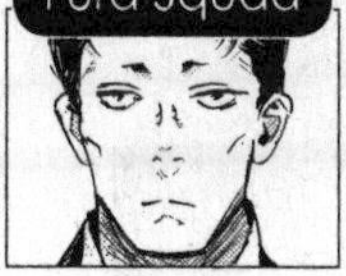

● Taishi Fura
富良太志
Senior Investigator
A veteran investigator who has known Ui for a long time. Disappointed with how smokers are treated. A loving husband.

Kijima Squad

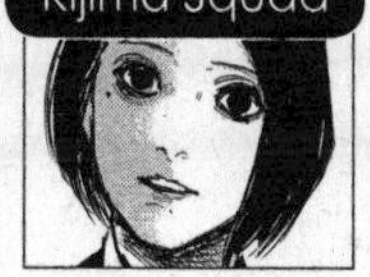

● Nimura Furuta
旧多二福
Rank 1 Investigator
Shiki Kijima's direct subordinate. A mysterious investigator whose true nature becomes clear after Kijima's death.

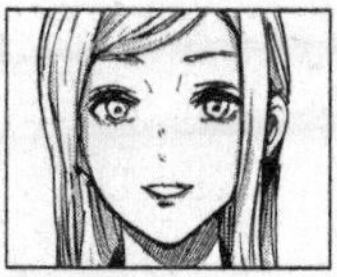

● Akira Mado
真戸 暁
Assistant Special Investigator
Mentors Haise. Takes after her father. Determined to eradicate Ghouls. Investigating the Aogiri Tree. Concerned about Fueguchi.

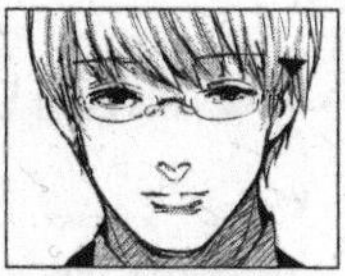

● Kisho Arima
有馬貴将
Special Investigator
An undefeated investigator respected by many at the CCG.

Ito Squad

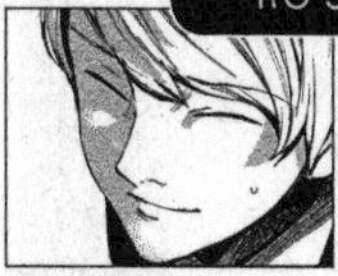

● Kuramoto Ito
伊東倉元
Senior Investigator
Took over as the leader of Hirako Squad. In high spirits, but feeling the pressure.

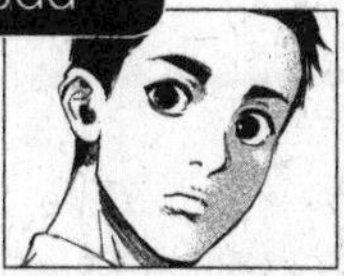

● Takeomi Kuroiwa
黒磐武臣
Rank 1 Investigator
The son of Special Investigator Iwao Kuroiwa. Has restrained Ghouls with his bare hands.

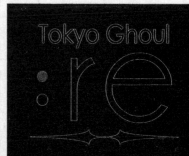

Tokyo Ghoul :re

T ● K Y ● G H ● U L

Tokyo Ghoul :re

Ghouls

They appear human, but have a unique predation organ called Kagune and can only survive by feeding on human flesh. They are the nemesis of humanity. Besides human flesh, the only other thing they can ingest is coffee. Ghouls can only be wounded by a Kagune or a Quinque made from a Kagune. One of the most prominent Ghoul factions is the Aogiri Tree, a hostile organization that is increasing its strength.

Rosewald Family Faction

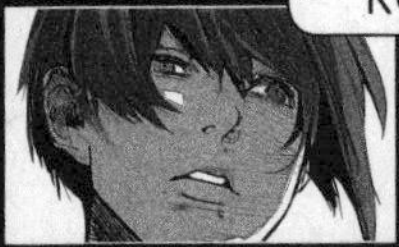

Shu Tsukiyama
月山 習

Seeks the gourmet. He has fed poorly since the disappearance of Ken Kaneki, but he begins taking action after seeing Ken's shadow in Haise.

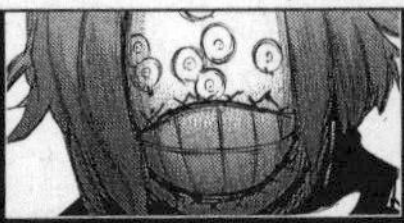

Kanae von Rosewald
カナエ=フォン・ロゼヴァルト

Tsukiyama family retainer and the youngest Rosewald child. He now wears a mask after receiving a "bone" from Eto .

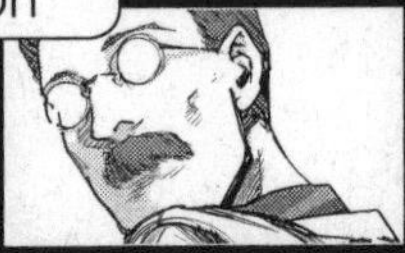

Mirumo Tsukiyama
月山観母

Shu's father and head of the Tsukiyama Family. Currently detained by the CCG.

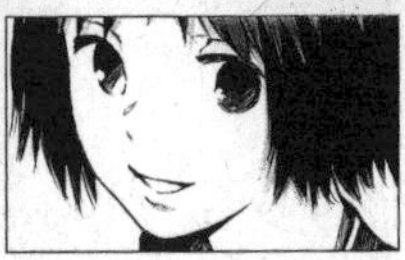

Chie Hori
掘 ちえ

A freelance photographer selling information. She interacts with the Tsukiyama family and provides useful information to Kanae, but...

Aogiri Tree

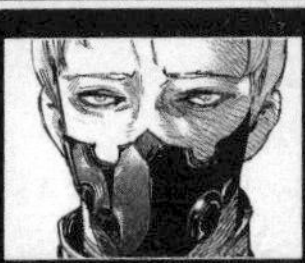

Tatara
タタラ

A leading member of the Aogiri Tree.

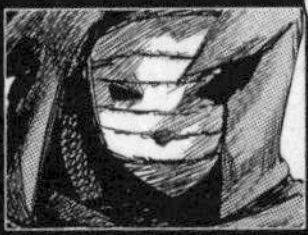

Eto
エト

Mysterious. A leading member of the Aogiri Tree. Recruits Kanae into the Aogiri Tree.

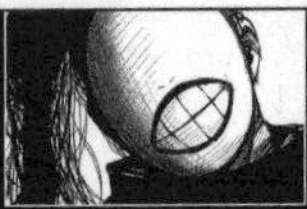

Noro
ノロ

Member of the Aogiri Tree. Rate SS with great regeneration abilities who has killed many investigators.

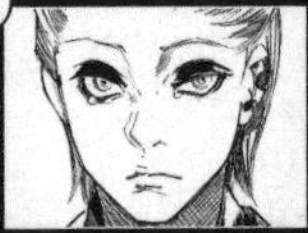

Naki
ナキ

Member of the Aogiri Tree. Rate S, but often loses control. Grieving Gaki and Guge.

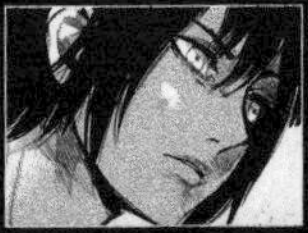

Ayato
アヤト

A leading member of the Aogiri Tree. A Rate SS Ghoul known as the Rabbit.

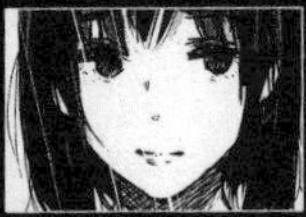

Hinami Fueguchi
フエグチヒナミ

Member of the Aogiri Tree. Captured during Operation Auction Sweep and sent to Cochlea. Awaiting disposal.

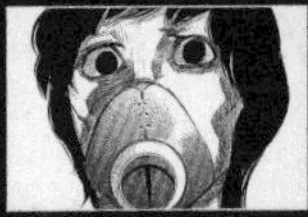

The Torso (Karao Saeki)
トルソー(冴木空男)

Rate A Ghoul. Abused his position as a taxi driver to prey on women with scars. Obsessed with Toru Mutsuki.

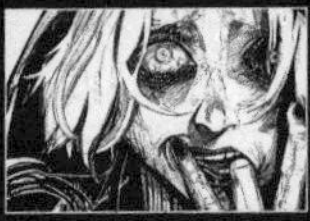

The Owl
オウル

The current incarnation of Investigator Seido Takizawa. Overwhelmingly powerful.

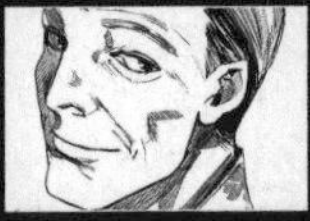

Professor Kano
嘉納教授

Aogiri Tree medical examiner. Researching transplanting Kakuho into humans to create artificial half-Ghouls.

Café.re

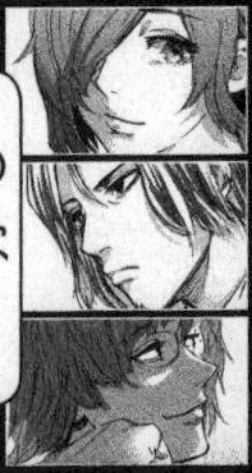

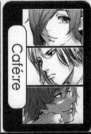

So far in :re

T ● K Y ● G H ● U L

The Quinx Project was implemented to develop investigators to surpass Kisho Arima in order to combat the growing strength of Ghoul organizations. The four Qs investigators and their mentor Haise Sasaki were promoted for their achievements during Operation Auction Sweep. Their current target is Rosé, but the voice in Haise's head has grown louder as the investigation progresses. Meanwhile, the Aogiri Tree crept up on Kanae while he was in relentless pursuit of Haise and the Qs. The resulting three-way battle at Lunatic Eclipse resulted in many casualties. Just as Haise was about to apprehend Shu Tsukiyama, the One-Eyed Owl suddenly appeared...

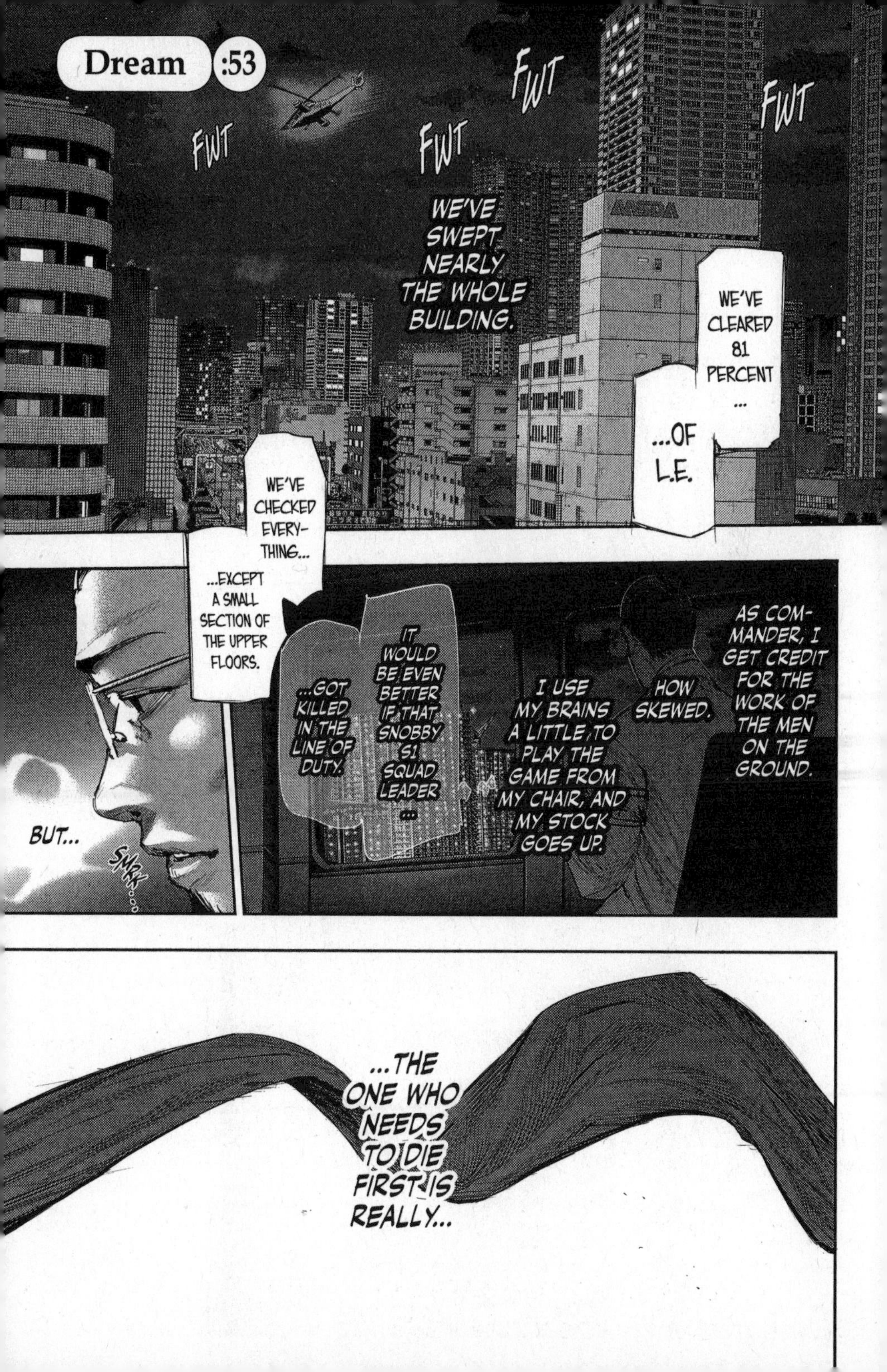
Dream :53
FWT
FWT
FWT
FWT
WE'VE CLEARED 81 PERCENT...
...OF L.E.
WE'VE SWEPT NEARLY THE WHOLE BUILDING.
WE'VE CHECKED EVERYTHING...
...EXCEPT A SMALL SECTION OF THE UPPER FLOORS.
AS COMMANDER, I GET CREDIT FOR THE WORK OF THE MEN ON THE GROUND.
HOW SKEWED.
I USE MY BRAINS A LITTLE TO PLAY THE GAME FROM MY CHAIR, AND MY STOCK GOES UP.
IT WOULD BE EVEN BETTER IF THAT SNOBBY S1 SQUAD LEADER...
...GOT KILLED IN THE LINE OF DUTY.
BUT...
SMRK...
...THE ONE WHO NEEDS TO DIE FIRST IS REALLY...

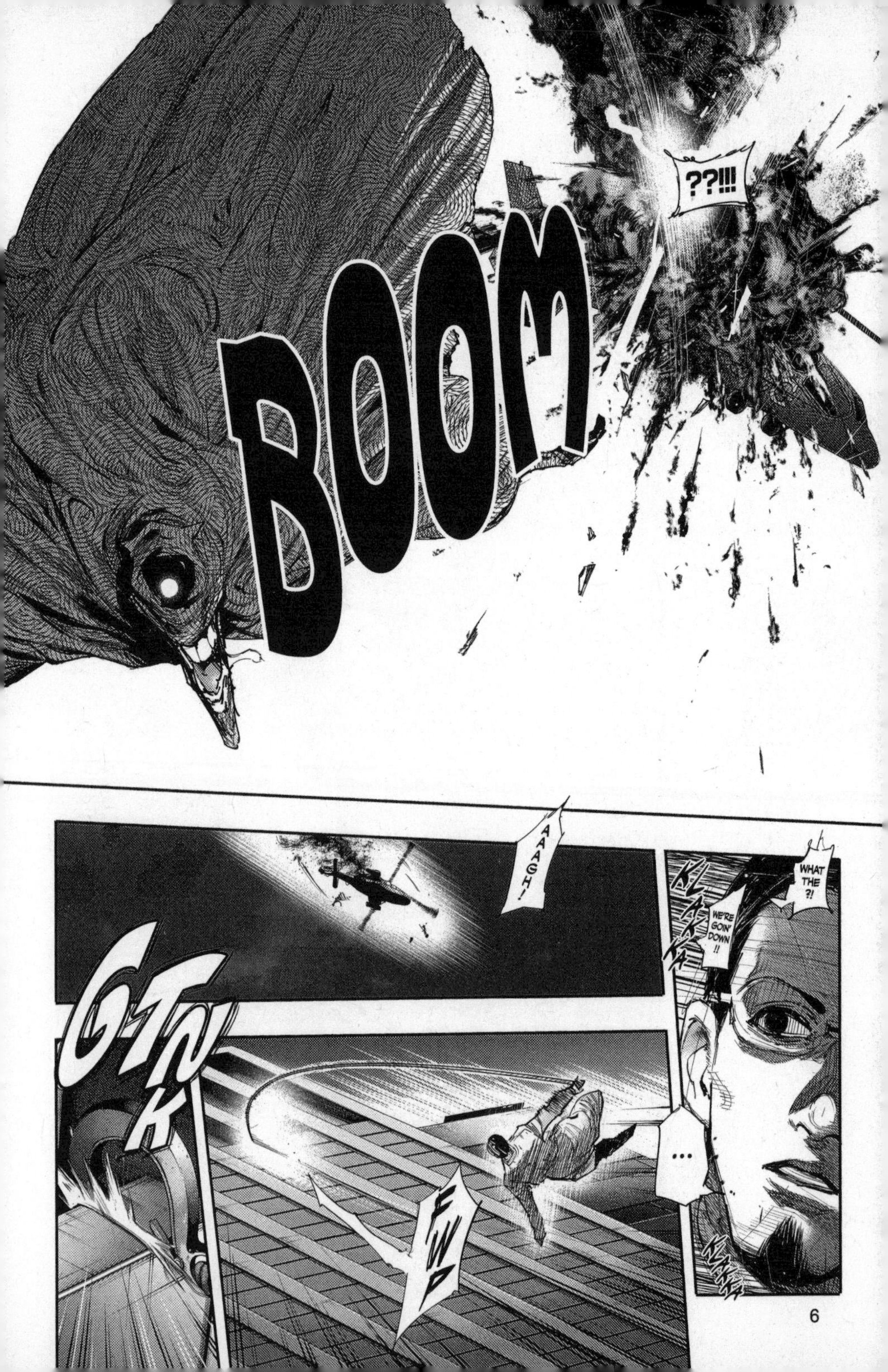

??!!!
BOOM
WHAT THE ?!
WE'RE GOIN' DOWN !!
KLAKAKA
...
KLAKAKA
AAAGH!
GTNK
FWP

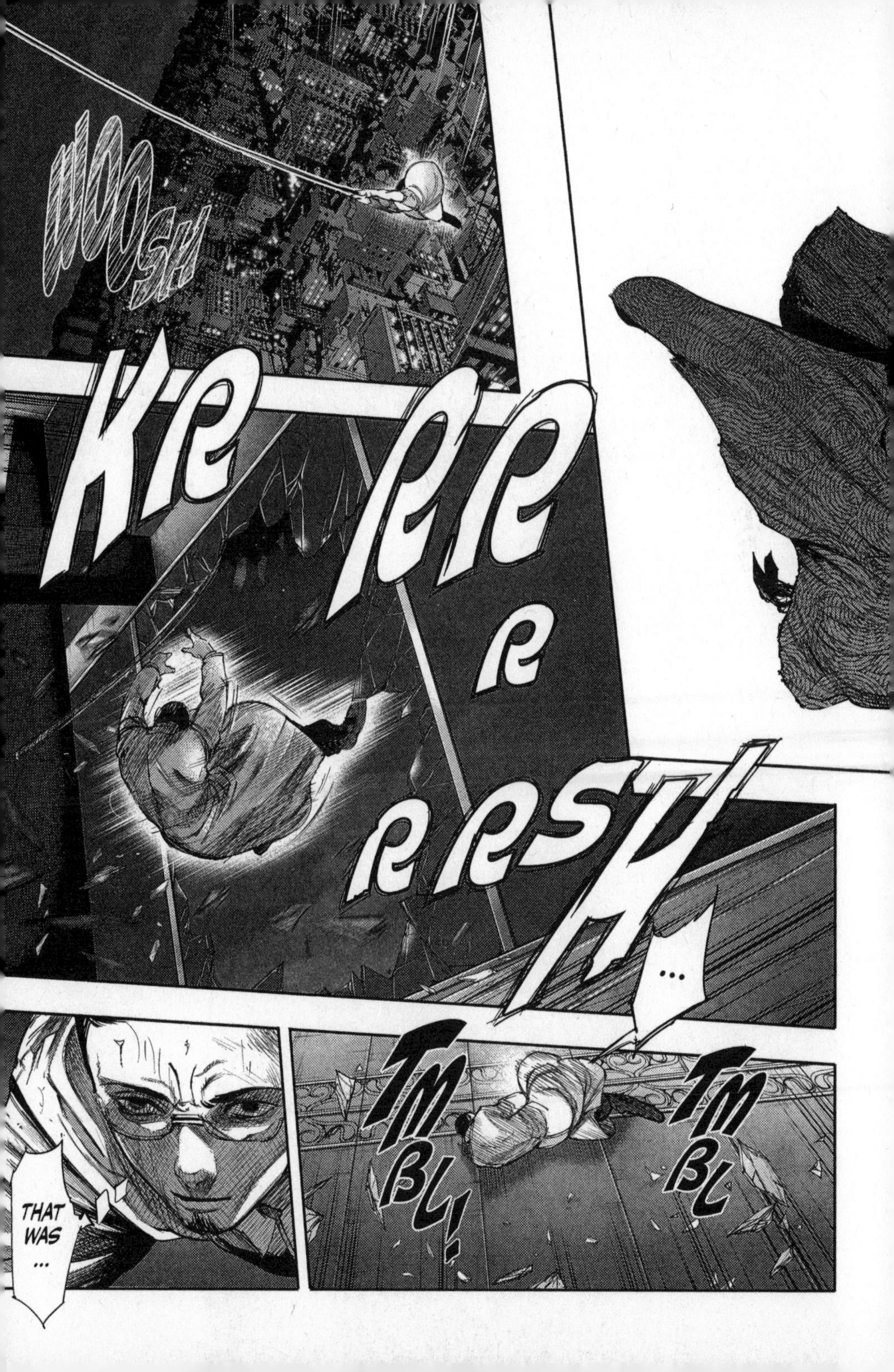
WHOOSH
KREEEEEESH
...
TMBL TMBL!
THAT WAS ...

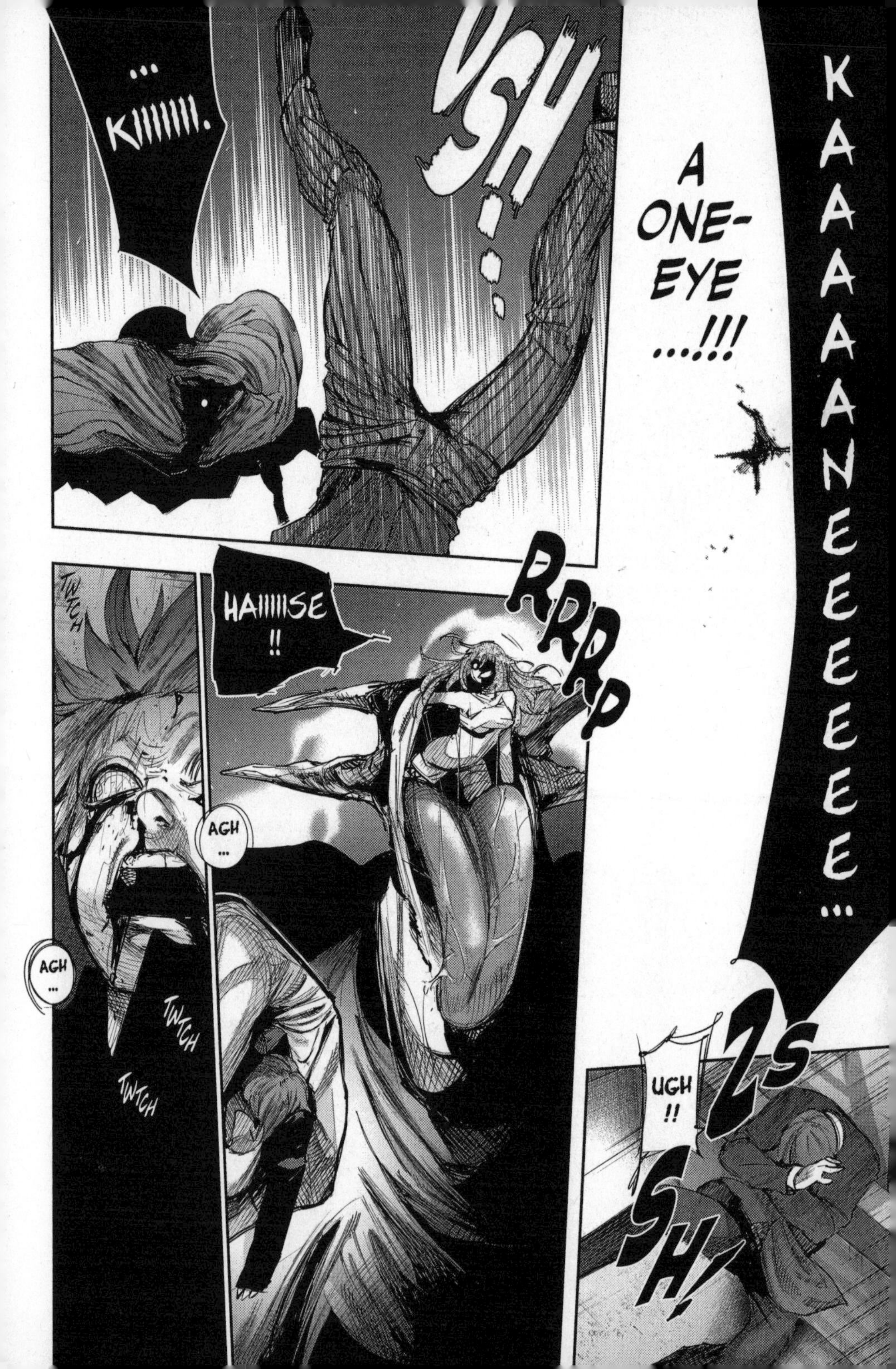
KAAAAANEEEEEE...
A ONE-EYE...!!!
VSH
...KIIIIIII.
UGH!!
ZSSH!
RRRP
HAIIIISE!!
AGH...
TWITCH
AGH...
TWITCH
TWITCH

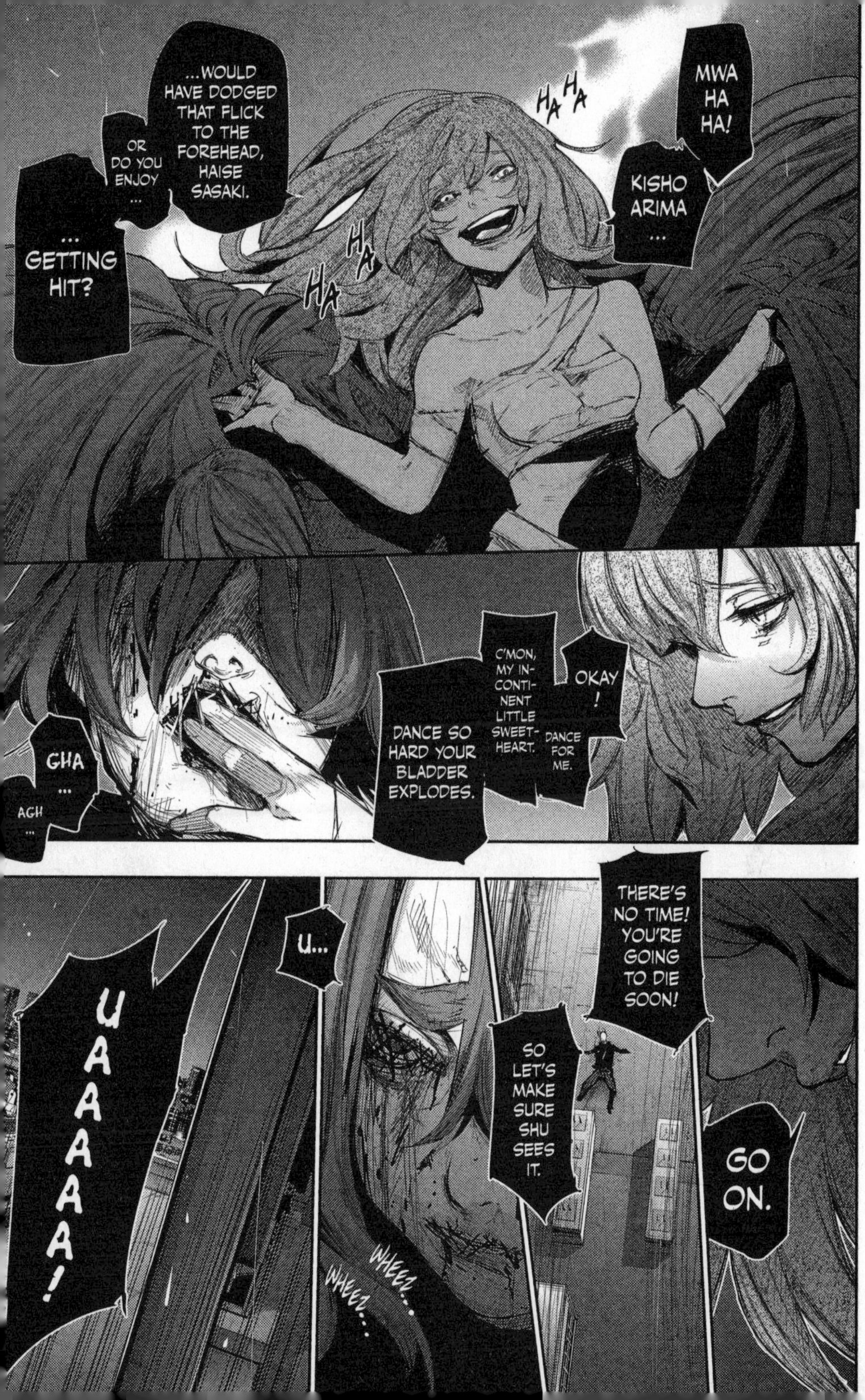
MWA HA HA!
KISHO ARIMA ...
HA HA
HA HA
...WOULD HAVE DODGED THAT FLICK TO THE FOREHEAD, HAISE SASAKI.
OR DO YOU ENJOY ...
... GETTING HIT?
OKAY!
DANCE FOR ME.
C'MON, MY IN-CONTINENT LITTLE SWEET-HEART.
DANCE SO HARD YOUR BLADDER EXPLODES.
GHA ...
AGH ...
THERE'S NO TIME! YOU'RE GOING TO DIE SOON!
SO LET'S MAKE SURE SHU SEES IT.
GO ON.
U...
WHEEZ...
WHEEZ...
UAAAAAA!

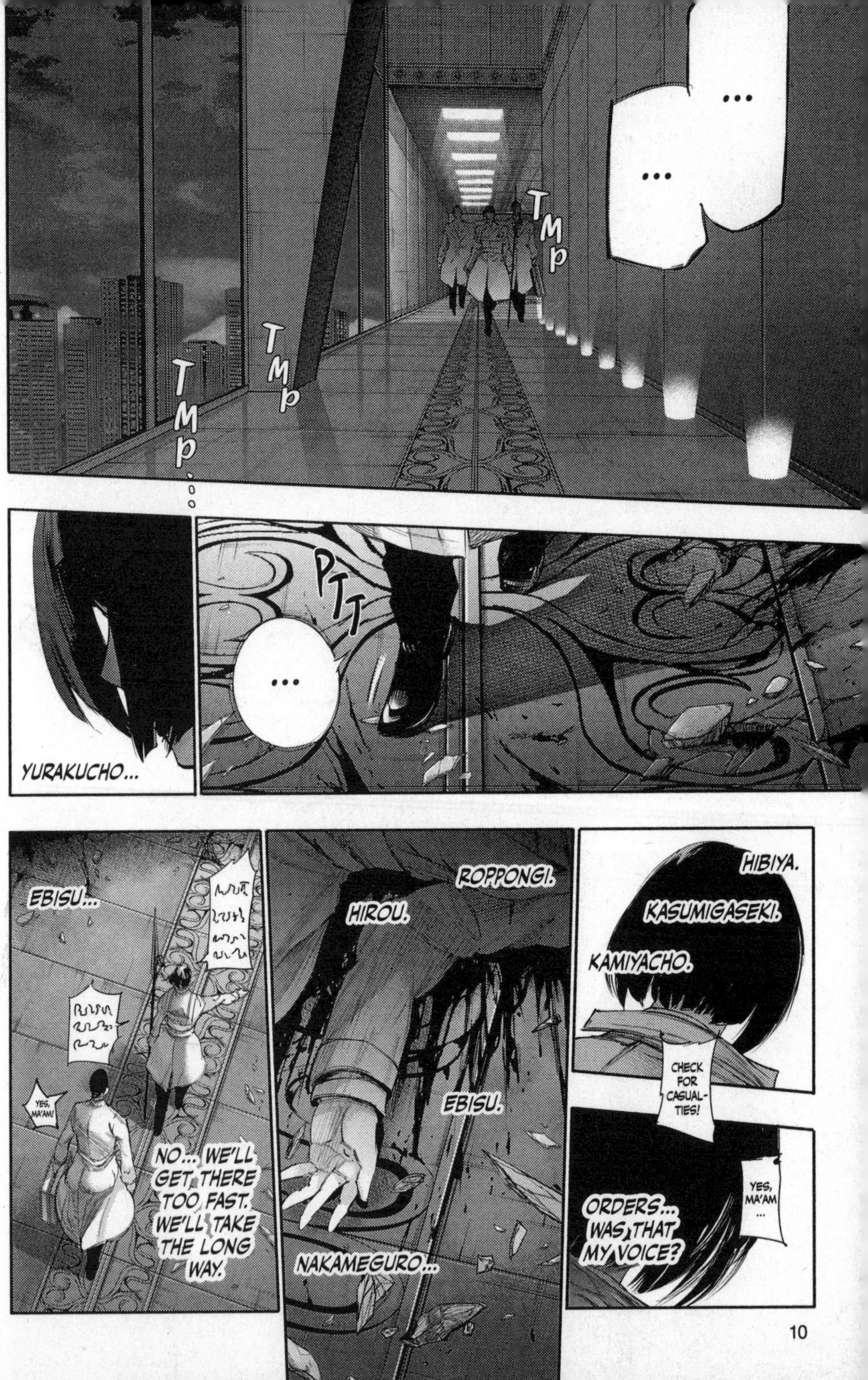
...
...
TMP
TMP
TMP...
PTT
...
YURAKUCHO...
HIBIYA.
KASUMIGASEKI.
KAMIYACHO.
CHECK FOR CASUALTIES!
YES, MA'AM...
ORDERS... WAS THAT MY VOICE?
ROPPONGI.
HIROU.
EBISU.
NAKAMEGURO...
EBISU...
YES, MA'AM!
NO... WE'LL GET THERE TOO FAST. WE'LL TAKE THE LONG WAY.

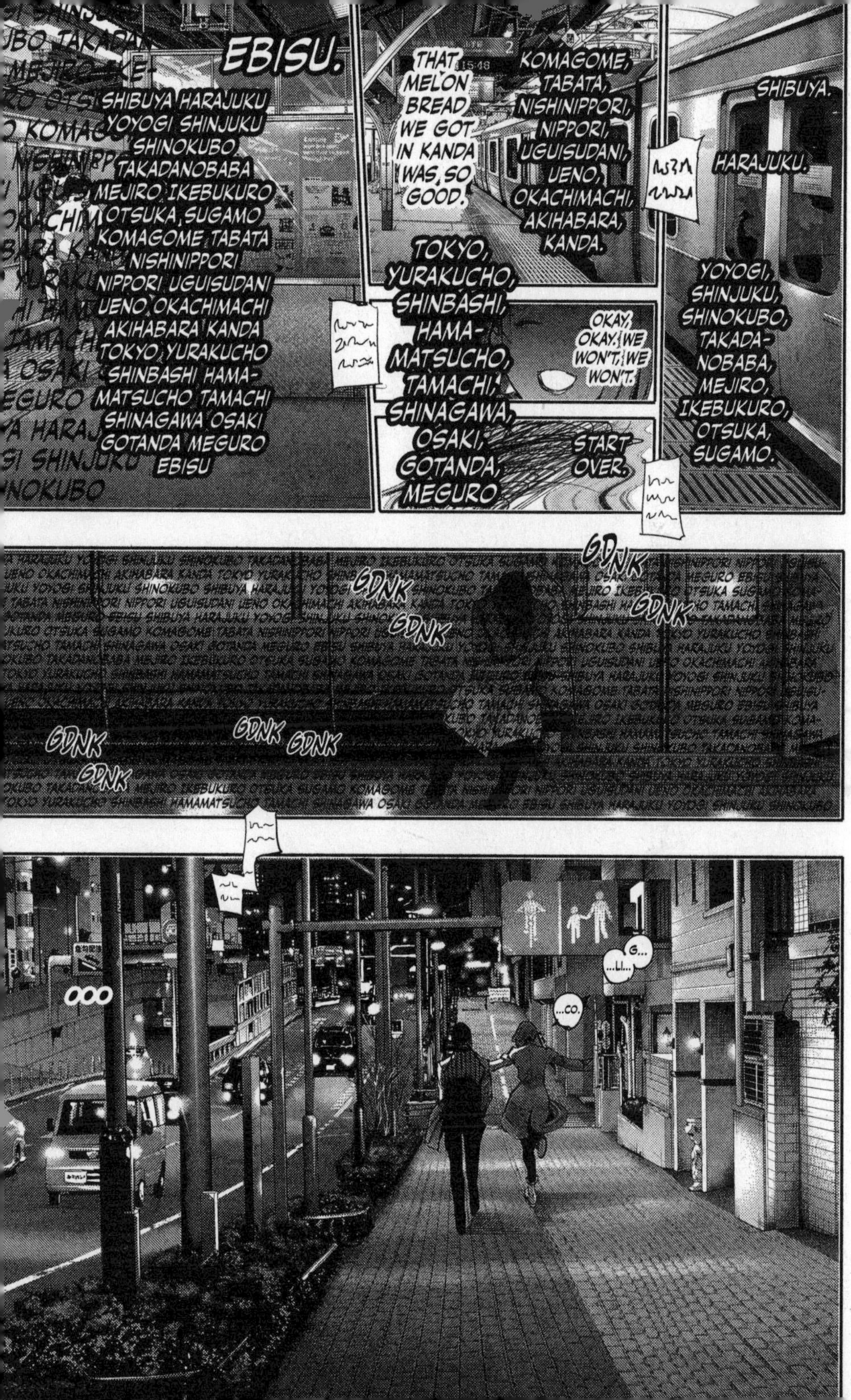
SHIBUYA.
HARAJUKU.
YOYOGI, SHINJUKU, SHINOKUBO, TAKADA-NOBABA, MEJIRO, IKEBUKURO, OTSUKA, SUGAMO.
KOMAGOME, TABATA, NISHINIPPORI, NIPPORI, UGUISUDANI, UENO, OKACHIMACHI, AKIHABARA, KANDA.
THAT MELON BREAD WE GOT IN KANDA WAS, SO GOOD.
TOKYO, YURAKUCHO, SHINBASHI, HAMA-MATSUCHO, TAMACHI, SHINAGAWA, OSAKI, GOTANDA, MEGURO
OKAY, OKAY. WE WON'T, WE WON'T.
START OVER.
EBISU.
SHIBUYA HARAJUKU YOYOGI SHINJUKU SHINOKUBO TAKADANOBABA MEJIRO IKEBUKURO OTSUKA, SUGAMO KOMAGOME TABATA NISHINIPPORI NIPPORI UGUISUDANI UENO OKACHIMACHI AKIHABARA KANDA TOKYO YURAKUCHO SHINBASHI HAMA-MATSUCHO TAMACHI SHINAGAWA OSAKI GOTANDA MEGURO EBISU
GDNK
GDNK
GDNK
GDNK
GDNK
GDNK
GDNK
GDNK
G...
...LI...
...CO.
OOO

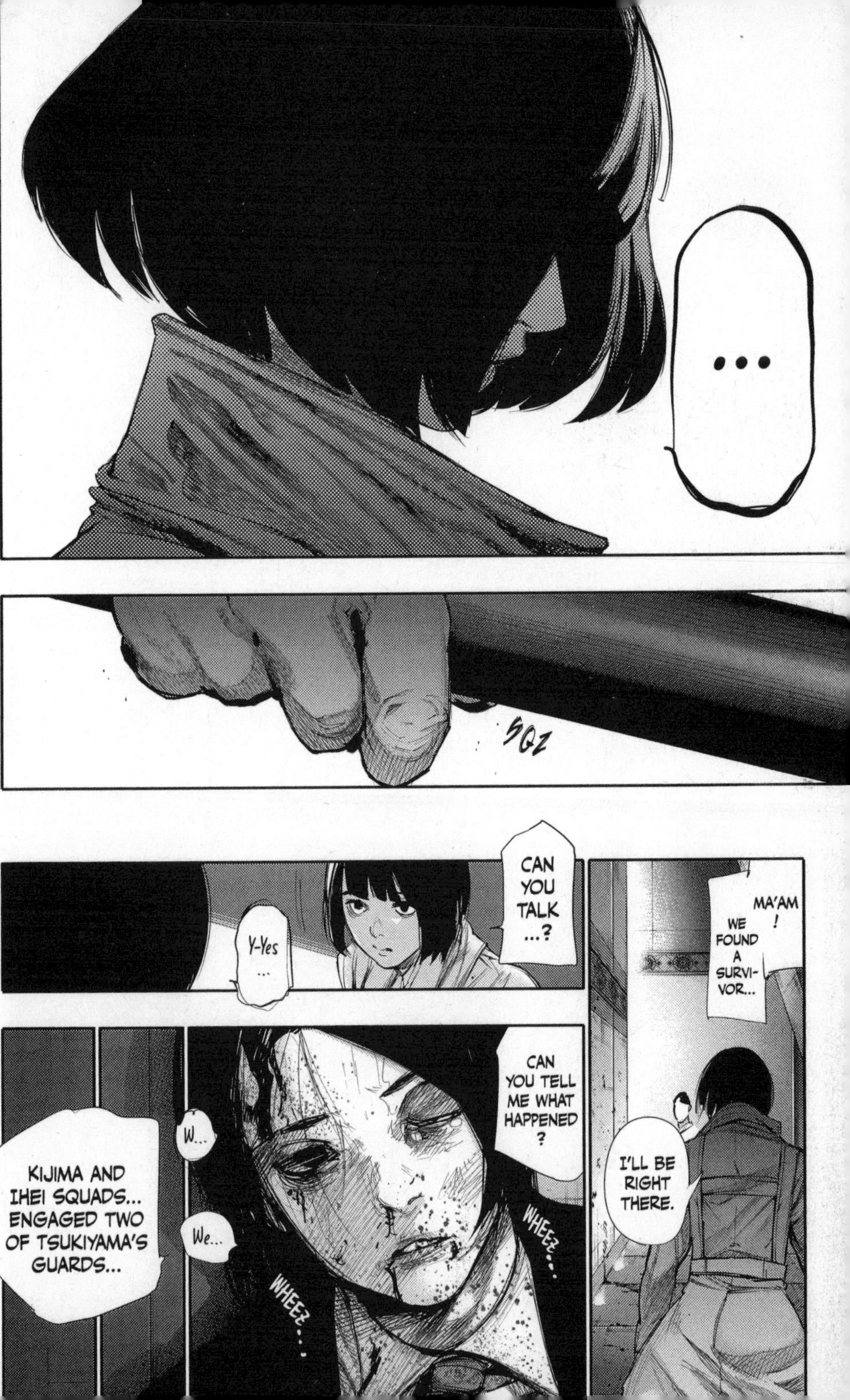
...
SQZ
MA'AM! WE FOUND A SURVIVOR...
I'LL BE RIGHT THERE.
CAN YOU TALK ...?
Y-Yes ...
CAN YOU TELL ME WHAT HAPPENED?
W...
WHEEZ...
We...
WHEEZ...
KIJIMA AND IHEI SQUADS... ENGAGED TWO OF TSUKIYAMA'S GUARDS...

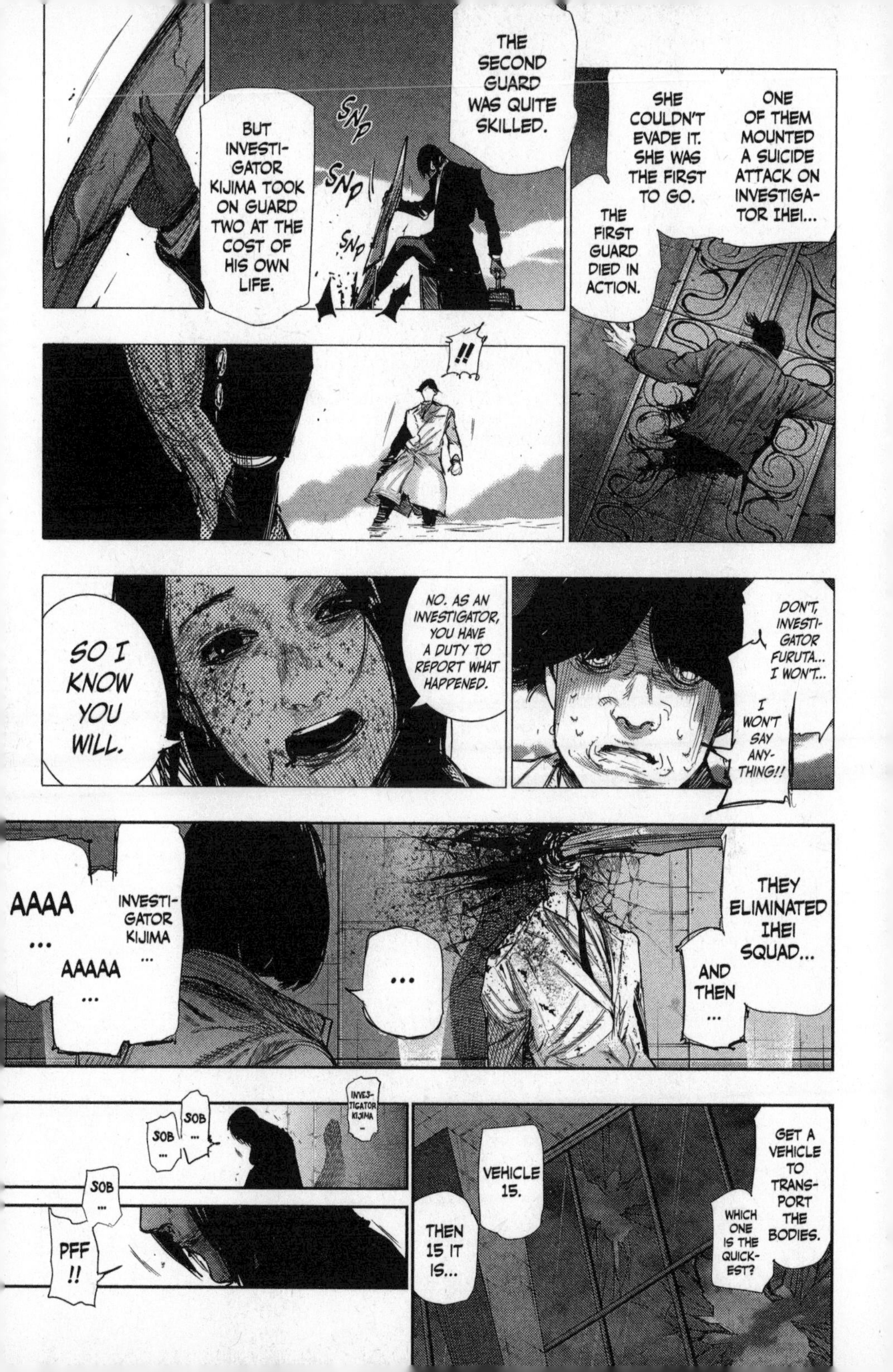
ONE OF THEM MOUNTED A SUICIDE ATTACK ON INVESTIGATOR IHEI...
SHE COULDN'T EVADE IT. SHE WAS THE FIRST TO GO.
THE FIRST GUARD DIED IN ACTION.
THE SECOND GUARD WAS QUITE SKILLED.
BUT INVESTIGATOR KIJIMA TOOK ON GUARD TWO AT THE COST OF HIS OWN LIFE.
SNP
SNP
SNP
!!
DON'T, INVESTIGATOR FURUTA... I WON'T...
I WON'T SAY ANYTHING!!
NO. AS AN INVESTIGATOR, YOU HAVE A DUTY TO REPORT WHAT HAPPENED.
SO I KNOW YOU WILL.
THEY ELIMINATED IHEI SQUAD...
AND THEN...
...
INVESTIGATOR KIJIMA...
AAAA...
AAAAA...
GET A VEHICLE TO TRANSPORT THE BODIES.
WHICH ONE IS THE QUICKEST?
VEHICLE 15.
THEN 15 IT IS...
INVESTIGATOR KIJIMA...
SOB...
SOB...
SOB...
PFF!!

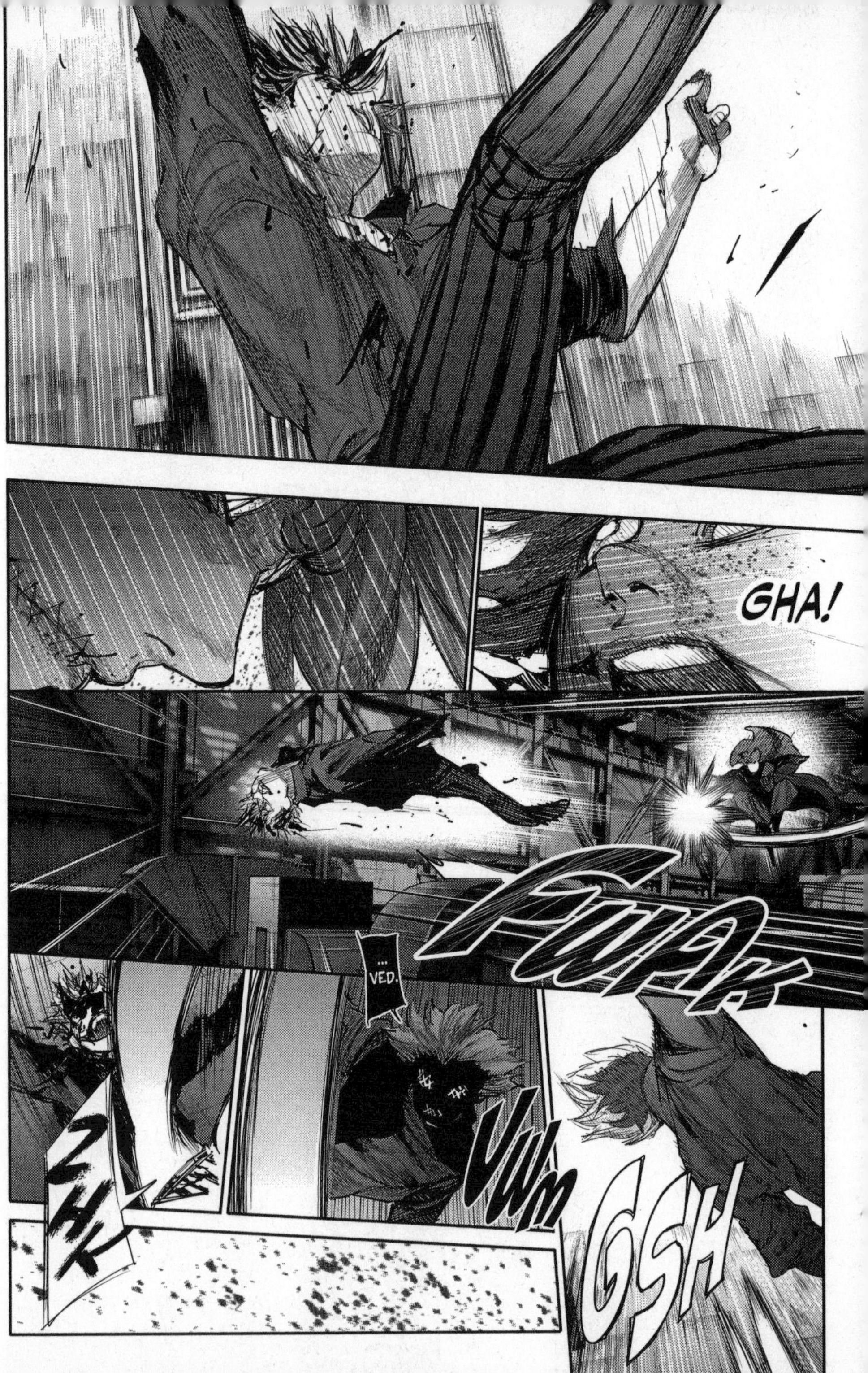
GHA!
FWAK
...VED.
GSH
VUM
ZNHK

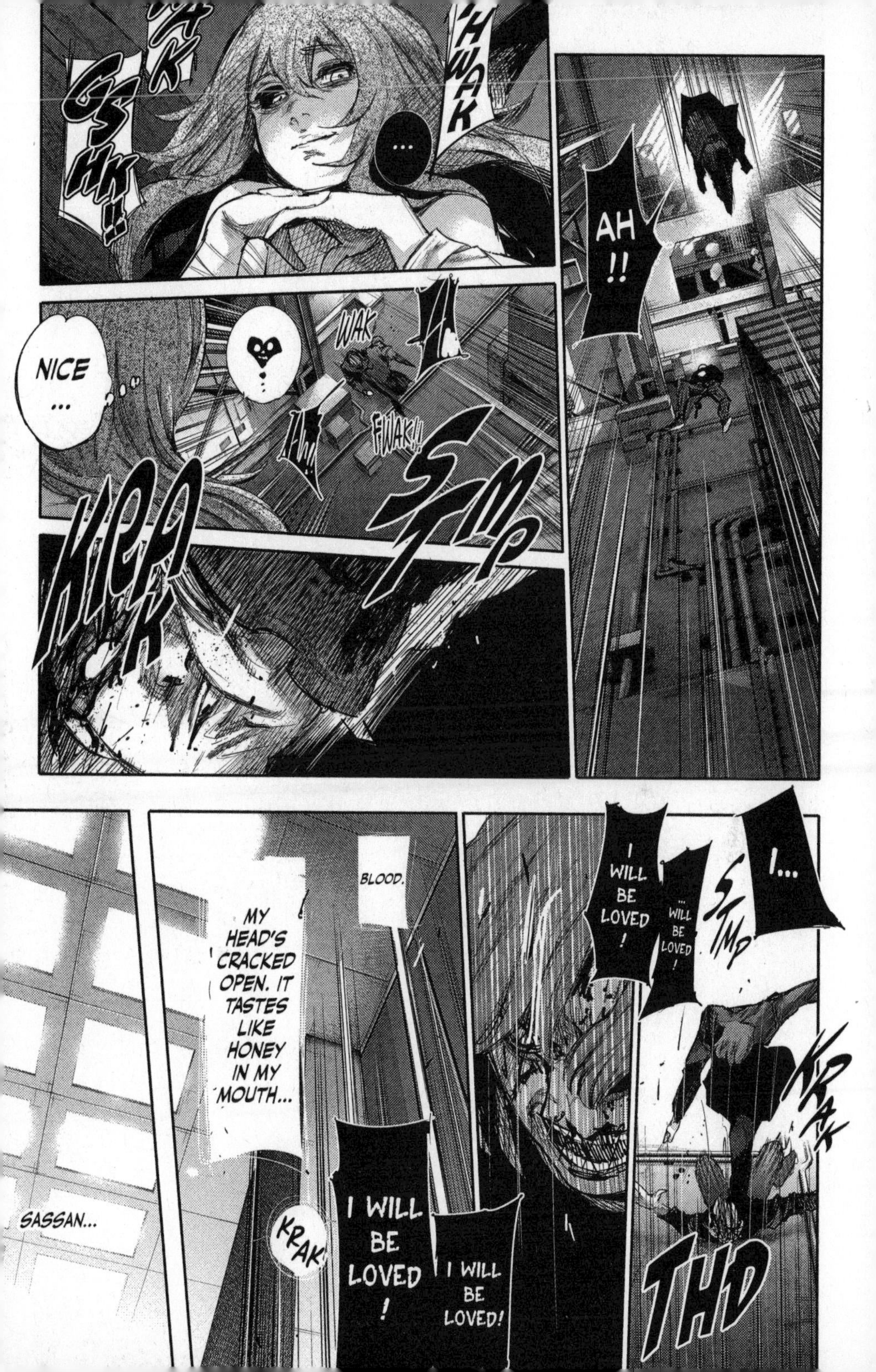

AH!!
HWAK
GSHK!!
...
NICE...
WAK
FWAK!!
STMP
I...
STMP
I WILL BE LOVED!
...WILL BE LOVED!
KRAK
THD
I WILL BE LOVED!
I WILL BE LOVED!
BLOOD.
MY HEAD'S CRACKED OPEN. IT TASTES LIKE HONEY IN MY MOUTH...
KRAK
SASSAN...

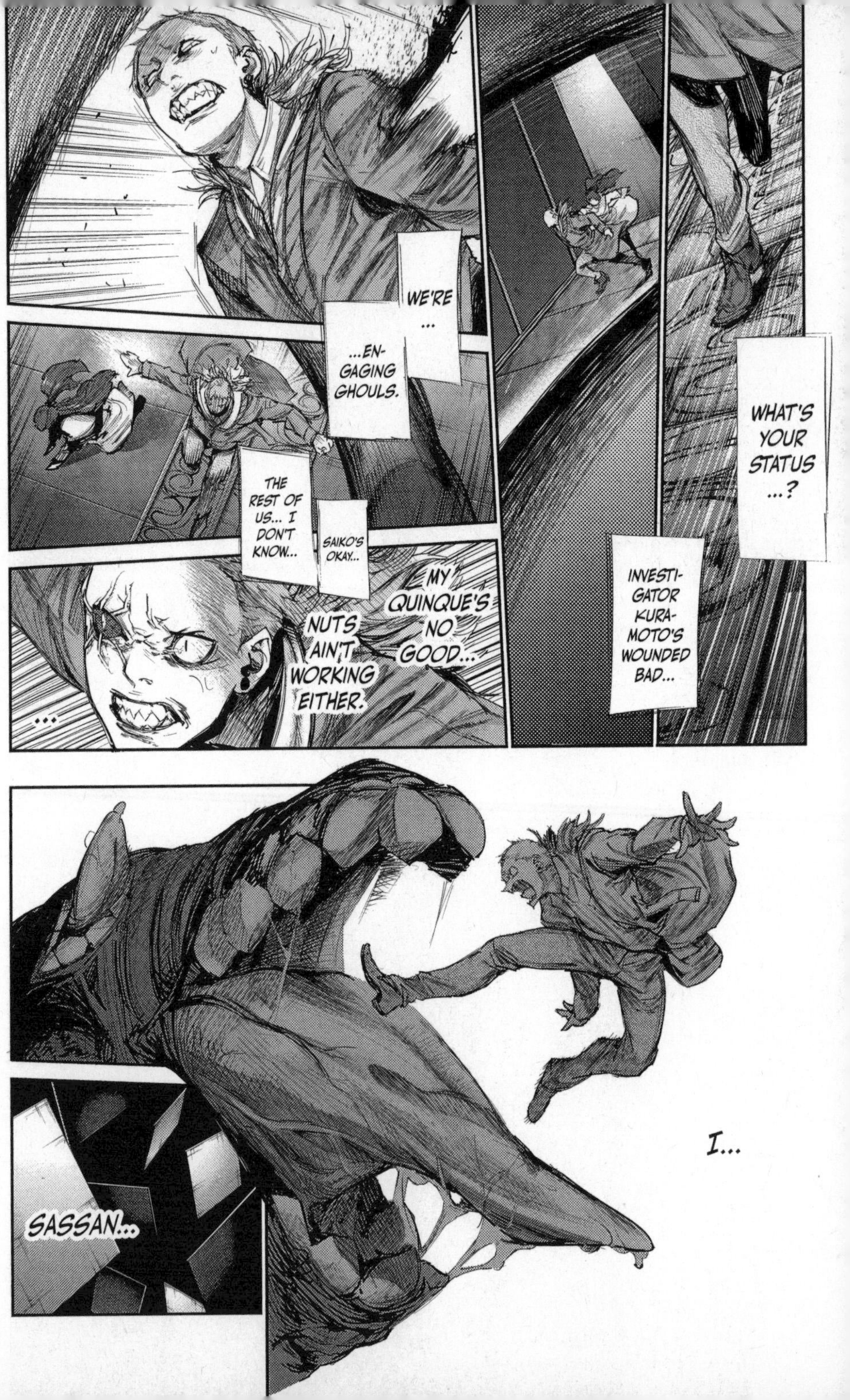
WHAT'S YOUR STATUS ...?
INVESTI-GATOR KURA-MOTO'S WOUNDED BAD...
WE'RE ...
...EN-GAGING GHOULS.
SAIKO'S OKAY...
THE REST OF US... I DON'T KNOW...
MY QUINQUE'S NO GOOD...
NUTS AIN'T WORKING EITHER.
...
I...
SASSAN...

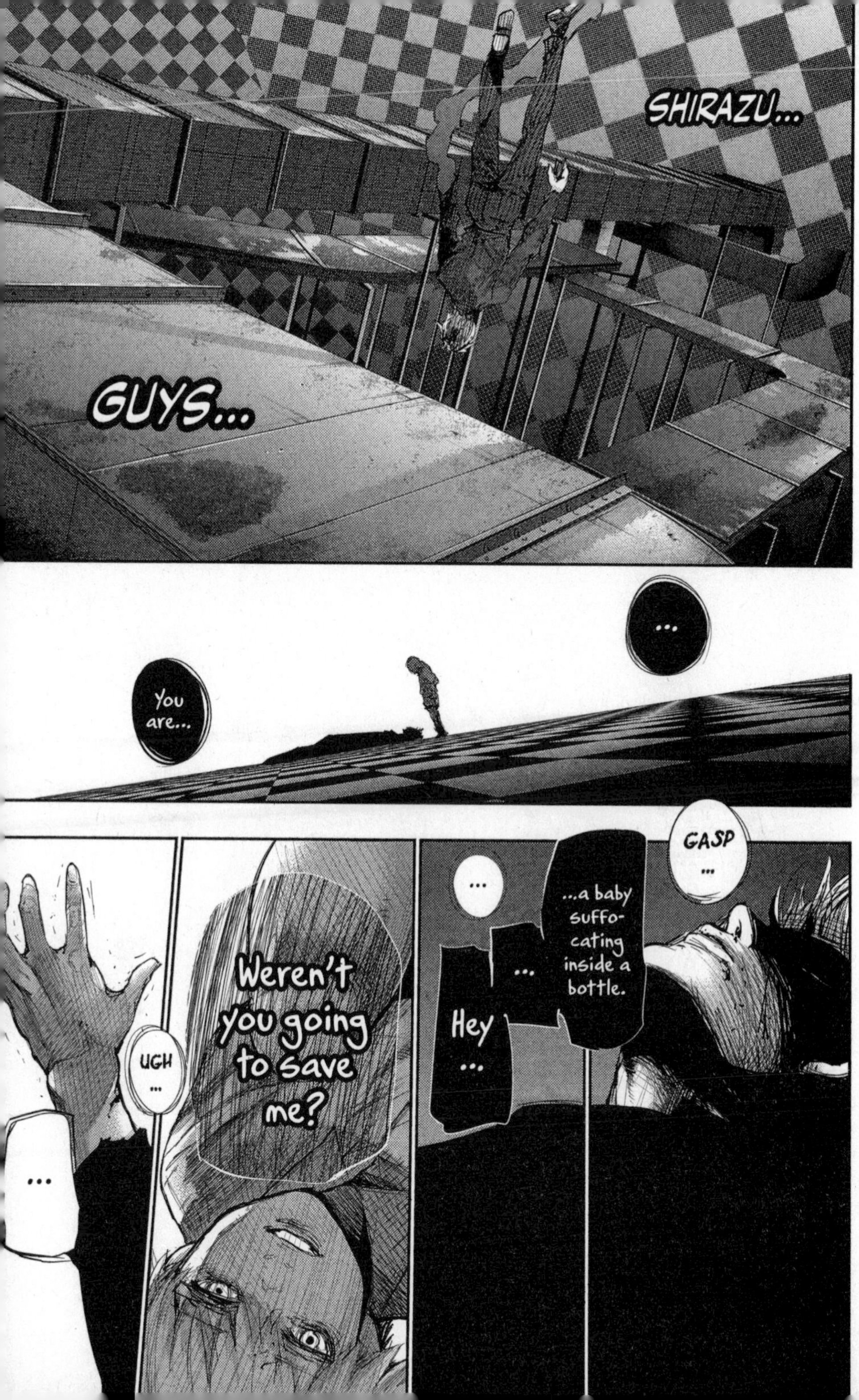

SHIRAZU...
GUYS...
...
You are...
GASP ...
...a baby suffocating inside a bottle.
...
...
Hey ...
Weren't you going to save me?
UGH ...
...

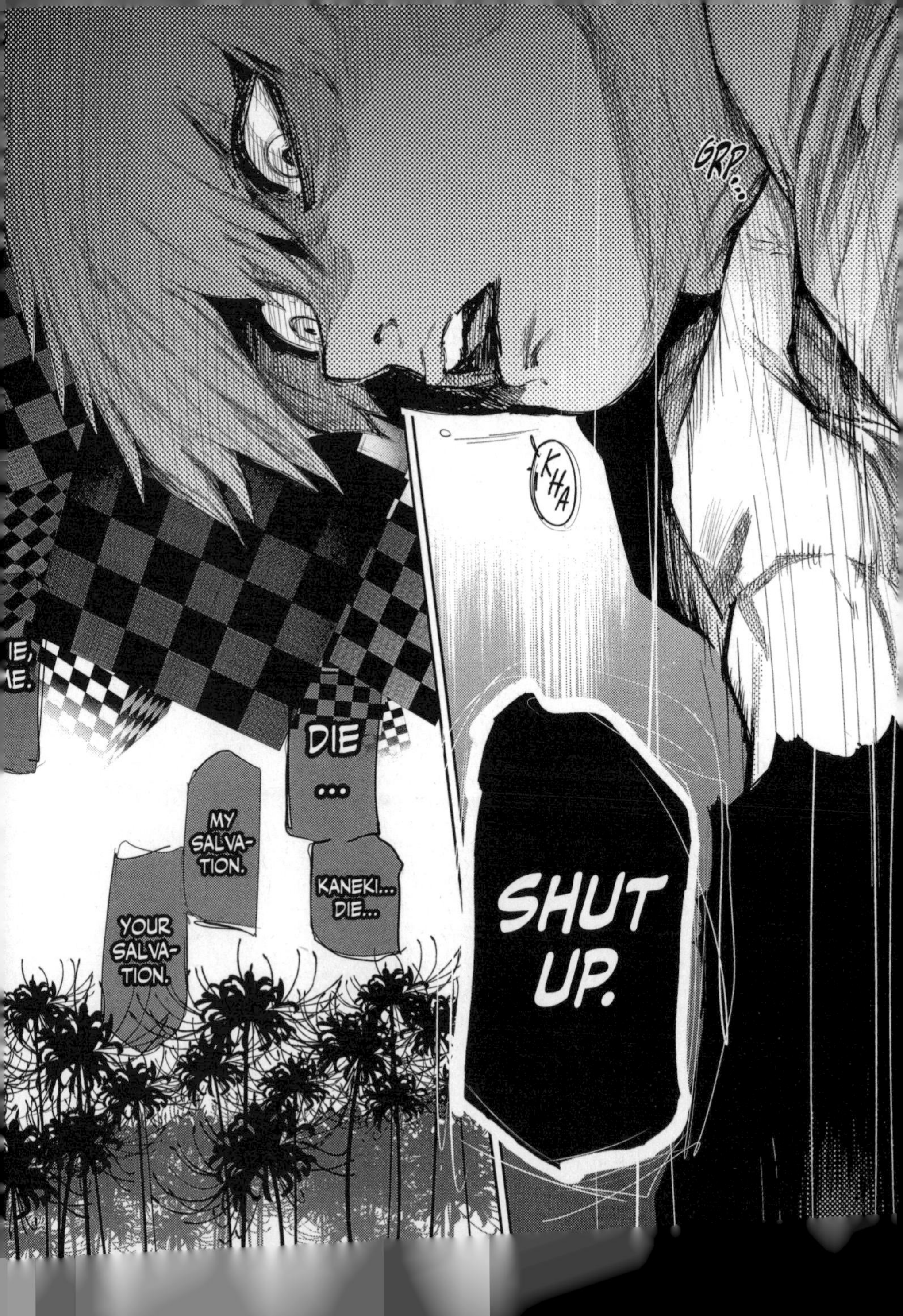
GRP...
KHA
SHUT UP.
DIE...
KANEKI... DIE...
MY SALVATION.
YOUR SALVATION.

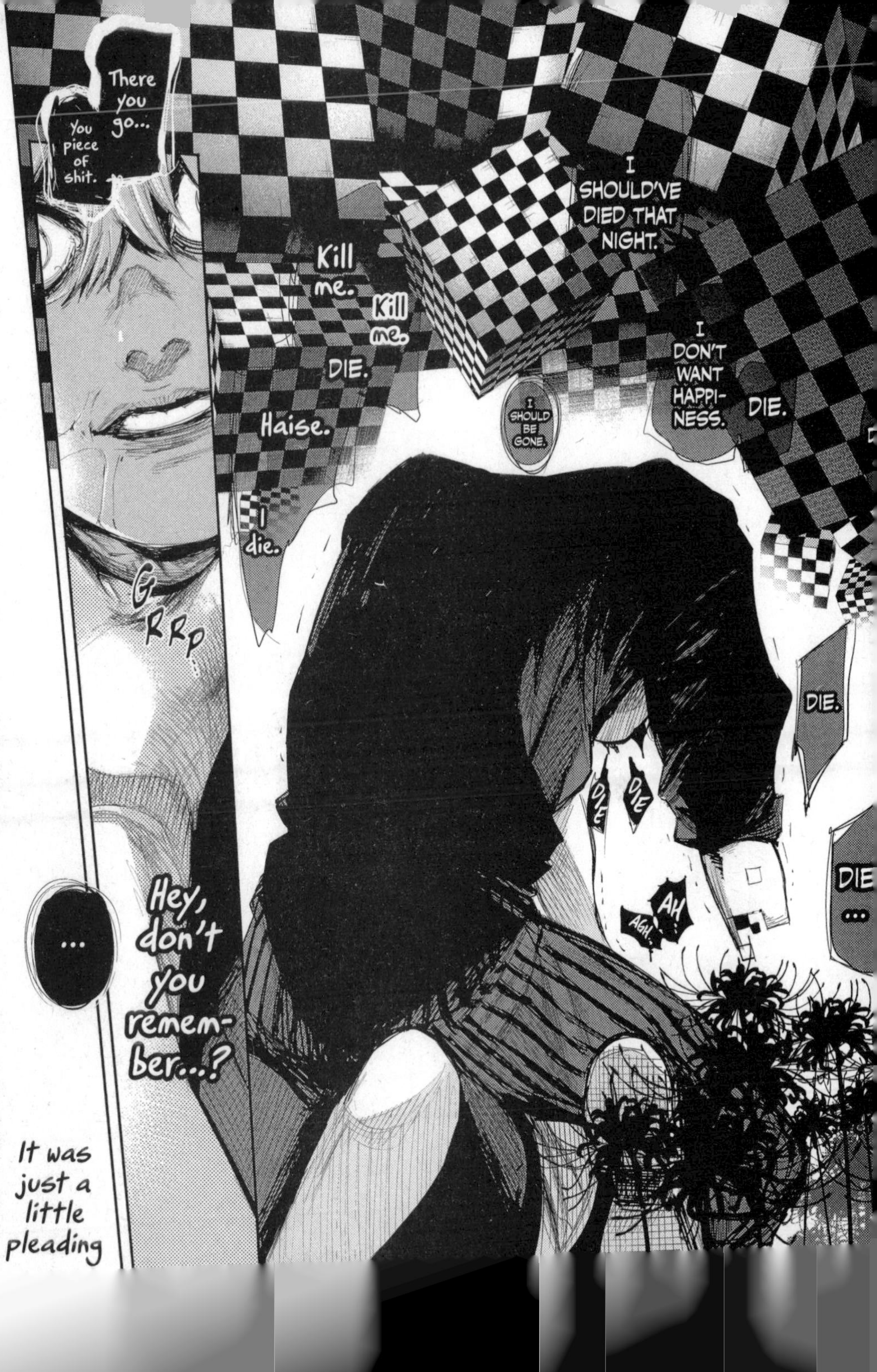

I SHOULD'VE DIED THAT NIGHT.
I DON'T WANT HAPPINESS.
DIE.
I SHOULD BE GONE.
Kill me.
Kill me.
DIE.
Haise.
I die.
DIE.
DIE
DIE
DIE...
AH
AGH
Hey, don't you remember...?
There you go...
You piece of shit.
GRRP
...
It was just a little pleading

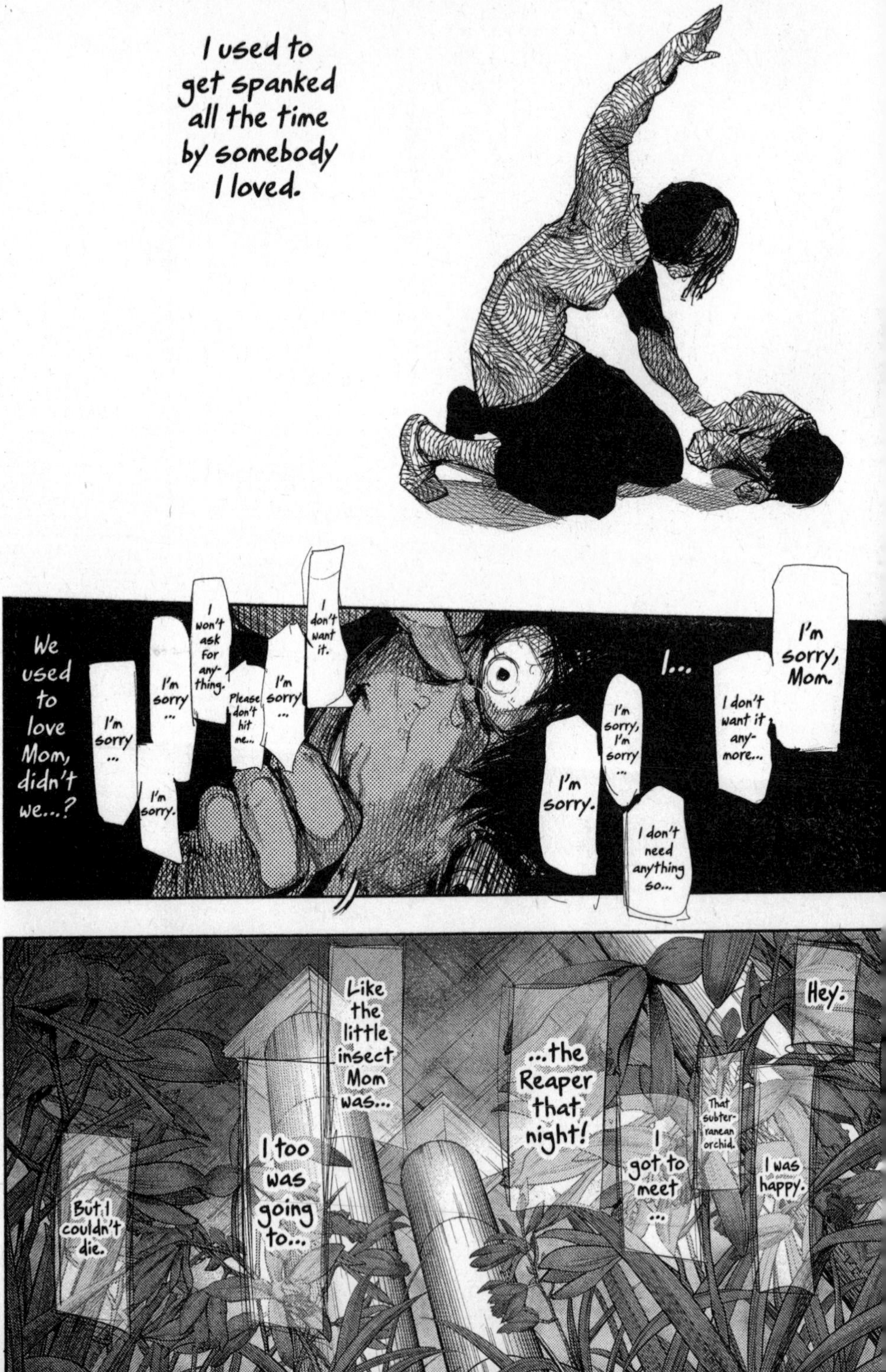
I used to get spanked all the time by somebody I loved.
I'm sorry, Mom.
I don't want it any-more...
I...
I'm sorry, I'm sorry...
I'm sorry.
I don't need anything so...
I don't want it.
I'm sorry...
Please don't hit me...
I won't ask for any-thing.
I'm sorry...
I'm sorry...
I'm sorry.
We used to love Mom, didn't we...?
Hey.
I was happy.
That subter-ranean orchid.
I got to meet...
...the Reaper that night!
Like the little insect Mom was...
I too was going to...
But I couldn't die.

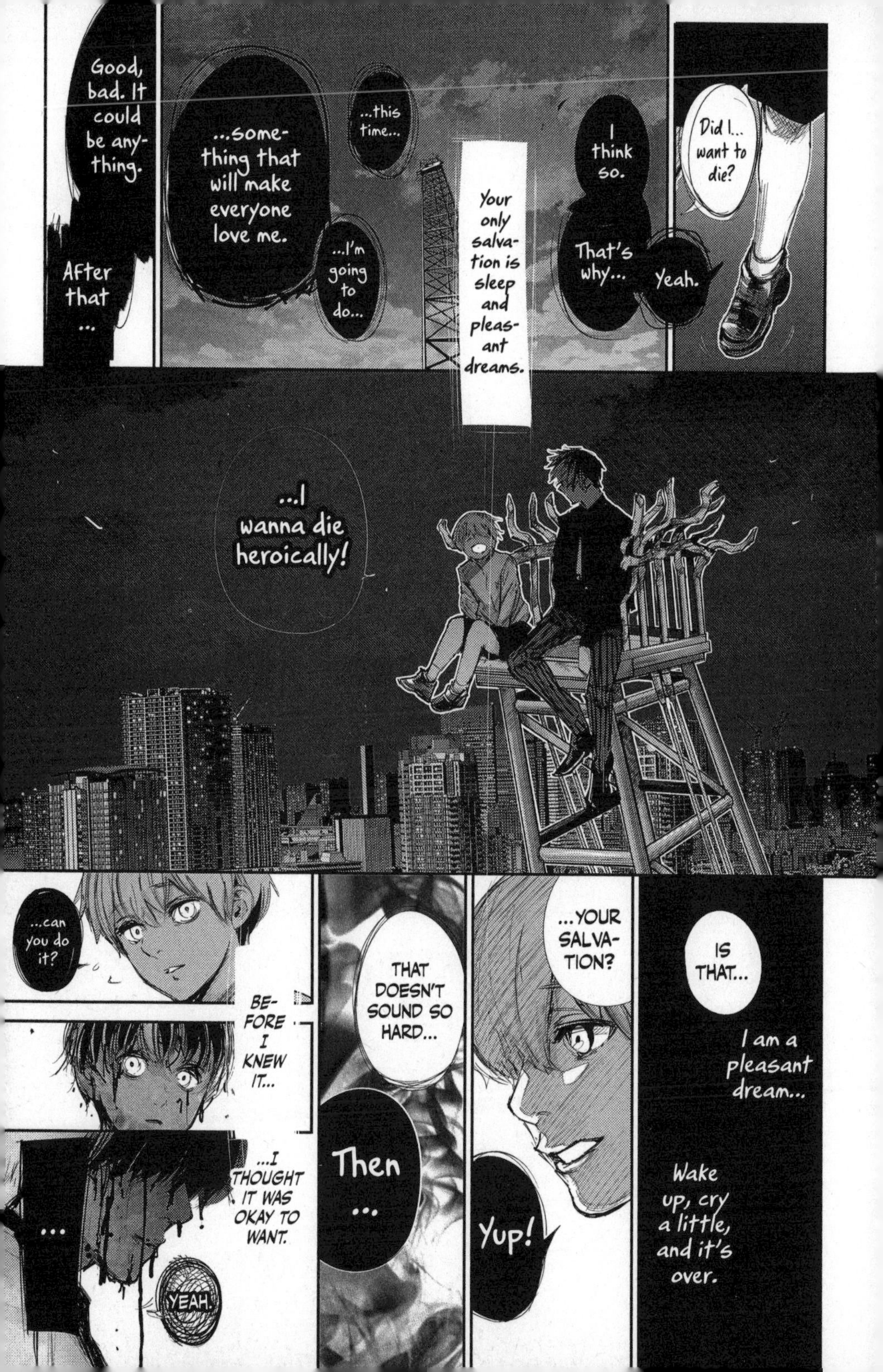
Did I... want to die?
I think so.
That's why...
Yeah.
Your only salvation is sleep and pleasant dreams.
...this time...
...something that will make everyone love me.
...I'm going to do...
Good, bad. It could be anything.
After that...
...I wanna die heroically!
IS THAT...
I am a pleasant dream...
Wake up, cry a little, and it's over.
...YOUR SALVATION?
Yup!
THAT DOESN'T SOUND SO HARD...
Then...
...can you do it?
BEFORE I KNEW IT...
...I THOUGHT IT WAS OKAY TO WANT.
...
YEAH.

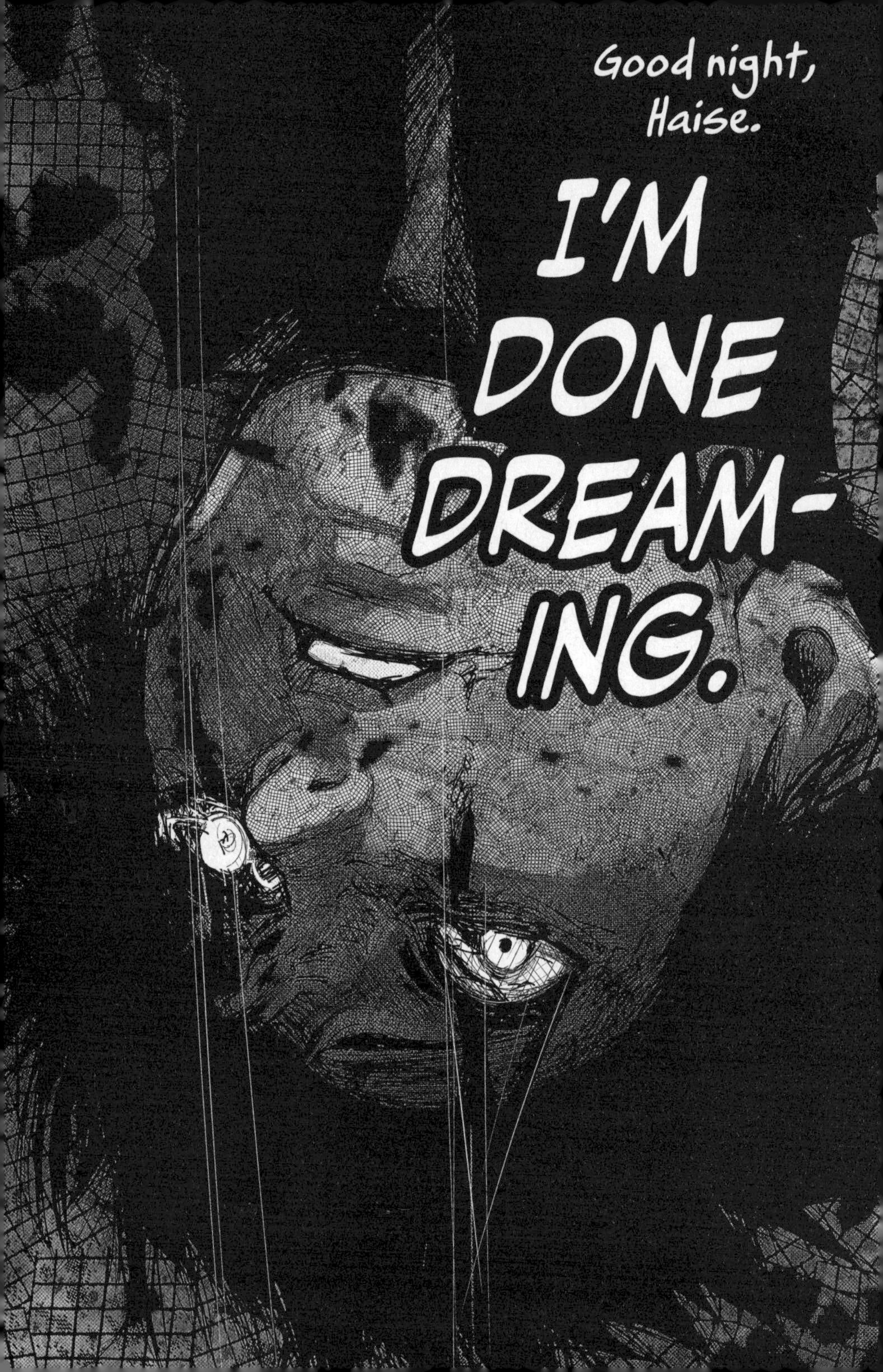
Good night, Haise.
I'M DONE DREAM-ING.

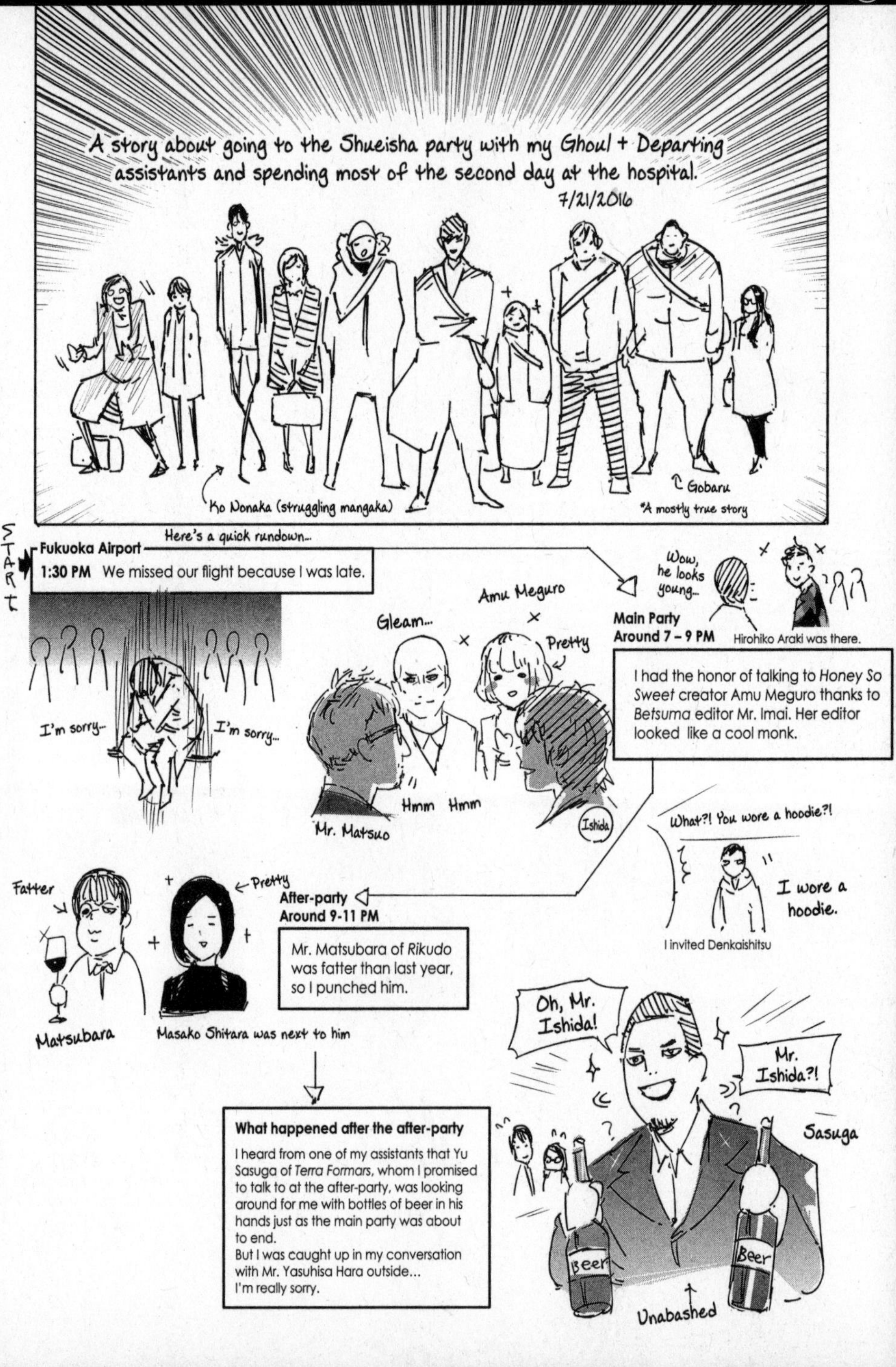
A story about going to the Shueisha party with my Ghoul + Departing assistants and spending most of the second day at the hospital.
7/21/2016
Ko Nonaka (struggling mangaka)
Gobaru
*A mostly true story
Here's a quick rundown...
START
Fukuoka Airport
1:30 PM We missed our flight because I was late.
I'm sorry...
I'm sorry...
Main Party
Around 7 – 9 PM
Wow, he looks young...
Hirohiko Araki was there.
Amu Meguro
Gleam...
Pretty
I had the honor of talking to Honey So Sweet creator Amu Meguro thanks to Betsuma editor Mr. Imai. Her editor looked like a cool monk.
Hmm Hmm
Mr. Matsuo
Ishida
What?! You wore a hoodie?!
I wore a hoodie.
I invited Denkaishitsu
After-party
Around 9-11 PM
Mr. Matsubara of Rikudo was fatter than last year, so I punched him.
Fatter
Pretty
Matsubara
Masako Shitara was next to him
What happened after the after-party
I heard from one of my assistants that Yu Sasuga of Terra Formars, whom I promised to talk to at the after-party, was looking around for me with bottles of beer in his hands just as the main party was about to end.
But I was caught up in my conversation with Mr. Yasuhisa Hara outside...
I'm really sorry.
Oh, Mr. Ishida!
Mr. Ishida?!
Sasuga
Beer
Beer
Unabashed

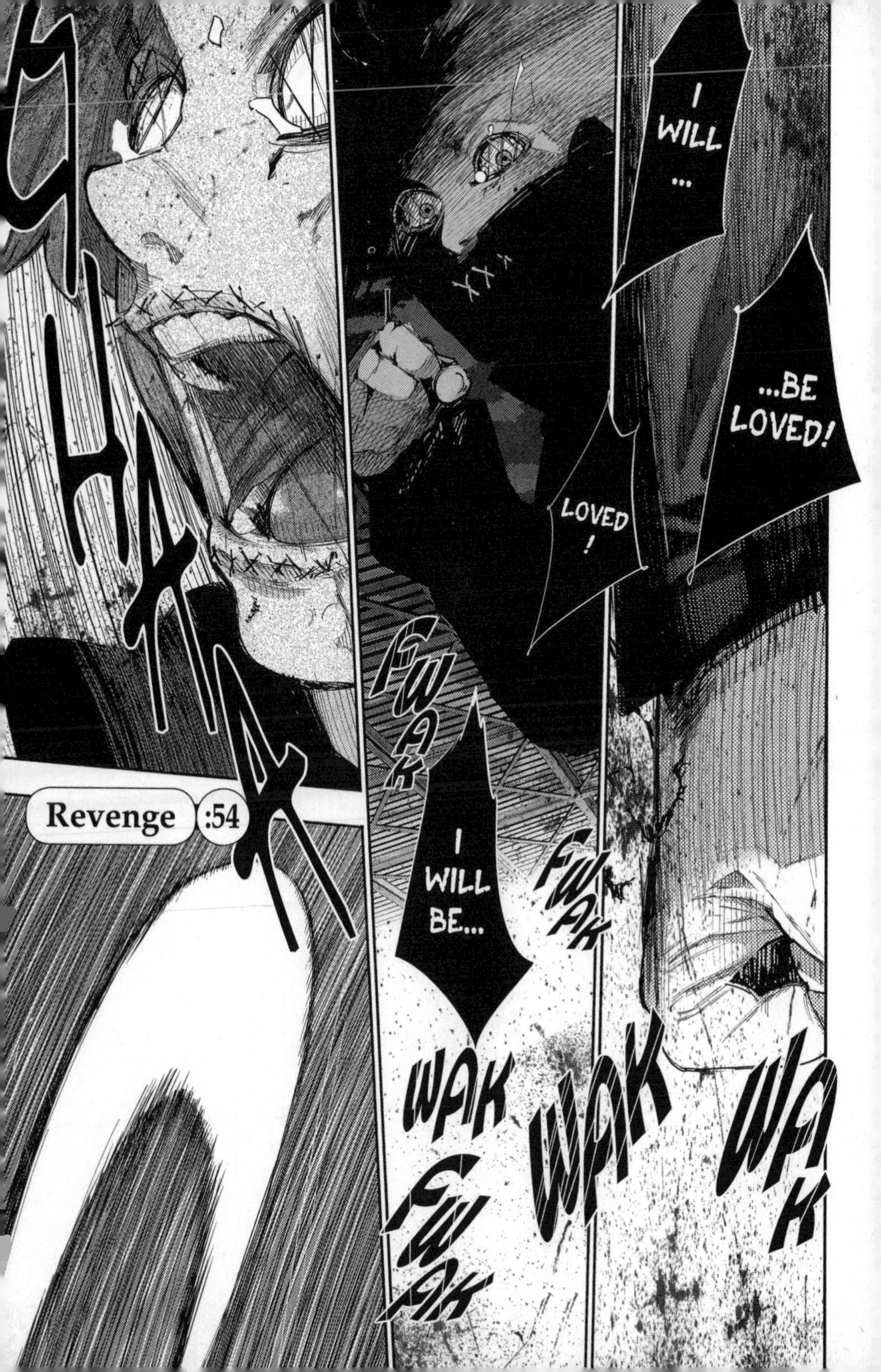
I WILL ...
...BE LOVED!
LOVED !
WAK
I WILL BE...
FWAK
FWAK
WAK
WAK
FWAK
Revenge :54

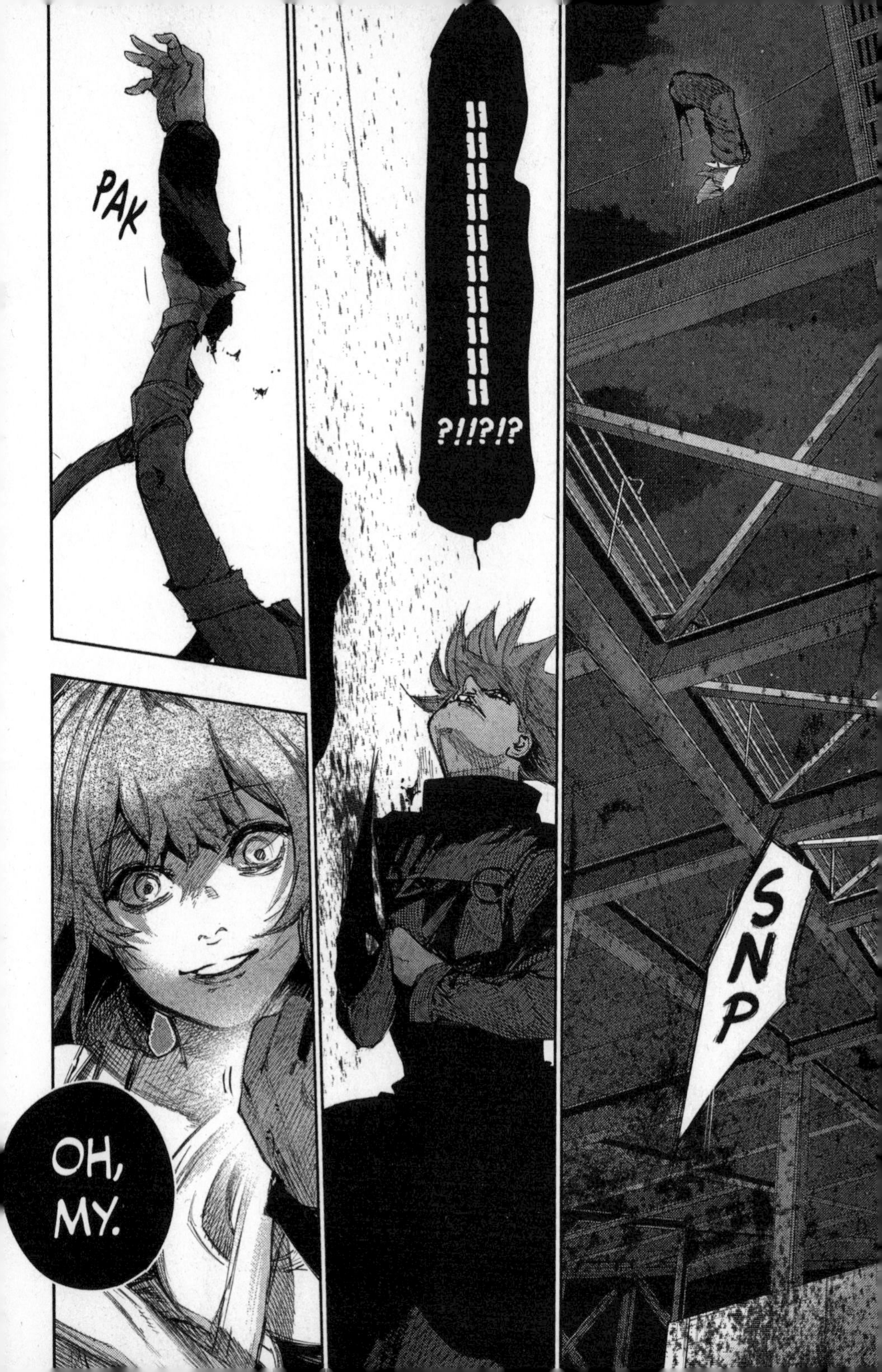
SNP
!!!!!!!!!!!!!!!!
?!!?!?
PAK
OH, MY.

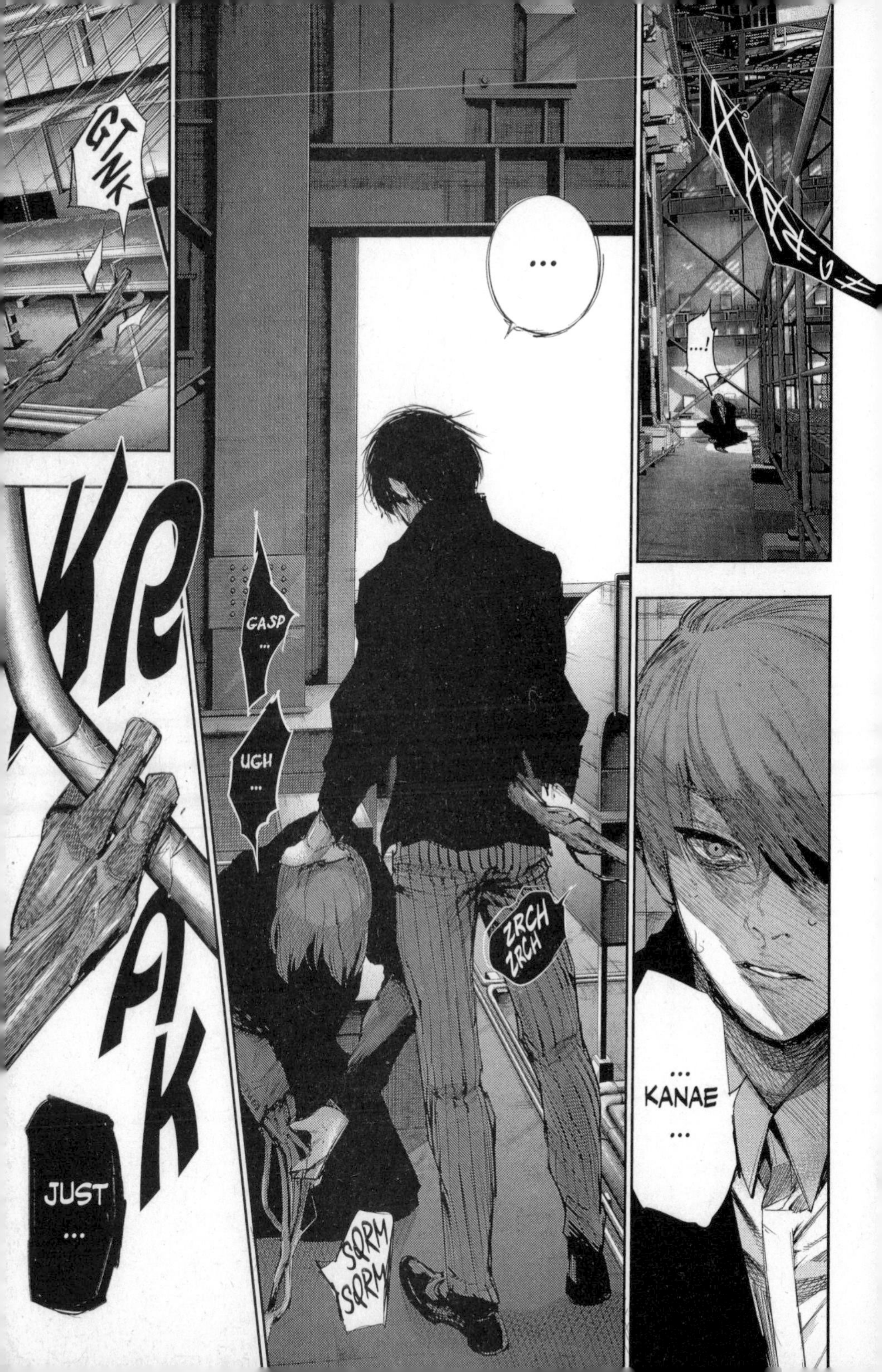

...!
... KANAE ...
...
GASP ...
UGH ...
ZRCH ZRCH
SQRM SQRM
GINK
JUST ...

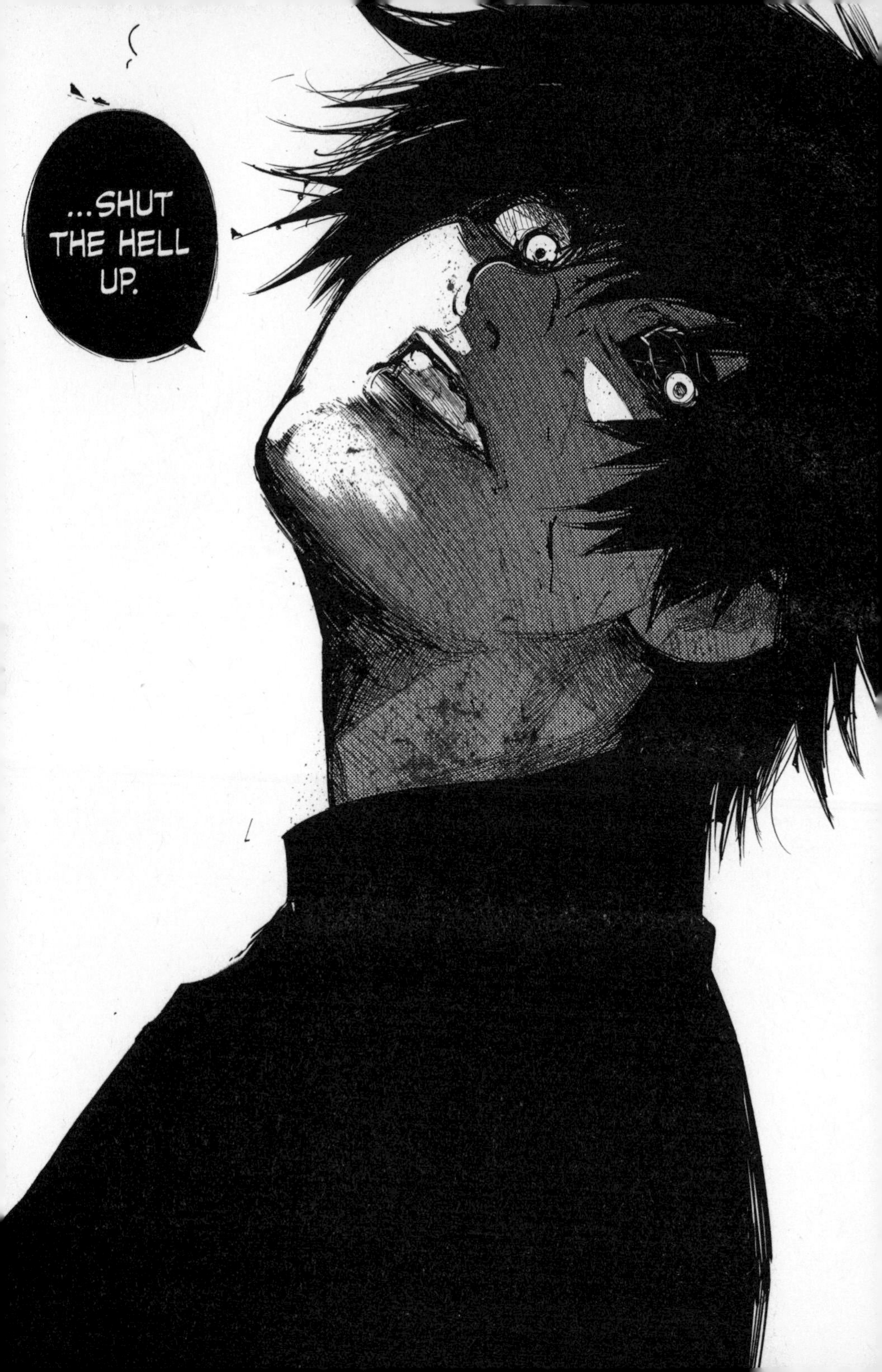
...SHUT THE HELL UP.

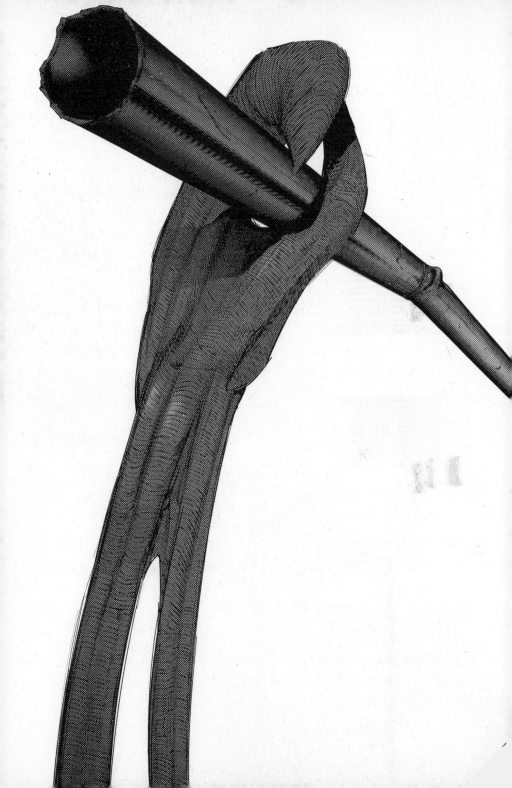

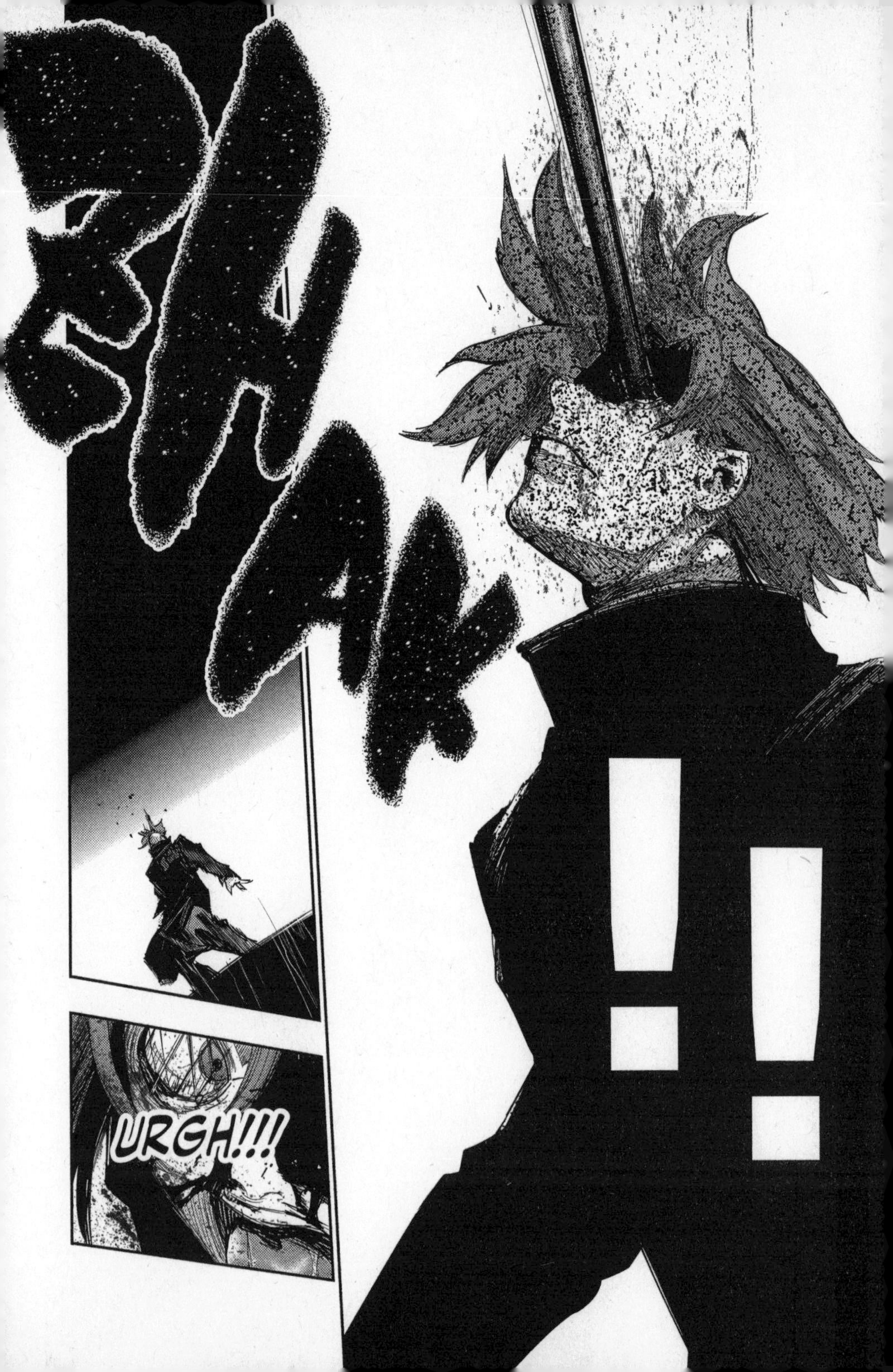
SHAK
!!
URGH!!!

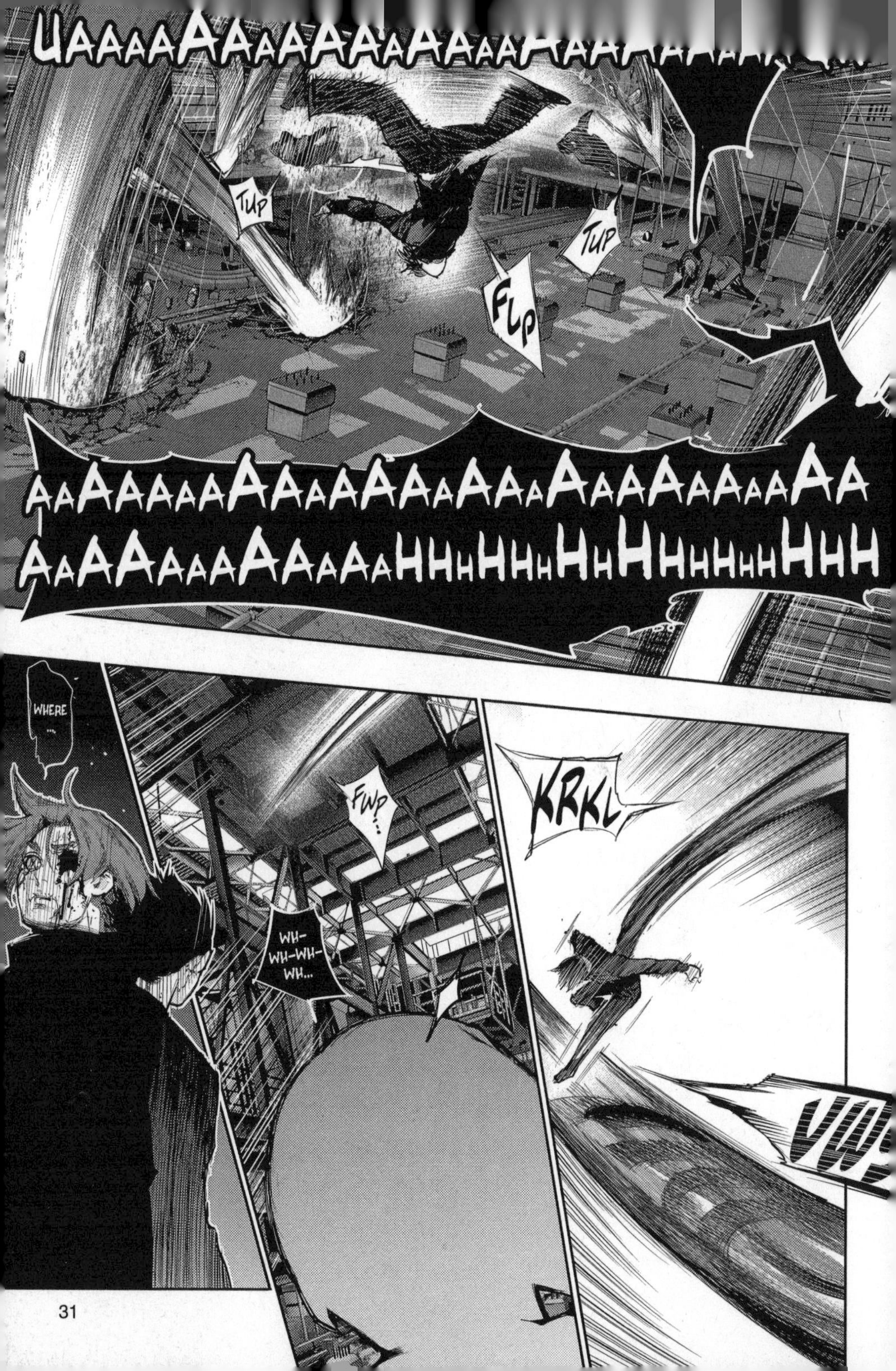
UAAAAAAAAAAAAAAAAAAAAAAA
TUP
TUP
FLUP
AAAAAAAAAAAAAAAAAAAAAAAAAAAA
AAAAAAAAAAAAHHHHHHHHHHHHHHHHH
KRKL
VWS
FWP...
WH-WH-WH-WH...
WHERE...

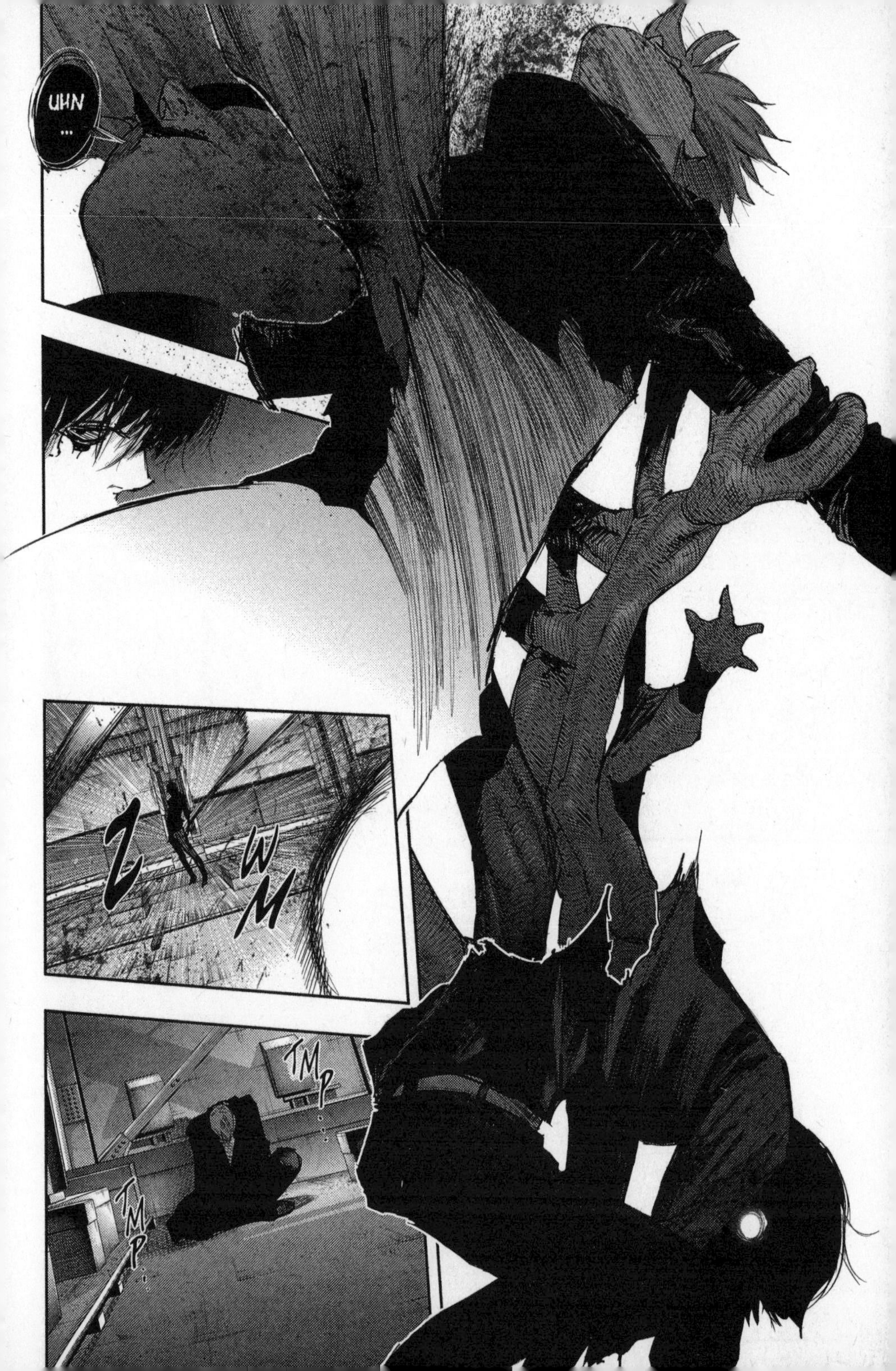
UHN
...
ZWM
TMP
TMP...

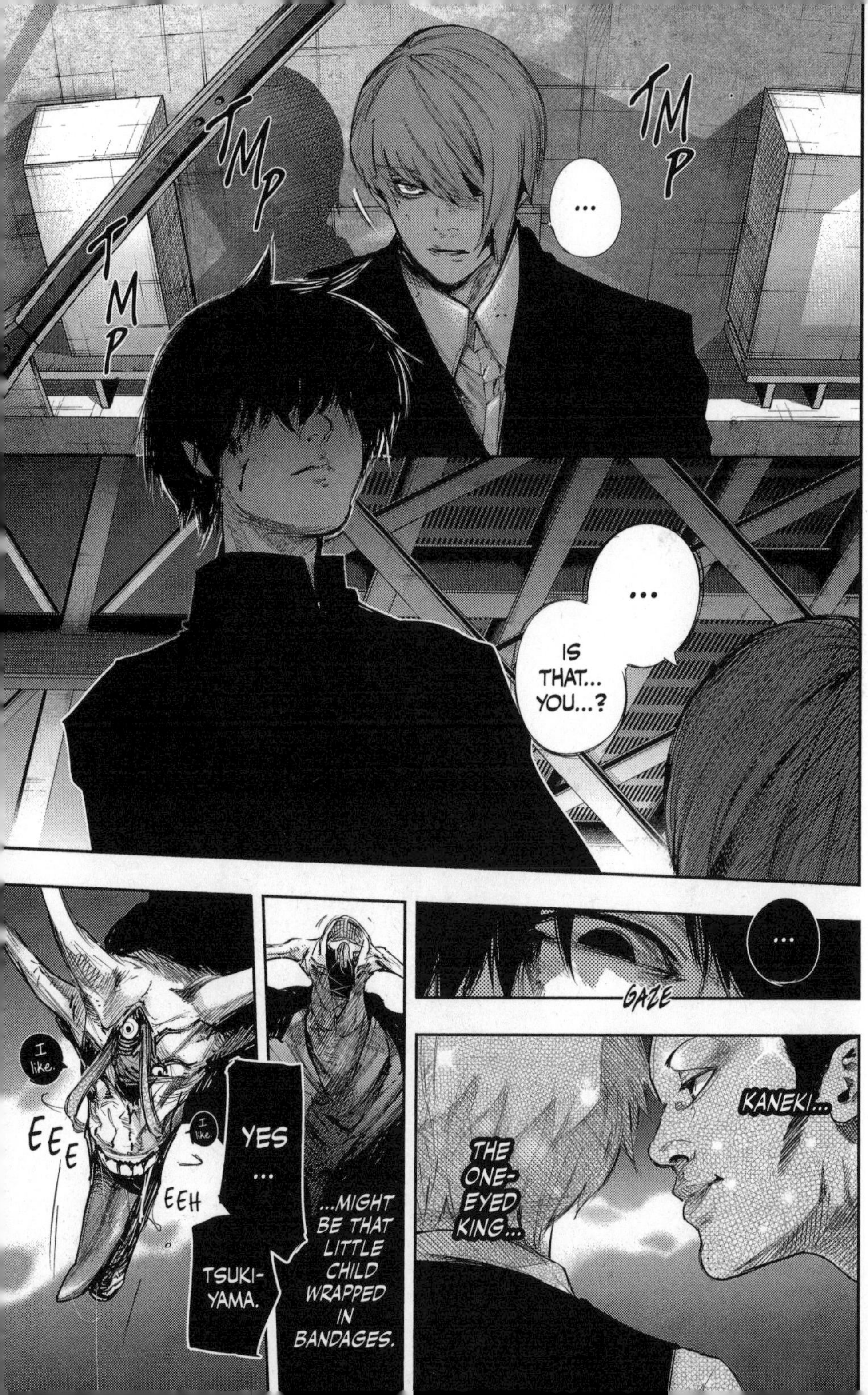
TMP
TMP
...
TMP
TMP
...
IS THAT... YOU...?
...
GAZE
KANEKI...
THE ONE-EYED KING...
YES...
TSUKI-YAMA.
...MIGHT BE THAT LITTLE CHILD WRAPPED IN BANDAGES.
I like.
I like.
EEE
EEH

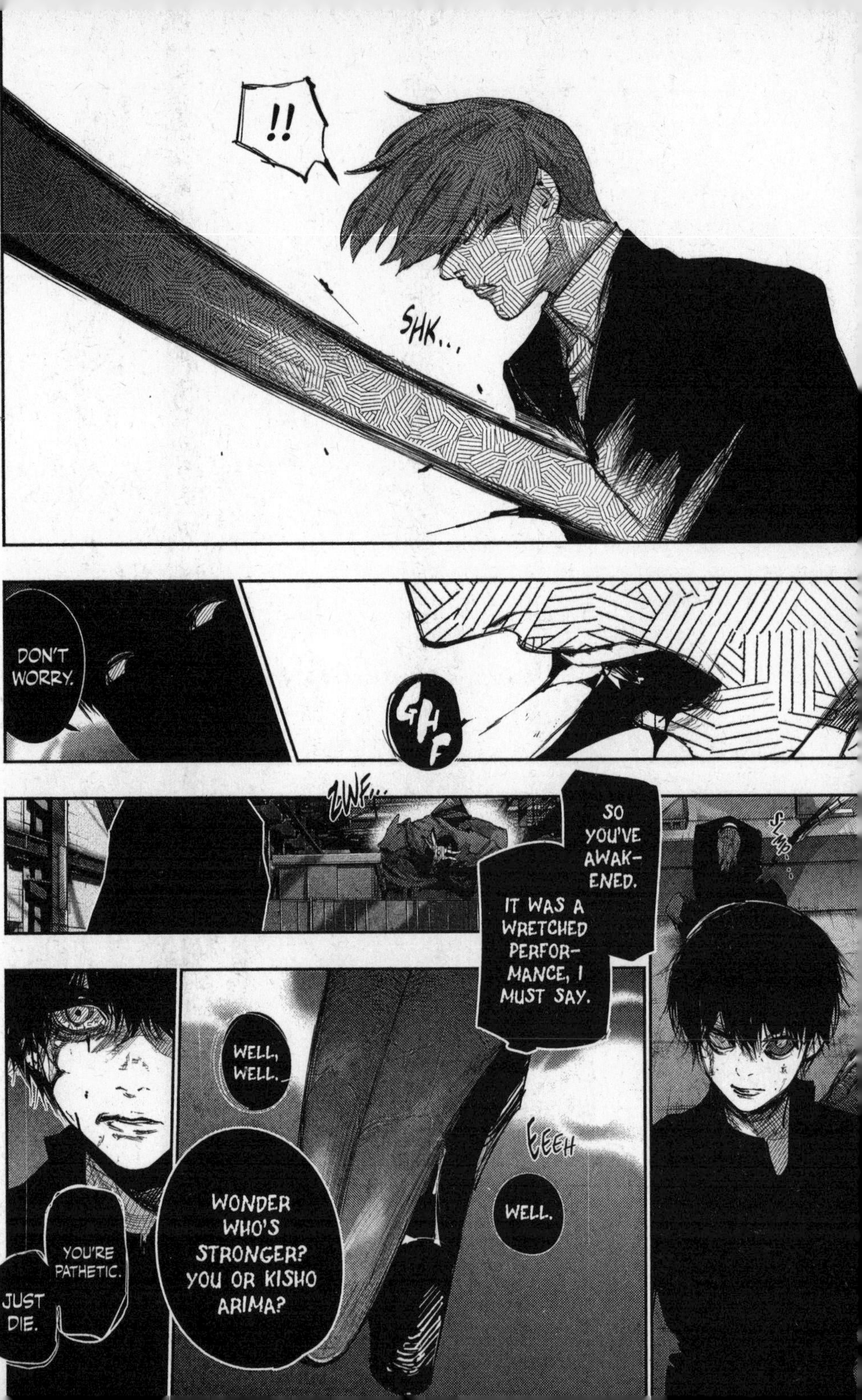
!!
SHK...
GHF
DON'T WORRY.
SLMP...
SO YOU'VE AWAKENED.
IT WAS A WRETCHED PERFORMANCE, I MUST SAY.
ZWF...
WELL, WELL.
EEEH
WELL.
WONDER WHO'S STRONGER? YOU OR KISHO ARIMA?
YOU'RE PATHETIC.
JUST DIE.

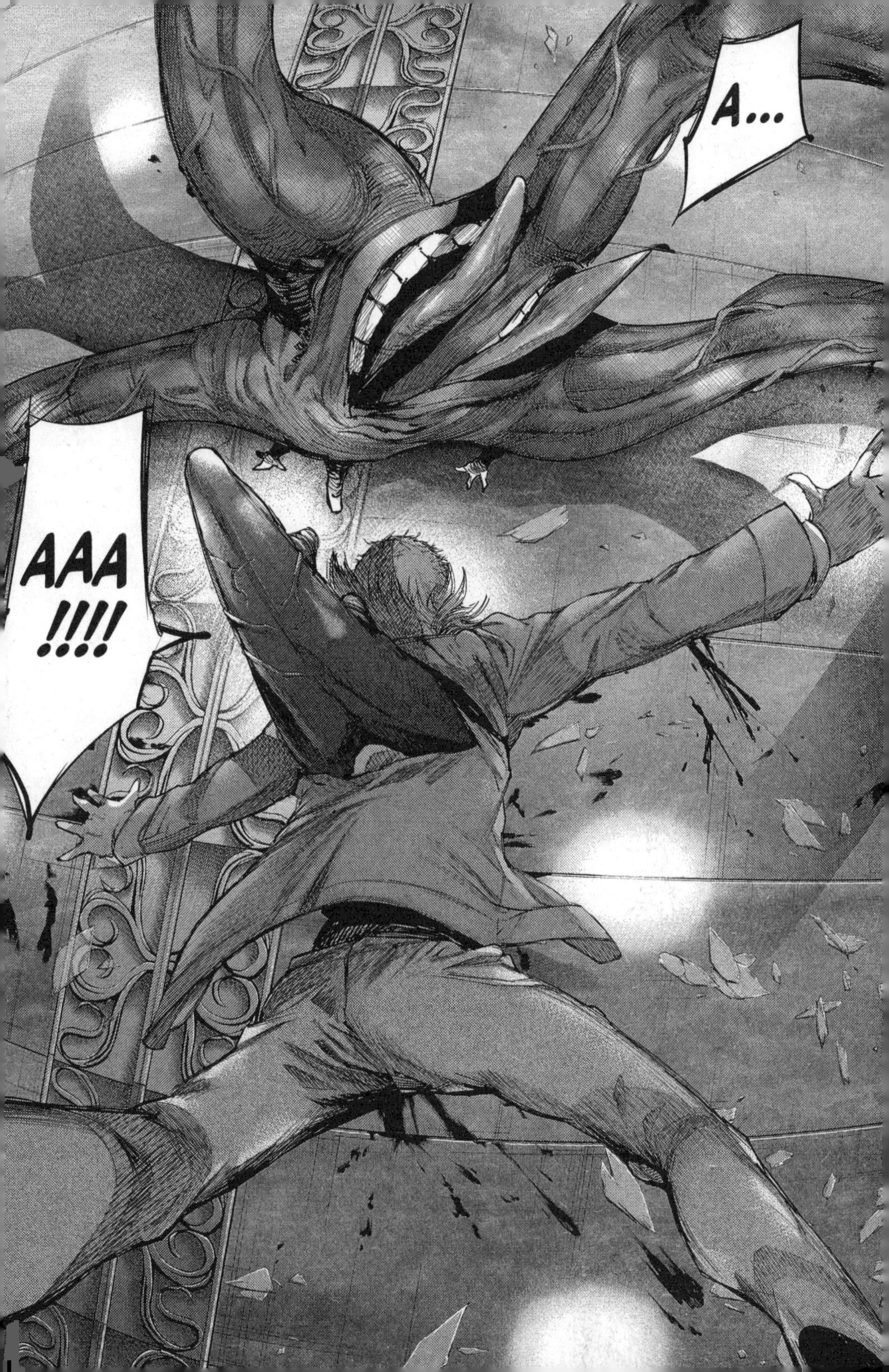
A...
AAA !!!!

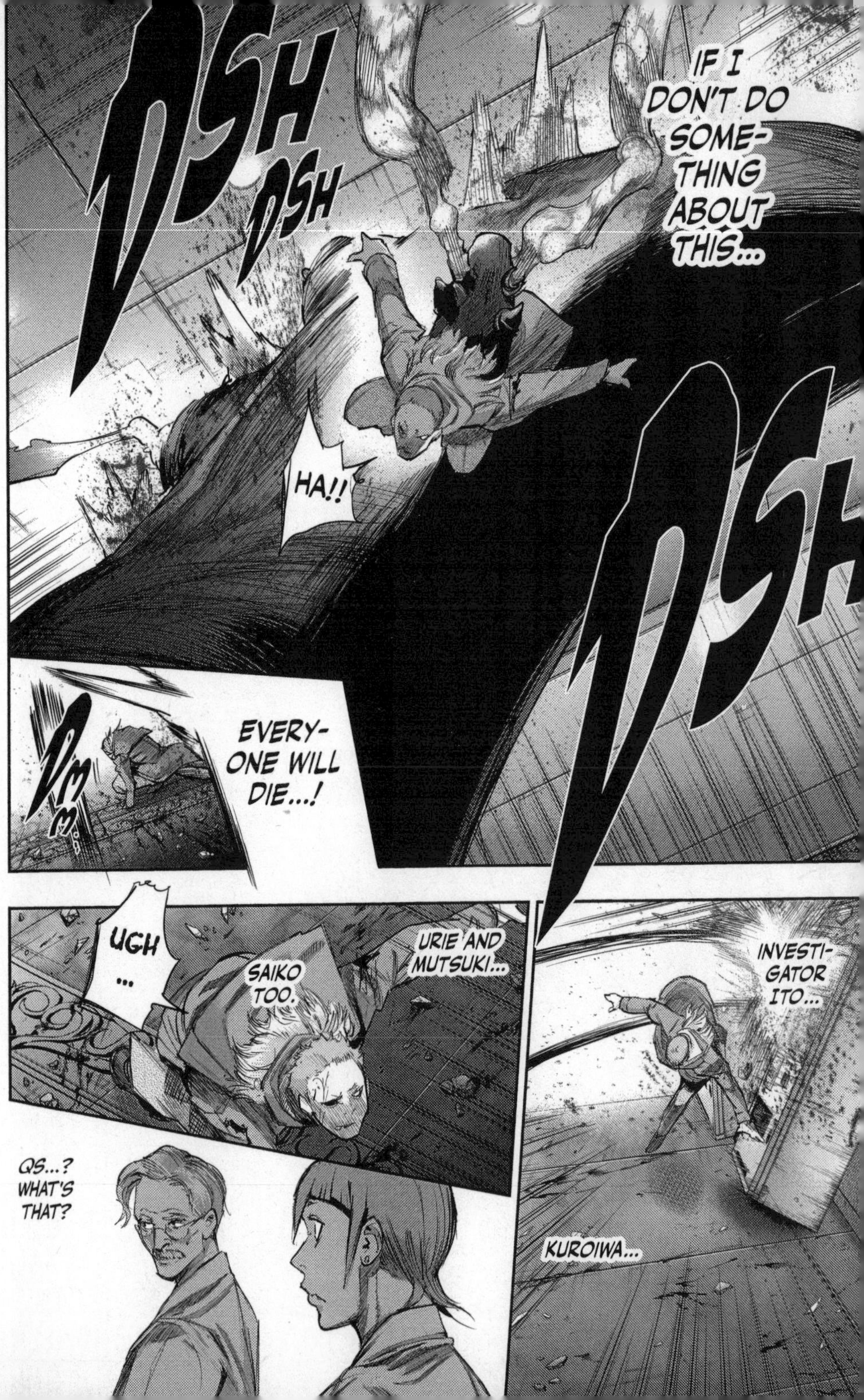
IF I DON'T DO SOME-THING ABOUT THIS...
DSH
DSH
HA!!
DSH
EVERY-ONE WILL DIE...!
INVESTI-GATOR ITO...
KUROIWA...
URIE AND MUTSUKI...
SAIKO TOO.
UGH ...
QS...? WHAT'S THAT?

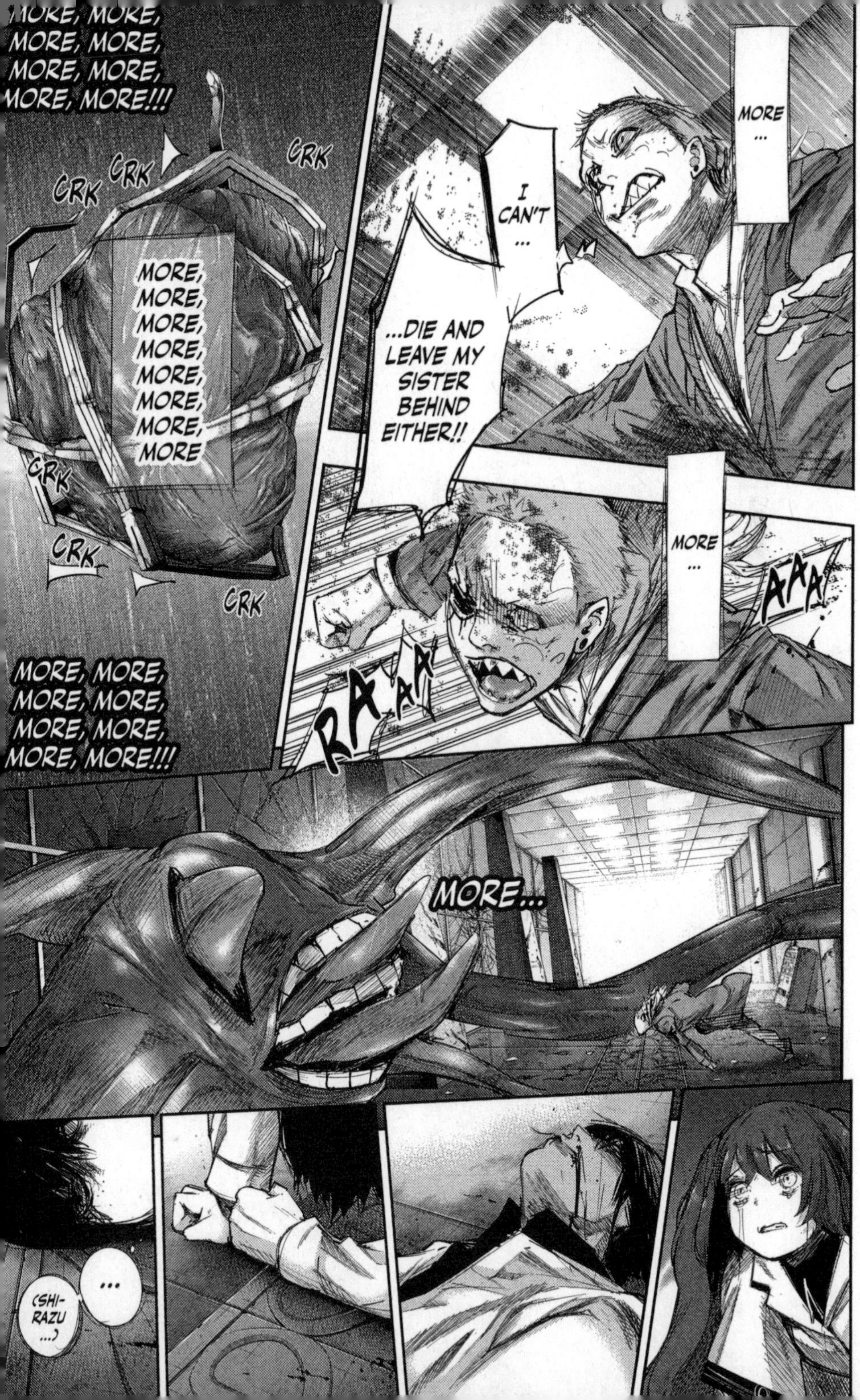
MORE ...
I CAN'T ...
...DIE AND LEAVE MY SISTER BEHIND EITHER!!
MORE ...
AAA!
RAAA!
MORE, MORE, MORE, MORE, MORE, MORE, MORE, MORE!!!
CRK
CRK
CRK
MORE, MORE, MORE, MORE, MORE, MORE, MORE, MORE
CRK
CRK
CRK
MORE, MORE, MORE, MORE, MORE, MORE, MORE, MORE!!!
MORE...
...
(SHIRAZU ...)

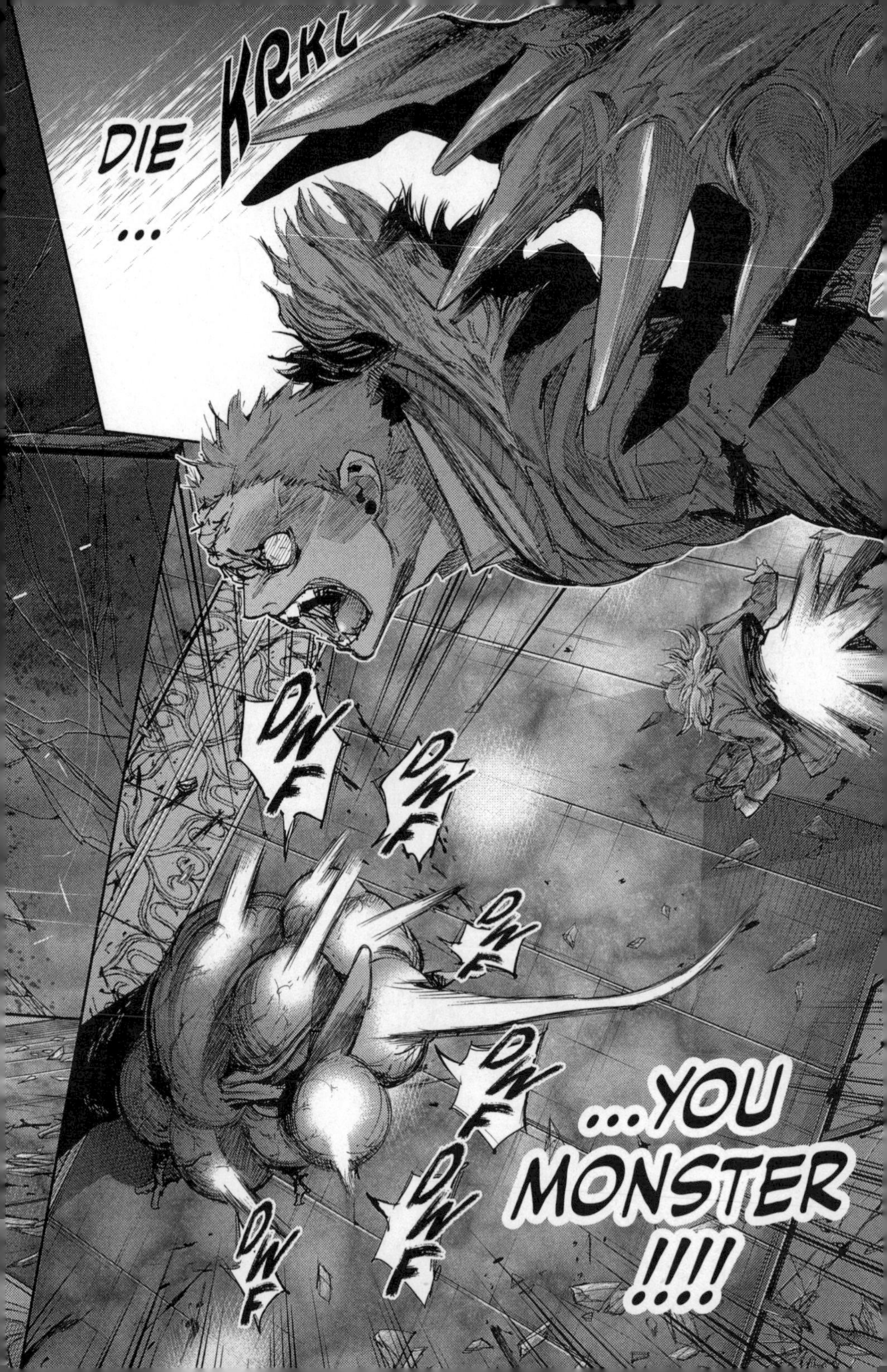

KRKL
DIE ...
DWF
DWF
DWF
...YOU MONSTER !!!!
DWF
DWF
DWF
DWF

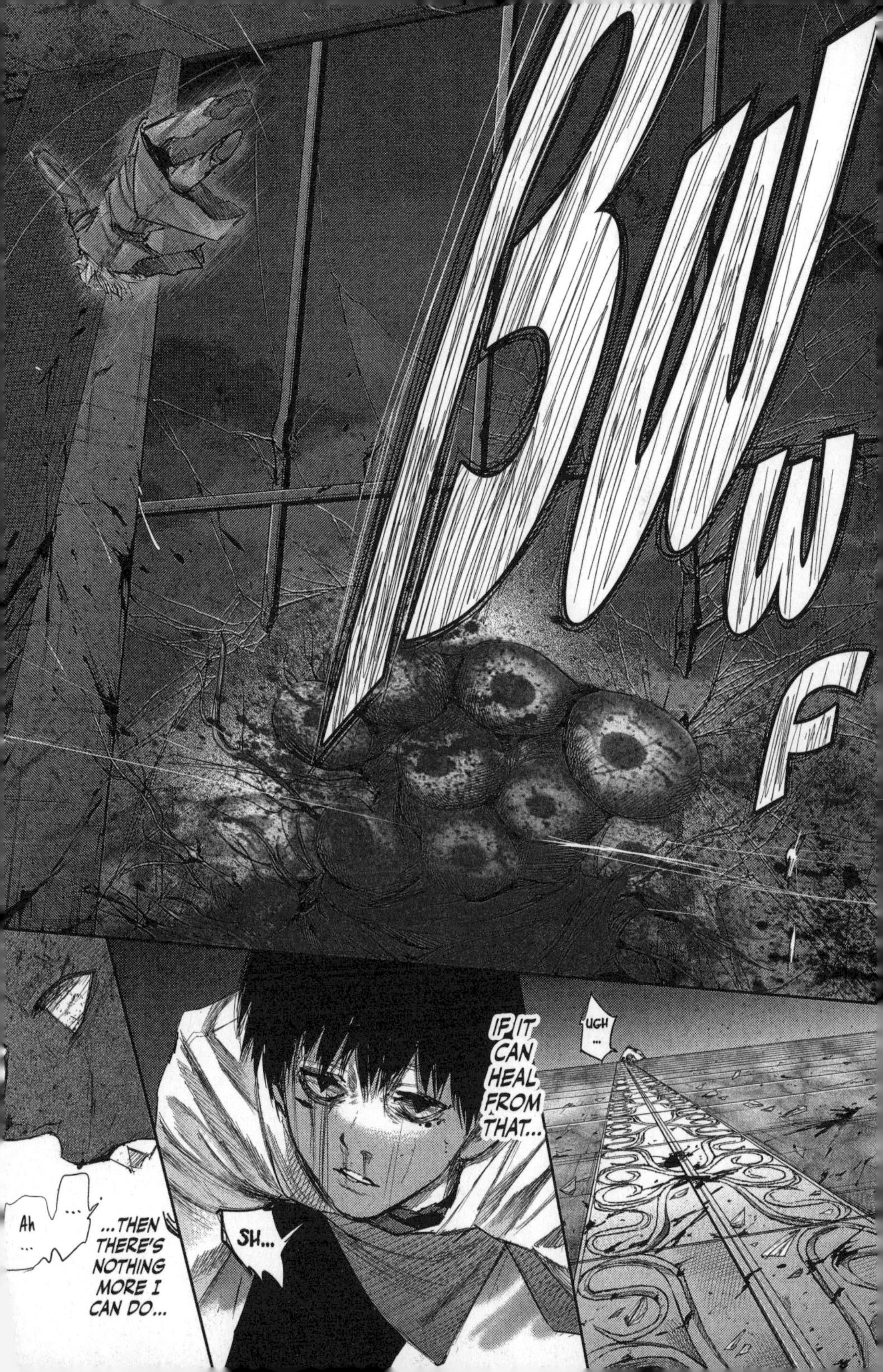
BUW
F
UGH ...
IF IT CAN HEAL FROM THAT...
SH...
...THEN THERE'S NOTHING MORE I CAN DO...
...
Ah ...

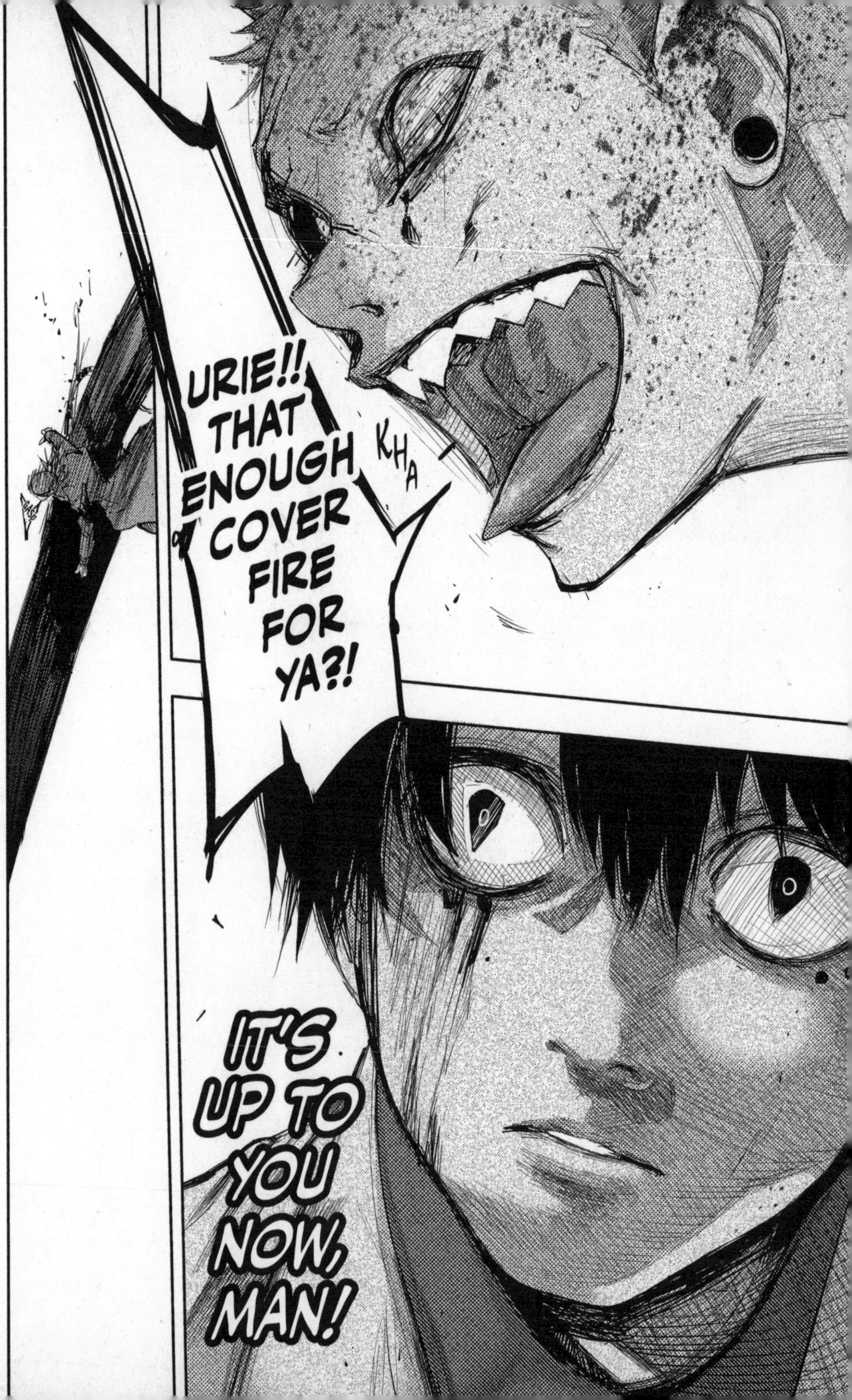
KHA
URIE!! THAT ENOUGH COVER FIRE FOR YA?!
IT'S UP TO YOU NOW, MAN!

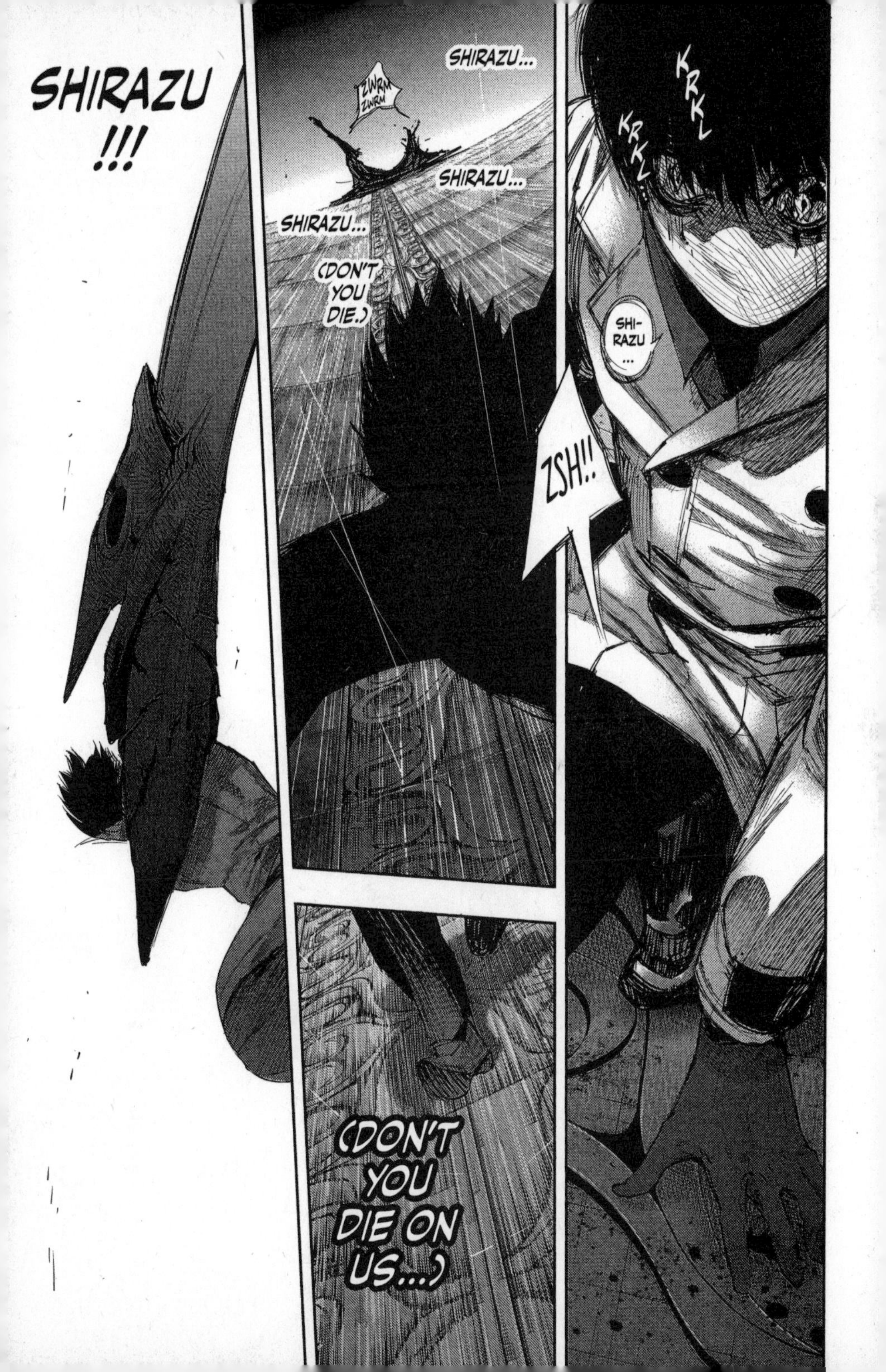
KRKL KRKL
SHI-RAZU...
ZSH!!
SHIRAZU...
ZWRM ZWRM
SHIRAZU...
SHIRAZU...
(DON'T YOU DIE.)
SHIRAZU !!!
(DON'T YOU DIE ON US...)

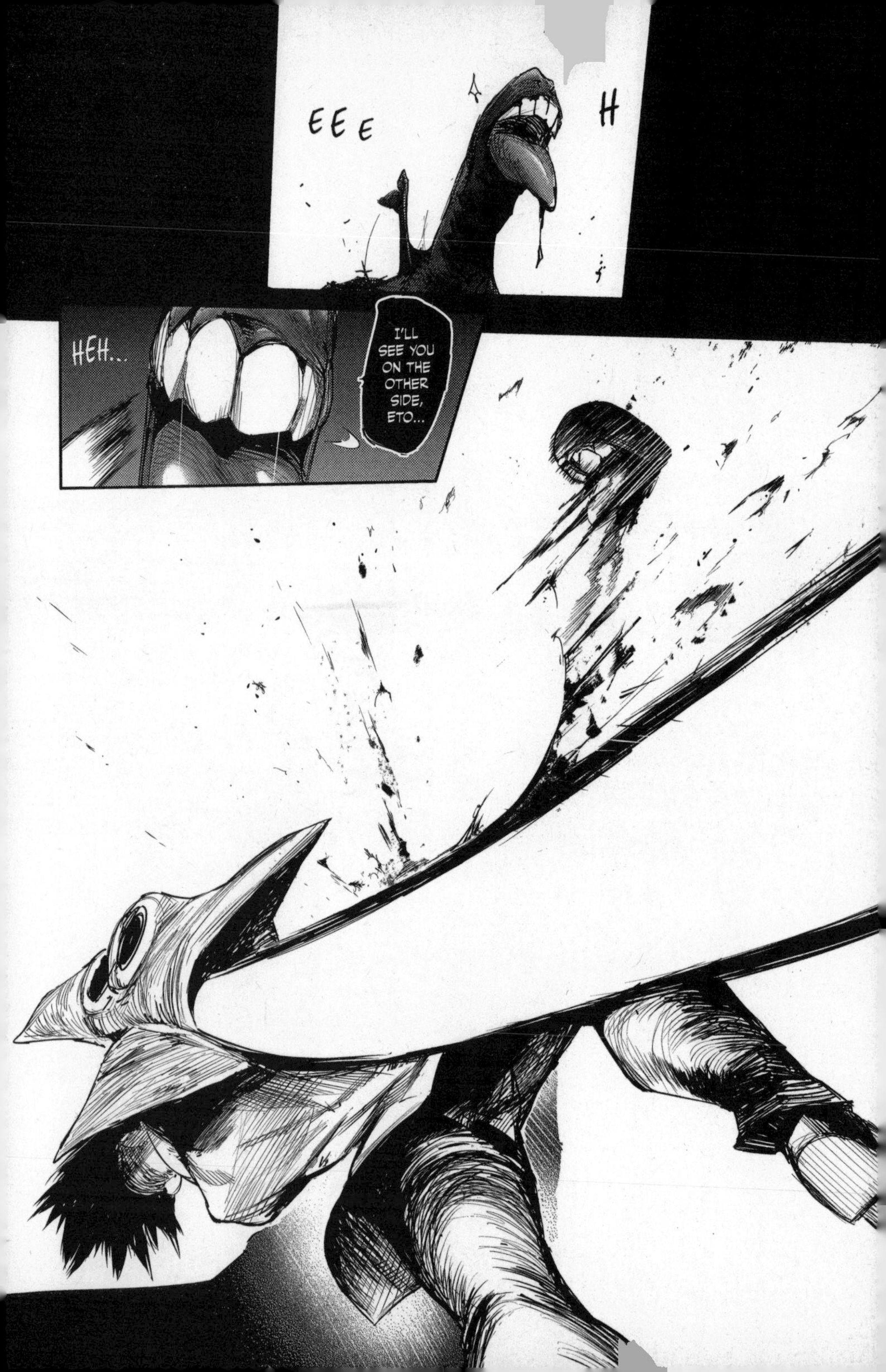
EEE
H
I'LL SEE YOU ON THE OTHER SIDE, ETO...
HEH...

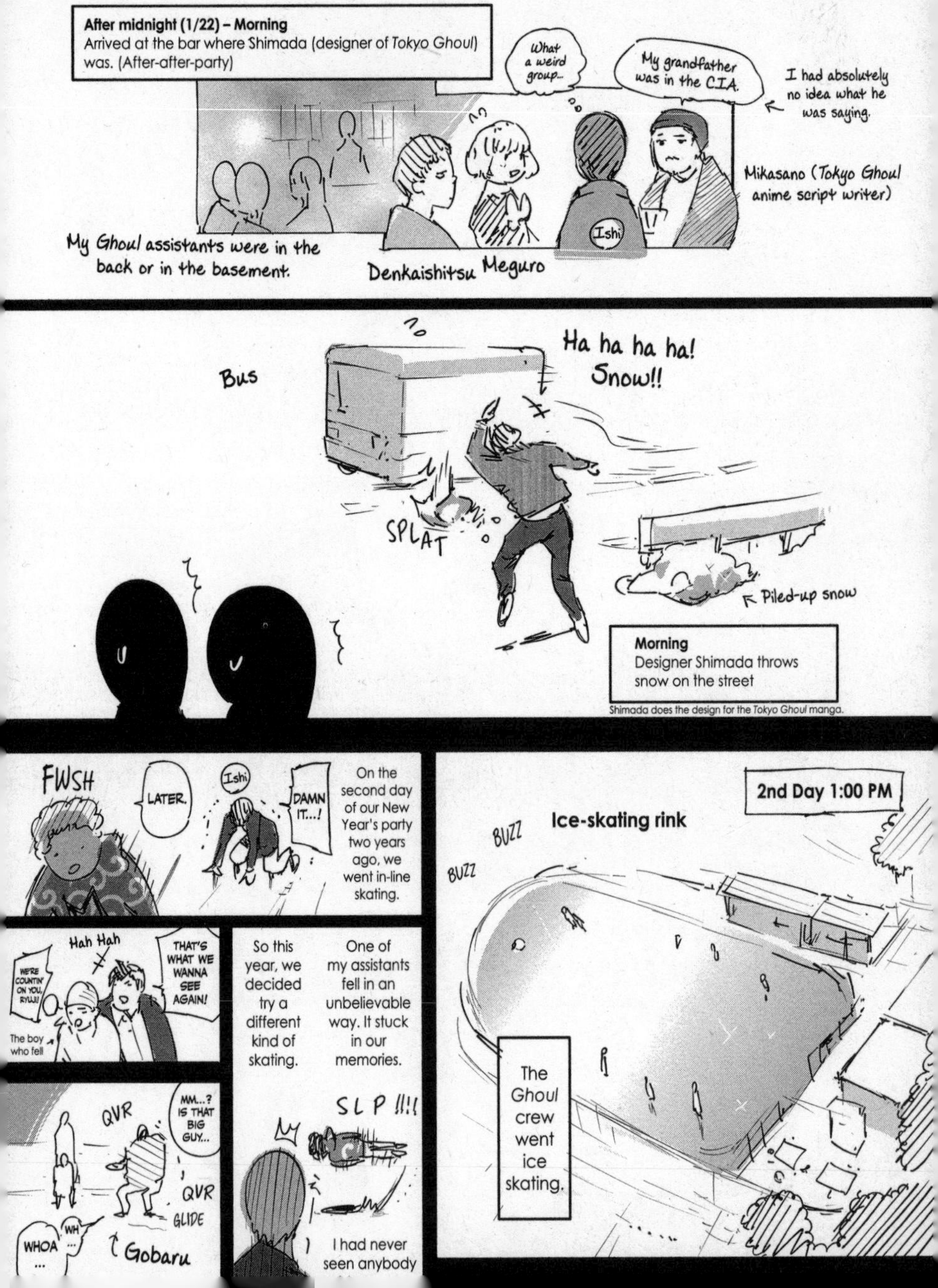

After midnight (1/22) – Morning
Arrived at the bar where Shimada (designer of Tokyo Ghoul) was. (After-after-party)
I had absolutely no idea what he was saying.
My grandfather was in the C.I.A.
What a weird group...
Mikasano (Tokyo Ghoul anime script writer)
Ishi
Meguro
Denkaishitsu
My Ghoul assistants were in the back or in the basement.
Ha ha ha ha! Snow!!
Bus
SPLAT
Piled-up snow
Morning
Designer Shimada throws snow on the street
Shimada does the design for the Tokyo Ghoul manga.
2nd Day 1:00 PM
Ice-skating rink
BUZZ
BUZZ
The Ghoul crew went ice skating.
On the second day of our New Year's party two years ago, we went in-line skating.
DAMN IT...!
Ishi
LATER.
FWSH
One of my assistants fell in an unbelievable way. It stuck in our memories.
So this year, we decided try a different kind of skating.
SLP !!!!
I had never seen anybody
THAT'S WHAT WE WANNA SEE AGAIN!
Hah Hah
WE'RE COUNTIN' ON YOU, RYUJI!
The boy who fell
MM...? IS THAT BIG GUY...
QVR
QVR
GLIDE
Gobaru
WH...
WHOA...

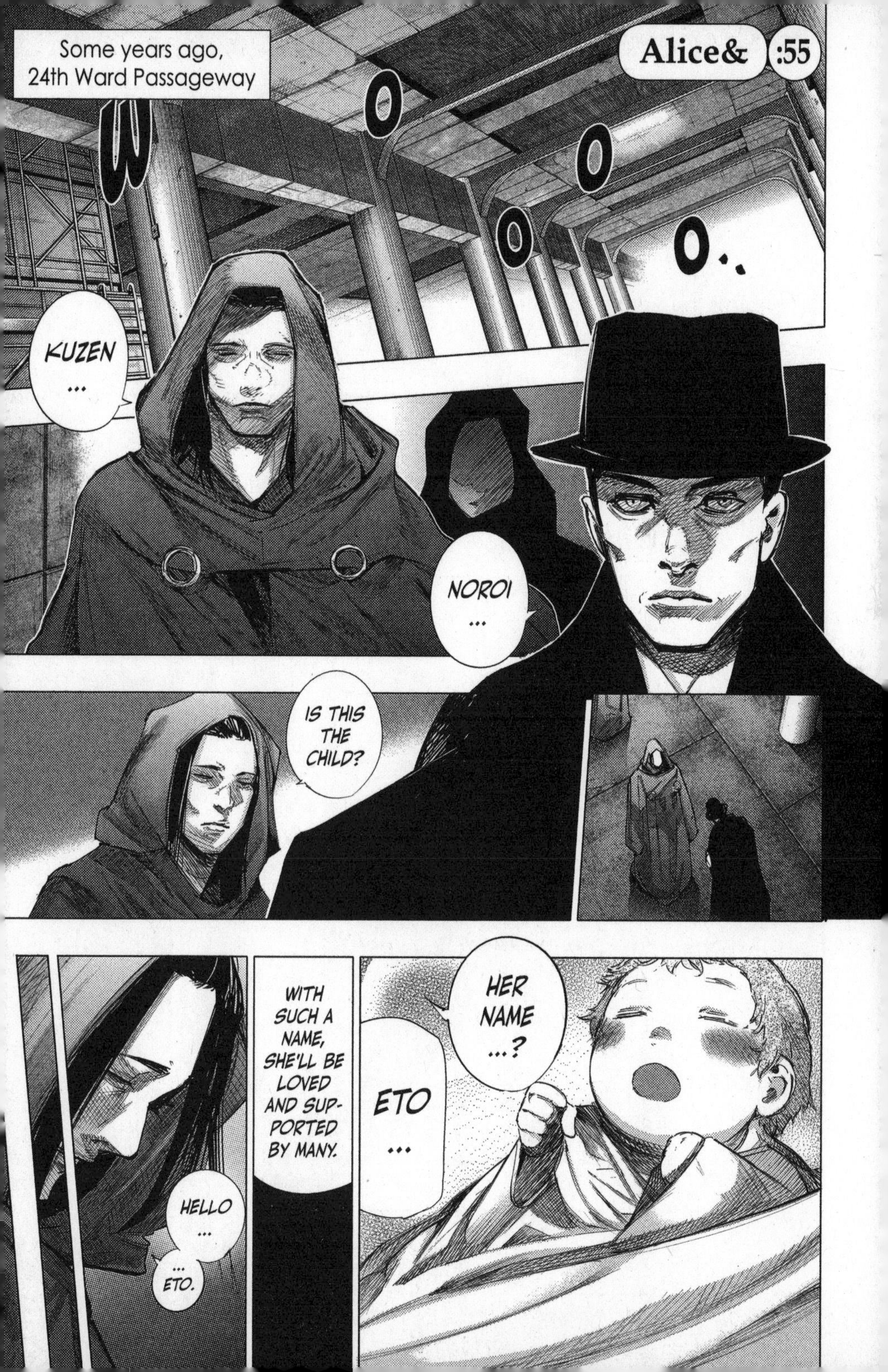
Alice& :55
Some years ago, 24th Ward Passageway
WOOOO..
KUZEN ...
NOROI ...
IS THIS THE CHILD?
HER NAME ...?
ETO ...
WITH SUCH A NAME, SHE'LL BE LOVED AND SUP-PORTED BY MANY.
HELLO ...
... ETO.

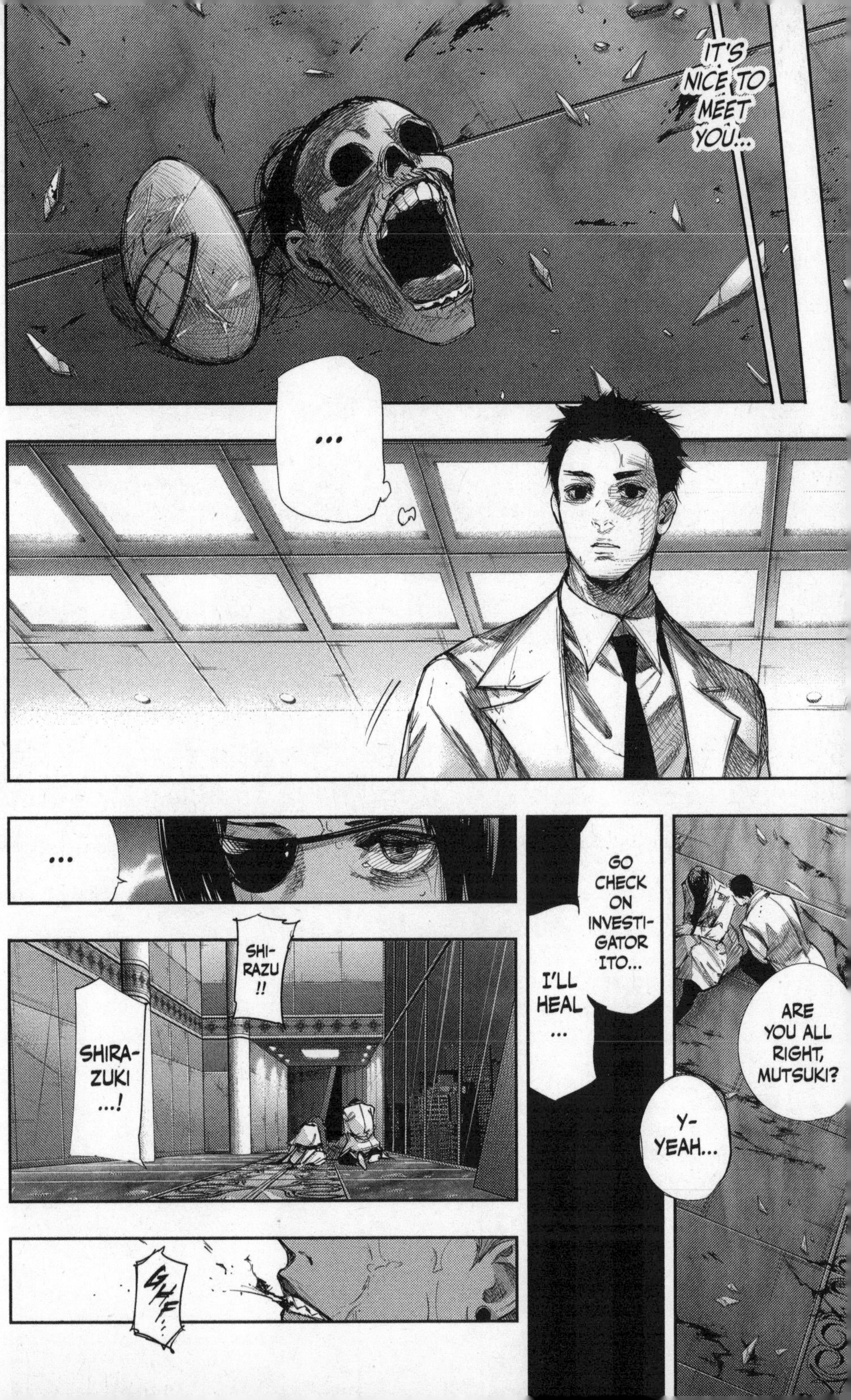
IT'S NICE TO MEET YOU...
...
ARE YOU ALL RIGHT, MUTSUKI?
Y-YEAH...
GO CHECK ON INVESTIGATOR ITO...
I'LL HEAL...
...
SHIRAZU!!
SHIRAZUKI...!
GHF...

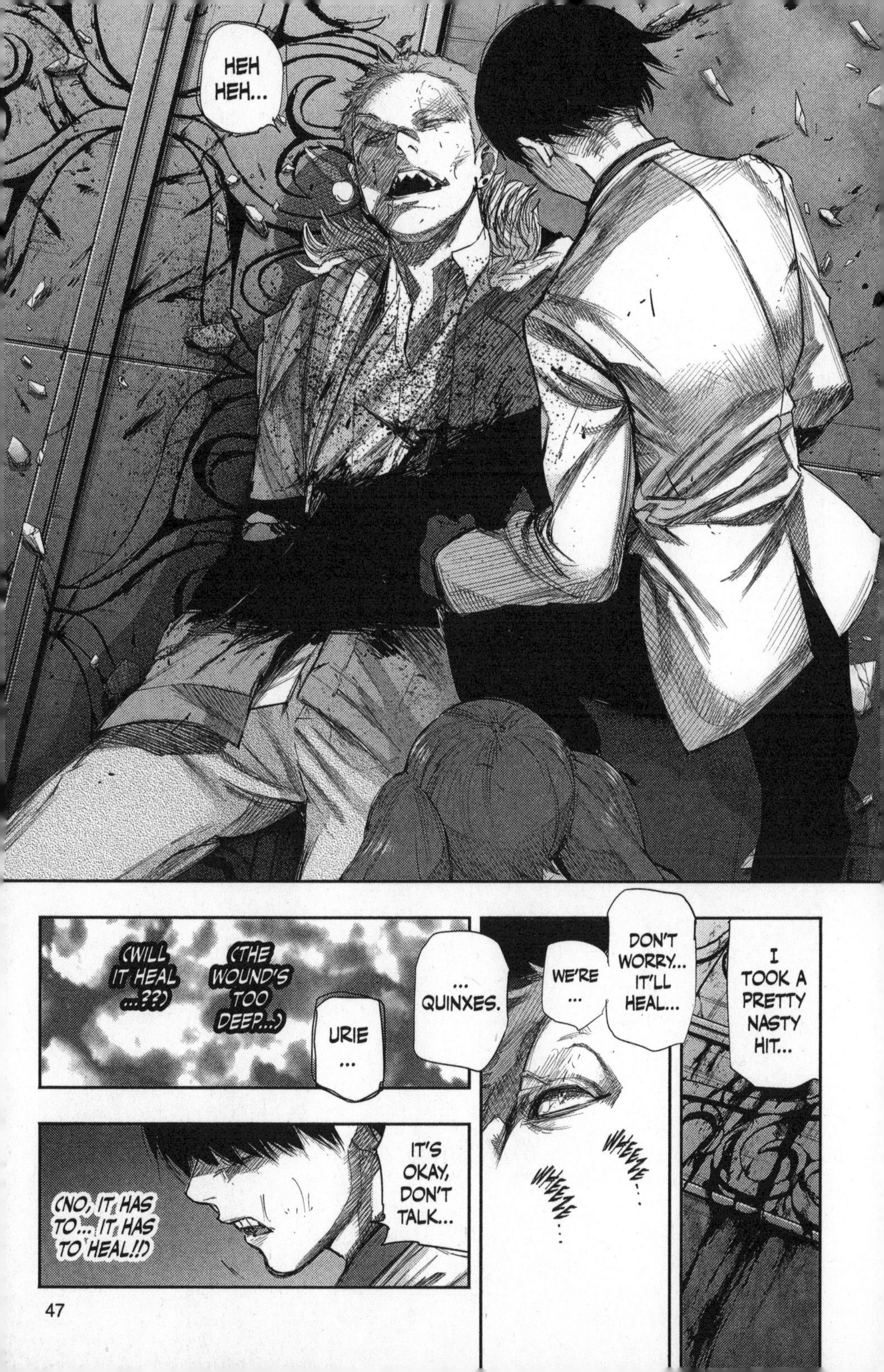
HEH HEH...
I TOOK A PRETTY NASTY HIT...
DON'T WORRY... IT'LL HEAL...
WE'RE ...
... QUINXES.
URIE ...
WHEEZE...
WHEEZE...
(THE WOUND'S TOO DEEP...)
(WILL IT HEAL ...??)
IT'S OKAY, DON'T TALK...
(NO, IT HAS TO... IT HAS TO HEAL!!)

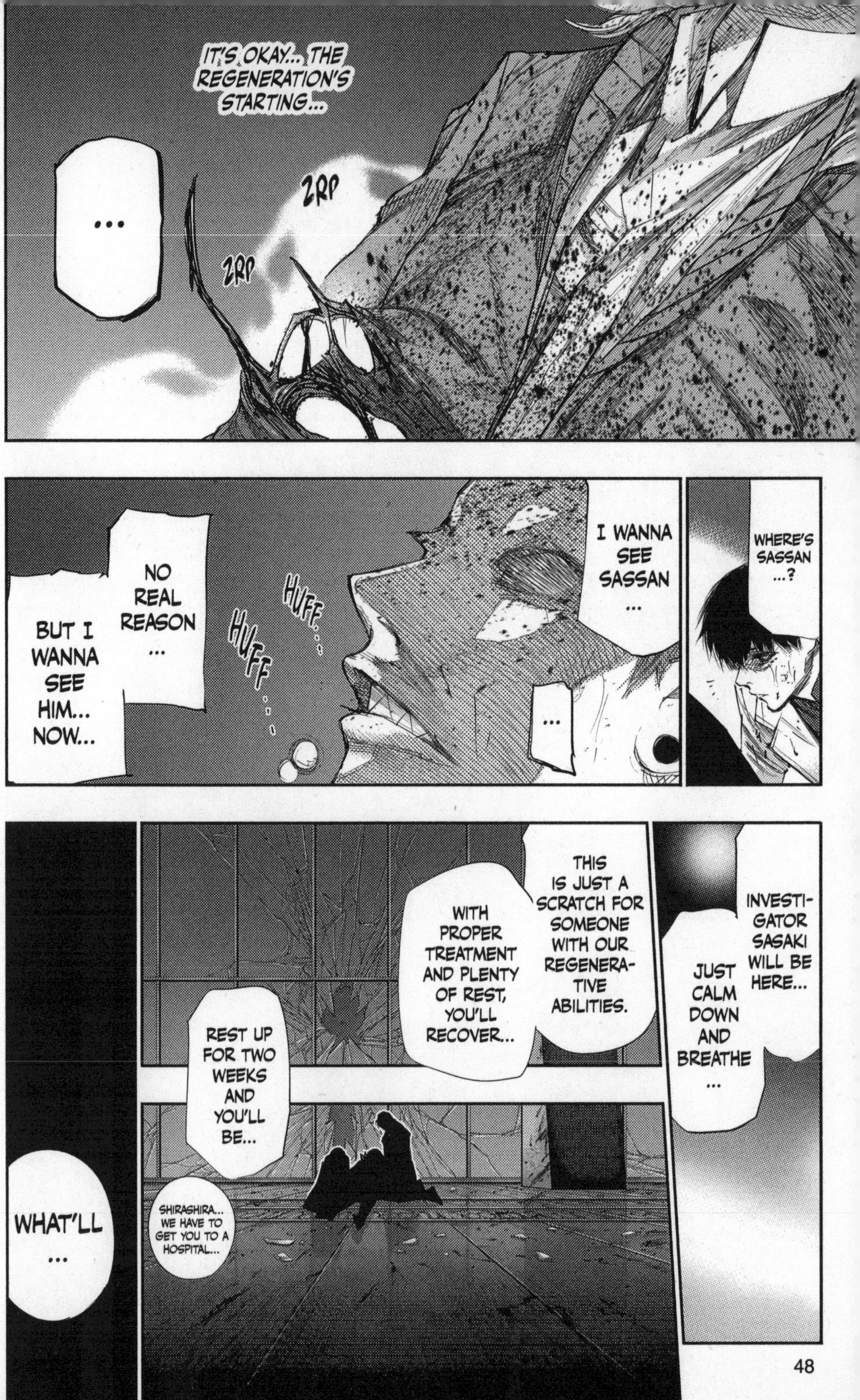
IT'S OKAY... THE REGENERATION'S STARTING...
ZRP
...
ZRP
WHERE'S SASSAN ...?
I WANNA SEE SASSAN ...
...
HUFF
HUFF
NO REAL REASON ...
BUT I WANNA SEE HIM... NOW...
INVESTI-GATOR SASAKI WILL BE HERE...
JUST CALM DOWN AND BREATHE ...
THIS IS JUST A SCRATCH FOR SOMEONE WITH OUR REGENERA-TIVE ABILITIES.
WITH PROPER TREATMENT AND PLENTY OF REST, YOU'LL RECOVER...
REST UP FOR TWO WEEKS AND YOU'LL BE...
SHIRASHIRA... WE HAVE TO GET YOU TO A HOSPITAL...
WHAT'LL ...

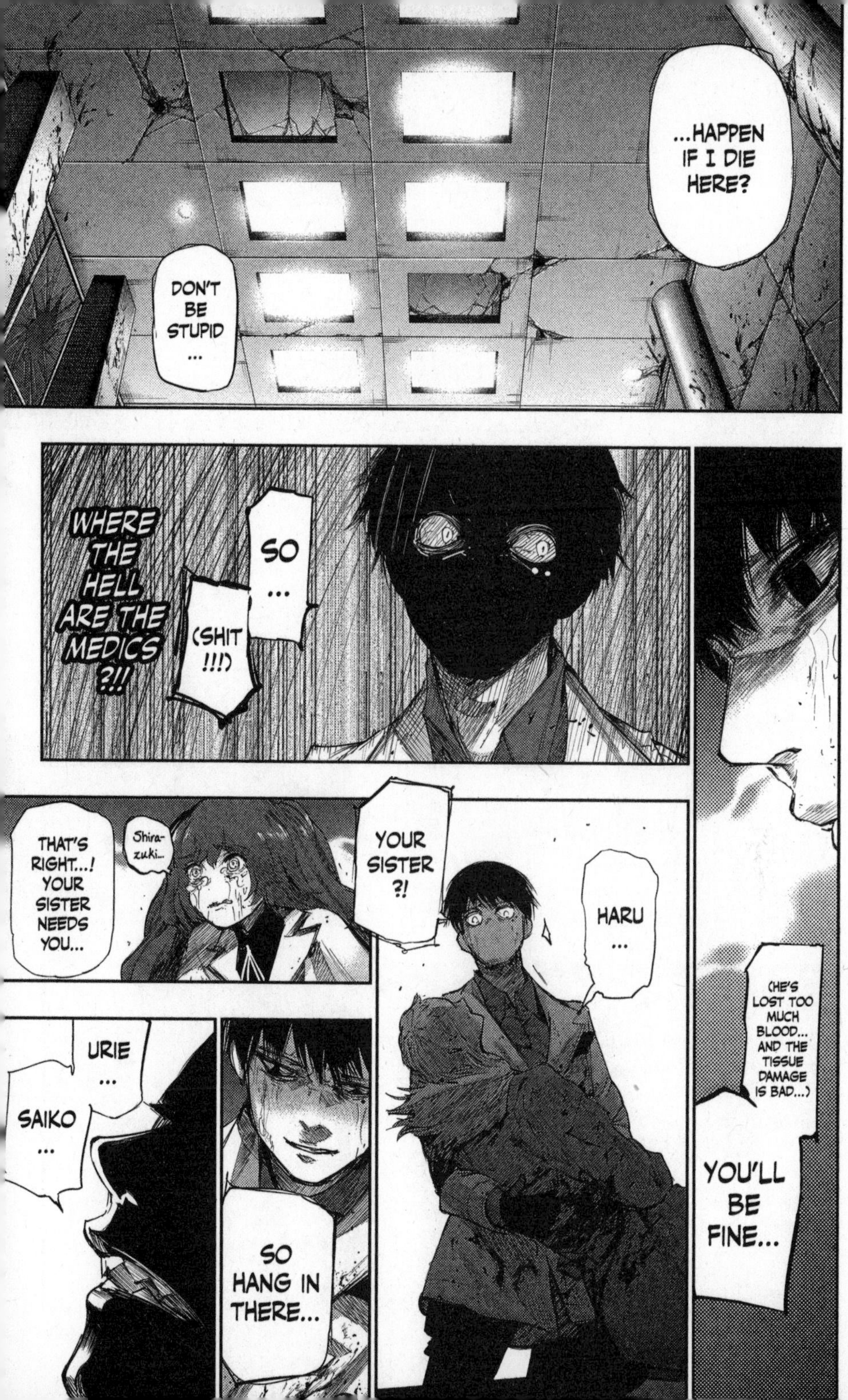
...HAPPEN IF I DIE HERE?
DON'T BE STUPID ...
(HE'S LOST TOO MUCH BLOOD... AND THE TISSUE DAMAGE IS BAD...)
YOU'LL BE FINE...
SO ...
(SHIT !!!)
WHERE THE HELL ARE THE MEDICS ?!!
HARU ...
YOUR SISTER ?!
Shira-zuki...
THAT'S RIGHT...! YOUR SISTER NEEDS YOU...
SO HANG IN THERE...
URIE ...
SAIKO ...

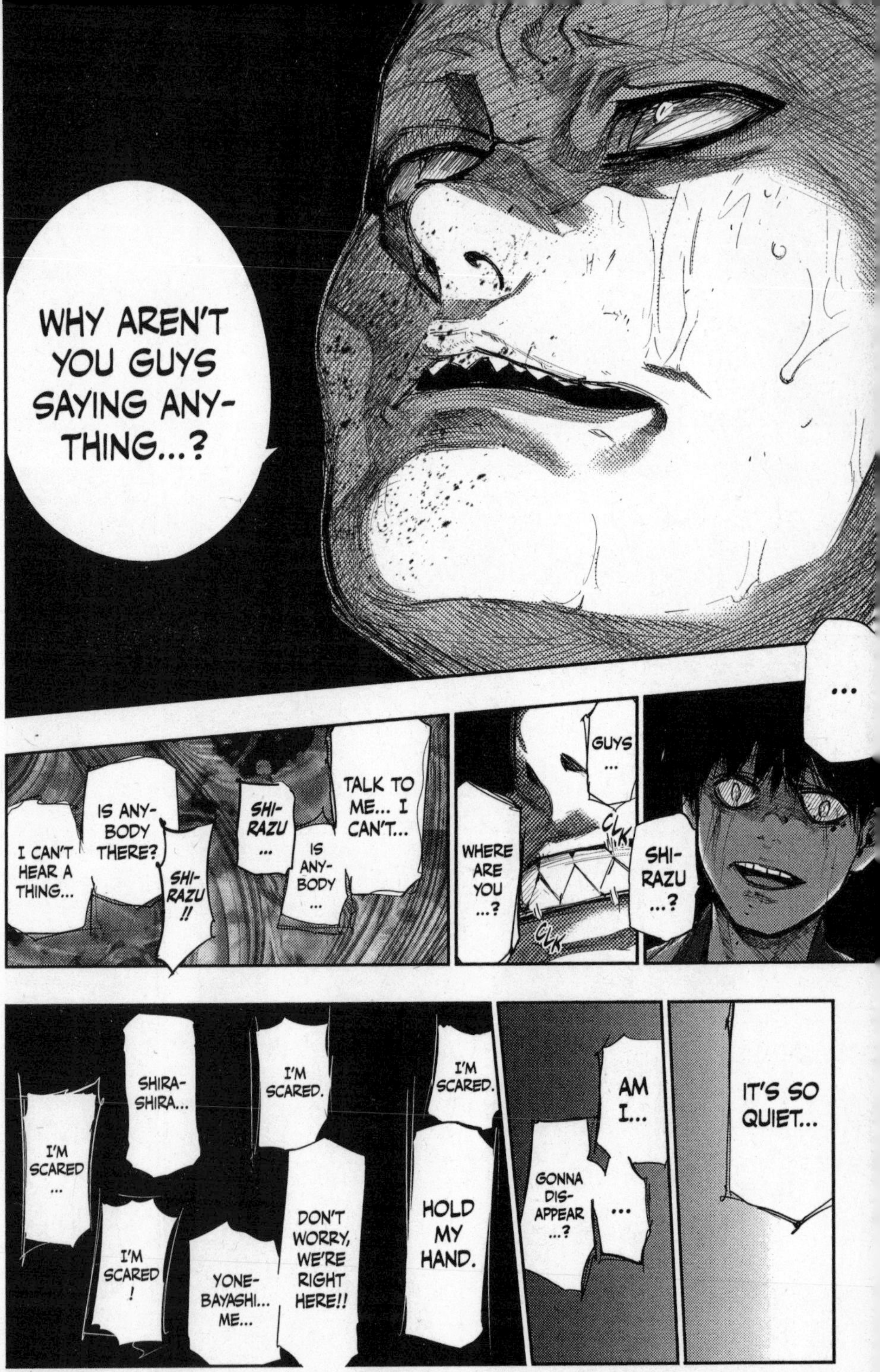
WHY AREN'T YOU GUYS SAYING ANY-THING...?
...
SHI-RAZU ...?
GUYS ...
CLK
WHERE ARE YOU ...?
CLK
TALK TO ME... I CAN'T...
SHI-RAZU ...
IS ANY-BODY ...
IS ANY-BODY THERE?
SHI-RAZU !!
I CAN'T HEAR A THING...
IT'S SO QUIET...
AM I...
GONNA DIS-APPEAR ...?
...
I'M SCARED.
HOLD MY HAND.
I'M SCARED.
DON'T WORRY, WE'RE RIGHT HERE!!
SHIRA-SHIRA...
YONE-BAYASHI... ME...
I'M SCARED !
I'M SCARED ...

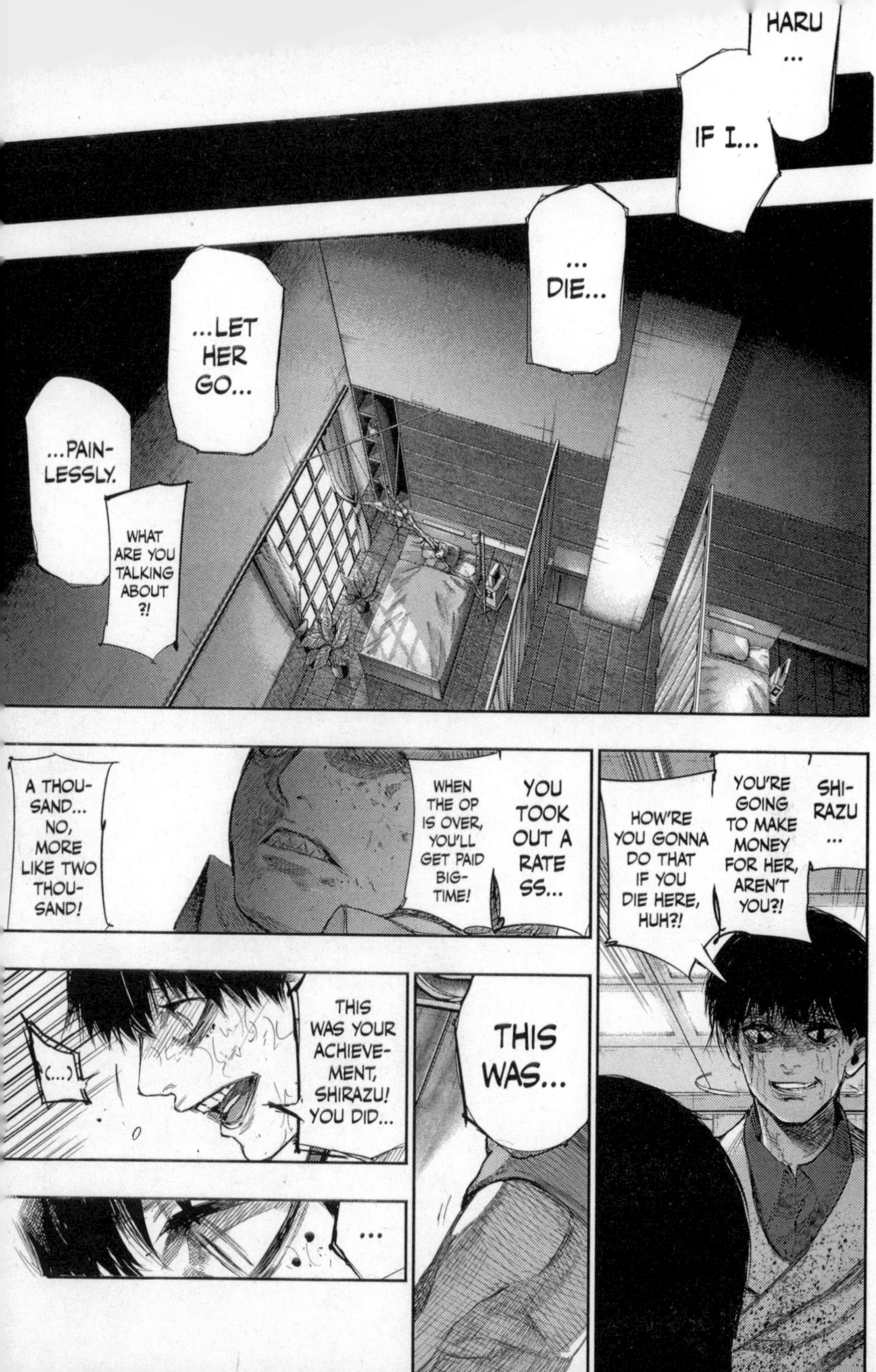
HARU...
IF I...
...DIE...
...LET HER GO...
...PAINLESSLY.
WHAT ARE YOU TALKING ABOUT?!
SHI-RAZU...
YOU'RE GOING TO MAKE MONEY FOR HER, AREN'T YOU?!
HOW'RE YOU GONNA DO THAT IF YOU DIE HERE, HUH?!
YOU TOOK OUT A RATE SS...
WHEN THE OP IS OVER, YOU'LL GET PAID BIG-TIME!
A THOUSAND... NO, MORE LIKE TWO THOUSAND!
THIS WAS...
THIS WAS YOUR ACHIEVEMENT, SHIRAZU! YOU DID...
(...)
...

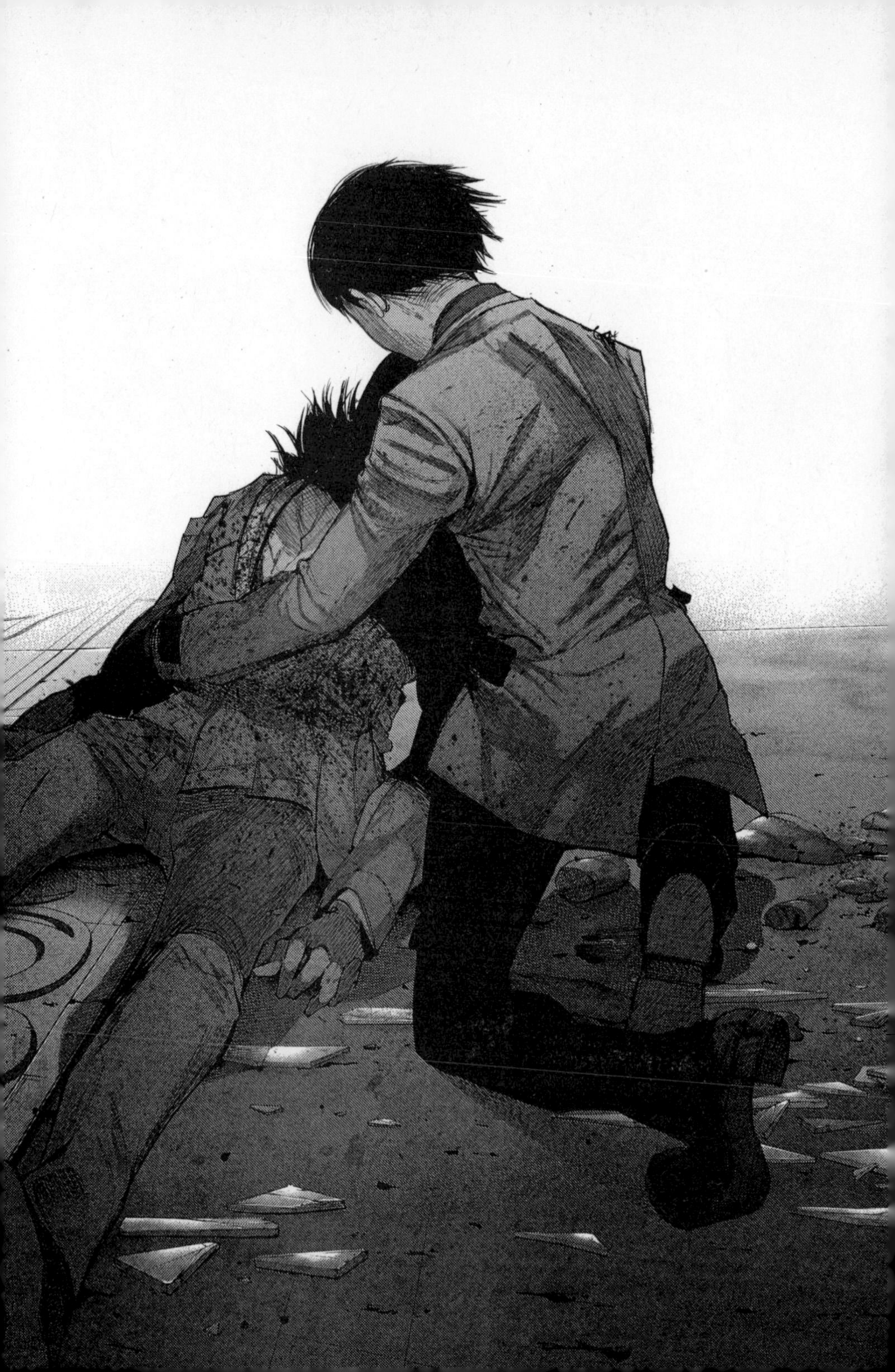

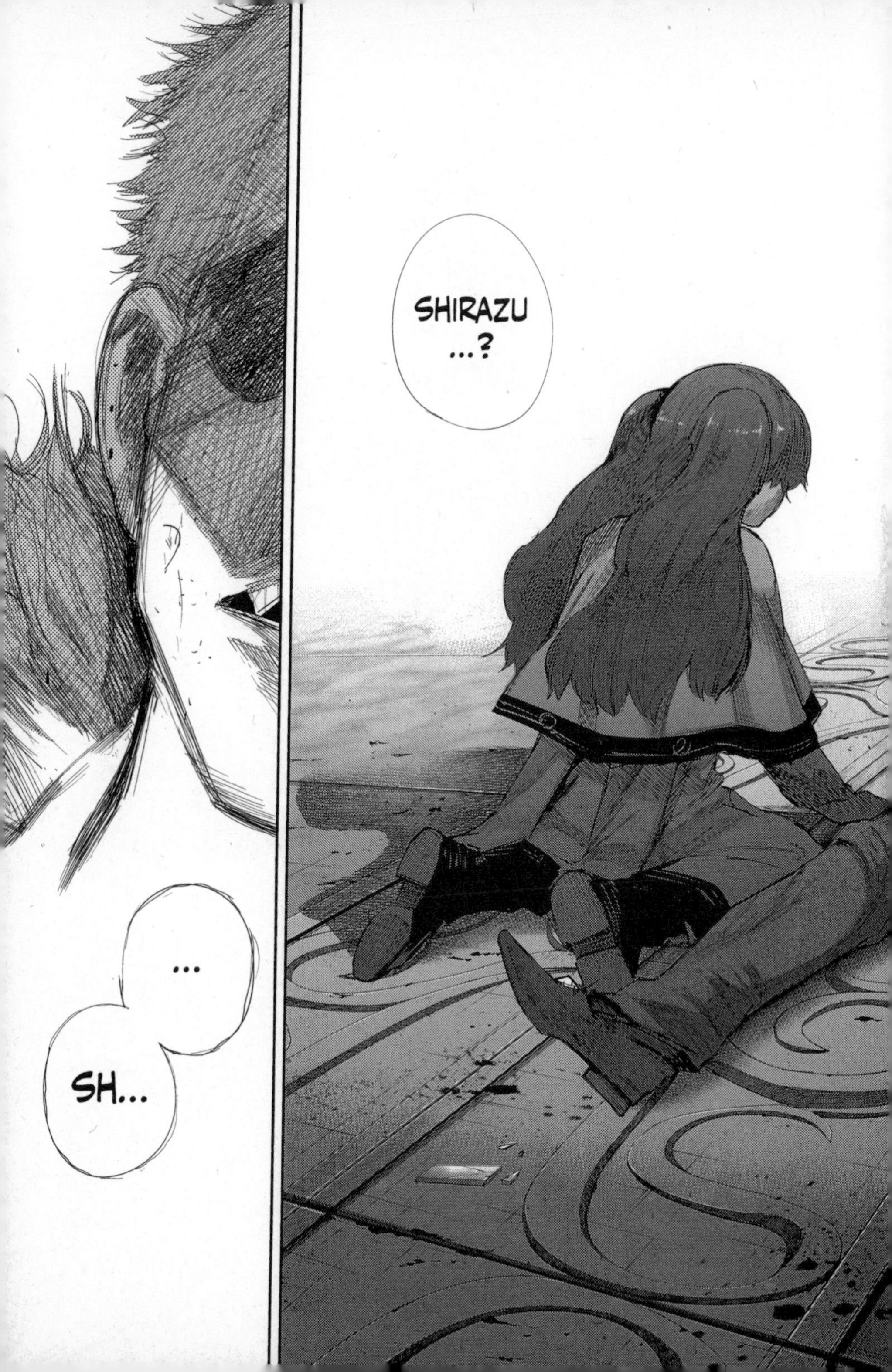
SHIRAZU ...?
...
SH...

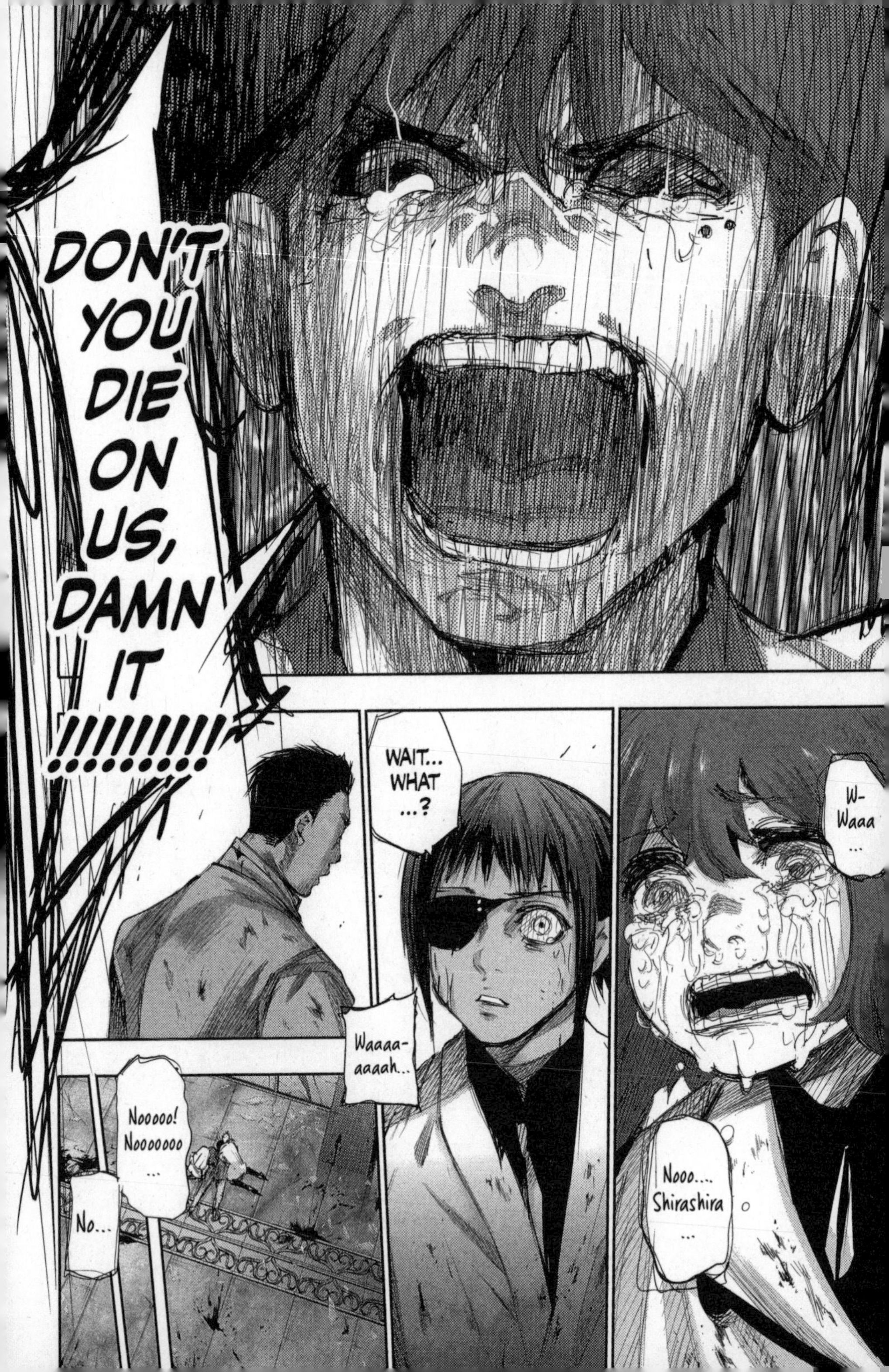
DON'T YOU DIE ON US, DAMN IT!!!!!!!!!!
W-Waaa...
Nooo.... Shirashira...
WAIT... WHAT...?
Waaaa-aaaah...
Nooooo! Noooooo...
No...

COLLECT THE BODIES...

WHAT THE HELL HAPPENED HERE...?

YEAH...

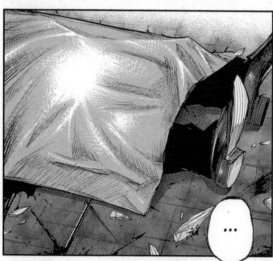

INVESTIGATOR ITO...?

...

INVESTIGATOR WASHU...?!

TMP TMP TMP TMP

WHAT ARE YOU DOING HERE?

ZSH

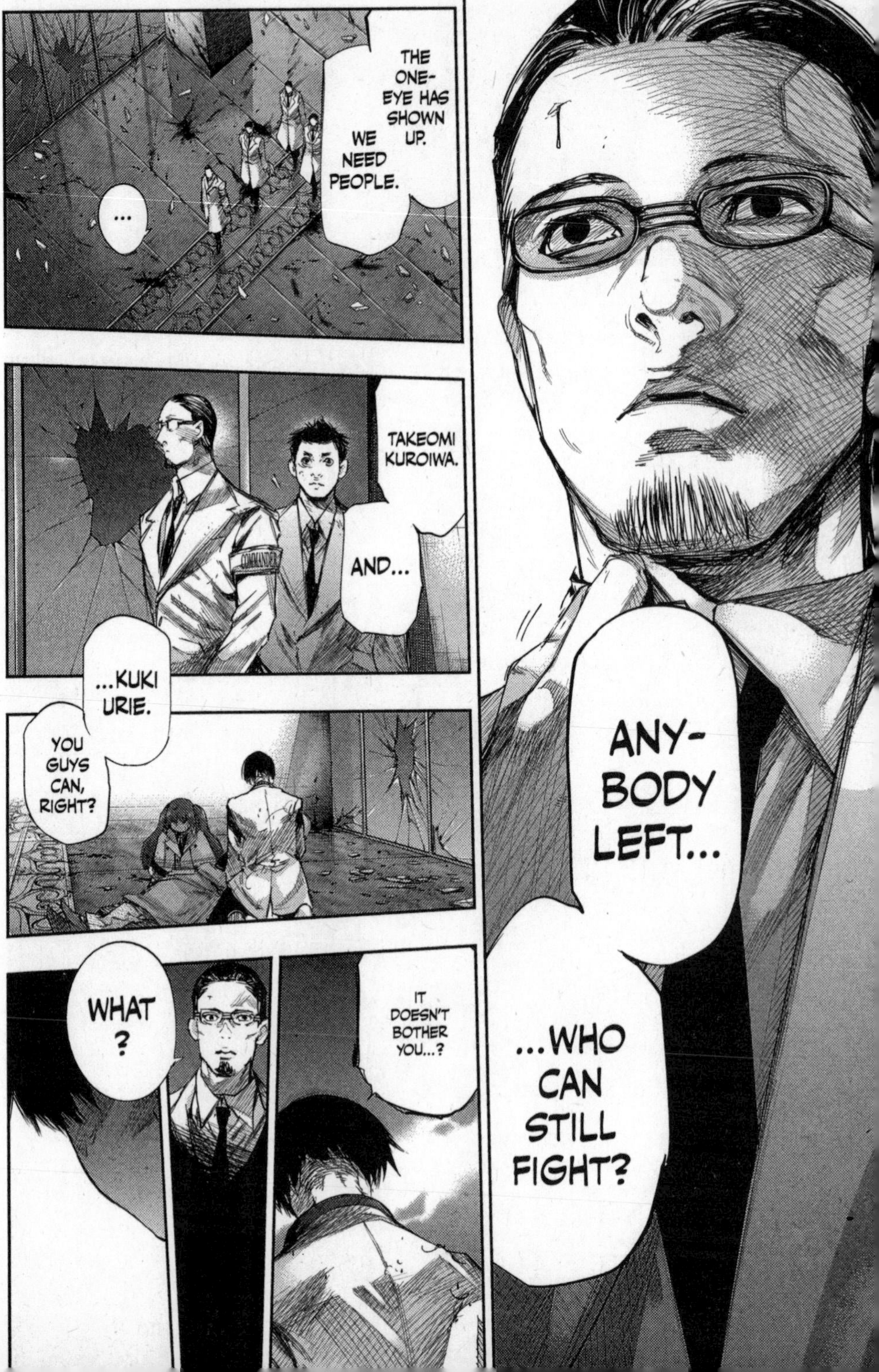
ANY-BODY LEFT...
...WHO CAN STILL FIGHT?
THE ONE-EYE HAS SHOWN UP.
WE NEED PEOPLE.
...
TAKEOMI KUROIWA.
AND...
COMMANDER
...KUKI URIE.
YOU GUYS CAN, RIGHT?
IT DOESN'T BOTHER YOU...?
WHAT?

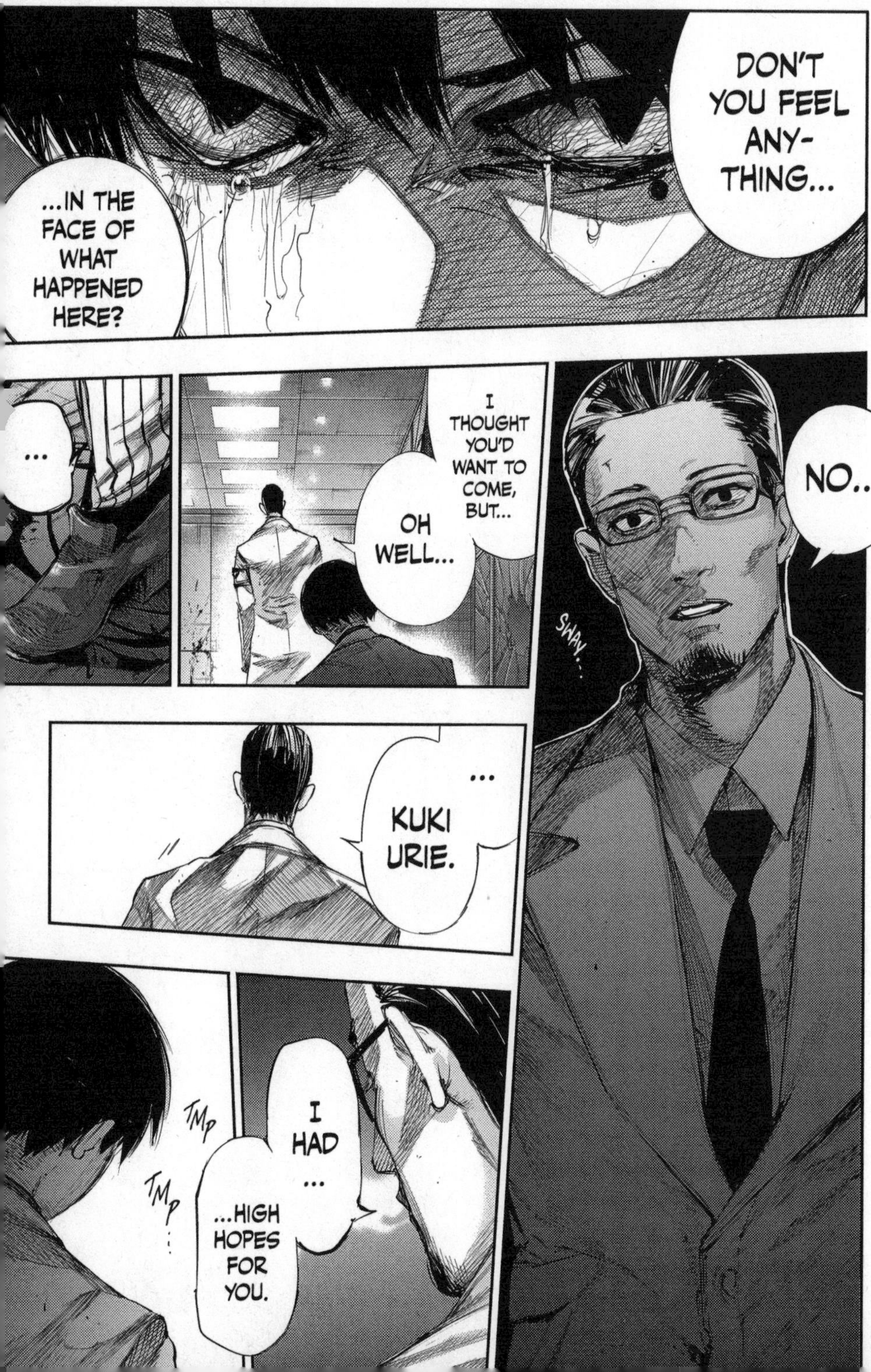
DON'T YOU FEEL ANYTHING...
...IN THE FACE OF WHAT HAPPENED HERE?
NO...
SWAY...
I THOUGHT YOU'D WANT TO COME, BUT...
OH WELL...
...
...
KUKI URIE.
I HAD...
...HIGH HOPES FOR YOU.
TMP
TMP...

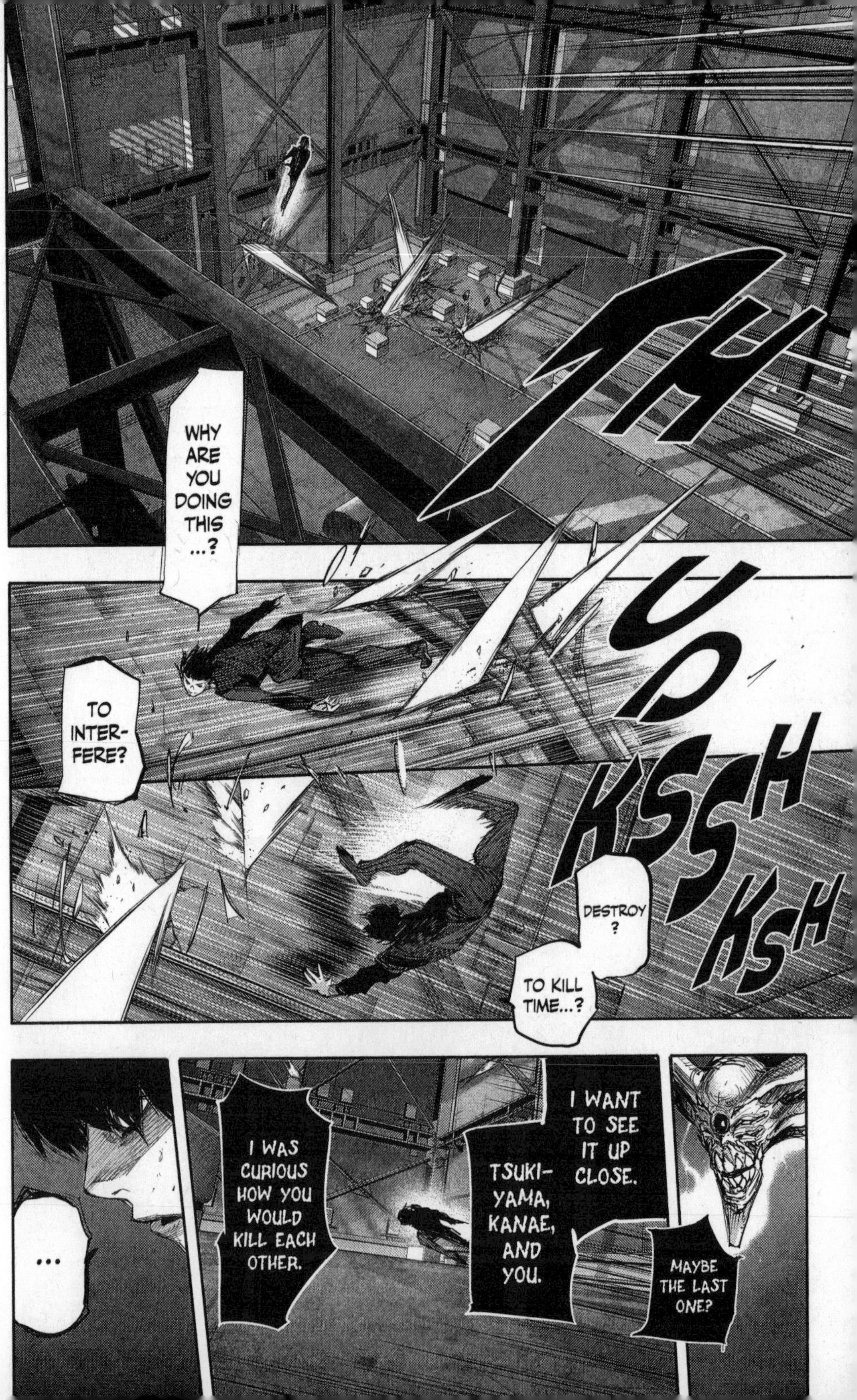
TH
WHY ARE YOU DOING THIS ...?
UD
KSSH
KSH
DESTROY?
TO KILL TIME...?
TO INTER-FERE?
MAYBE THE LAST ONE?
I WANT TO SEE IT UP CLOSE.
TSUKI-YAMA, KANAE, AND YOU.
I WAS CURIOUS HOW YOU WOULD KILL EACH OTHER.
...

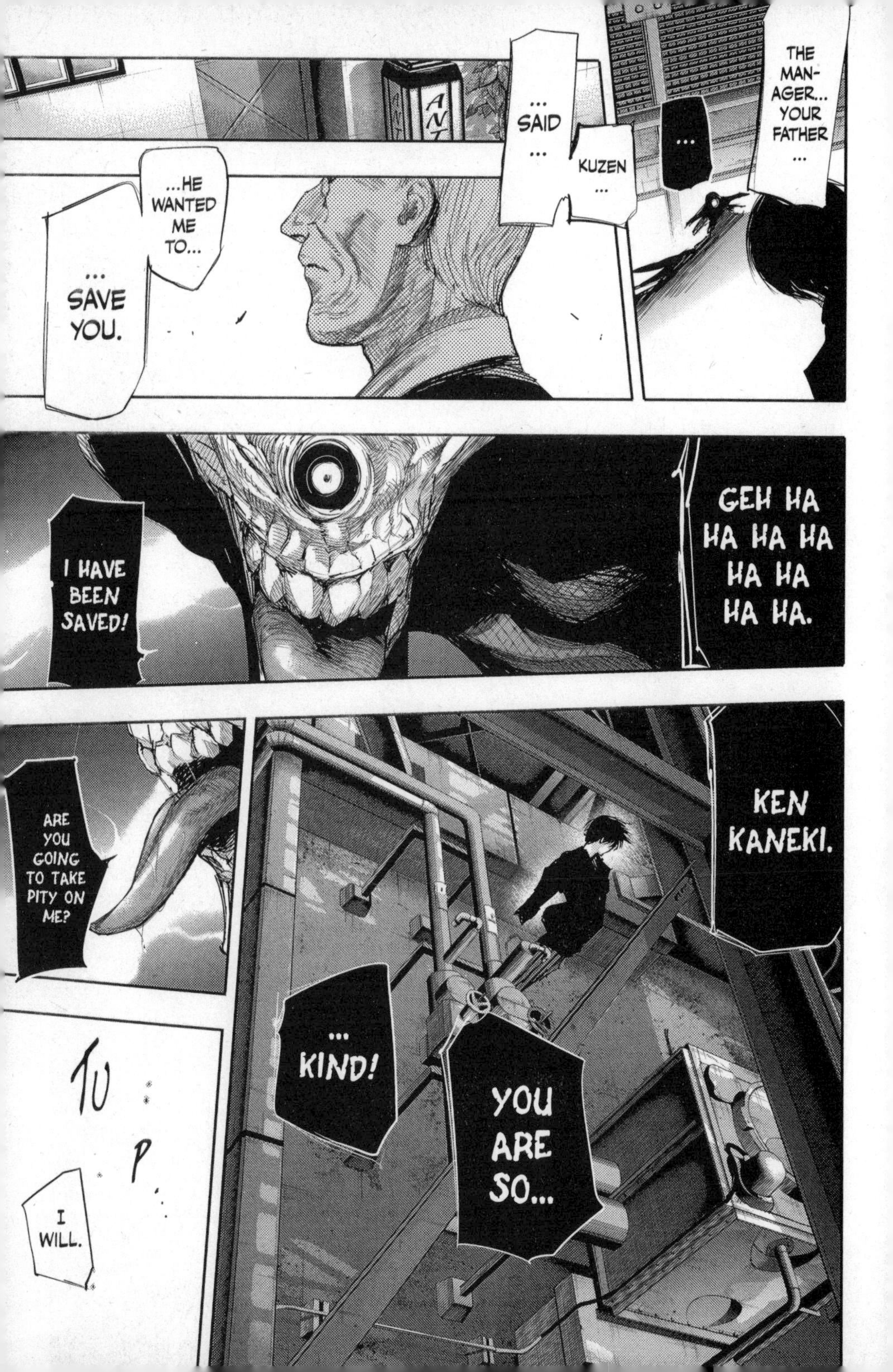
THE MAN-AGER... YOUR FATHER ...
...
KUZEN ...
... SAID ...
...HE WANTED ME TO...
... SAVE YOU.
GEH HA HA HA HA HA HA HA HA.
I HAVE BEEN SAVED!
KEN KANEKI.
YOU ARE SO...
... KIND!
ARE YOU GOING TO TAKE PITY ON ME?
TUP
I WILL.

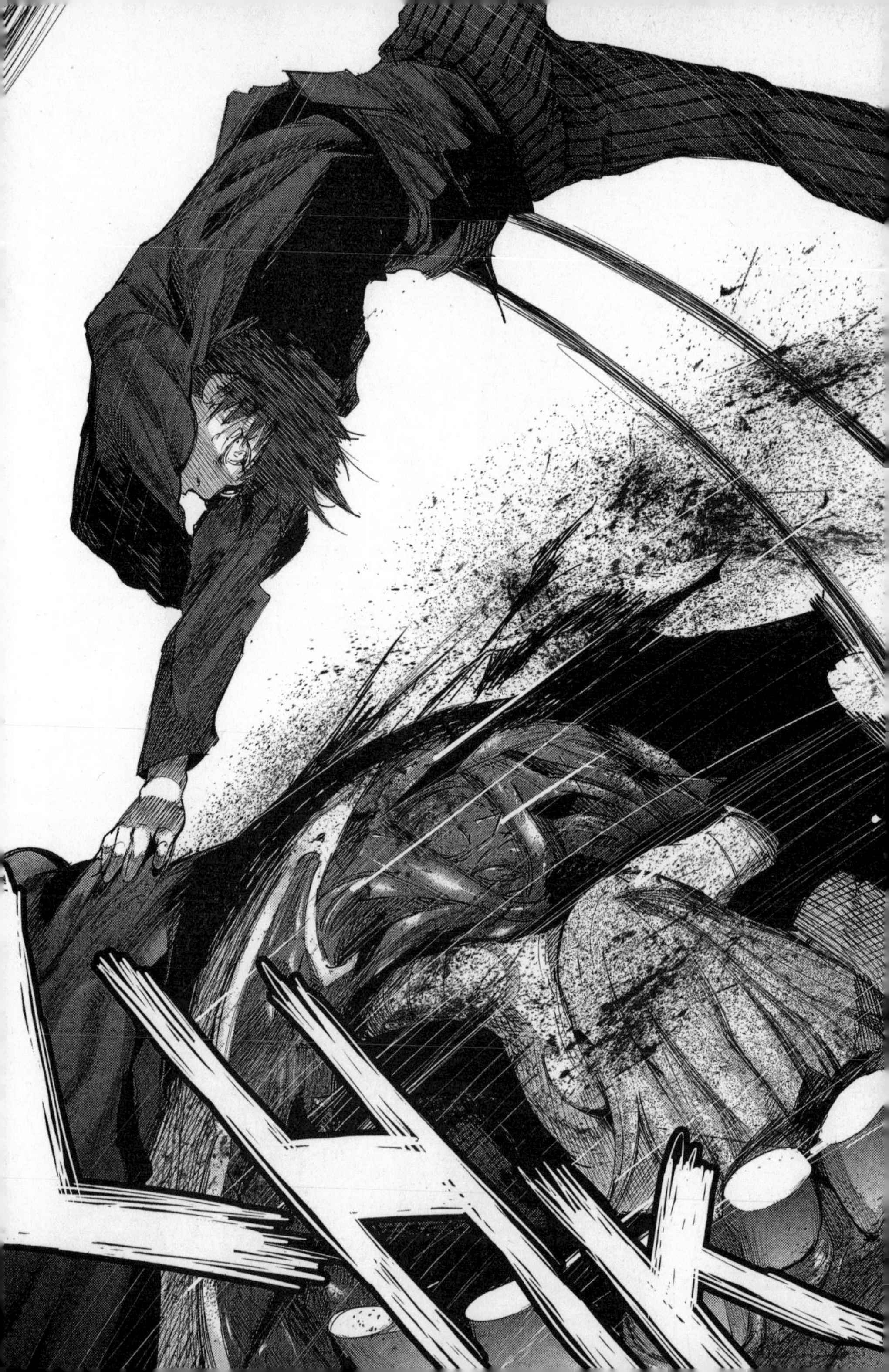

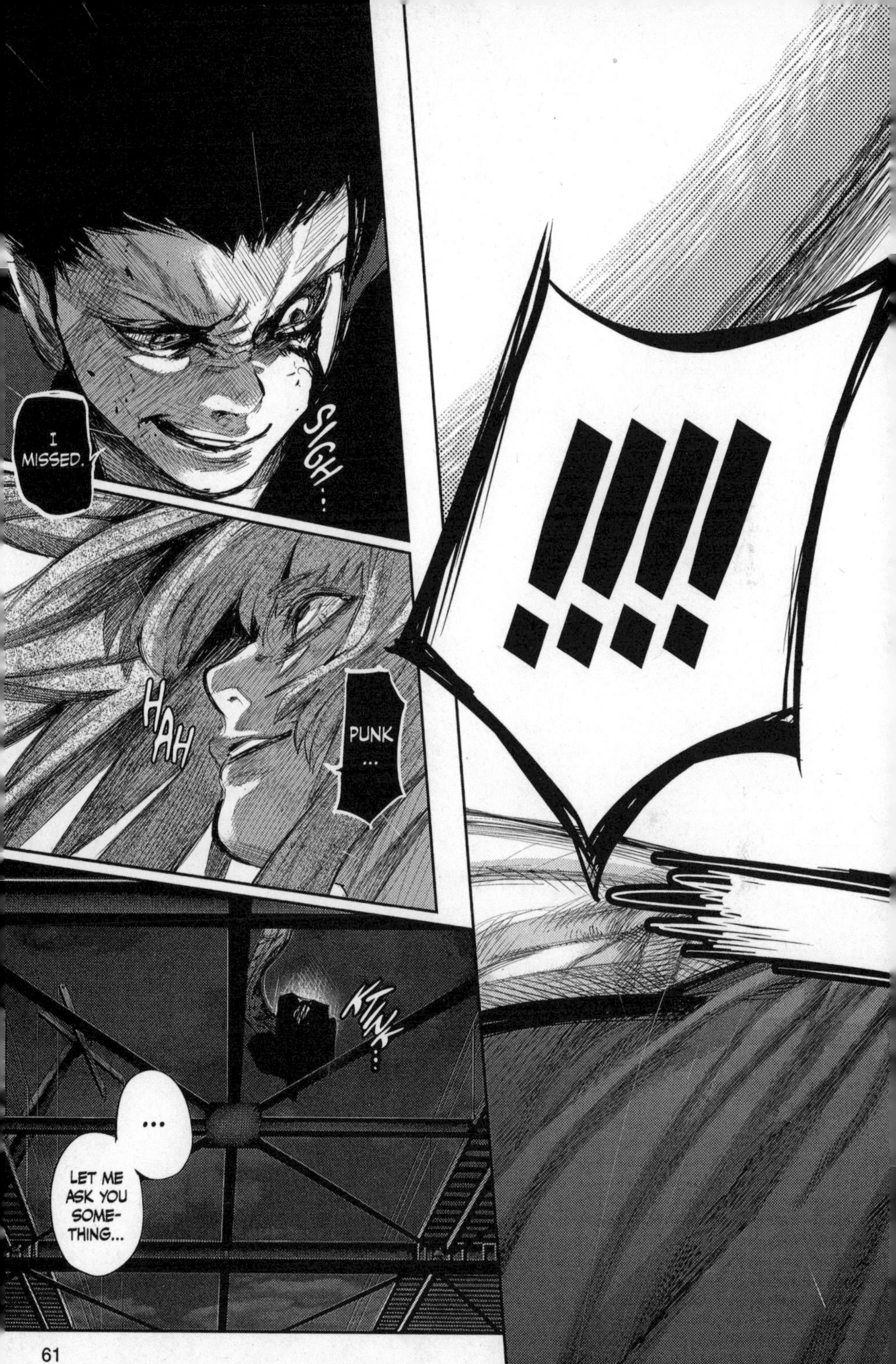
!!!!
SIGH...
I MISSED.
HAH HAH
PUNK...
KLINK...
...
LET ME ASK YOU SOME-THING...

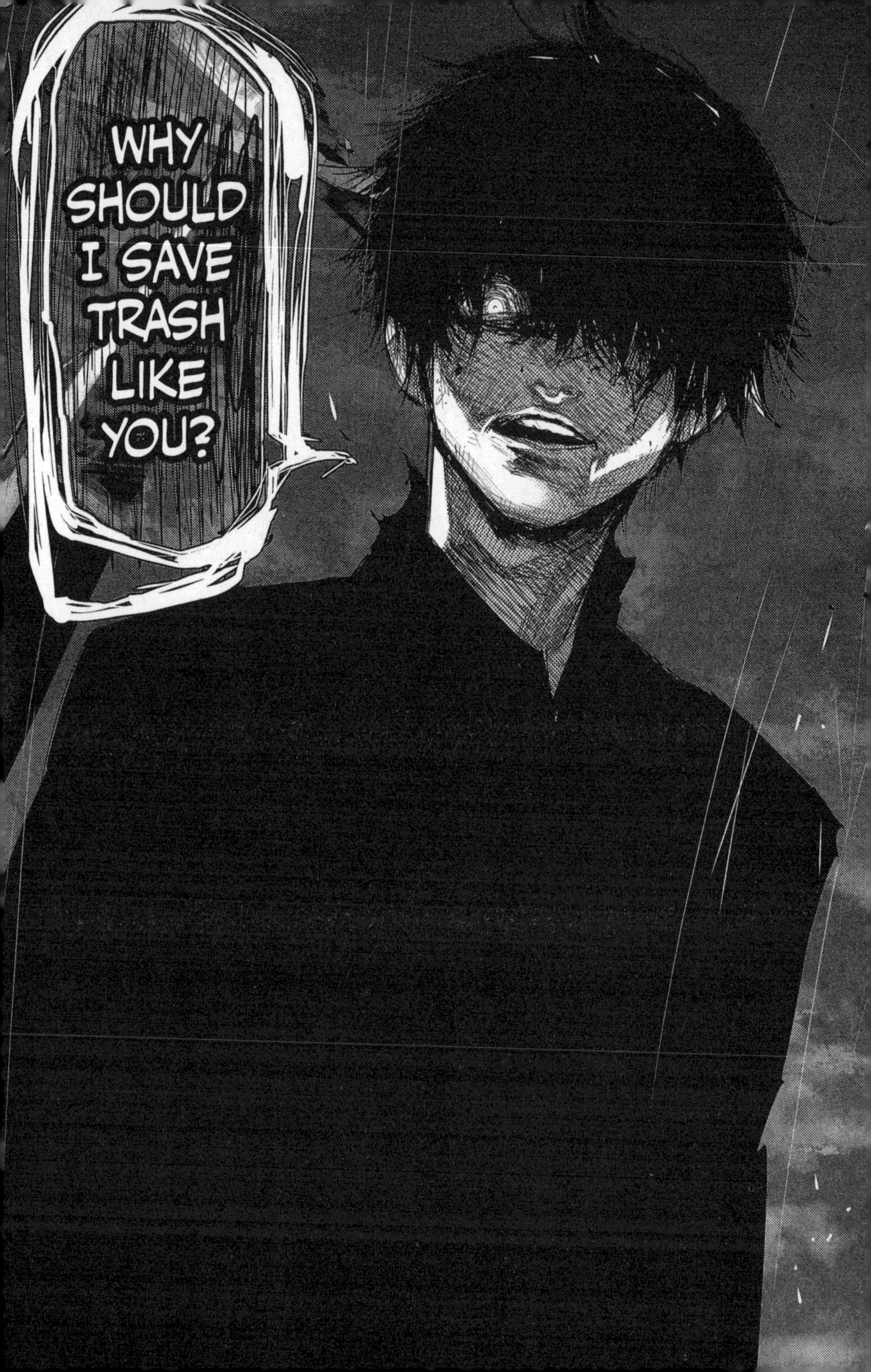
WHY SHOULD I SAVE TRASH LIKE YOU?

The Second King :56

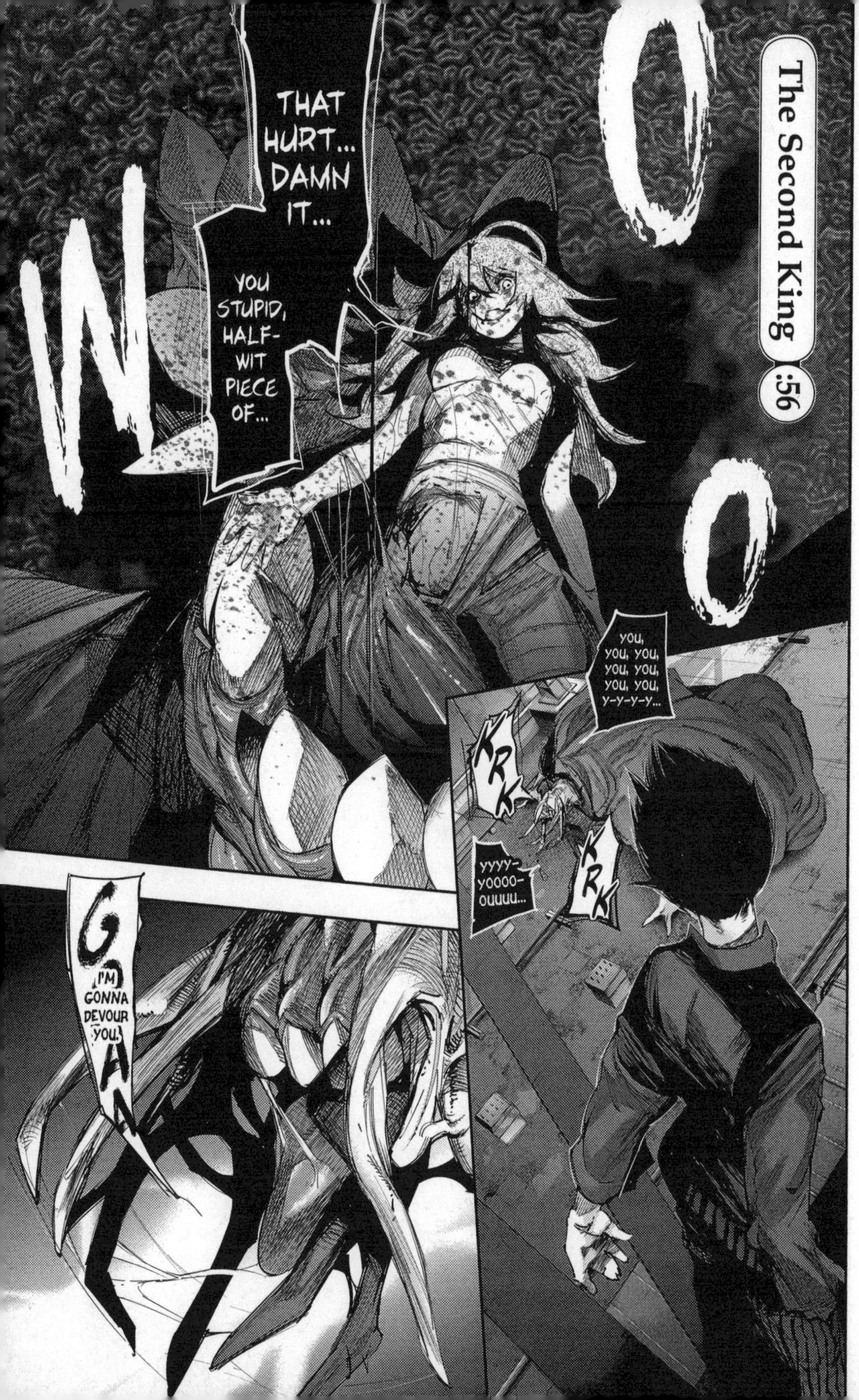
W O O
THAT HURT... DAMN IT...
YOU STUPID, HALF-WIT PIECE OF...
you, you, you, you, you, you, you, y-y-y-y...
KRK
yyyy-yoooo-ouuuu...
KRK
I'M GONNA DEVOUR YOU.
G A N

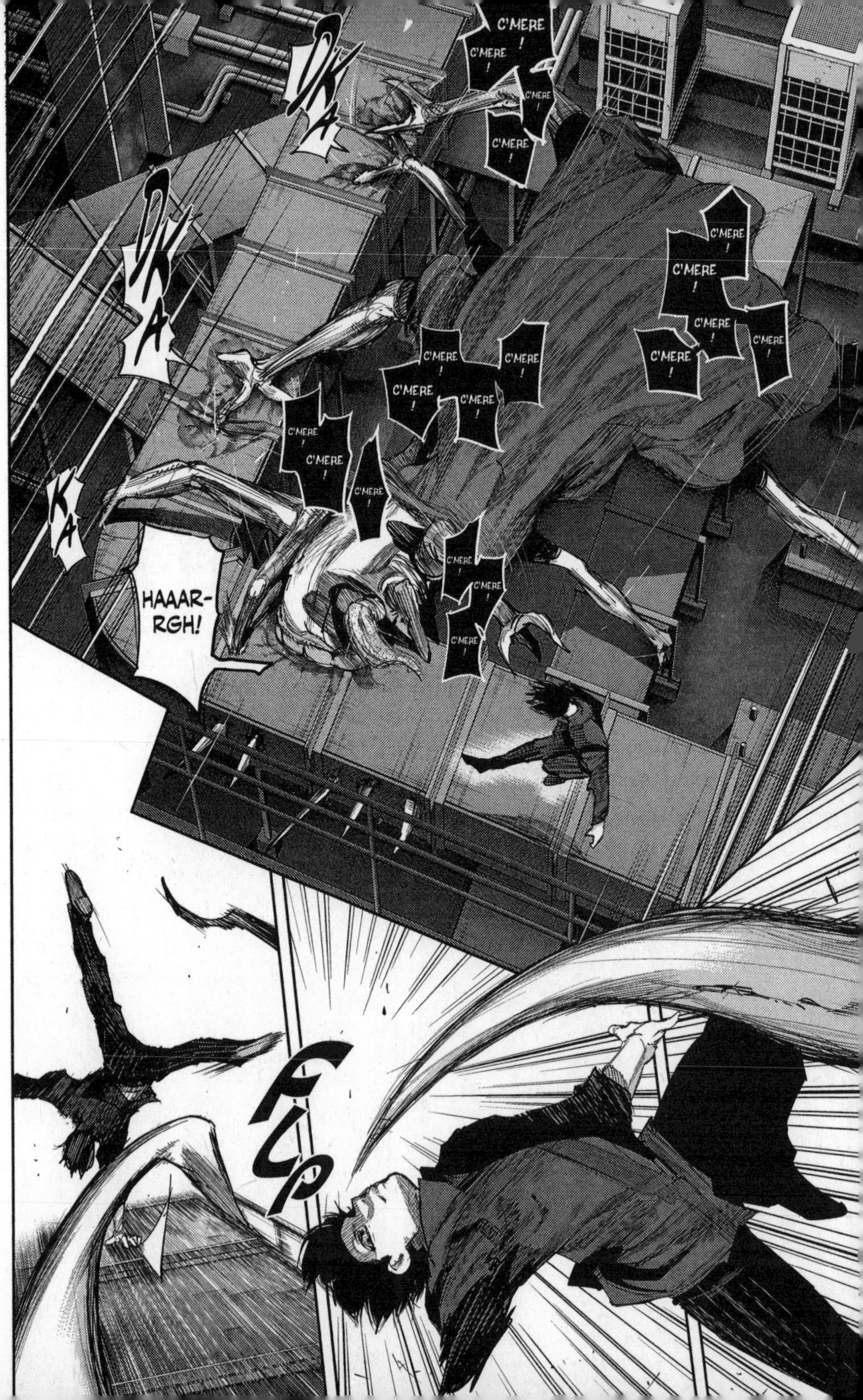

C'MERE!
C'MERE!
C'MERE!
C'MERE!
C'MERE!
C'MERE!
C'MERE!
C'MERE!
C'MERE!
C'MERE!
C'MERE!
C'MERE!
C'MERE!
C'MERE!
C'MERE!
C'MERE!
DOKA
DOKA
C'MERE!
C'MERE!
C'MERE!
KA
HAAAR-RGH!
FLIP

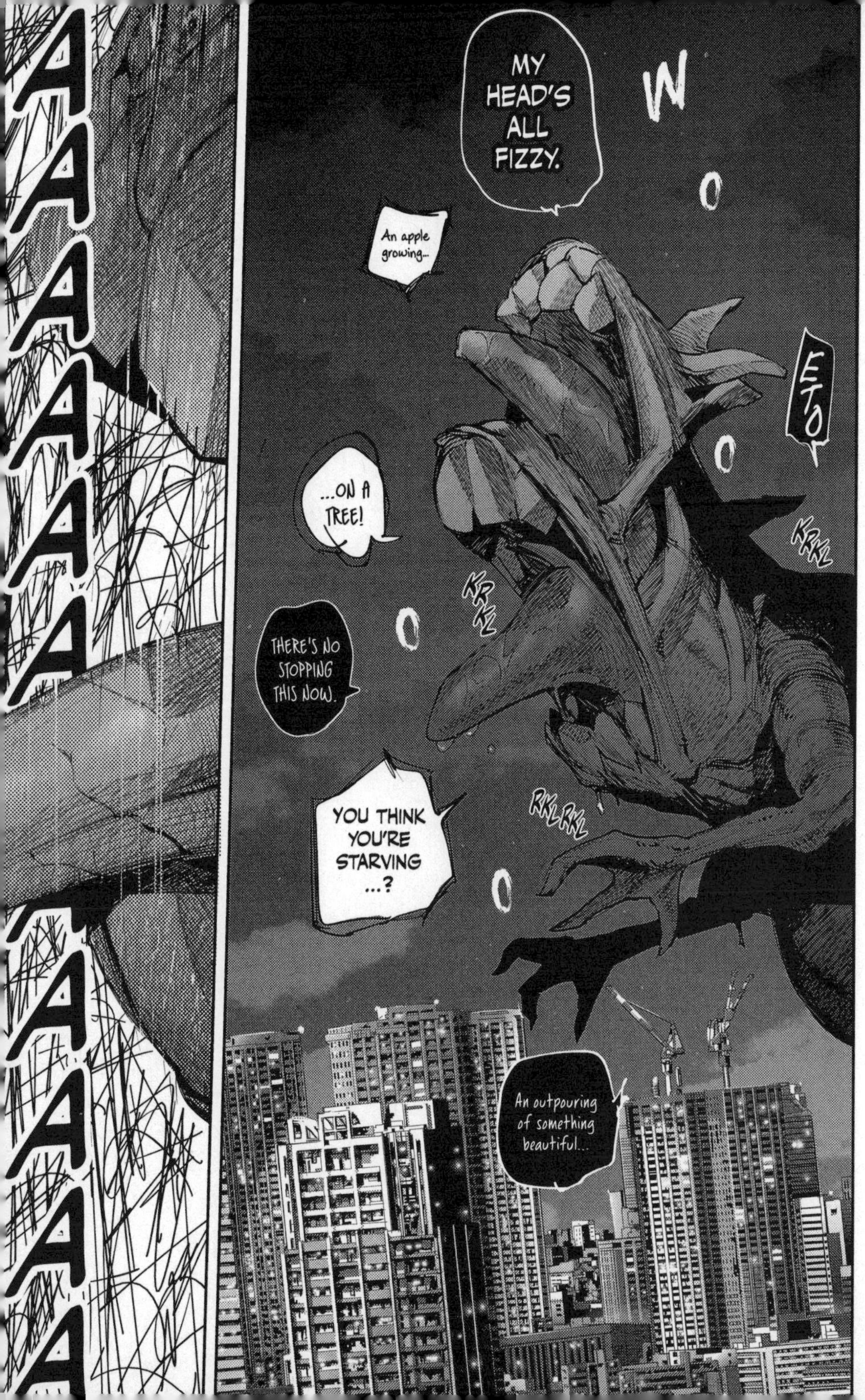
WOOOO
MY HEAD'S ALL FIZZY.
ETO
An apple growing...
KRKL
...ON A TREE!
KRKL
THERE'S NO STOPPING THIS NOW.
RKLRKL
YOU THINK YOU'RE STARVING ...?
An outpouring of something beautiful...
AAAAAAAAAAAAAAAAAA

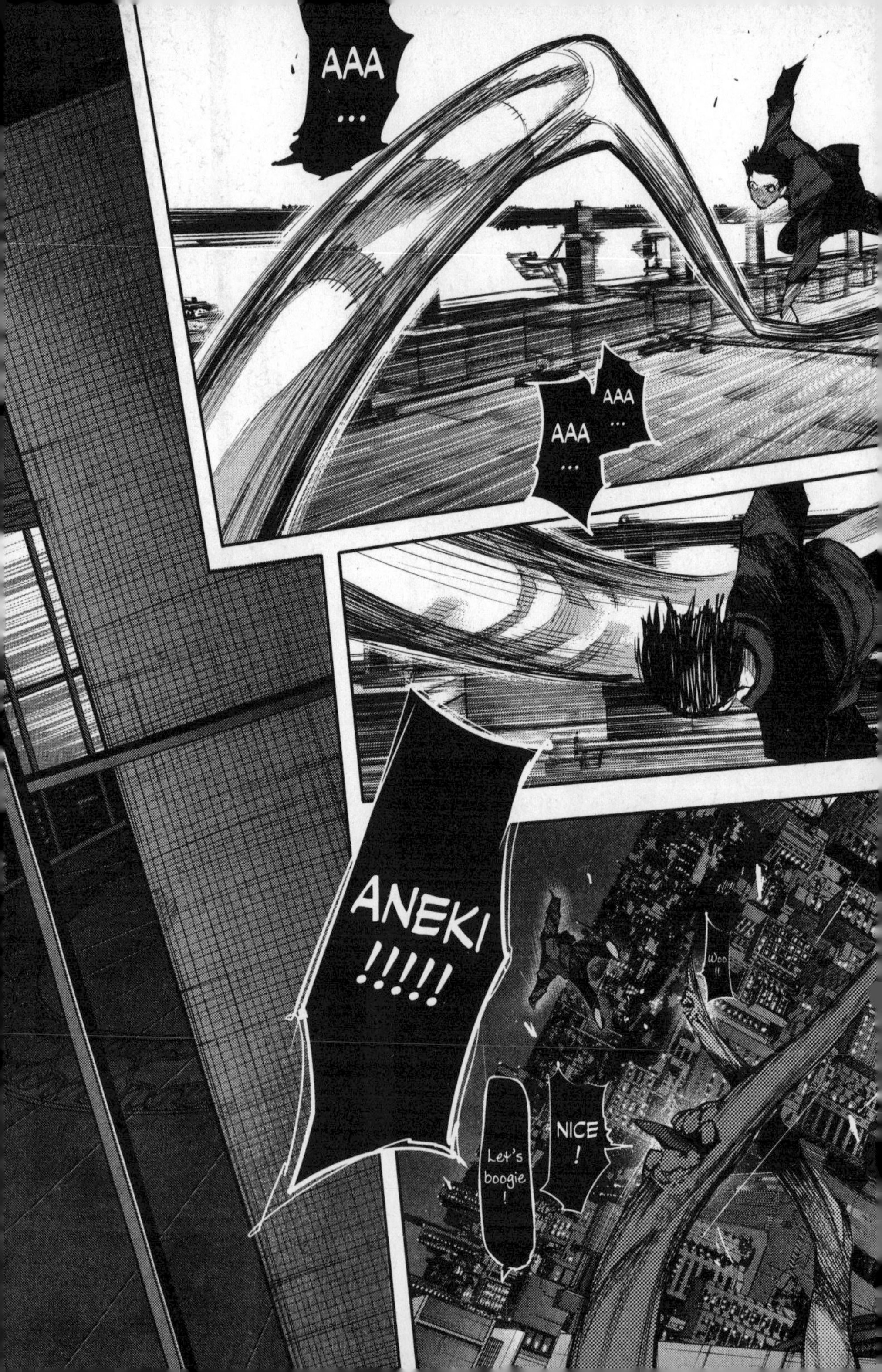
AAA...
AAA...
AAA...
ANEKI!!!!!
Woo!!
NICE!
Let's boogie!

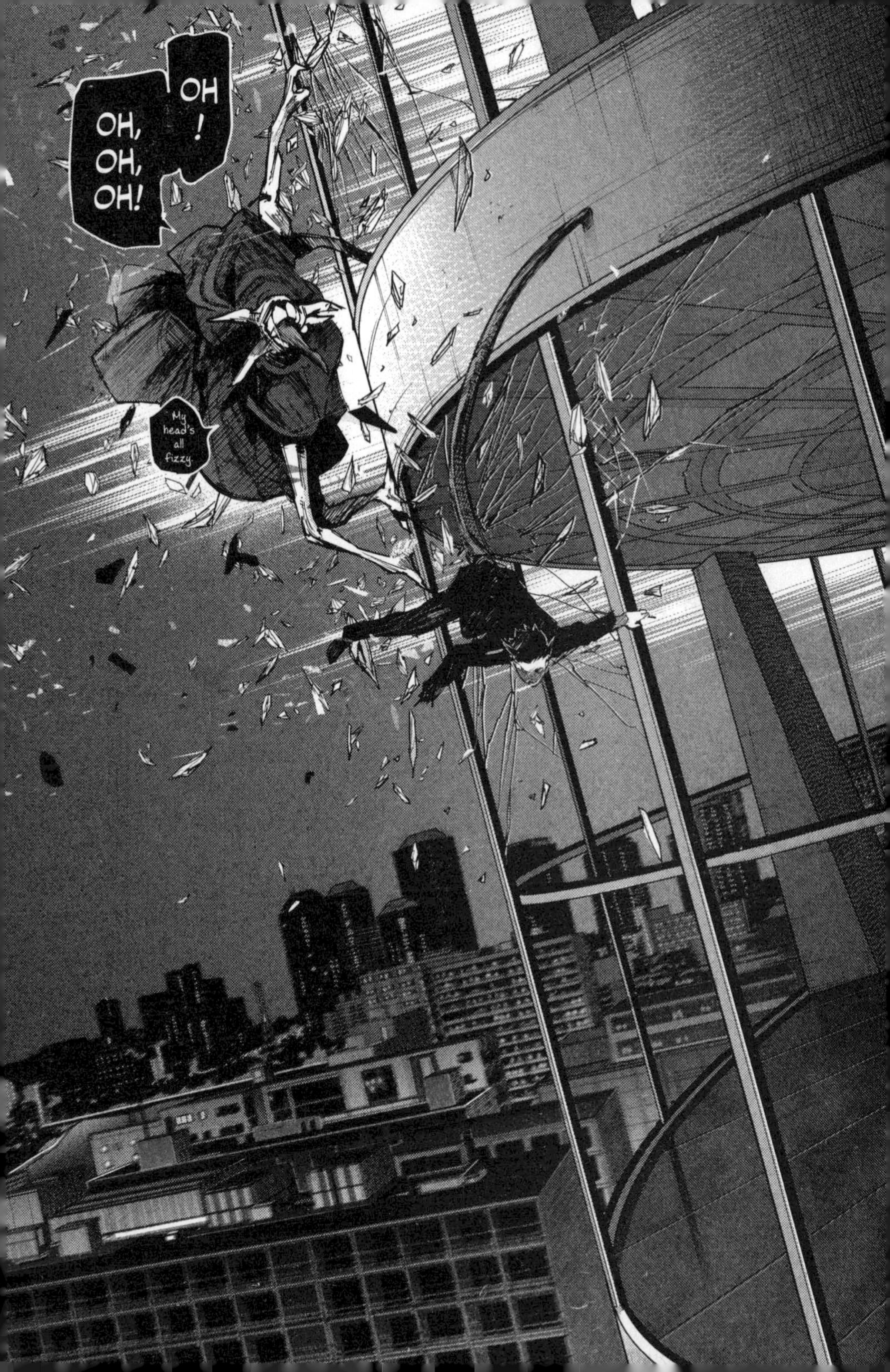
OH!
OH, OH, OH!
My head's all fizzy.

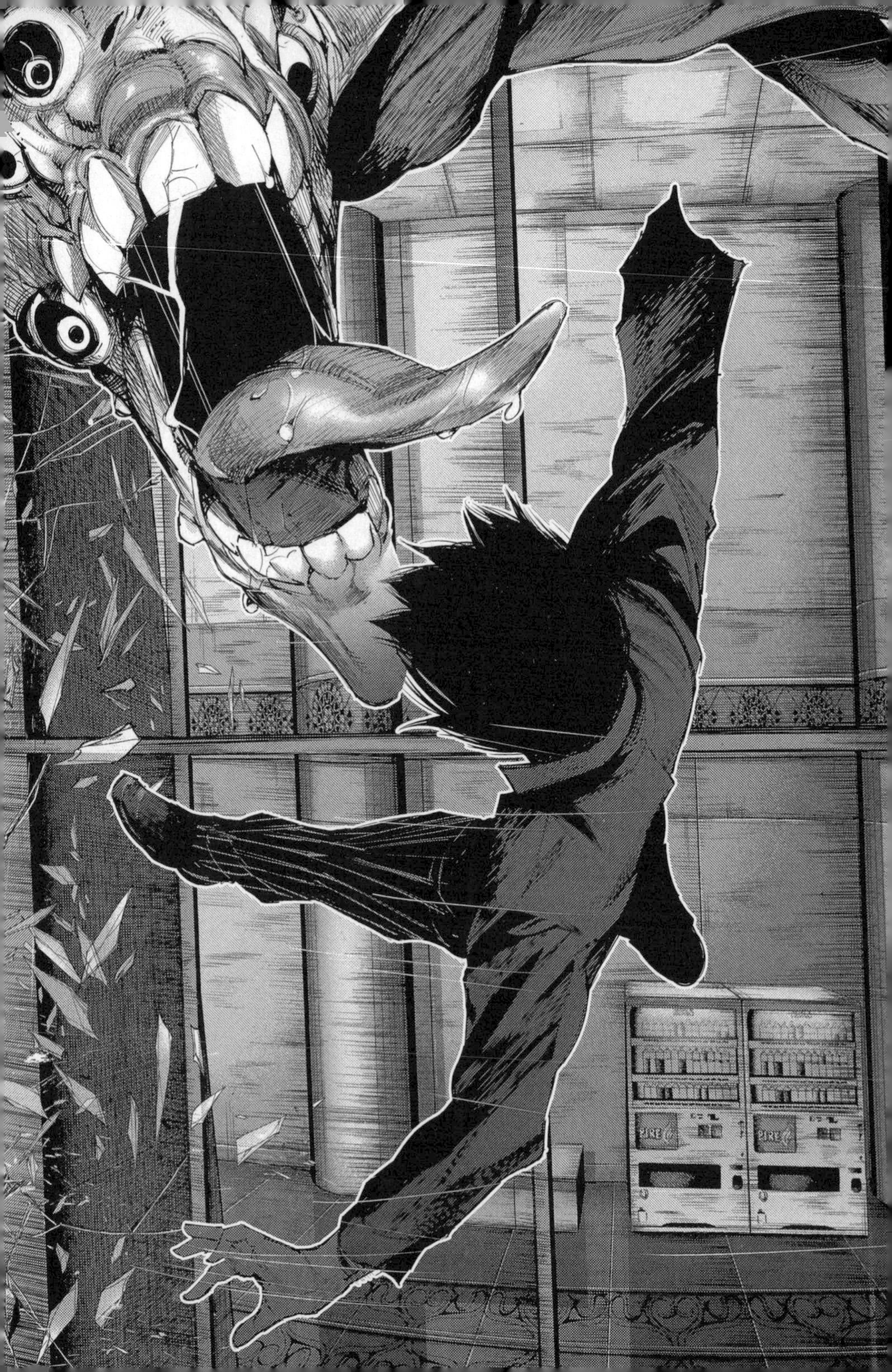

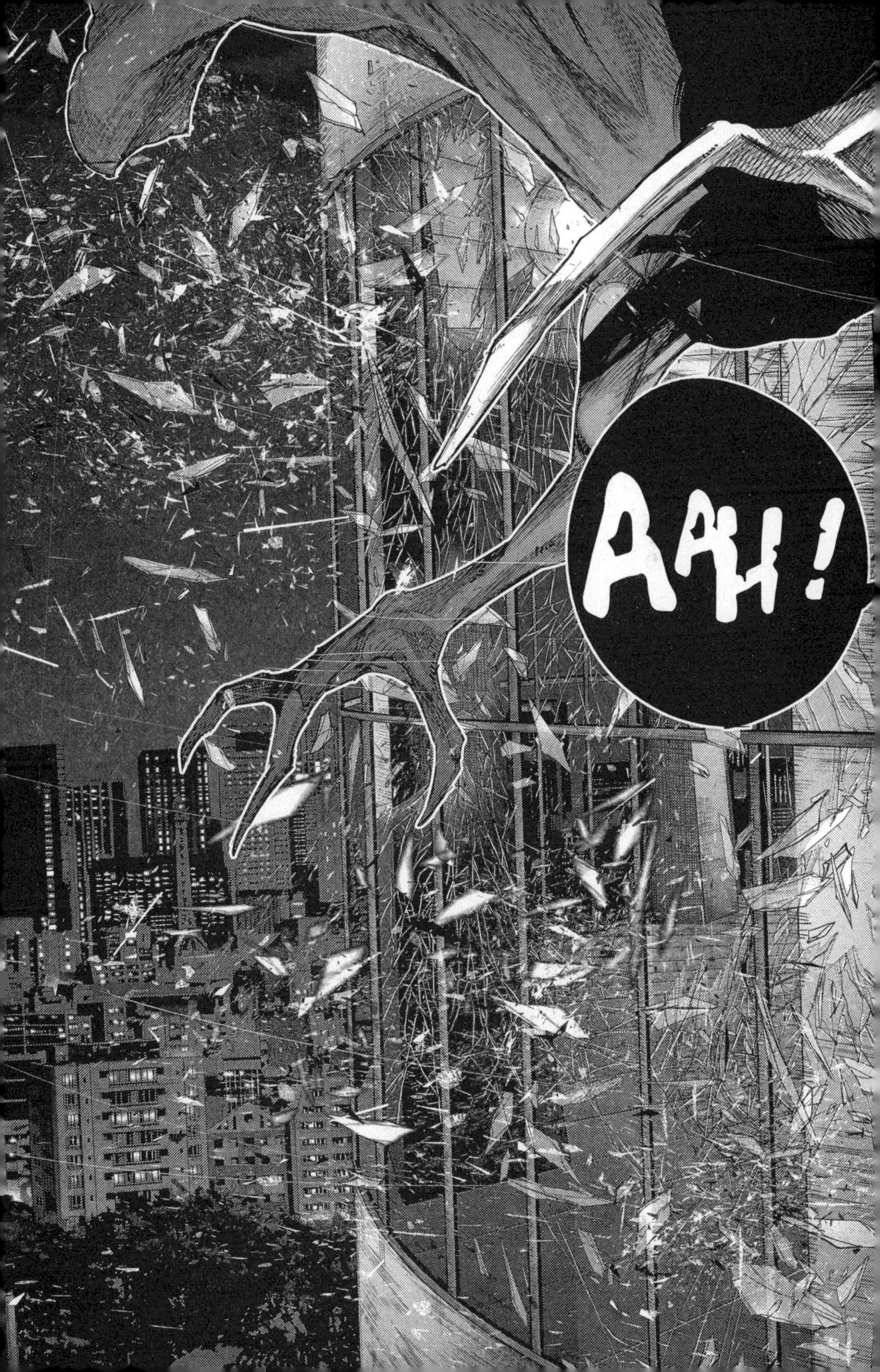
AAH!

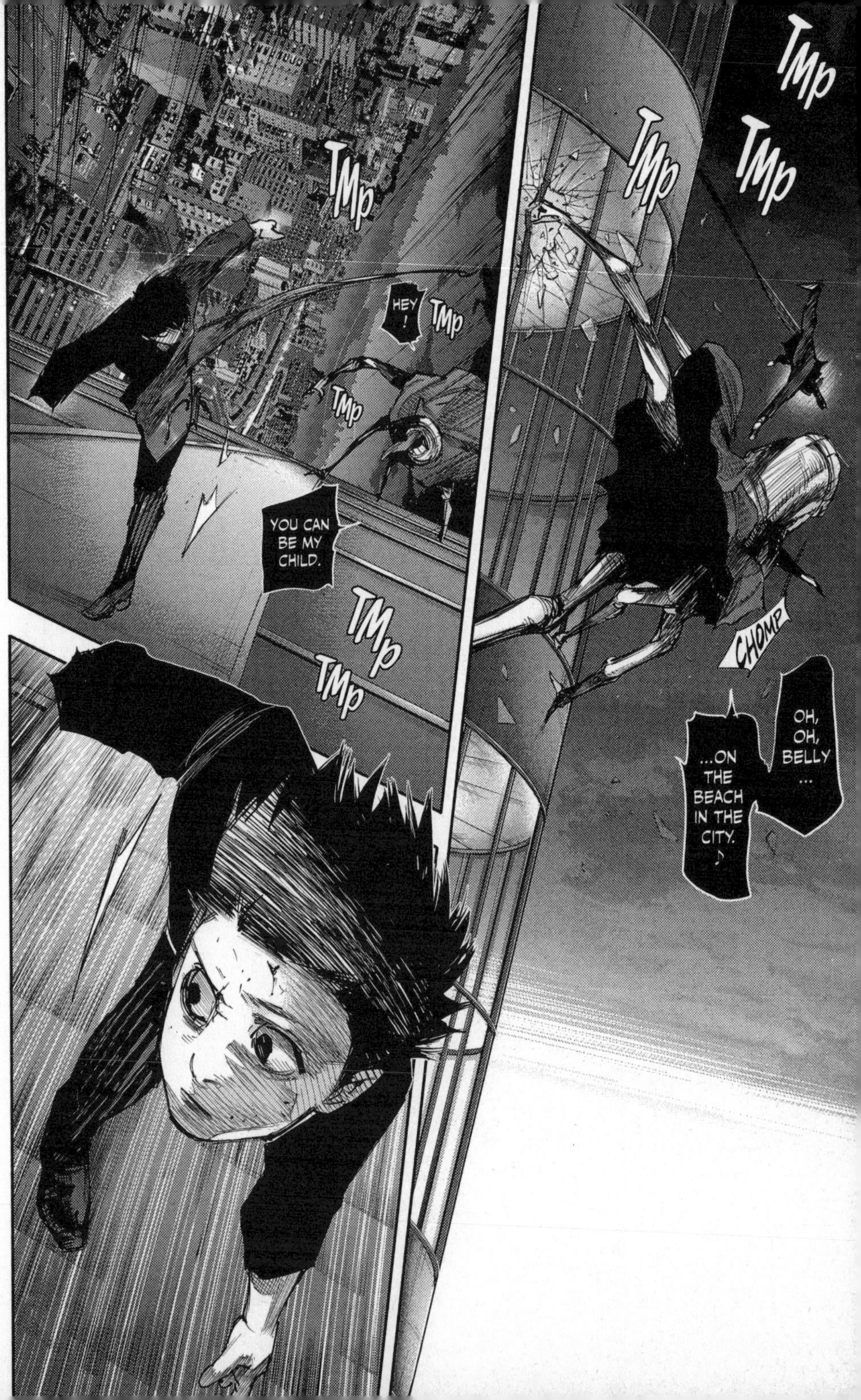
TMp
TMp
TMp
CHOMP
OH, OH, BELLY ...
...ON THE BEACH IN THE CITY. ♪
TMp
HEY!
TMp
TMp
YOU CAN BE MY CHILD.
TMp
TMp

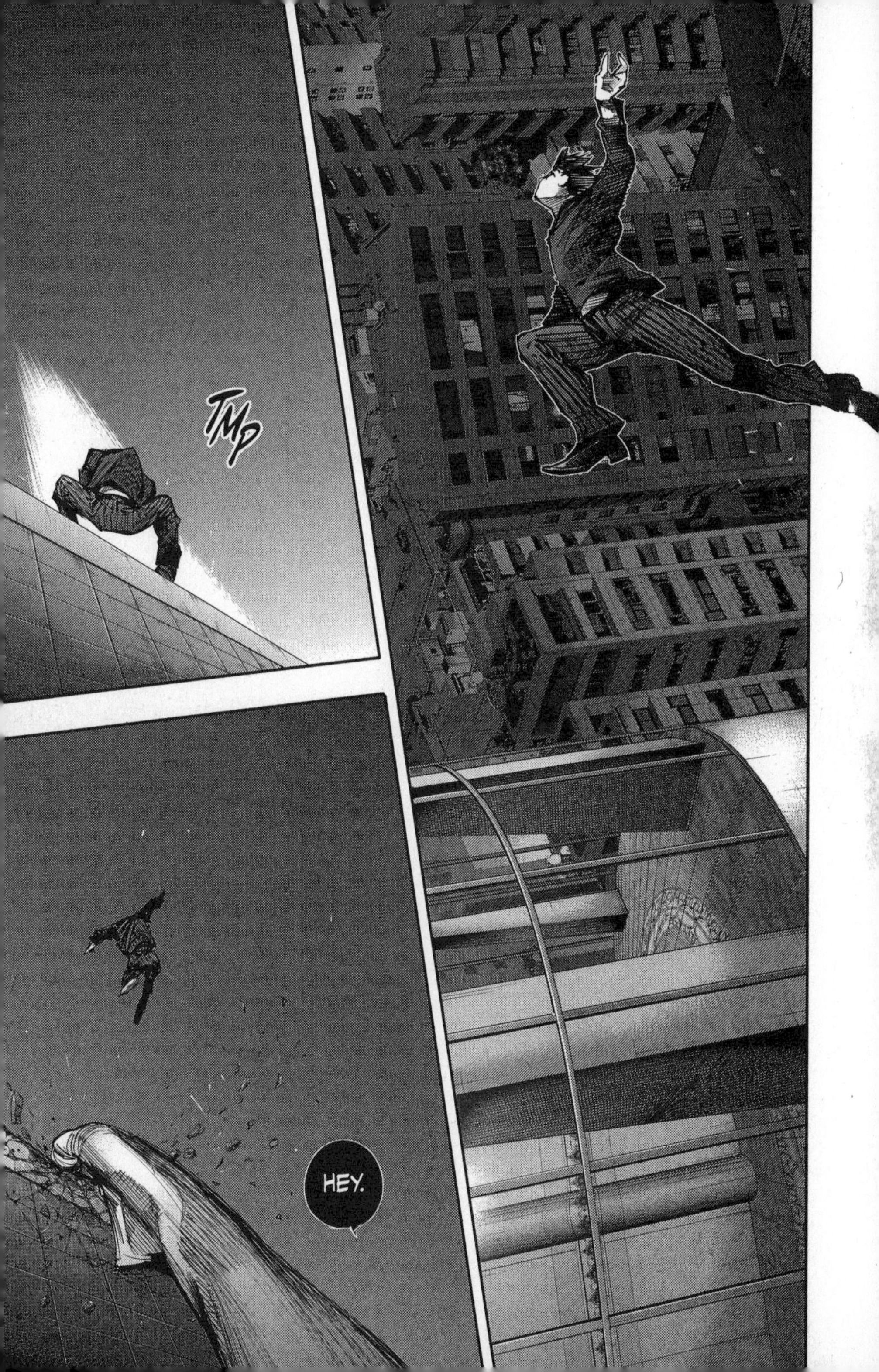
TMP
HEY.

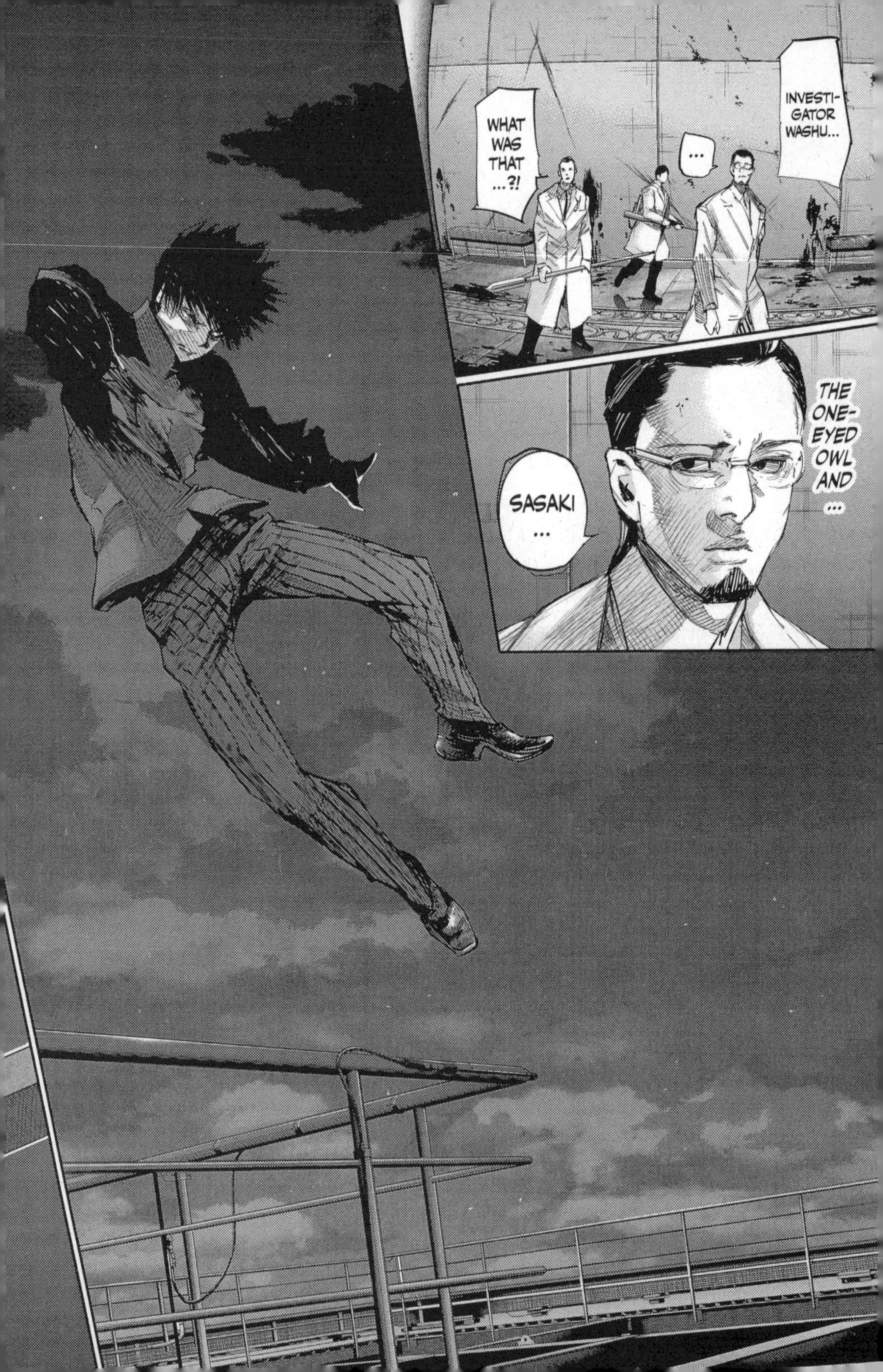
INVESTI-GATOR WASHU...
...
WHAT WAS THAT ...?!
THE ONE-EYED OWL AND ...
SASAKI ...

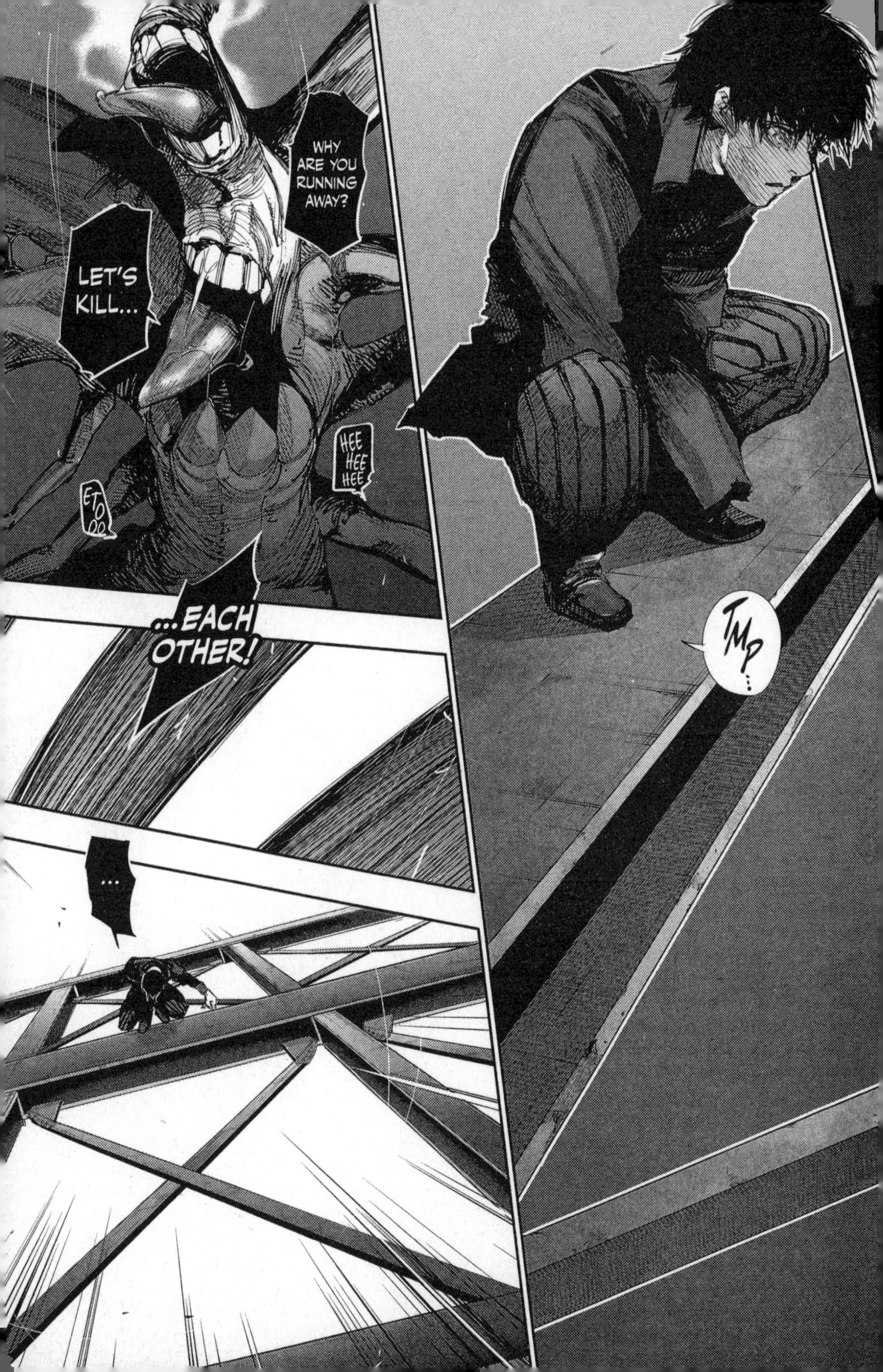

TMP...
WHY ARE YOU RUNNING AWAY?
LET'S KILL...
HEE HEE HEE
ETOOO
...EACH OTHER!
...

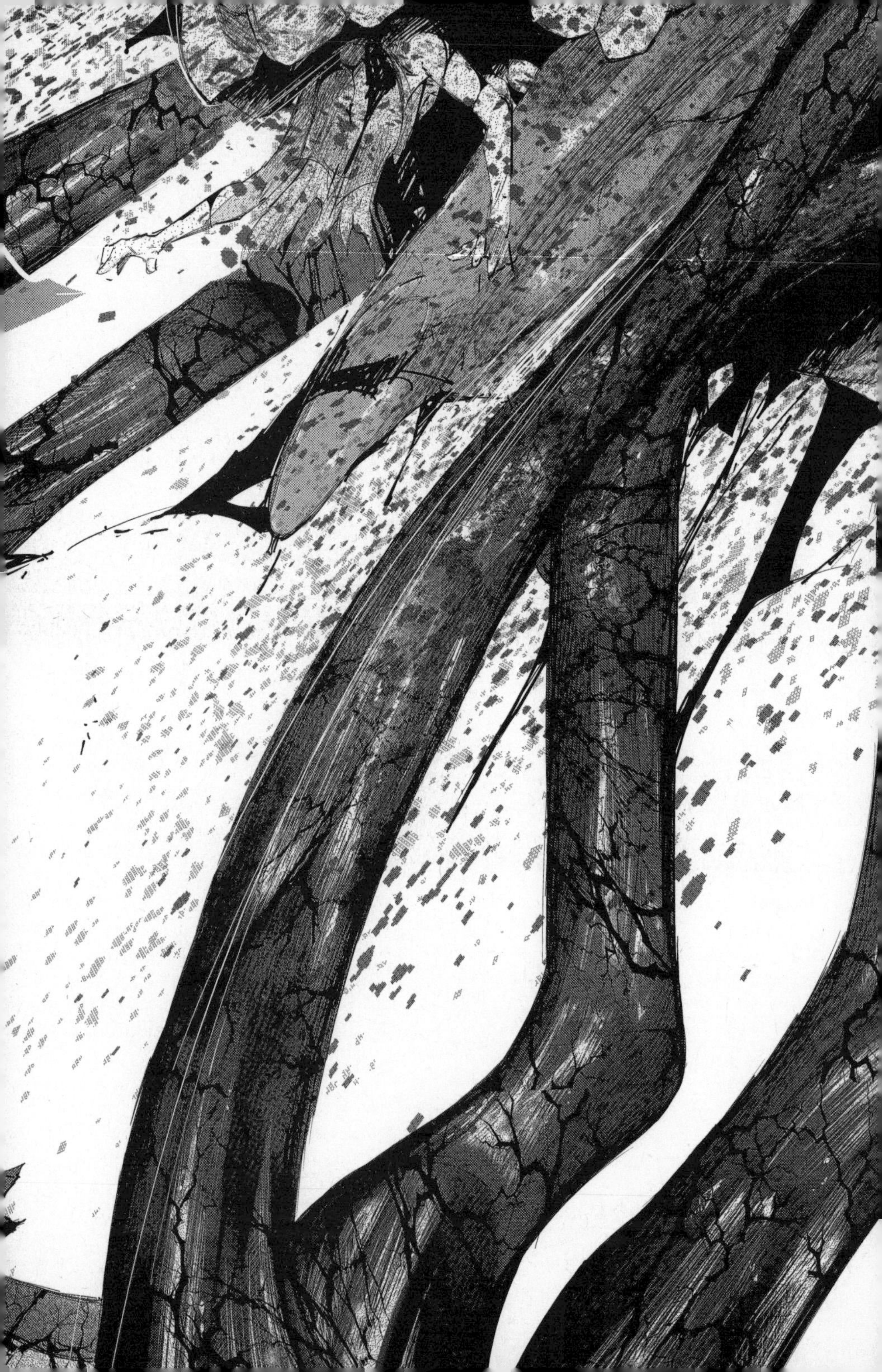

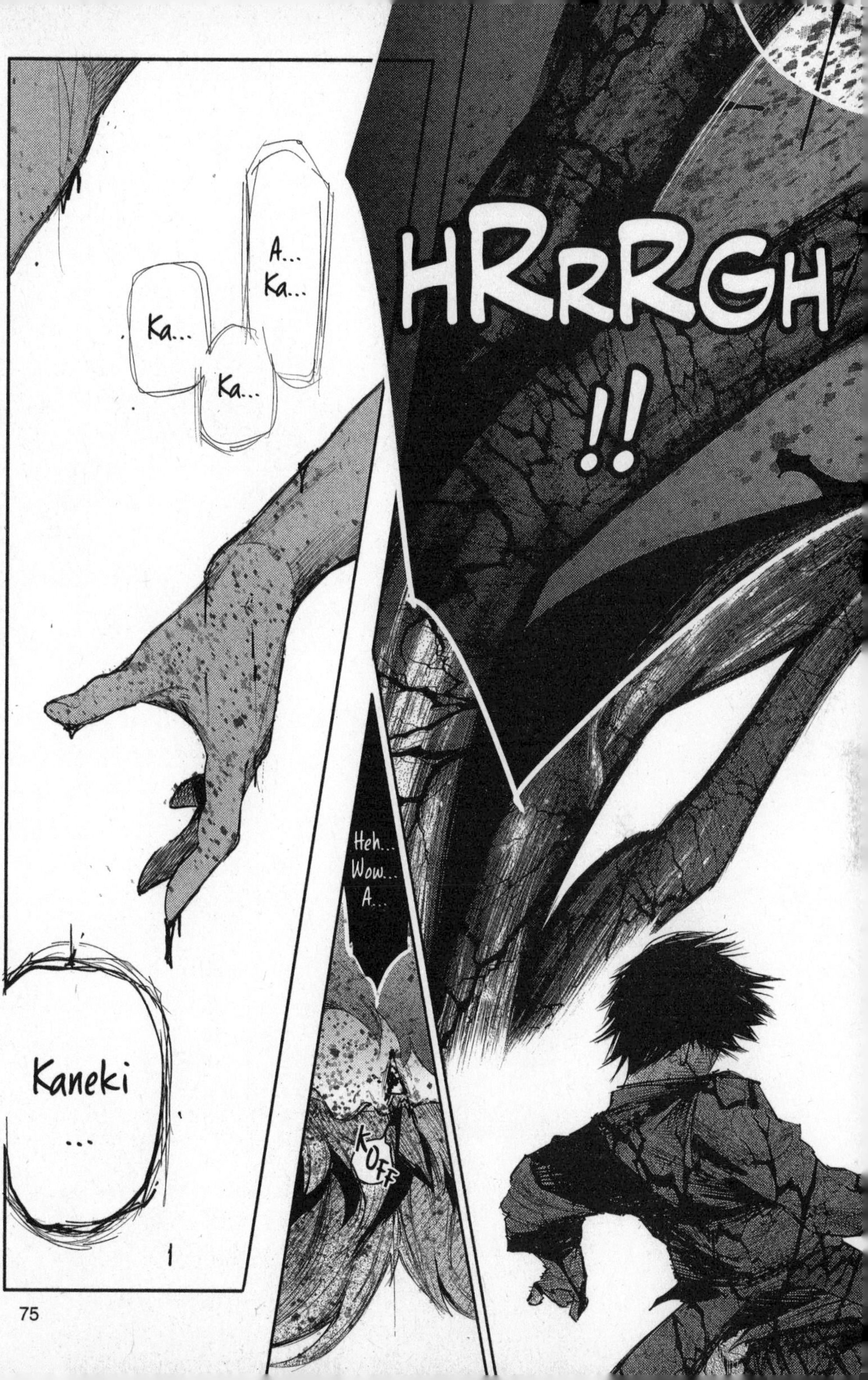

HRrRGH !!
Heh... Wow... A...
KOFF
A... Ka...
Ka...
Ka...
Kaneki ...

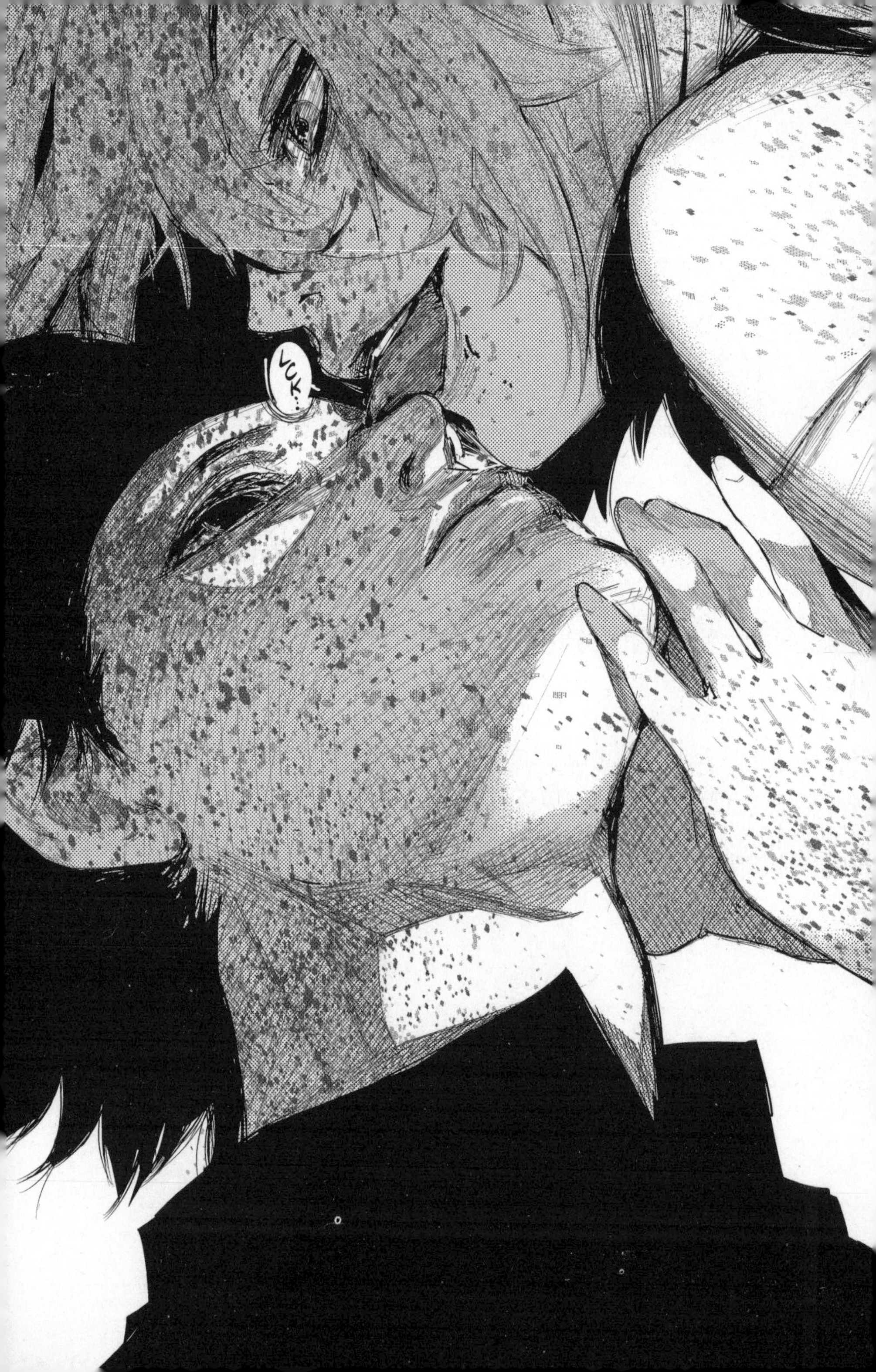
LICK...

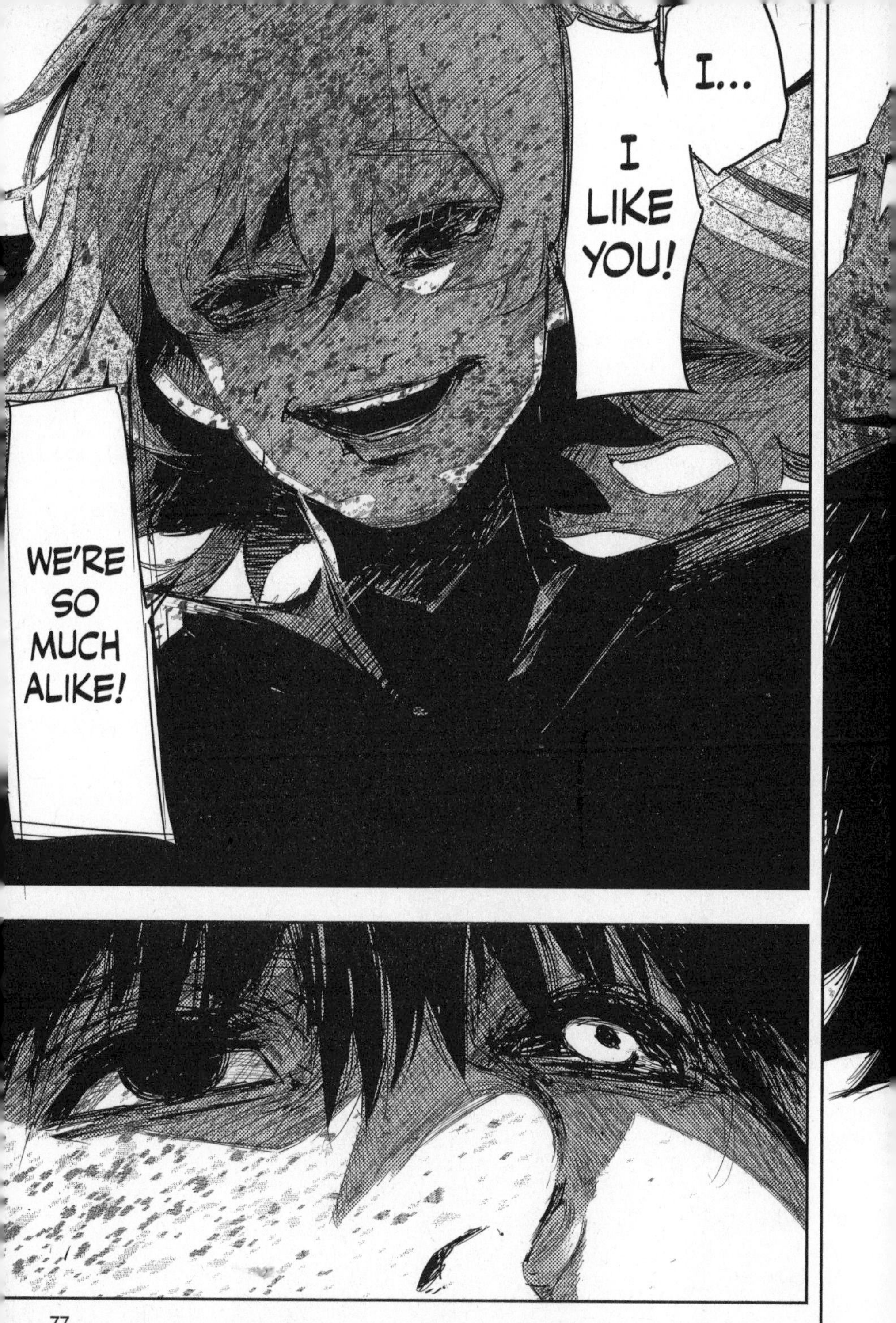
I...
I LIKE YOU!
WE'RE SO MUCH ALIKE!

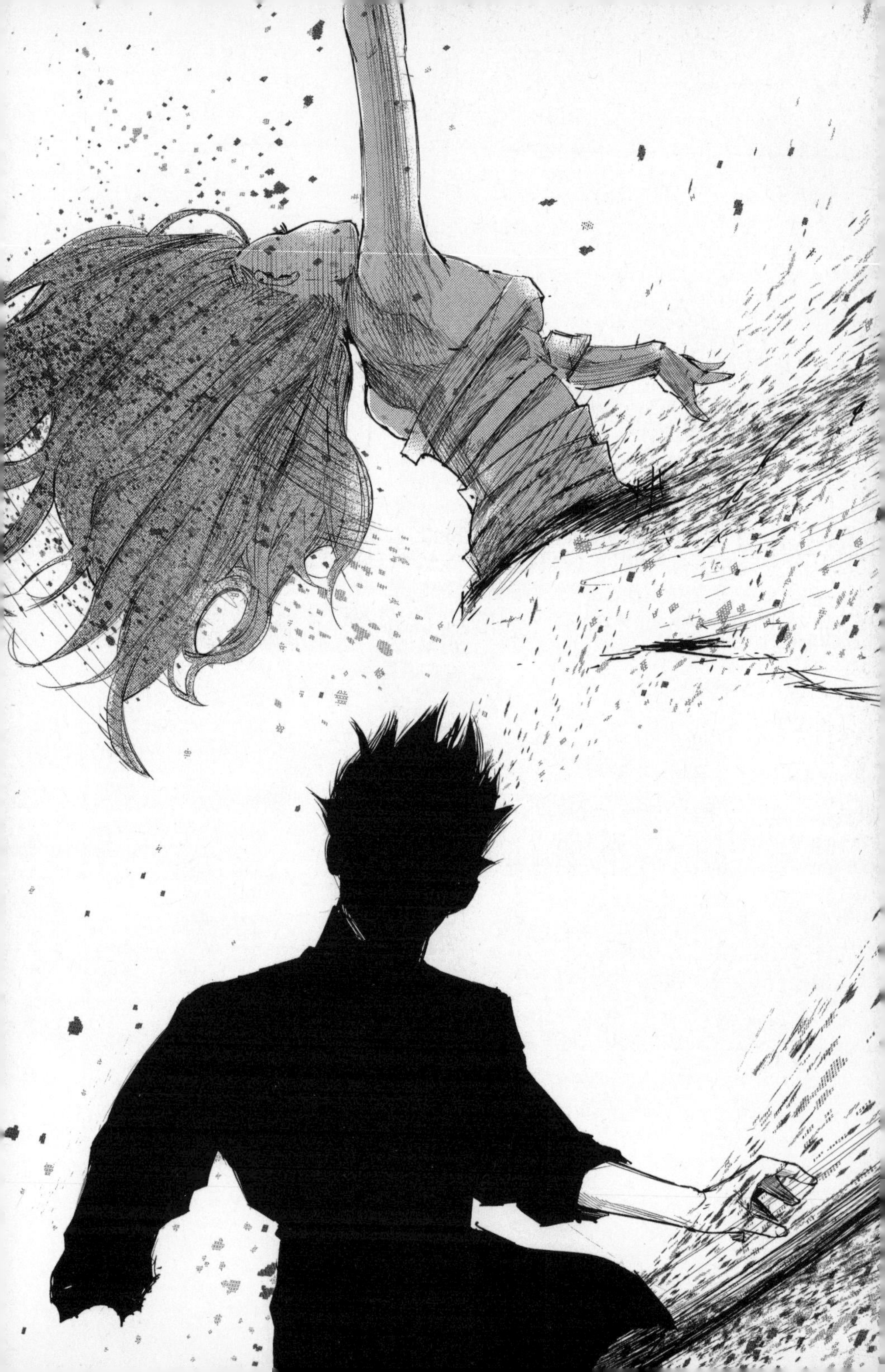

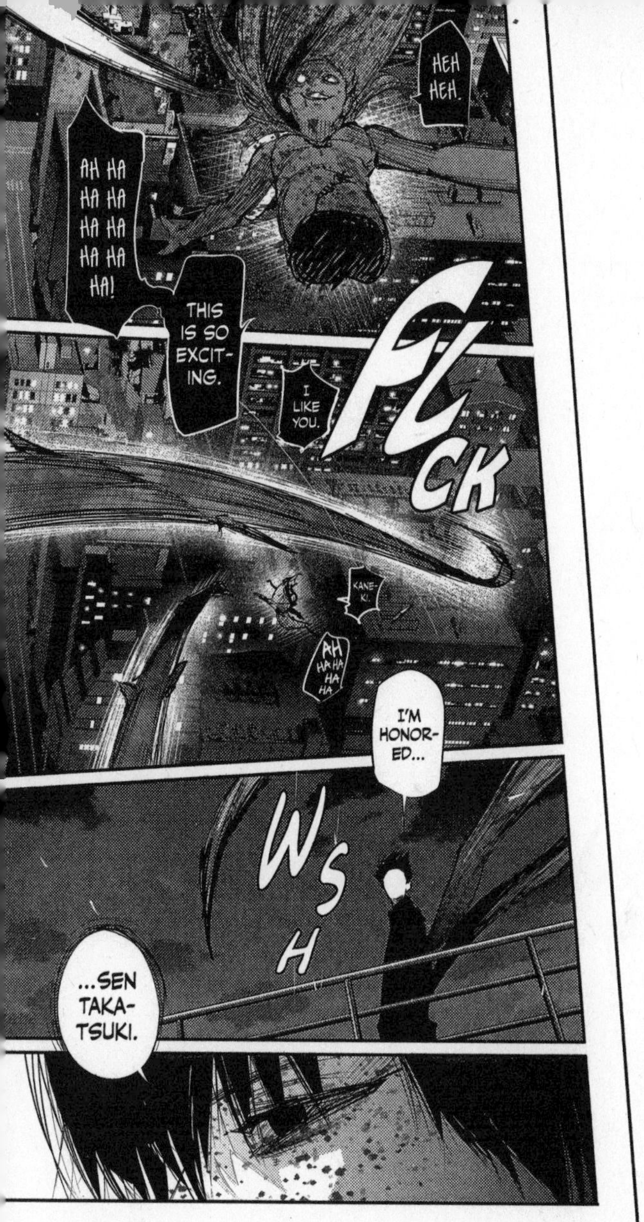
HEH HEH.
AH HA HA HA HA HA HA HA HA!
I LIKE YOU.
THIS IS SO EXCIT-ING.
FLCK
KANE-KI.
AH HA HA HA HA
I'M HONOR-ED...
WSH
...SEN TAKA-TSUKI.

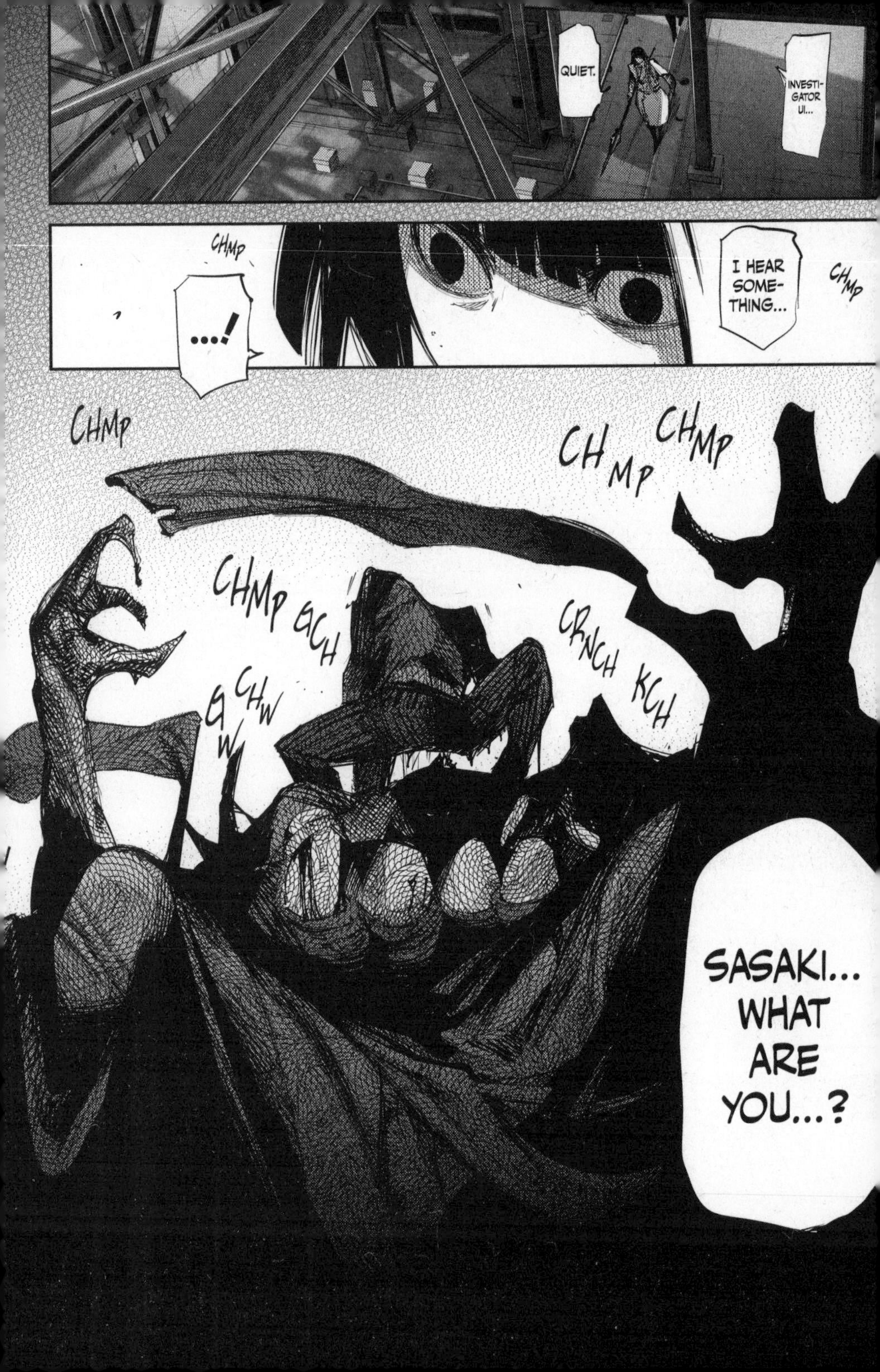
INVESTI-
GATOR
UI...
QUIET.
CHMP
I HEAR
SOME-
THING...
CHMP
...!
CHMP
CH MP
CRNCH KCH
CHMP
CHW
CHMP
SASAKI...
WHAT
ARE
YOU...?

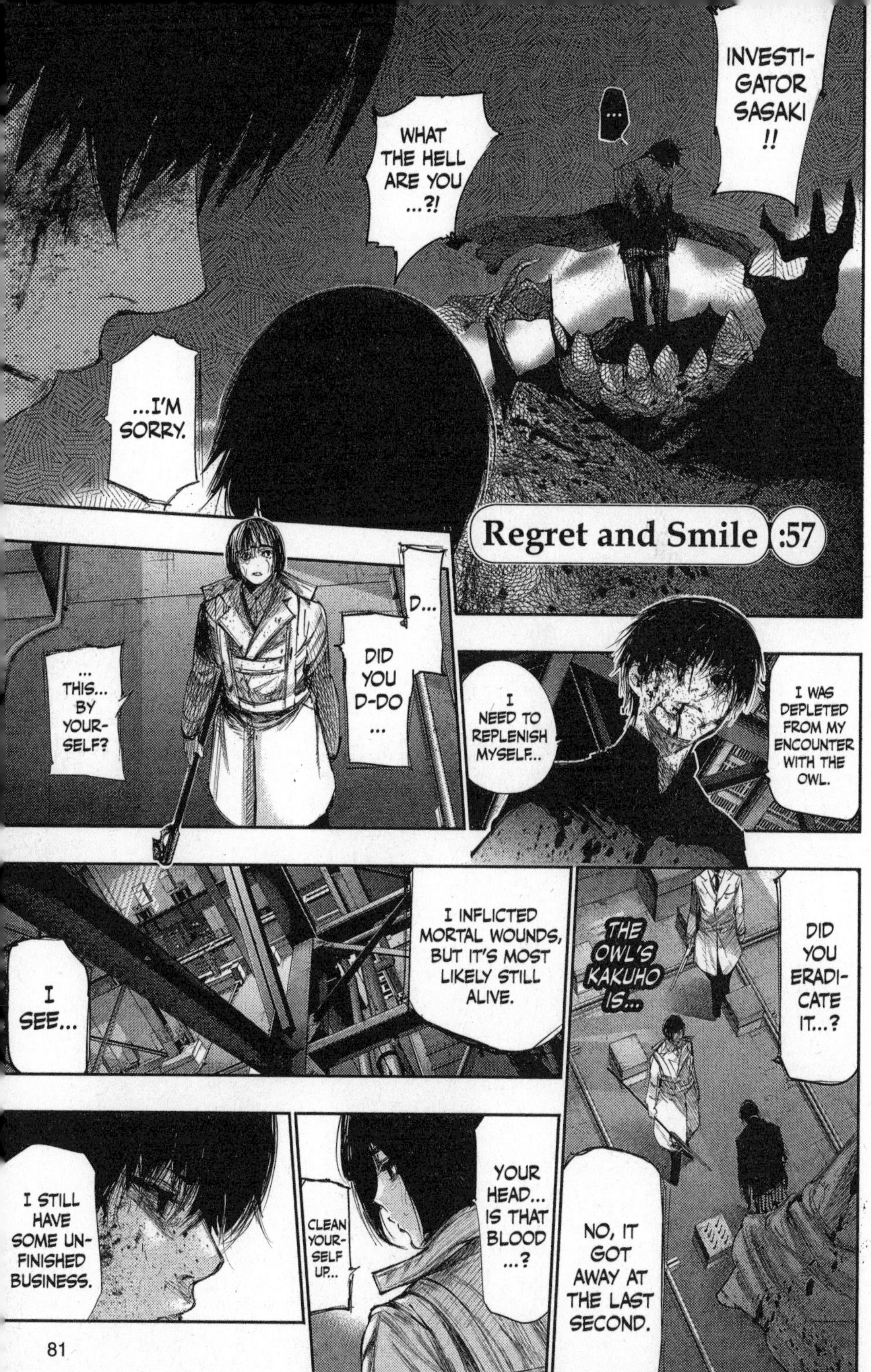
INVESTI-GATOR SASAKI !!
...
WHAT THE HELL ARE YOU ...?!
...I'M SORRY.
Regret and Smile :57
I WAS DEPLETED FROM MY ENCOUNTER WITH THE OWL.
I NEED TO REPLENISH MYSELF...
D...
DID YOU D-DO ...
... THIS... BY YOUR-SELF?
DID YOU ERADI-CATE IT...?
THE OWL'S KAKUHO IS...
NO, IT GOT AWAY AT THE LAST SECOND.
I INFLICTED MORTAL WOUNDS, BUT IT'S MOST LIKELY STILL ALIVE.
I SEE...
YOUR HEAD... IS THAT BLOOD ...?
CLEAN YOUR-SELF UP...
I STILL HAVE SOME UN-FINISHED BUSINESS.

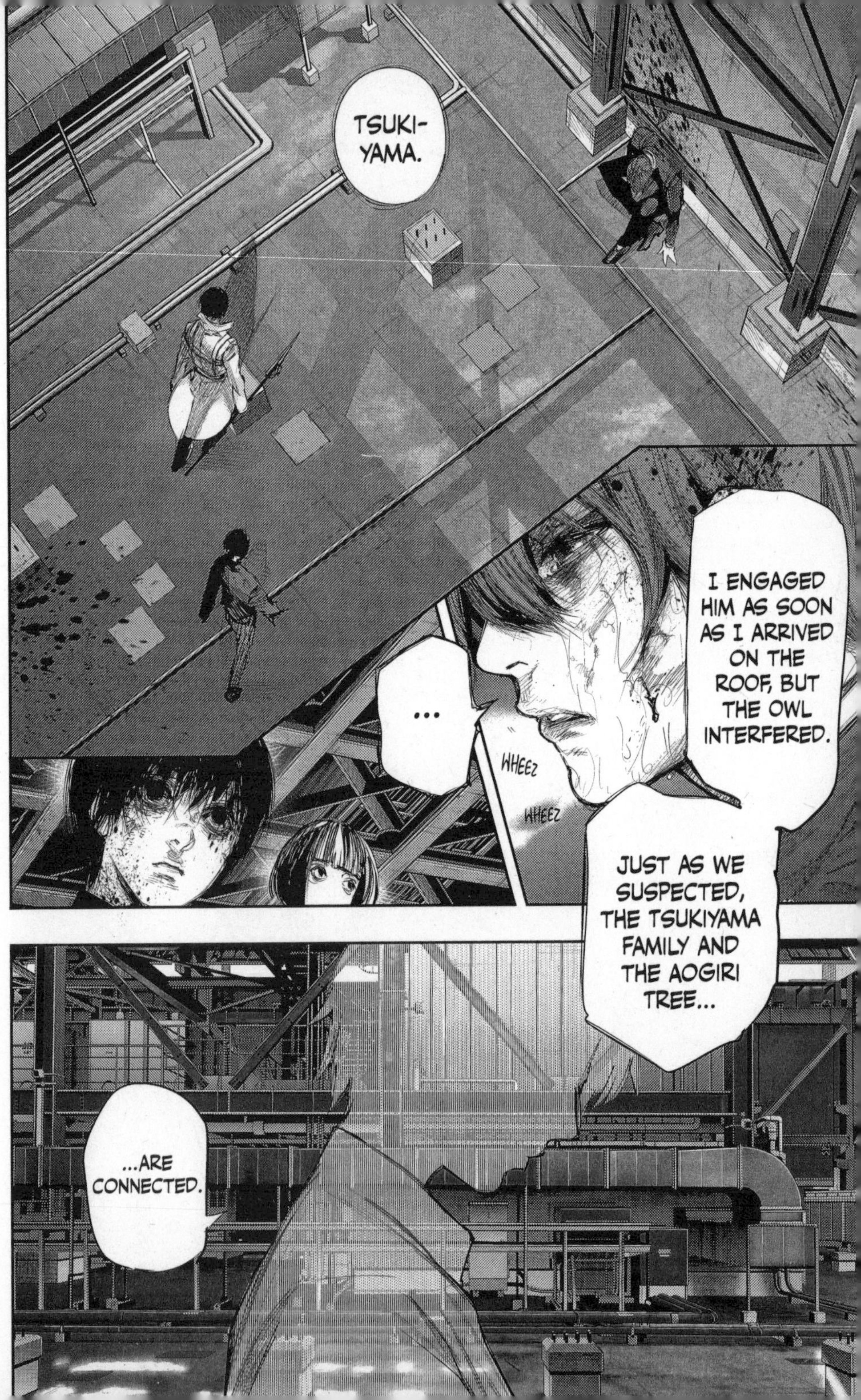
TSUKI-YAMA.
I ENGAGED HIM AS SOON AS I ARRIVED ON THE ROOF, BUT THE OWL INTERFERED.
...
WHEEZ
WHEEZ
JUST AS WE SUSPECTED, THE TSUKIYAMA FAMILY AND THE AOGIRI TREE...
...ARE CONNECTED.

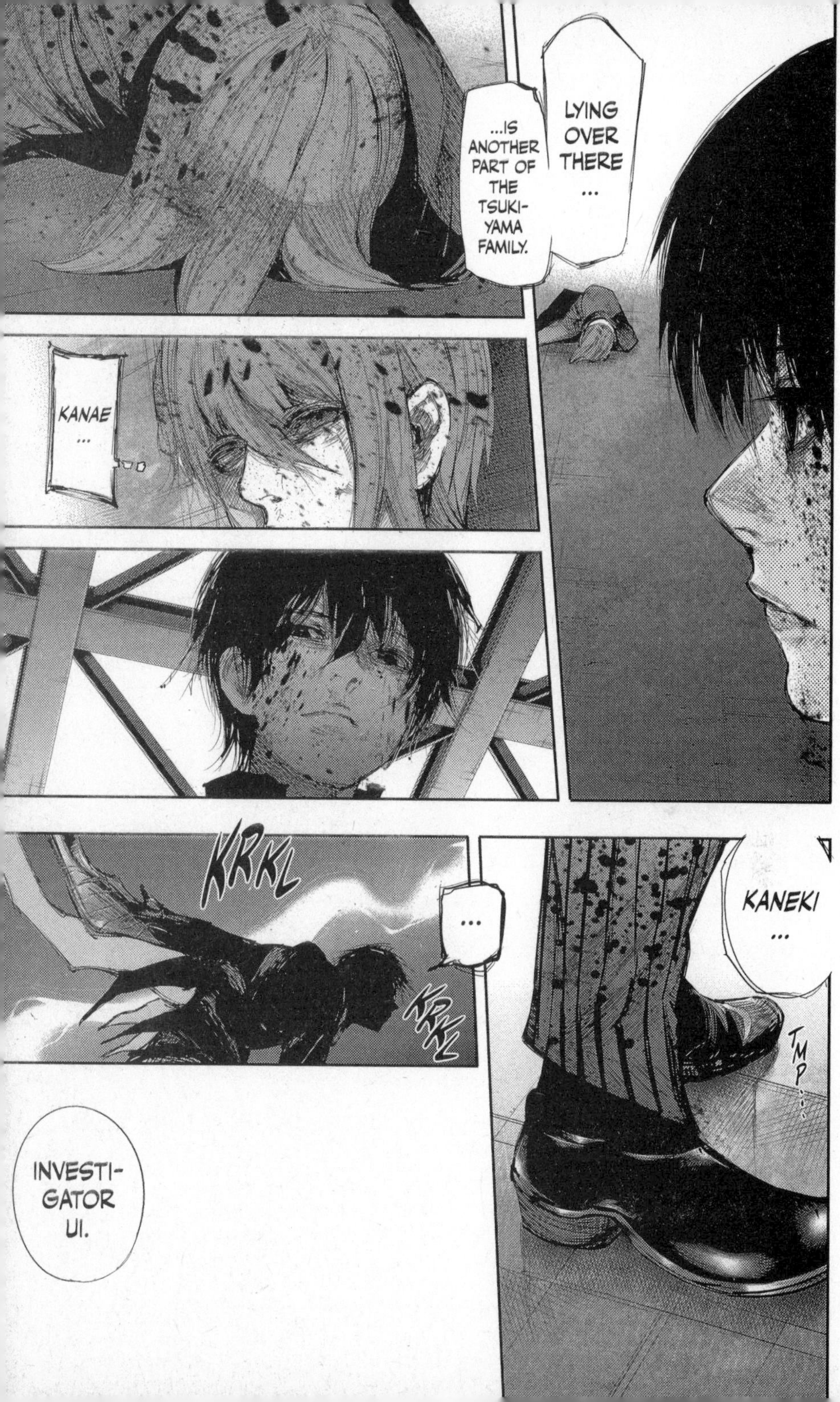
LYING OVER THERE ...
...IS ANOTHER PART OF THE TSUKI-YAMA FAMILY.
KANAE ...
KANEKI ...
TMP...
KRKL
...
KRKL
INVESTI-GATOR UI.

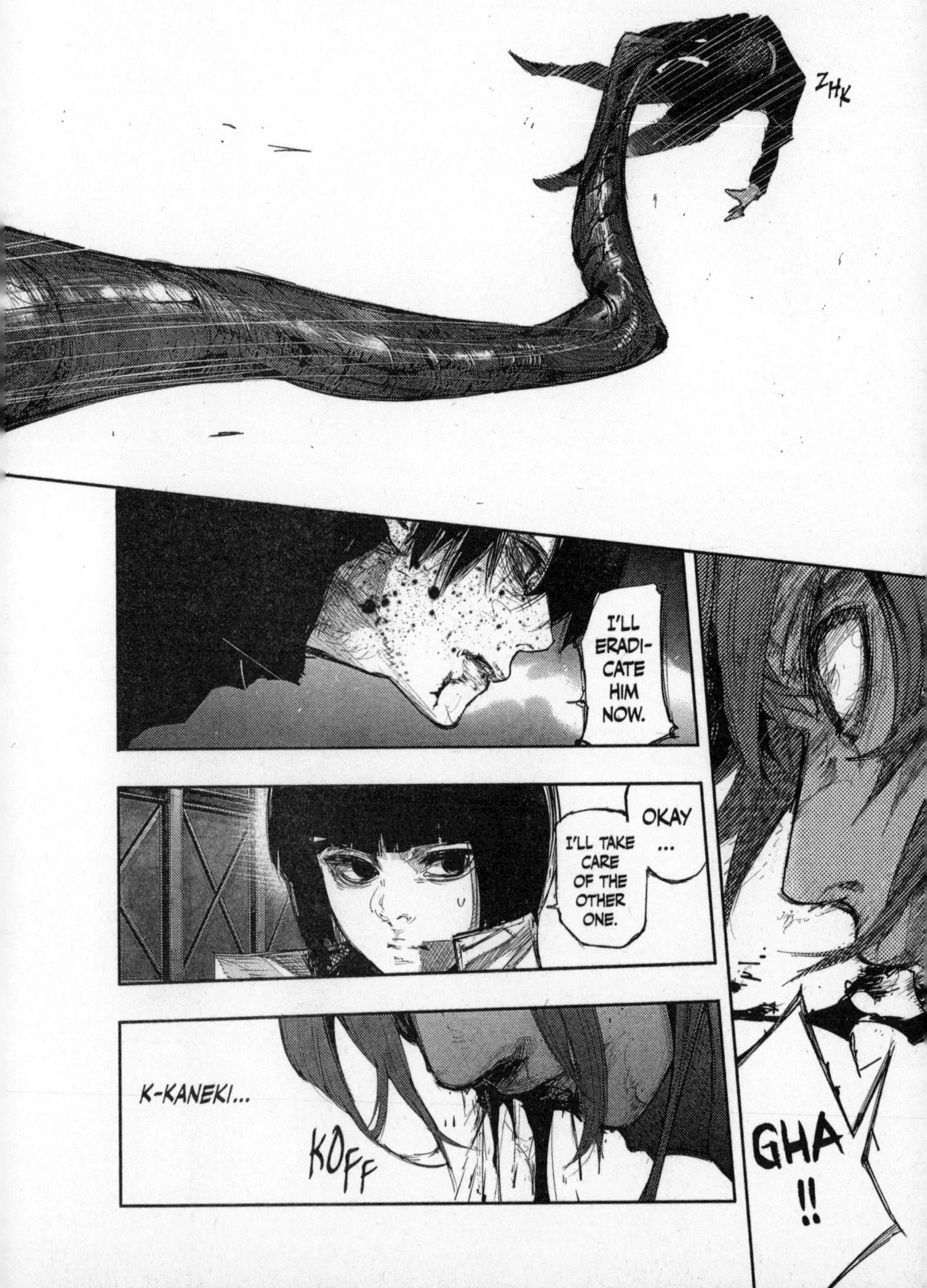
ZHK
GHA!!
I'LL ERADICATE HIM NOW.
OKAY ...
I'LL TAKE CARE OF THE OTHER ONE.
K-KANEKI...
KOFF

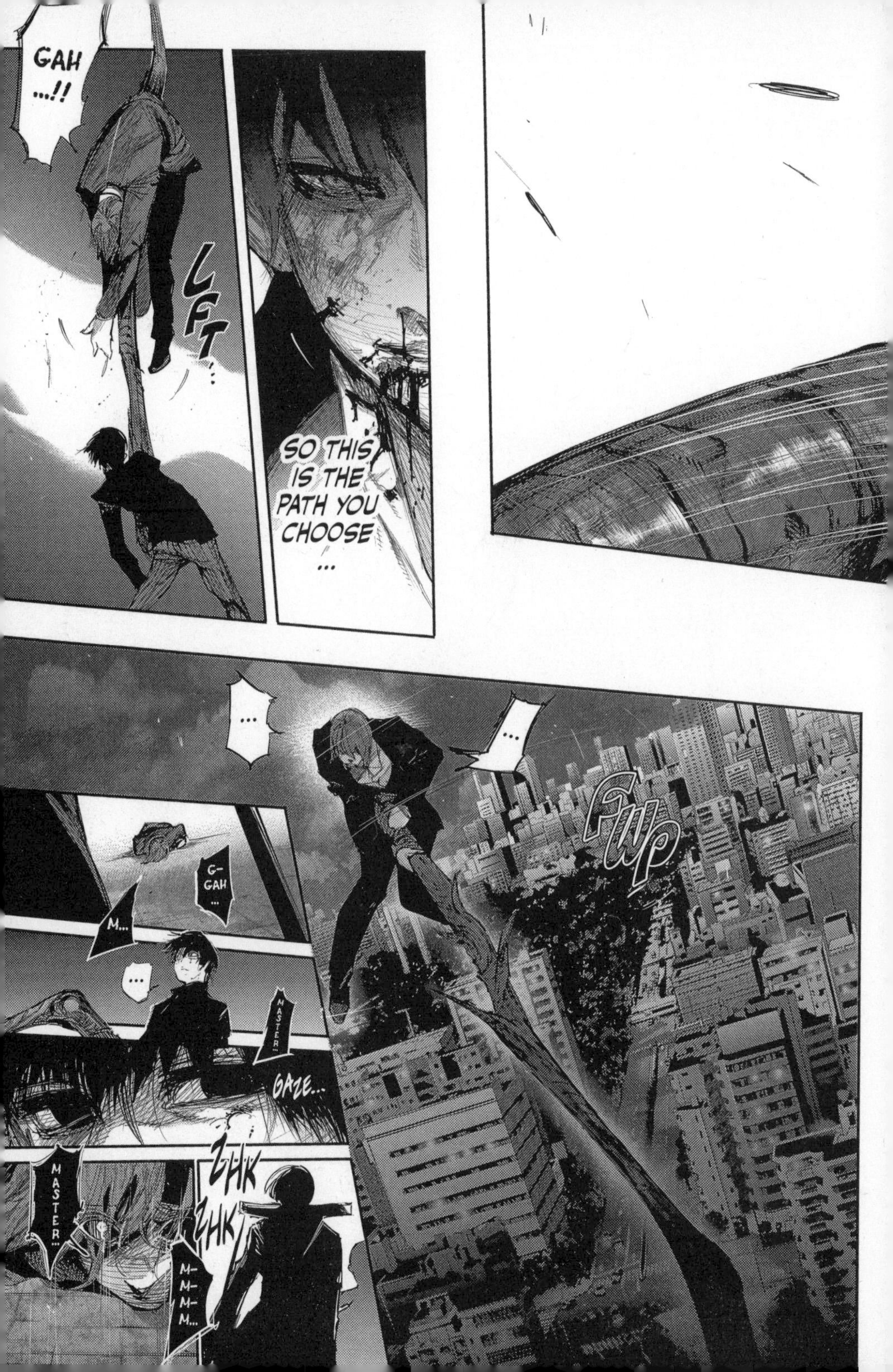
SO THIS IS THE PATH YOU CHOOSE...
GAH...!!
LFT
...
...
FWP
G-GAH...
M...
...
MASTER...
GAZE...
ZHK ZHK
MASTER...
M-M-M-M...

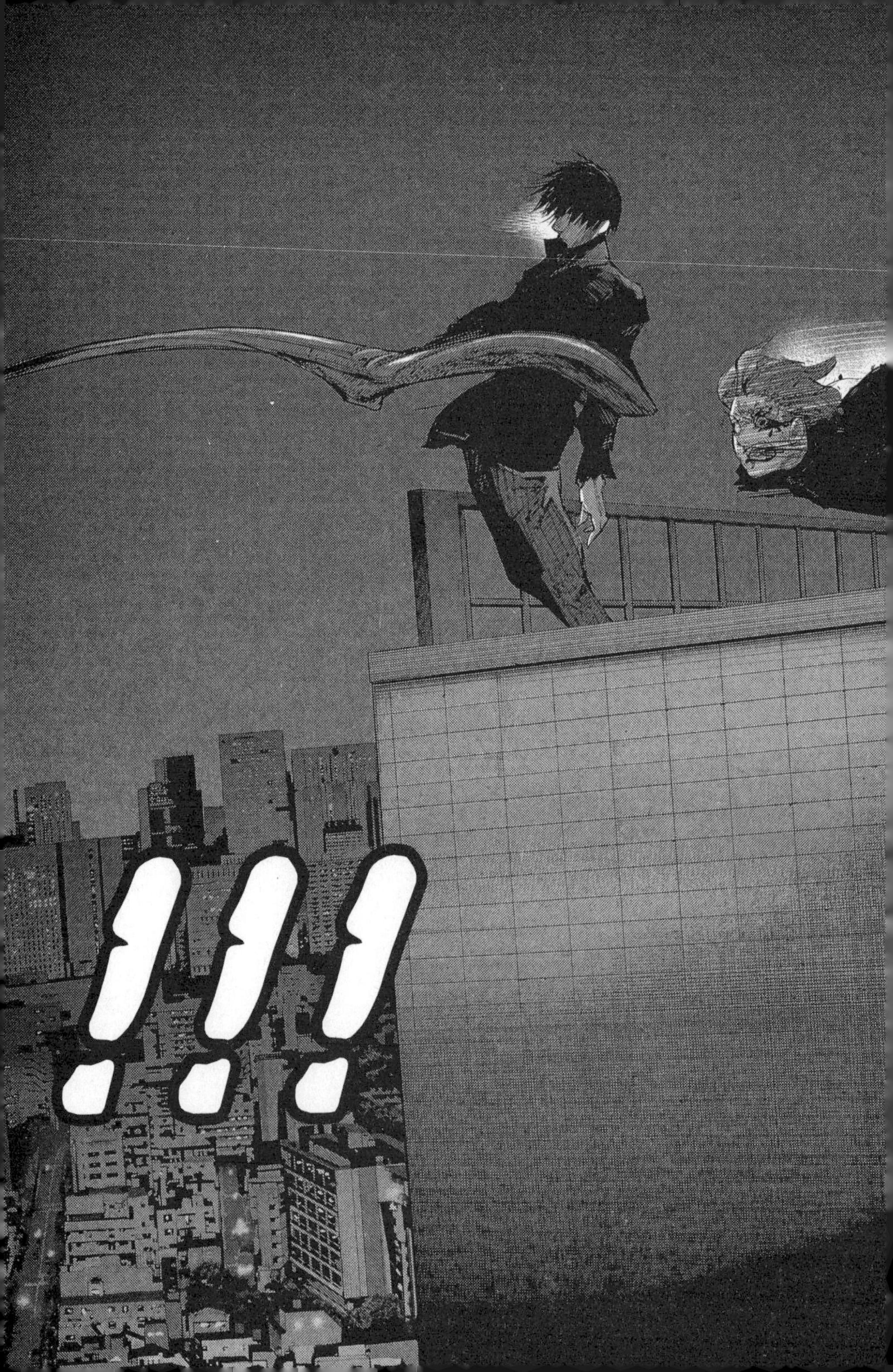
!!!

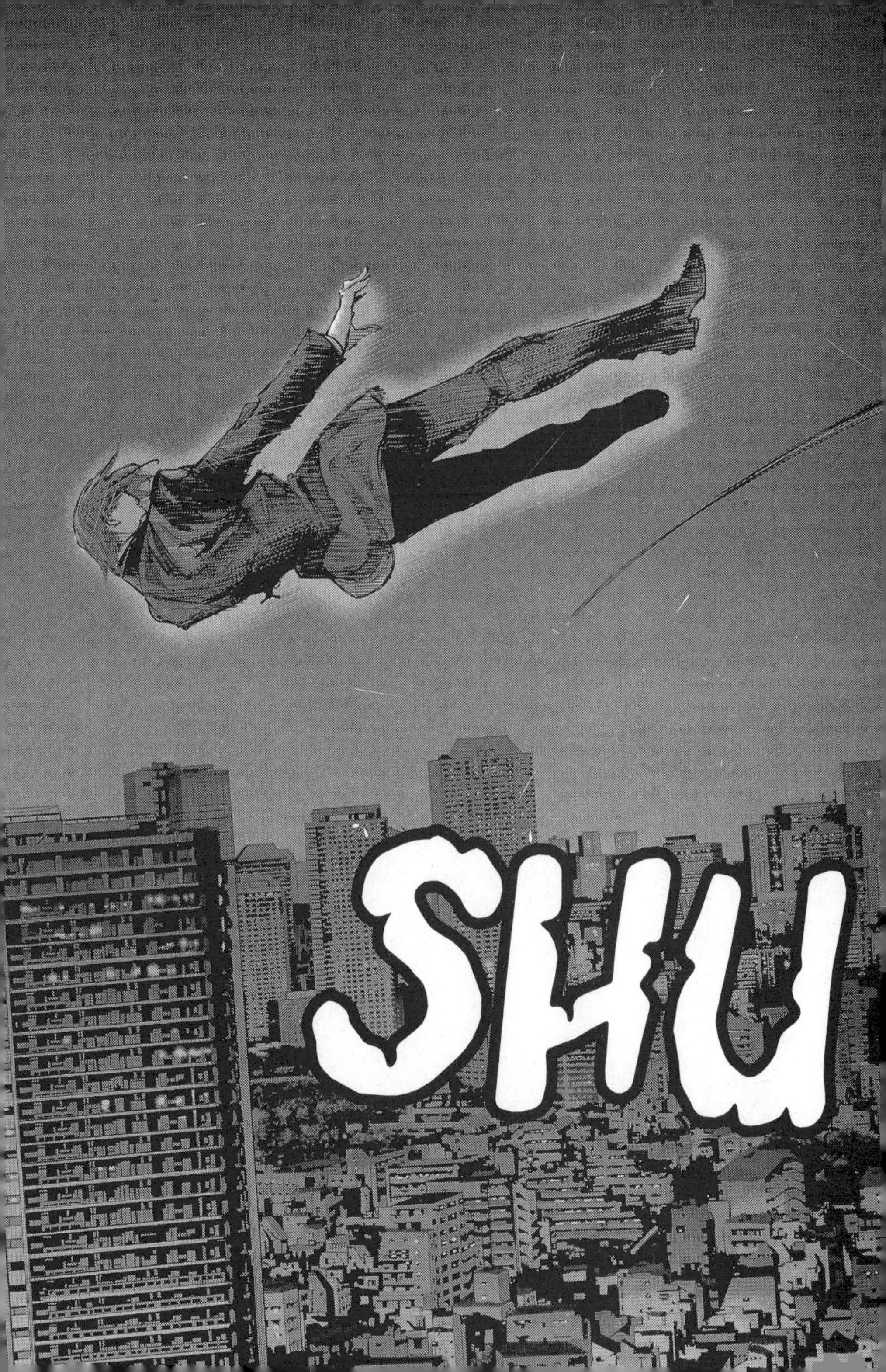
SHU

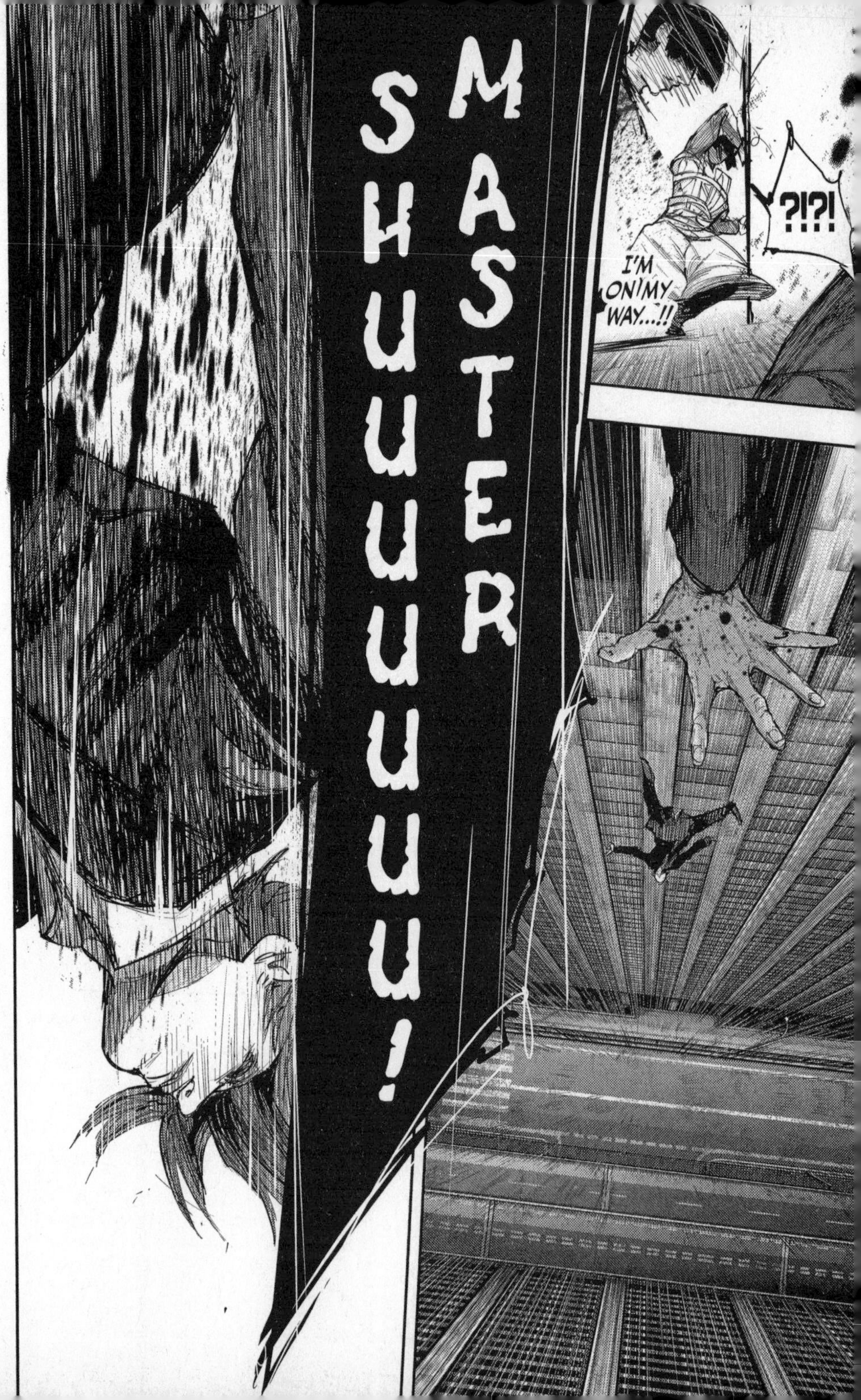
?!?!
I'M ON MY WAY...!!
MASTER
SHUUUUUUU!

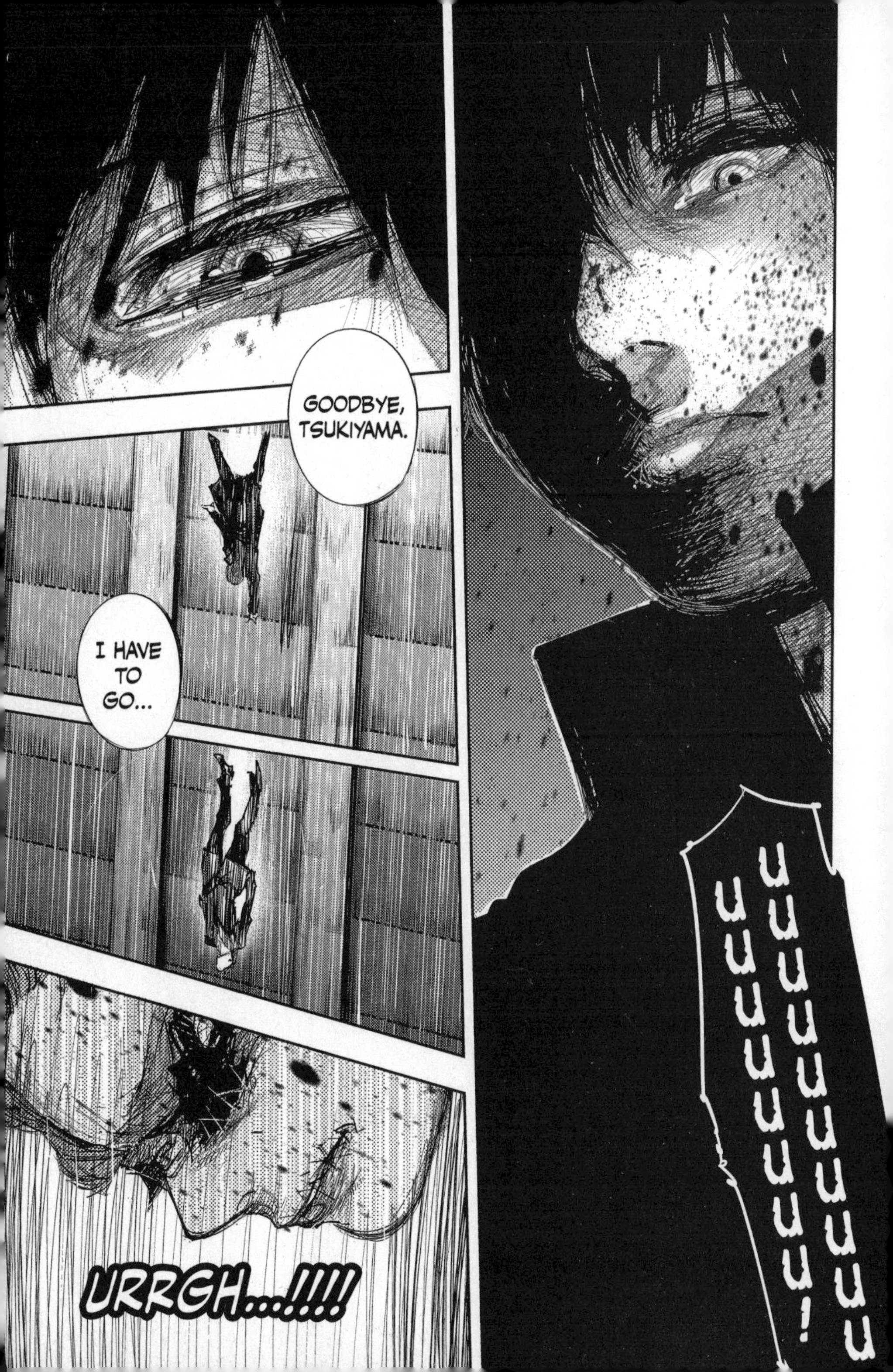
UUUUUUUUUUUUUUUUUU!
GOODBYE, TSUKIYAMA.
I HAVE TO GO...
URRGH...!!!!!

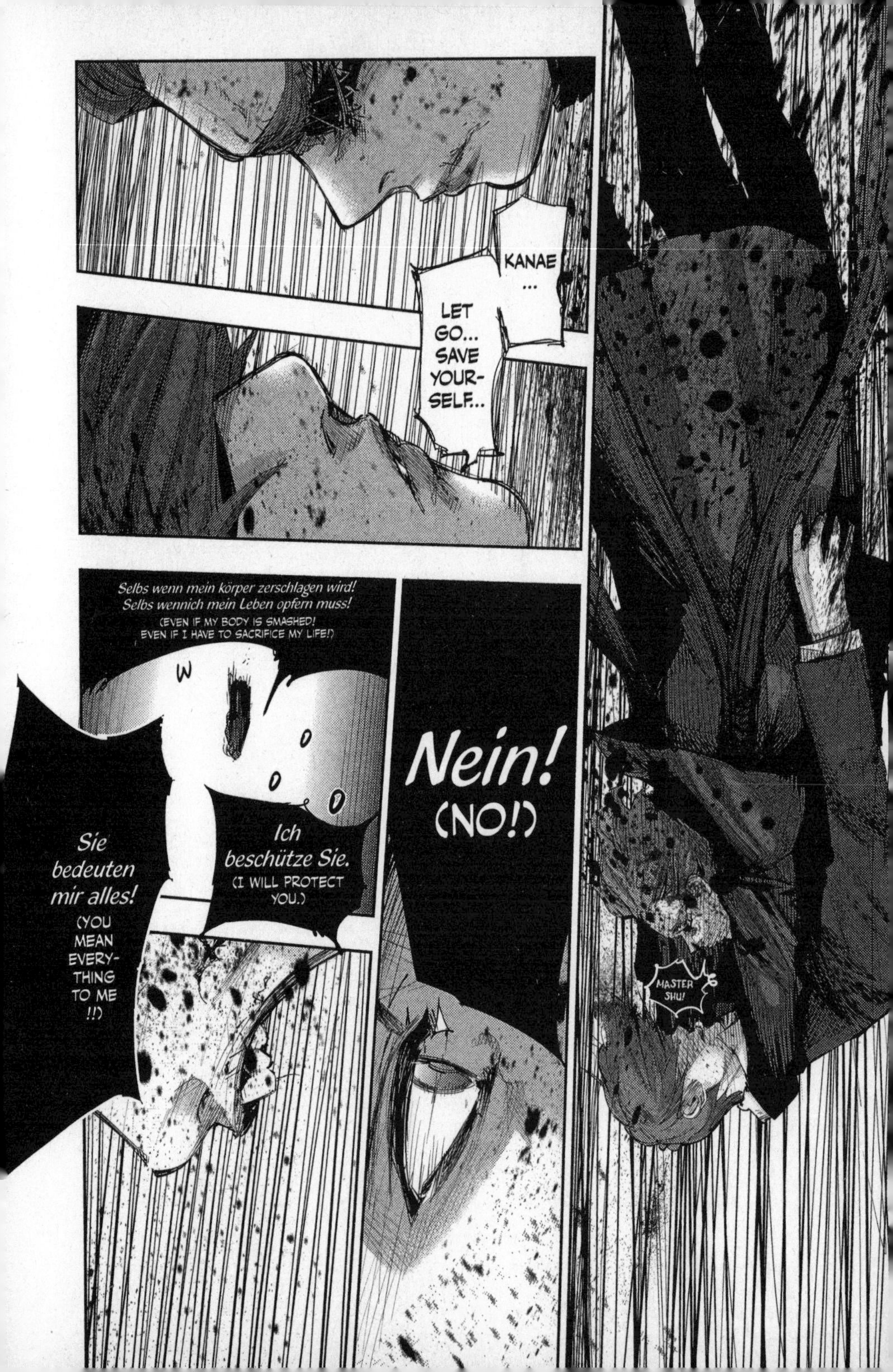
MASTER SHU!
KANAE ...
LET GO... SAVE YOURSELF...
Nein!
(NO!)
Selbs wenn mein körper zerschlagen wird!
Selbs wennich mein Leben opfern muss!
(EVEN IF MY BODY IS SMASHED!
EVEN IF I HAVE TO SACRIFICE MY LIFE!)
Ich beschütze Sie.
(I WILL PROTECT YOU.)
Sie bedeuten mir alles!
(YOU MEAN EVERYTHING TO ME!!)

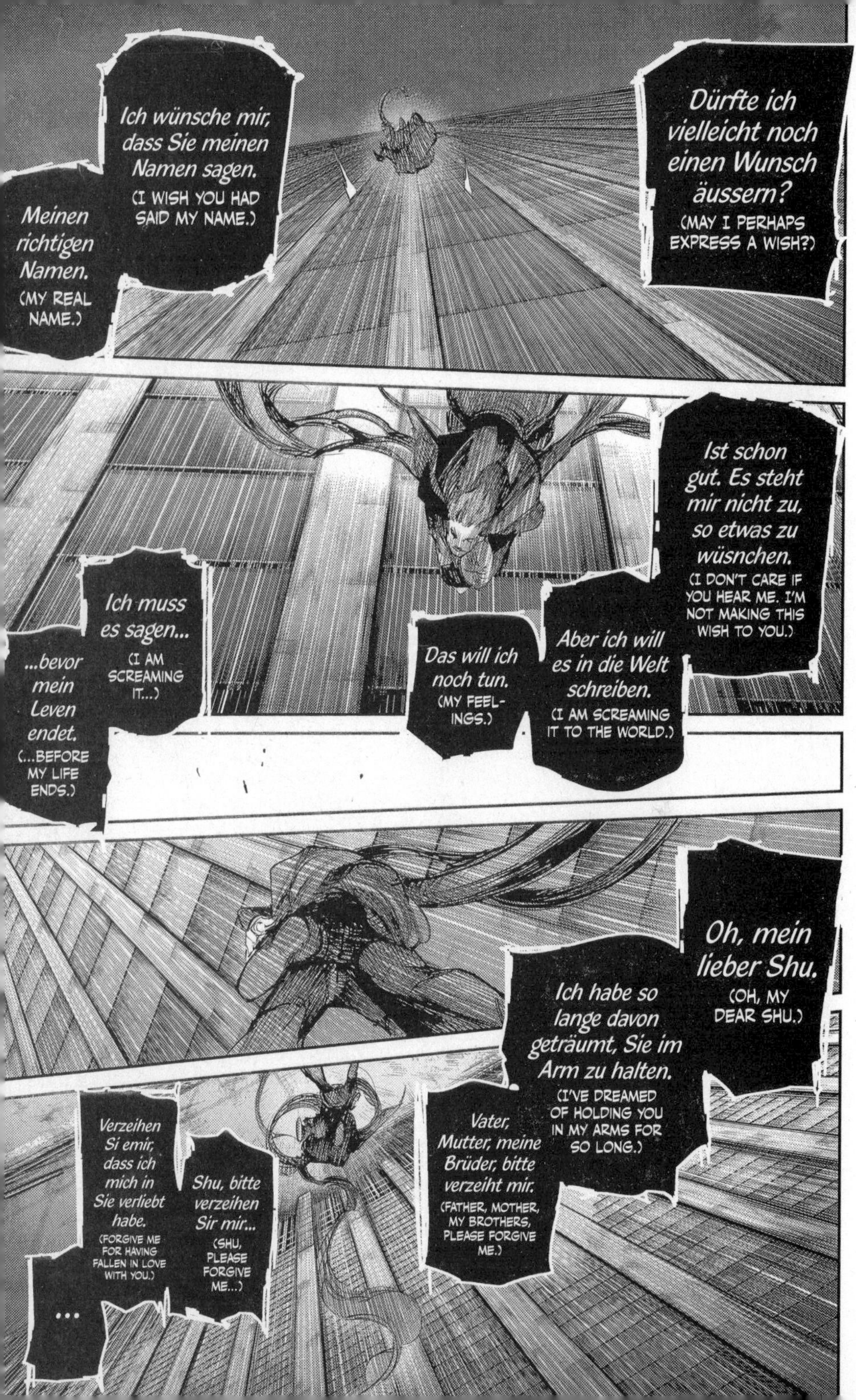
Dürfte ich vielleicht noch einen Wunsch äussern? (MAY I PERHAPS EXPRESS A WISH?)
Ich wünsche mir, dass Sie meinen Namen sagen. (I WISH YOU HAD SAID MY NAME.)
Meinen richtigen Namen. (MY REAL NAME.)
Ist schon gut. Es steht mir nicht zu, so etwas zu wüsnchen. (I DON'T CARE IF YOU HEAR ME. I'M NOT MAKING THIS WISH TO YOU.)
Aber ich will es in die Welt schreiben. (I AM SCREAMING IT TO THE WORLD.)
Das will ich noch tun. (MY FEEL-INGS.)
Ich muss es sagen... (I AM SCREAMING IT...)
...bevor mein Leven endet. (...BEFORE MY LIFE ENDS.)
Oh, mein lieber Shu. (OH, MY DEAR SHU.)
Ich habe so lange davon geträumt, Sie im Arm zu halten. (I'VE DREAMED OF HOLDING YOU IN MY ARMS FOR SO LONG.)
Vater, Mutter, meine Brüder, bitte verzeiht mir. (FATHER, MOTHER, MY BROTHERS, PLEASE FORGIVE ME.)
Shu, bitte verzeihen Sir mir... (SHU, PLEASE FORGIVE ME...)
Verzeihen Si emir, dass ich mich in Sie verliebt habe. (FORGIVE ME FOR HAVING FALLEN IN LOVE WITH YOU.)
...

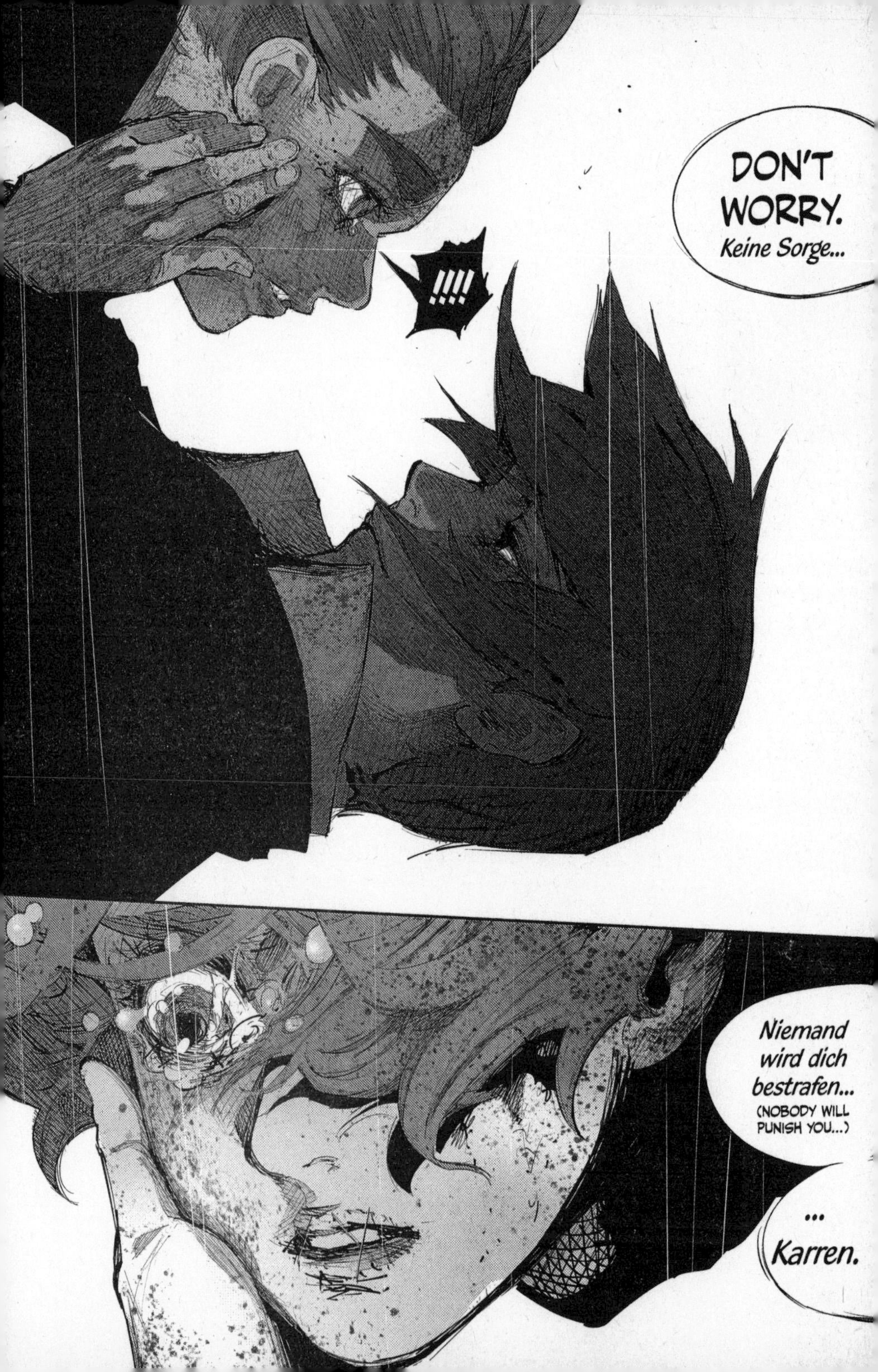
DON'T WORRY.
Keine Sorge...
!!!!
Niemand wird dich bestrafen...
(NOBODY WILL PUNISH YOU...)
... Karren.

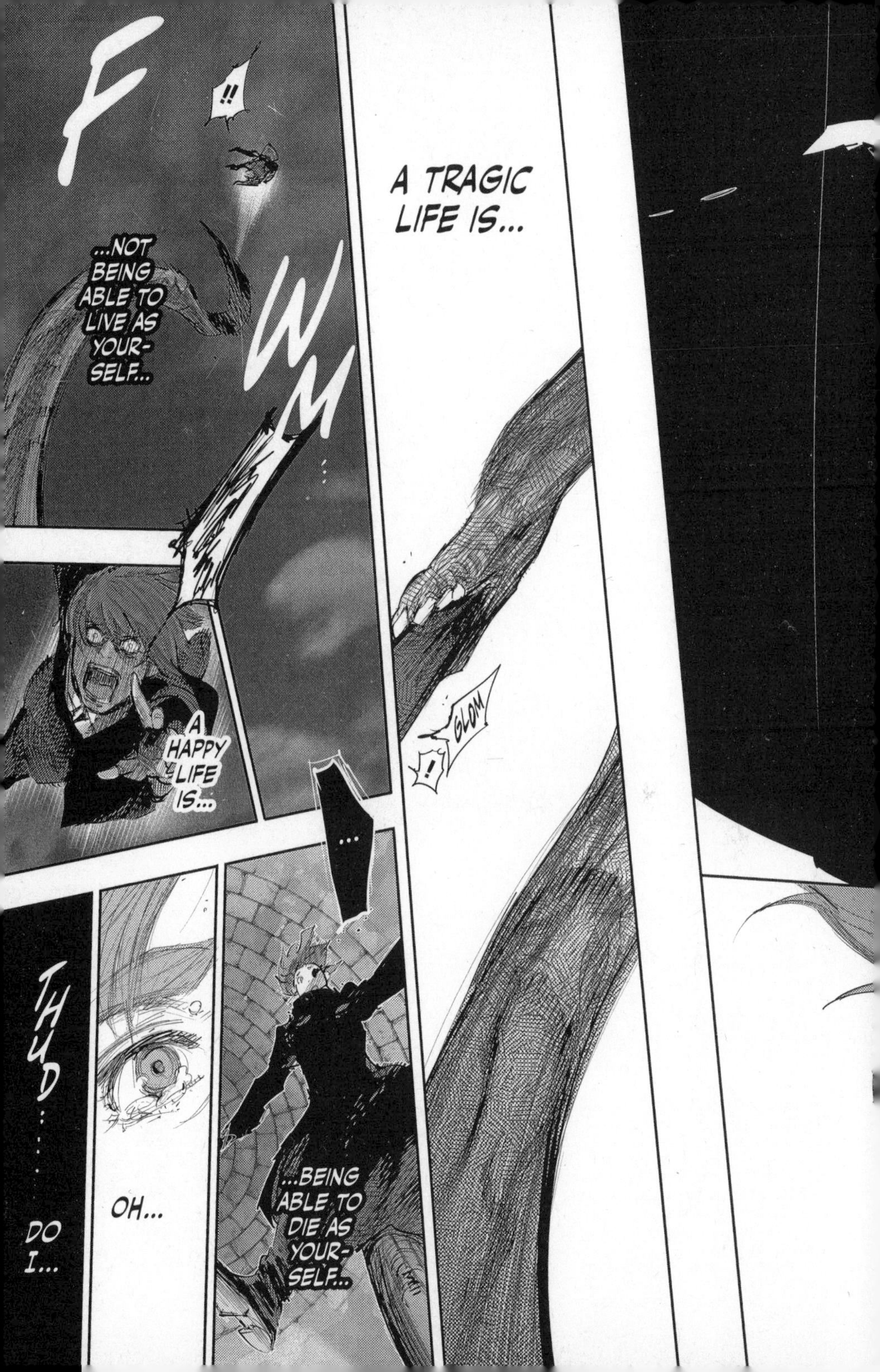
A TRAGIC LIFE IS...
GLOM
!
F
!!
...NOT BEING ABLE TO LIVE AS YOUR-SELF...
WWM
...
A HAPPY LIFE IS...
...
...BEING ABLE TO DIE AS YOUR-SELF...
OH...
THUD......
DO I...

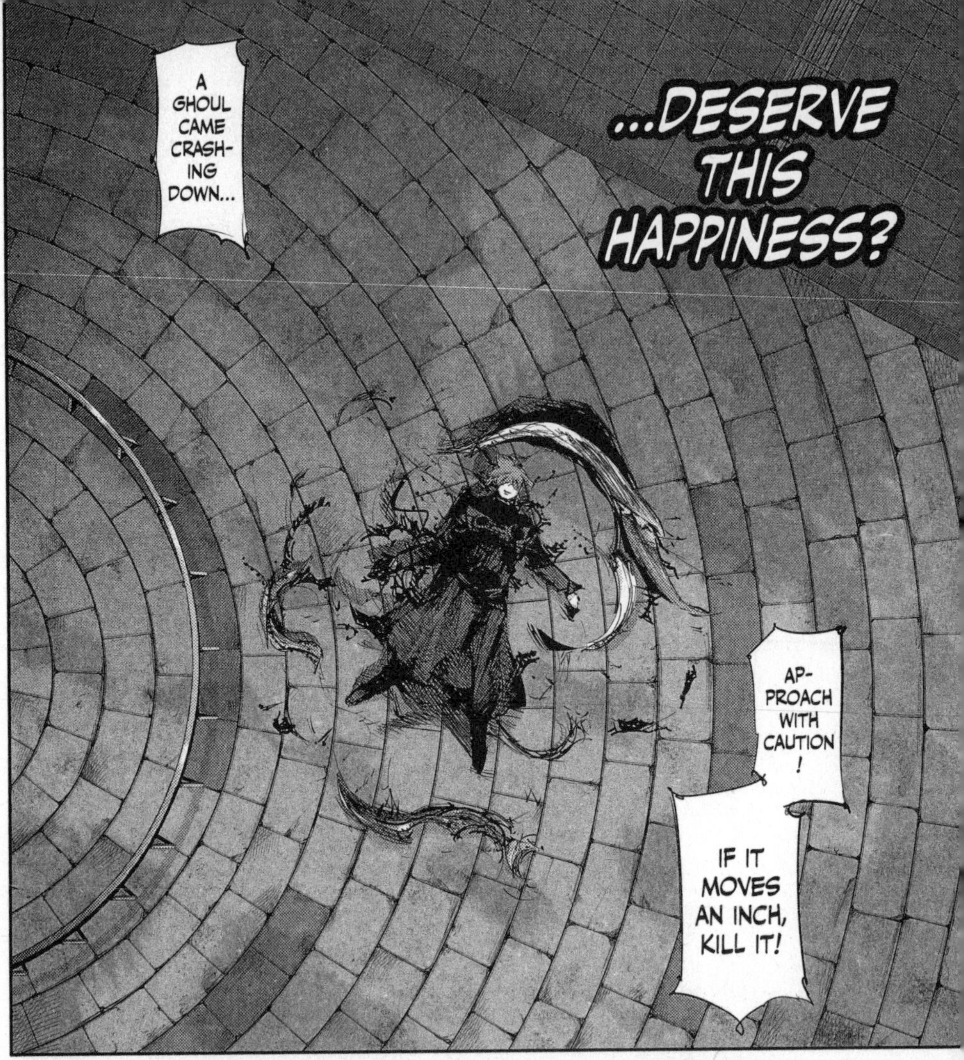
...DESERVE THIS HAPPINESS?
A GHOUL CAME CRASHING DOWN...
APPROACH WITH CAUTION!
IF IT MOVES AN INCH, KILL IT!

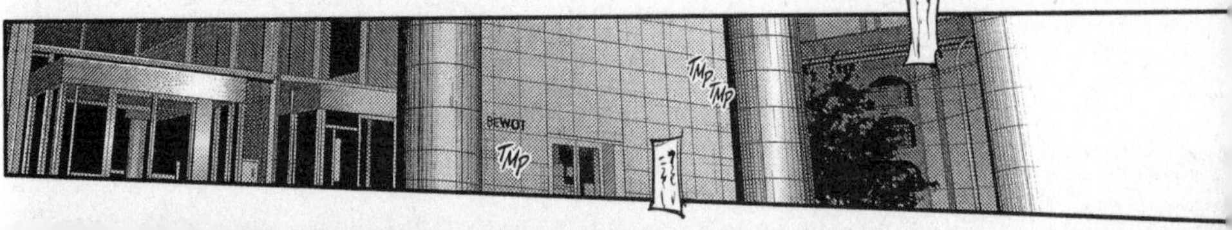
TMP TMP
TMP

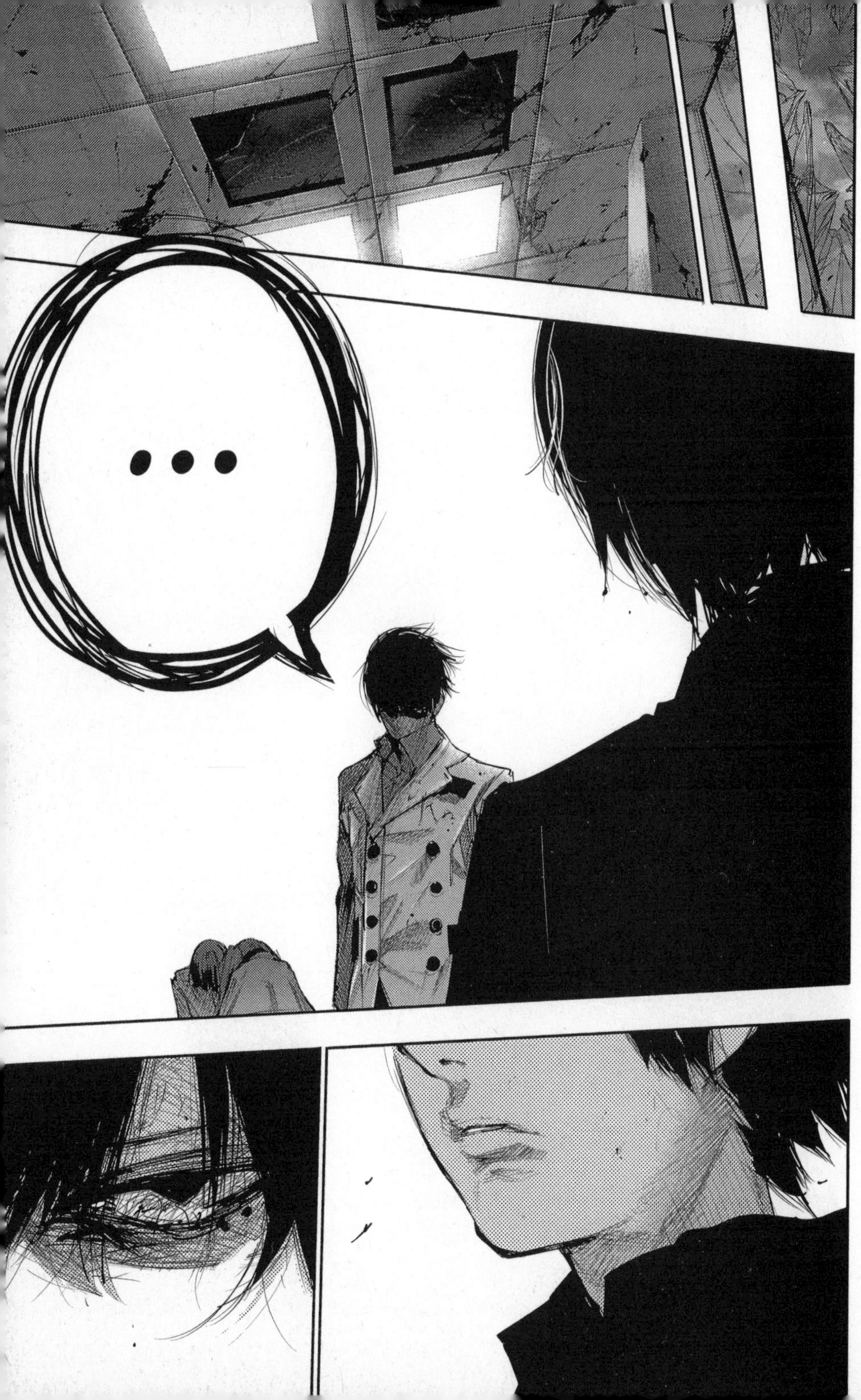
...

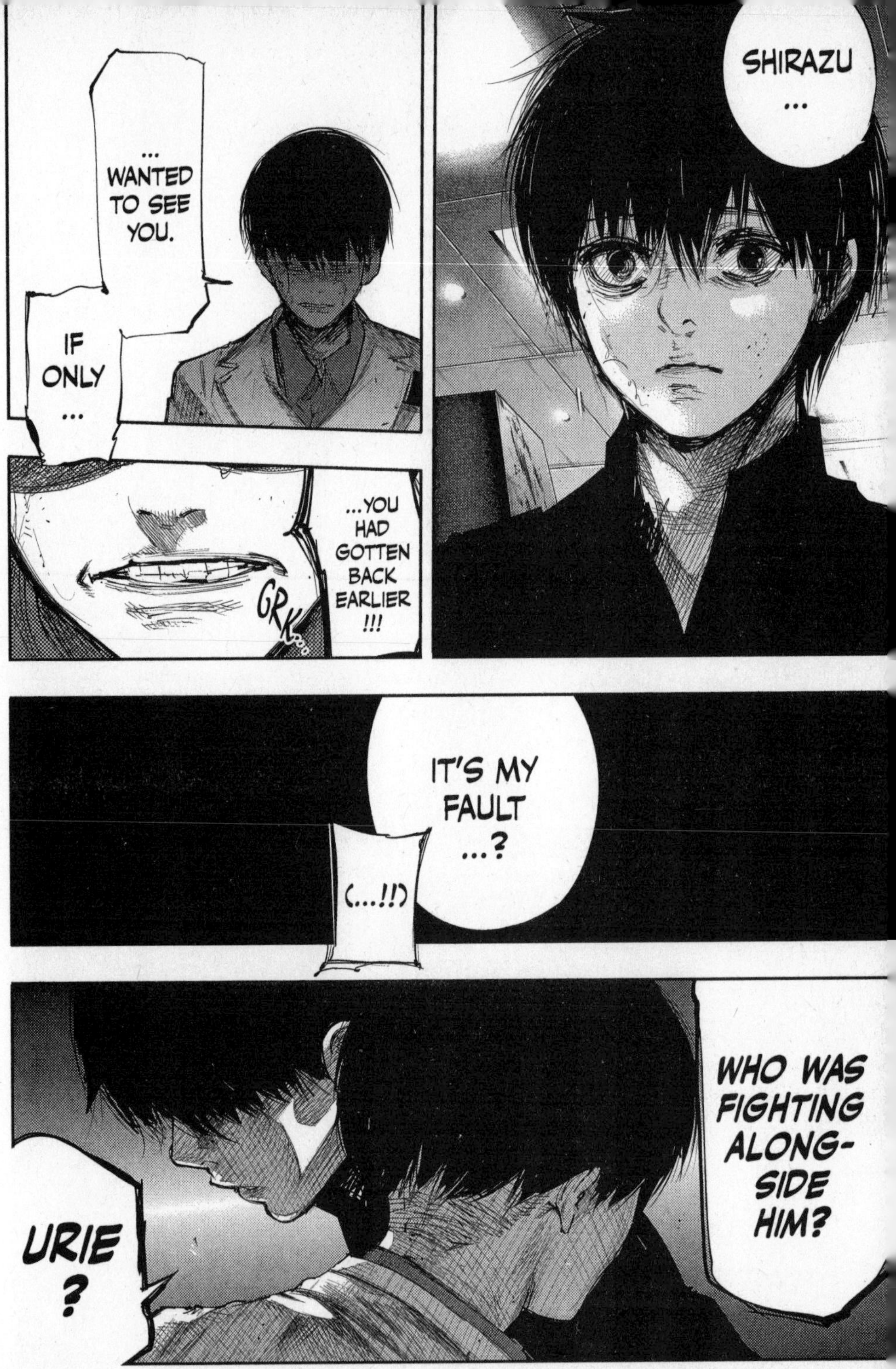
SHIRAZU ...
... WANTED TO SEE YOU.
IF ONLY ...
...YOU HAD GOTTEN BACK EARLIER !!!
GRK...
IT'S MY FAULT ...?
(...!!)
WHO WAS FIGHTING ALONG-SIDE HIM?
URIE ?

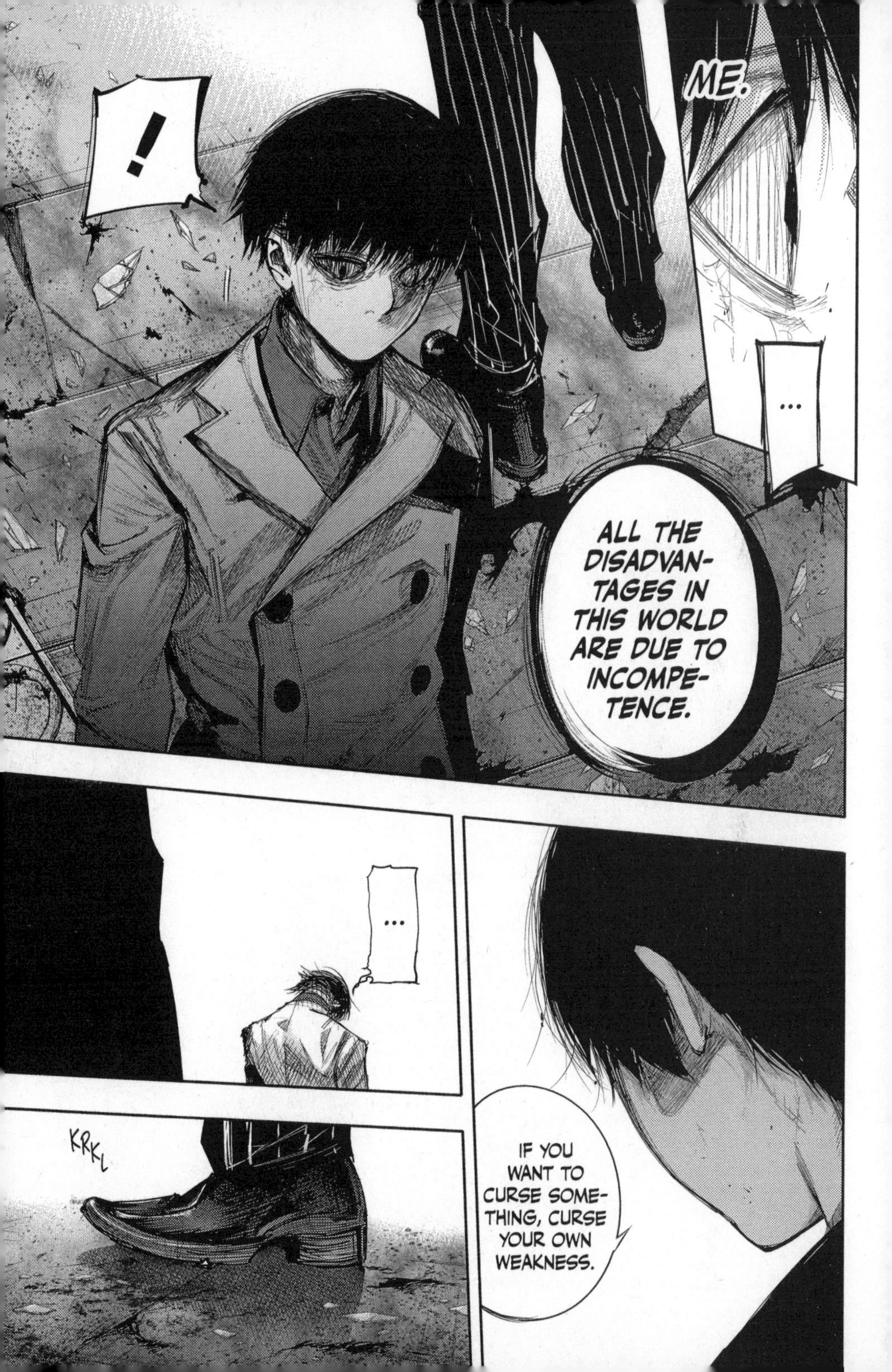

ME.
...
!
ALL THE DISADVANTAGES IN THIS WORLD ARE DUE TO INCOMPETENCE.
IF YOU WANT TO CURSE SOMETHING, CURSE YOUR OWN WEAKNESS.
...
KRKL

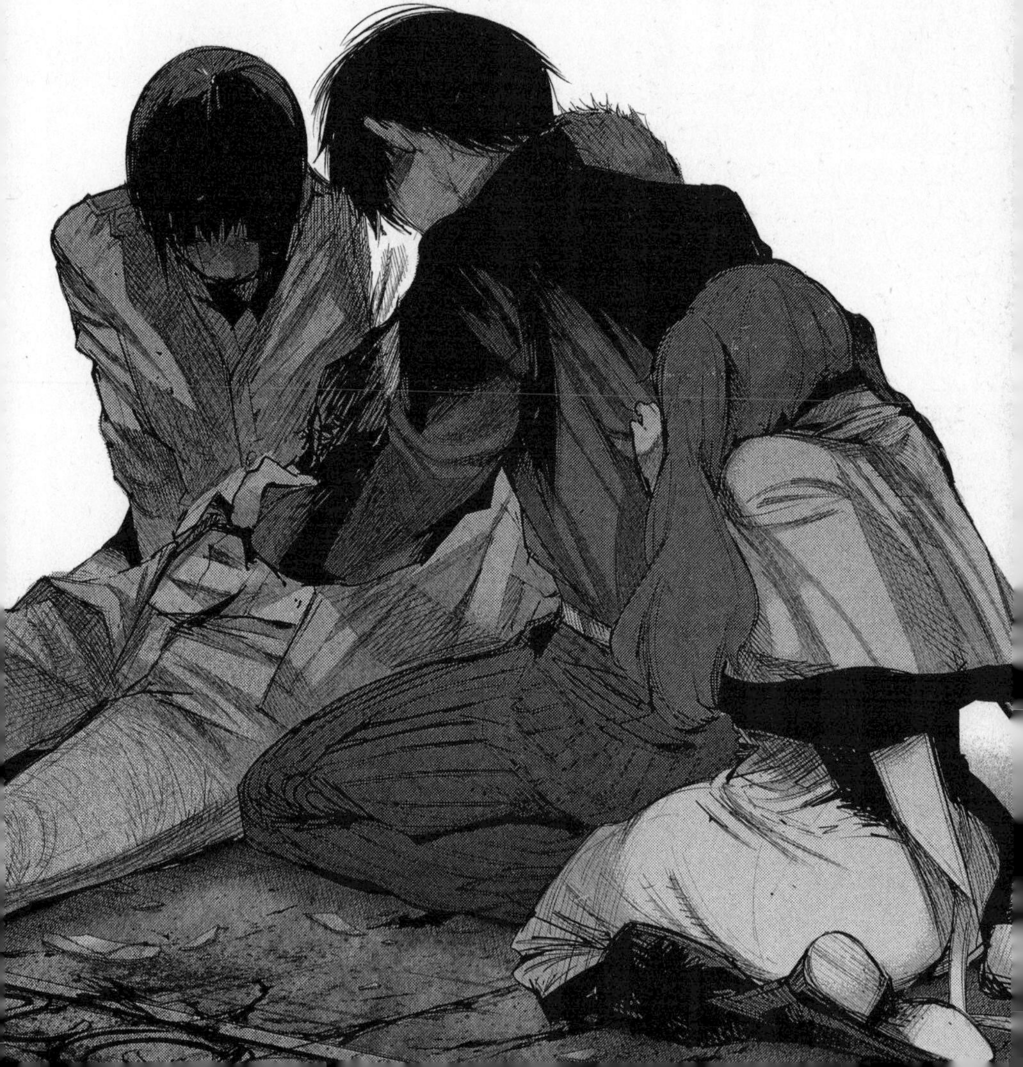

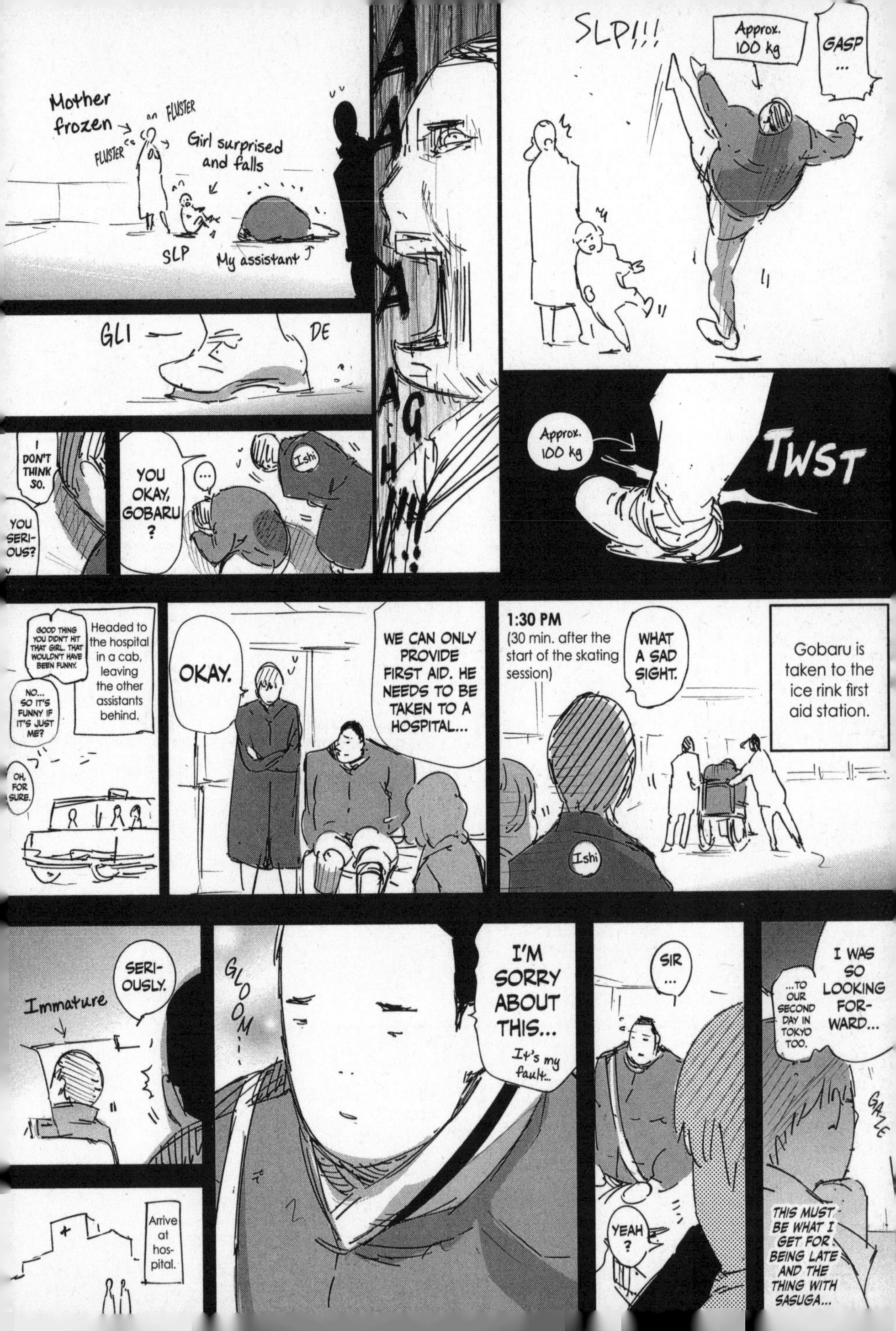

SLP!!!
Approx. 100 kg
GASP ...
Approx. 100 kg
TWST
AAAGH!!!
Mother frozen
FLUSTER
FLUSTER
Girl surprised and falls
SLP
My assistant
GLI — DE
YOU OKAY, GOBARU?
...
I DON'T THINK SO.
YOU SERIOUS?
Gobaru is taken to the ice rink first aid station.
1:30 PM
(30 min. after the start of the skating session)
WHAT A SAD SIGHT.
Ishi
WE CAN ONLY PROVIDE FIRST AID. HE NEEDS TO BE TAKEN TO A HOSPITAL...
OKAY.
Headed to the hospital in a cab, leaving the other assistants behind.
GOOD THING YOU DIDN'T HIT THAT GIRL. THAT WOULDN'T HAVE BEEN FUNNY.
NO... SO IT'S FUNNY IF IT'S JUST ME?
OH, FOR SURE.
I WAS SO LOOKING FOR-WARD...
...TO OUR SECOND DAY IN TOKYO TOO.
GAZE
THIS MUST BE WHAT I GET FOR BEING LATE AND THE THING WITH SASUGA...
SIR ...
YEAH?
I'M SORRY ABOUT THIS...
It's my fault...
GLOOM...
SERI-OUSLY.
Immature
Arrive at hos-pital.

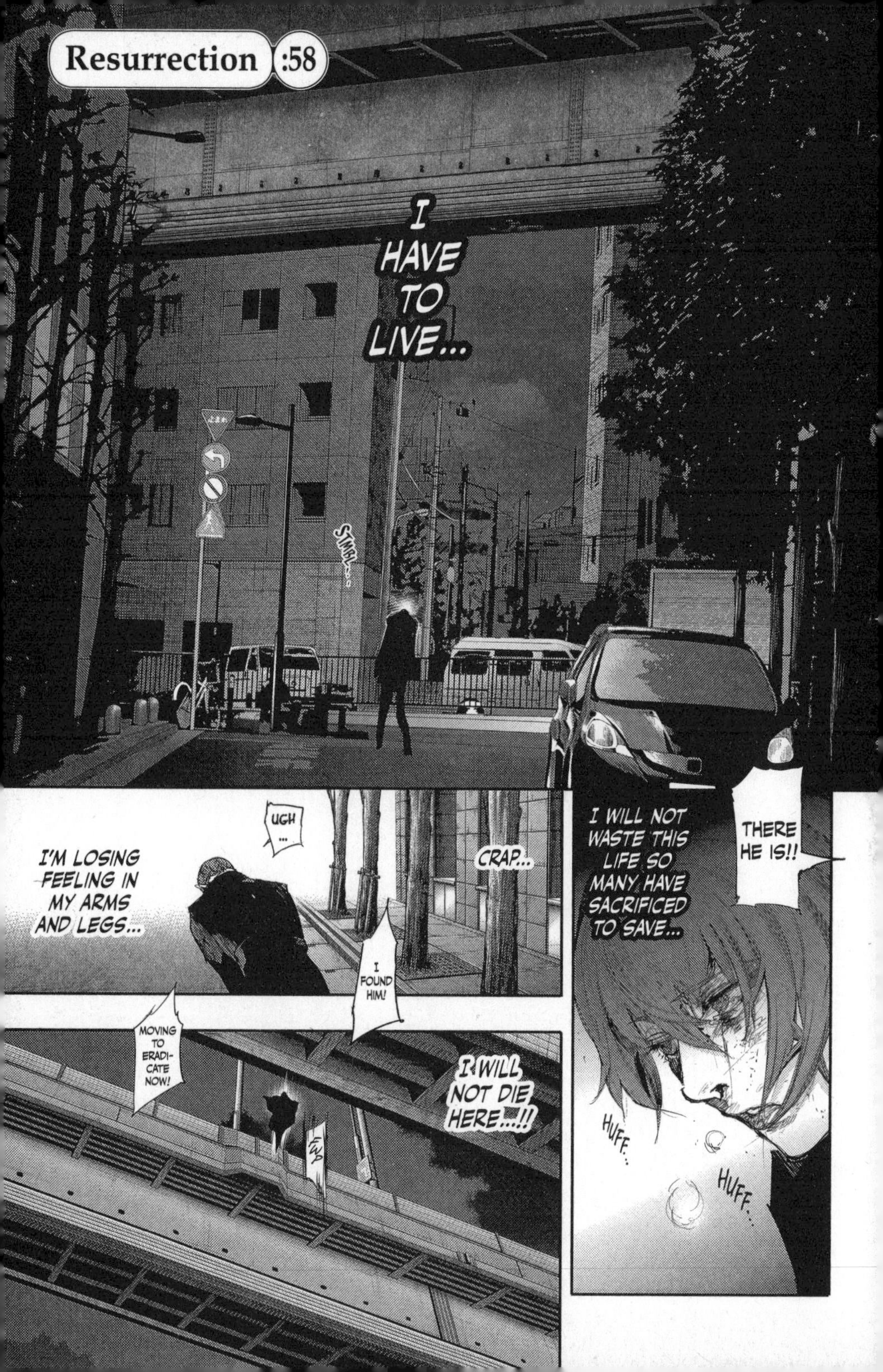
Resurrection :58
I HAVE TO LIVE...
THERE HE IS!!
I WILL NOT WASTE THIS LIFE SO MANY HAVE SACRIFICED TO SAVE...
HUFF...
HUFF...
CRAP...
UGH ...
I'M LOSING FEELING IN MY ARMS AND LEGS...
I FOUND HIM!
I WILL NOT DIE HERE...!!
MOVING TO ERADICATE NOW!

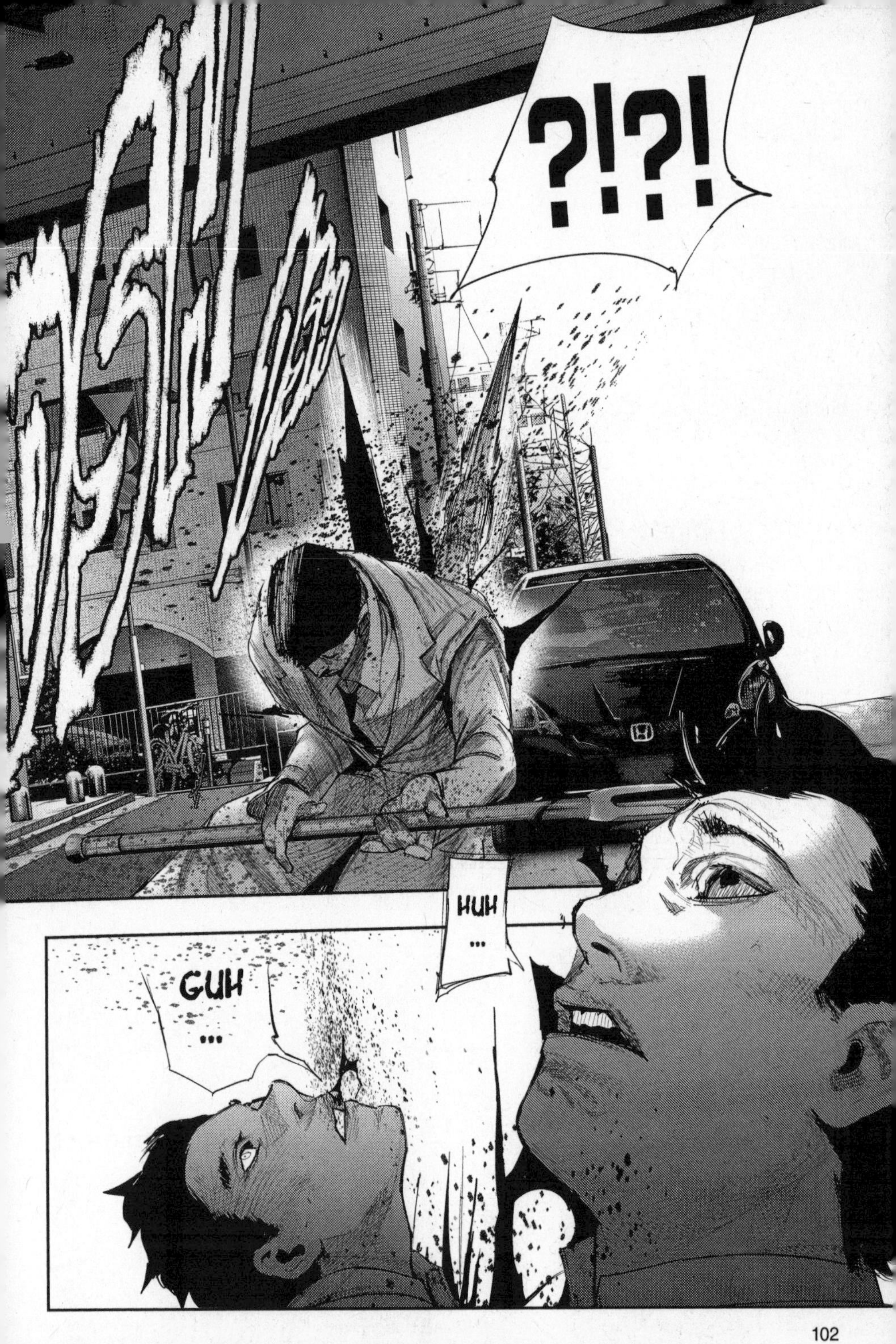
?!?!
HUH ...
GUH ...

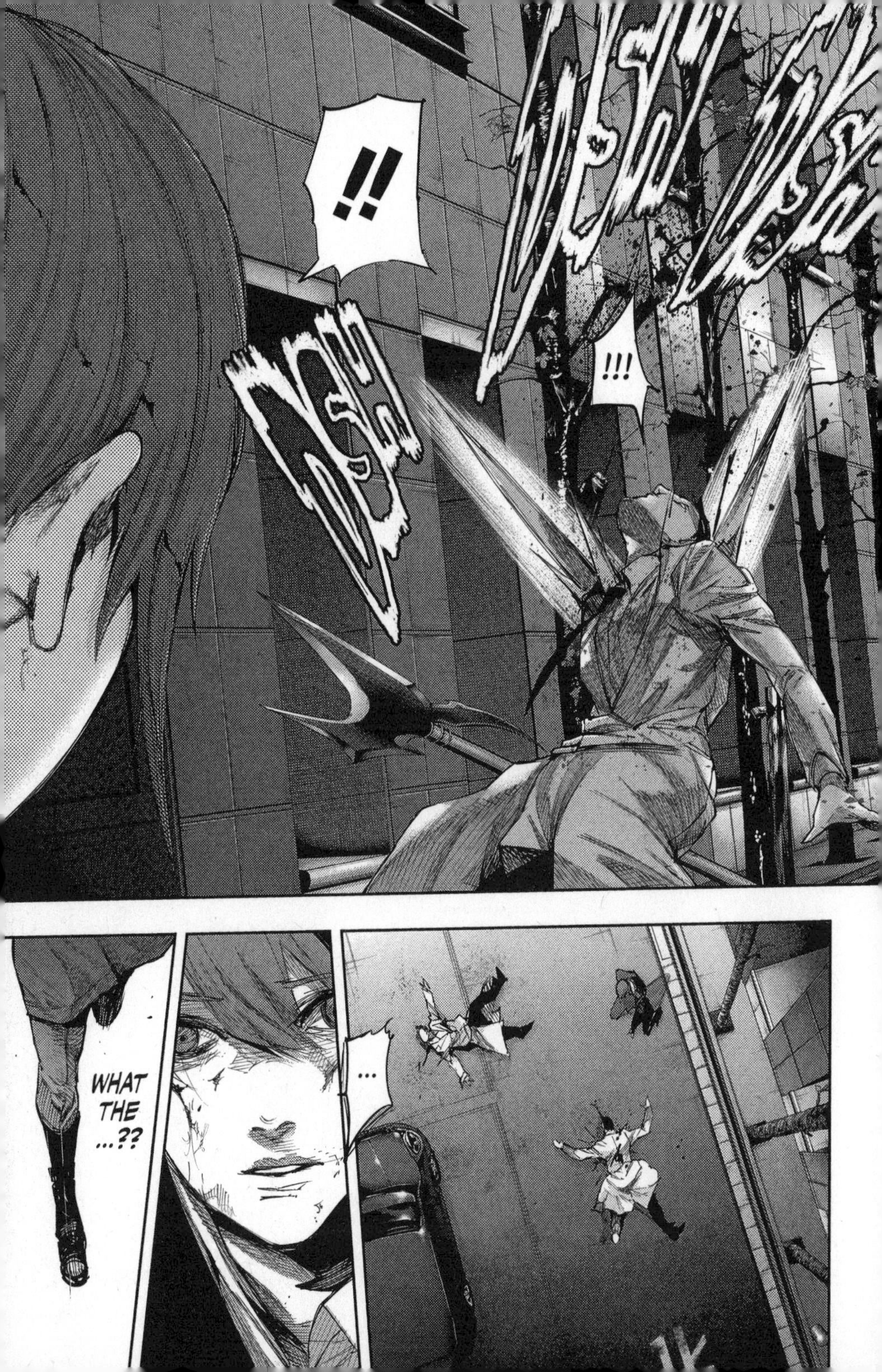
!!
!!!
...
WHAT THE ...??

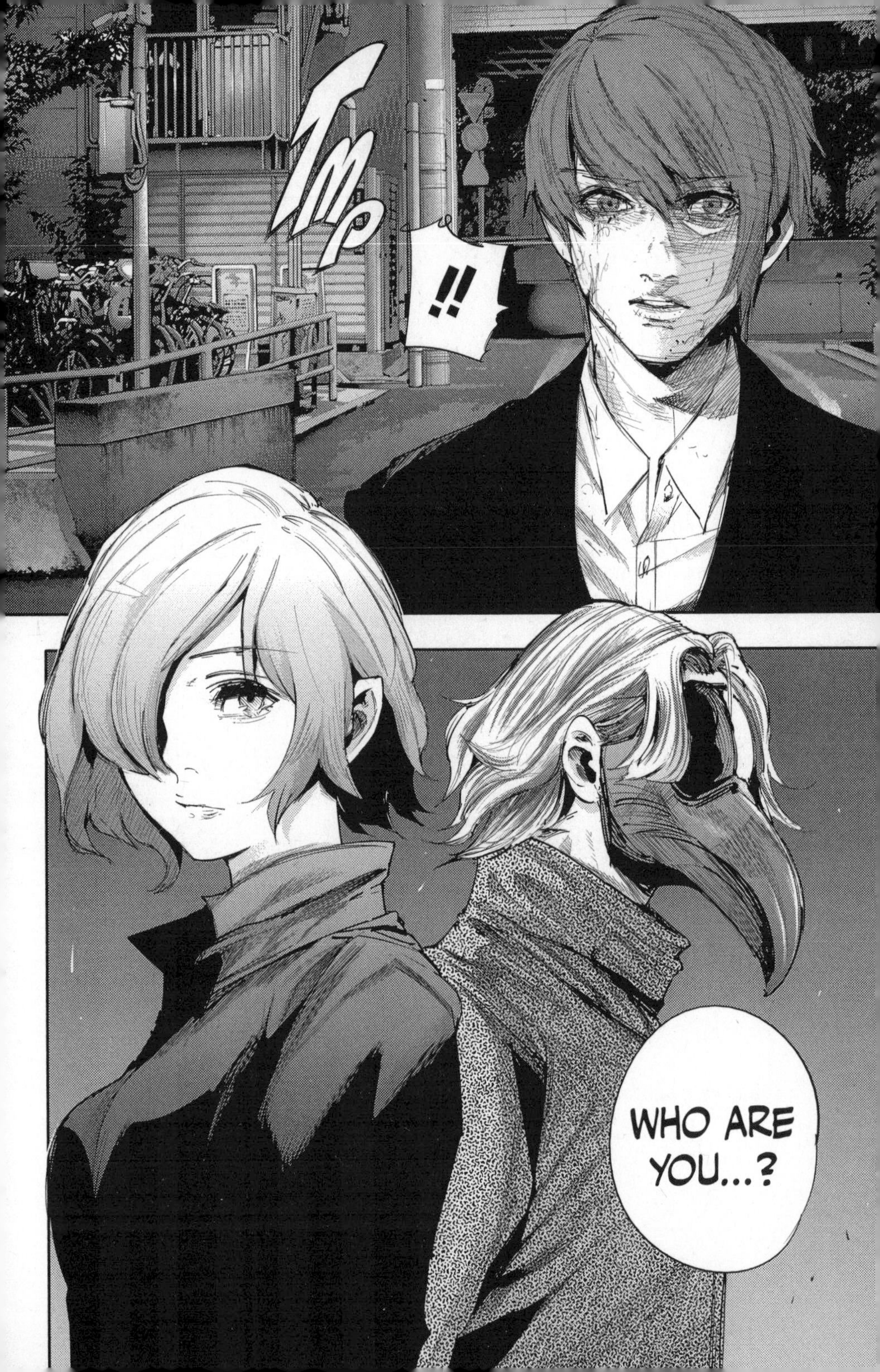
Tmp
!!
WHO ARE YOU...?

TSUKI-
YAMA.

GET
IN.

HORI...

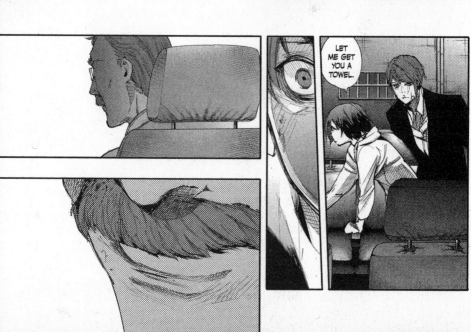

LET
ME GET
YOU A
TOWEL.

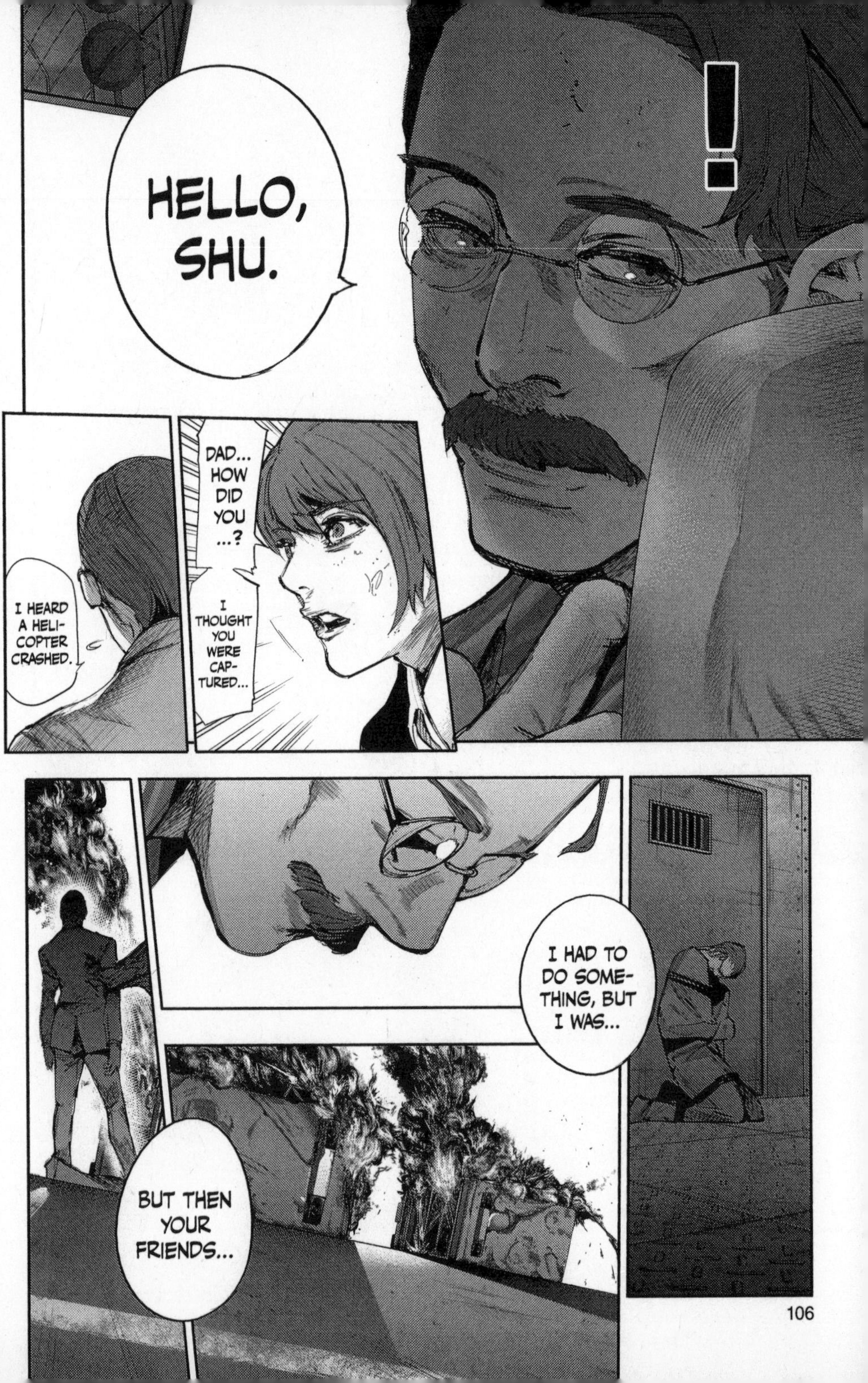
!
HELLO, SHU.
DAD... HOW DID YOU ...?
I THOUGHT YOU WERE CAP-TURED...
I HEARD A HELI-COPTER CRASHED.
I HAD TO DO SOME-THING, BUT I WAS...
BUT THEN YOUR FRIENDS...

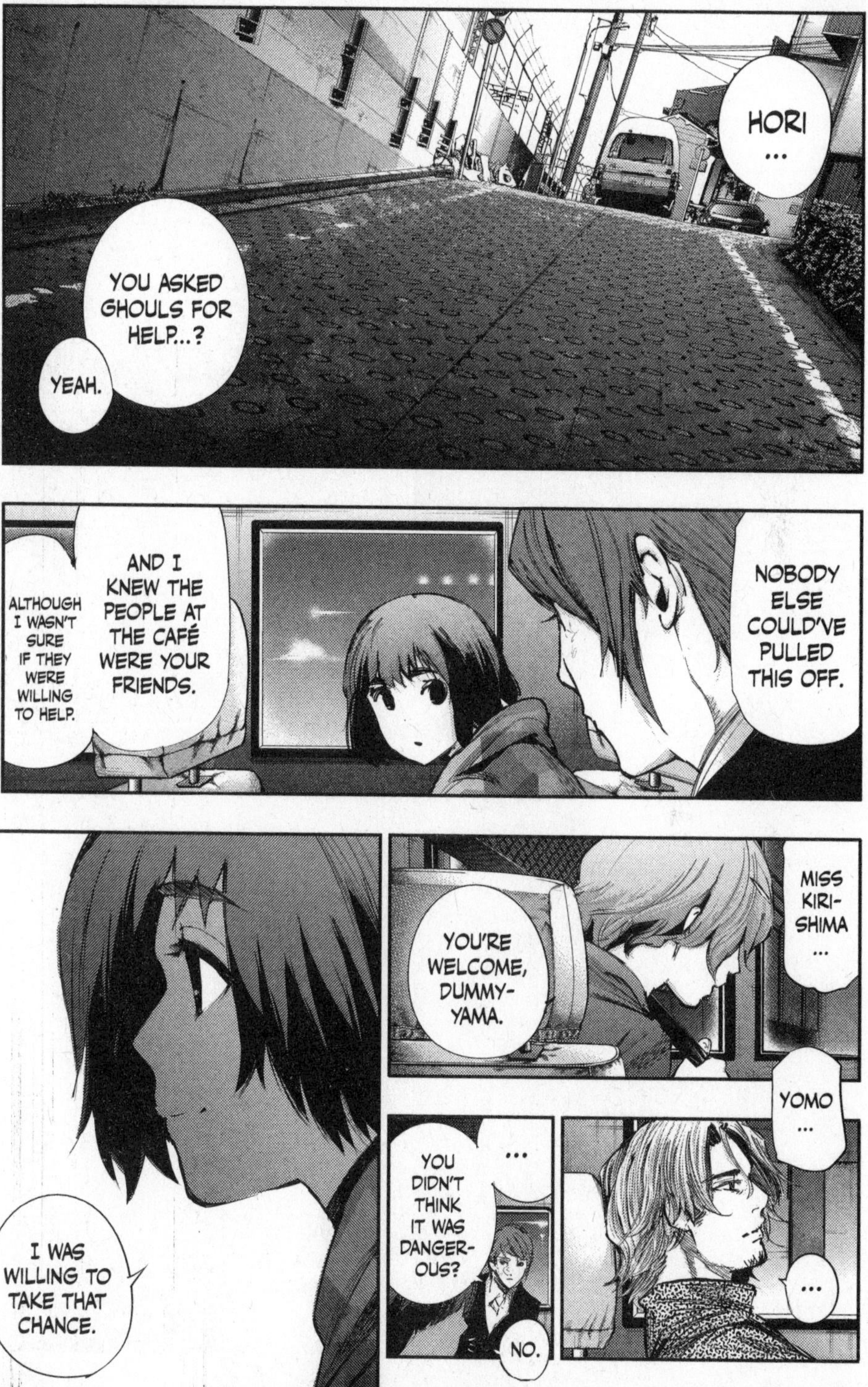
HORI ...
YOU ASKED GHOULS FOR HELP...?
YEAH.
NOBODY ELSE COULD'VE PULLED THIS OFF.
AND I KNEW THE PEOPLE AT THE CAFÉ WERE YOUR FRIENDS.
ALTHOUGH I WASN'T SURE IF THEY WERE WILLING TO HELP.
MISS KIRI-SHIMA ...
YOU'RE WELCOME, DUMMY-YAMA.
YOMO ...
...
...
YOU DIDN'T THINK IT WAS DANGER-OUS?
NO.
I WAS WILLING TO TAKE THAT CHANCE.

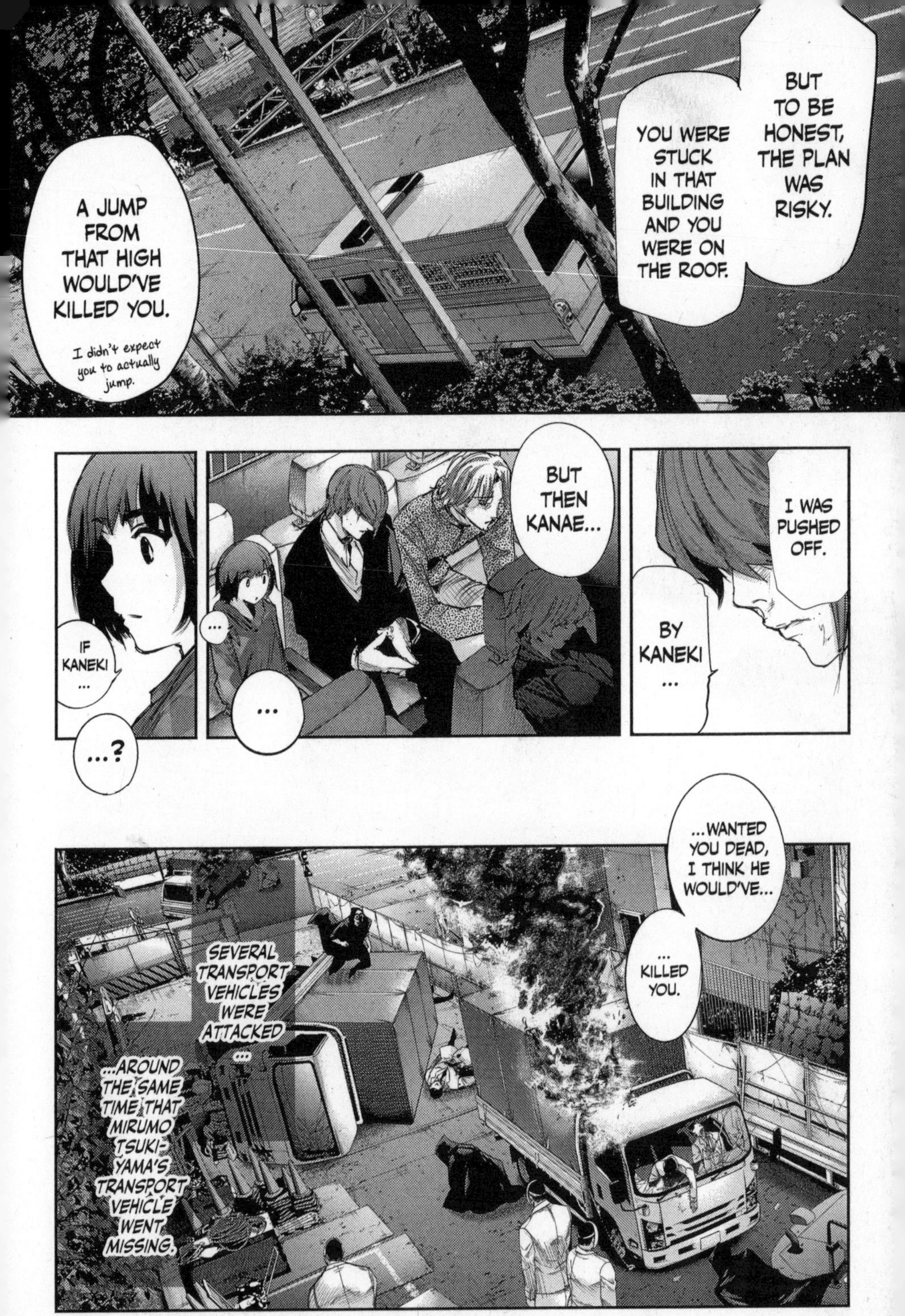
BUT TO BE HONEST, THE PLAN WAS RISKY.
YOU WERE STUCK IN THAT BUILDING AND YOU WERE ON THE ROOF.
A JUMP FROM THAT HIGH WOULD'VE KILLED YOU.
I didn't expect you to actually jump.
I WAS PUSHED OFF.
BY KANEKI ...
BUT THEN KANAE...
...
...
IF KANEKI ...
...?
...WANTED YOU DEAD, I THINK HE WOULD'VE...
... KILLED YOU.
SEVERAL TRANSPORT VEHICLES WERE ATTACKED ...
...AROUND THE SAME TIME THAT MIRUMO TSUKI-YAMA'S TRANSPORT VEHICLE WENT MISSING.

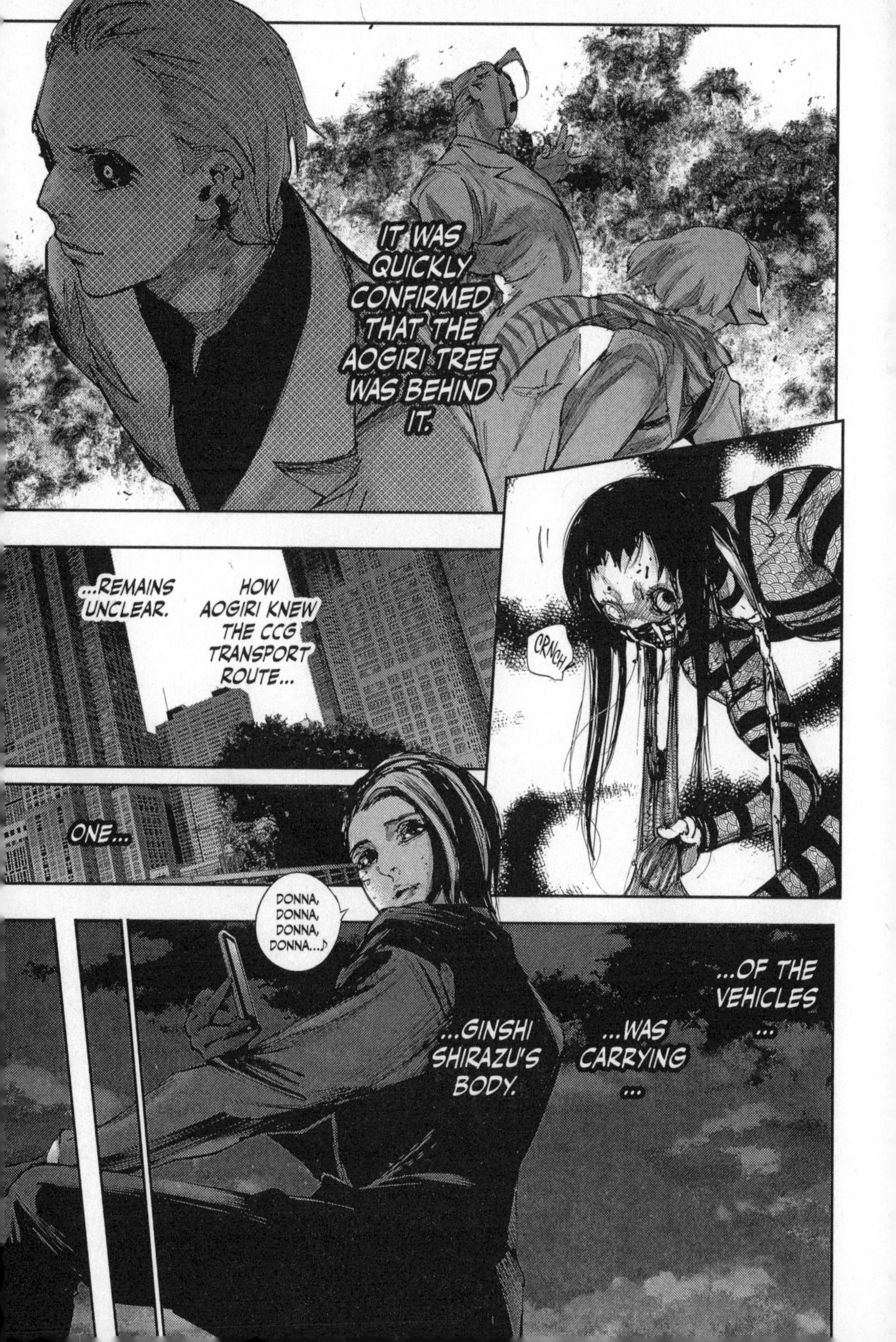
IT WAS QUICKLY CONFIRMED THAT THE AOGIRI TREE WAS BEHIND IT.
CRNCH
HOW AOGIRI KNEW THE CCG TRANSPORT ROUTE...
...REMAINS UNCLEAR.
ONE...
DONNA, DONNA, DONNA, DONNA...♪
...OF THE VEHICLES...
...WAS CARRYING...
...GINSHI SHIRAZU'S BODY.

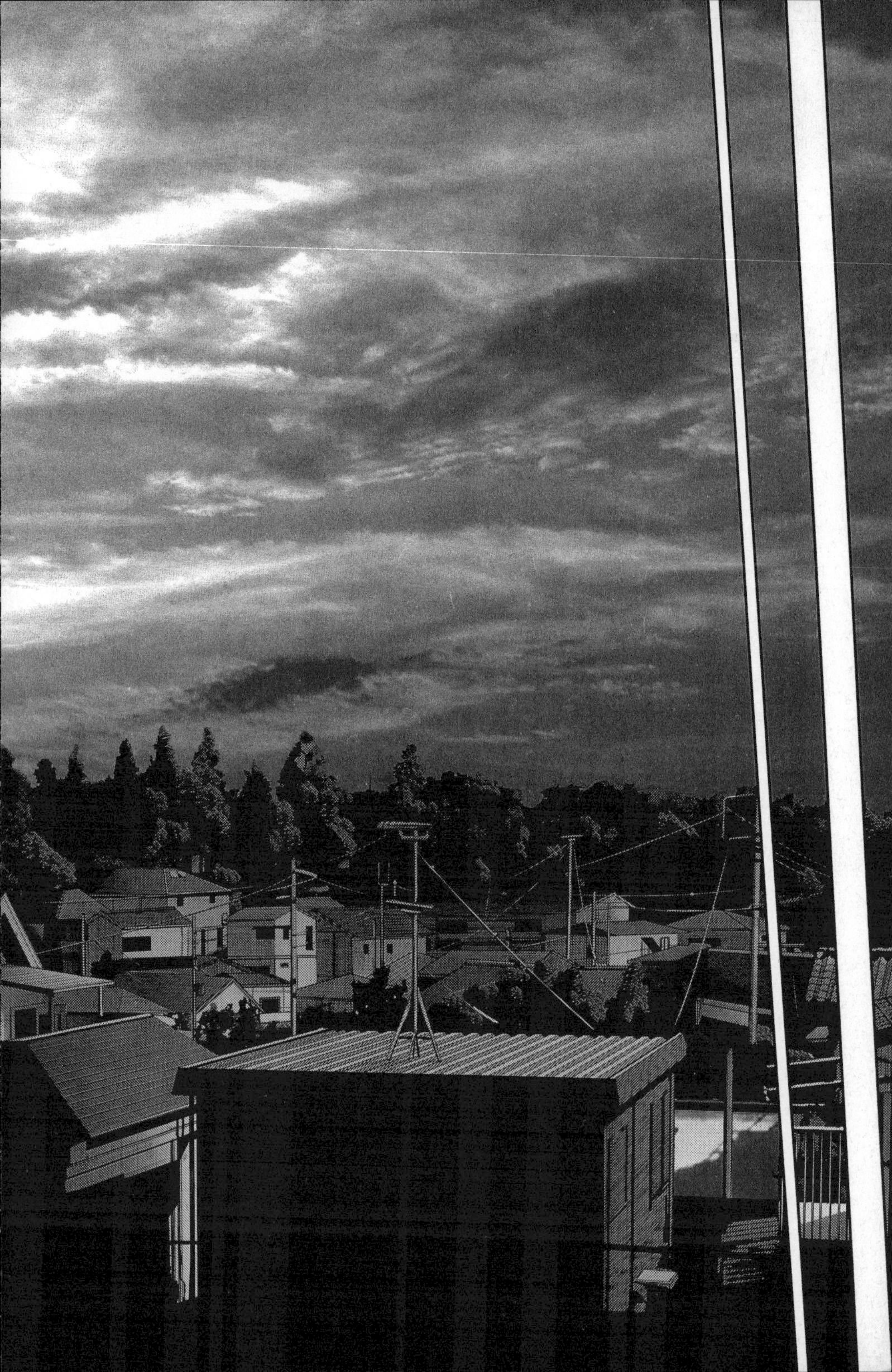

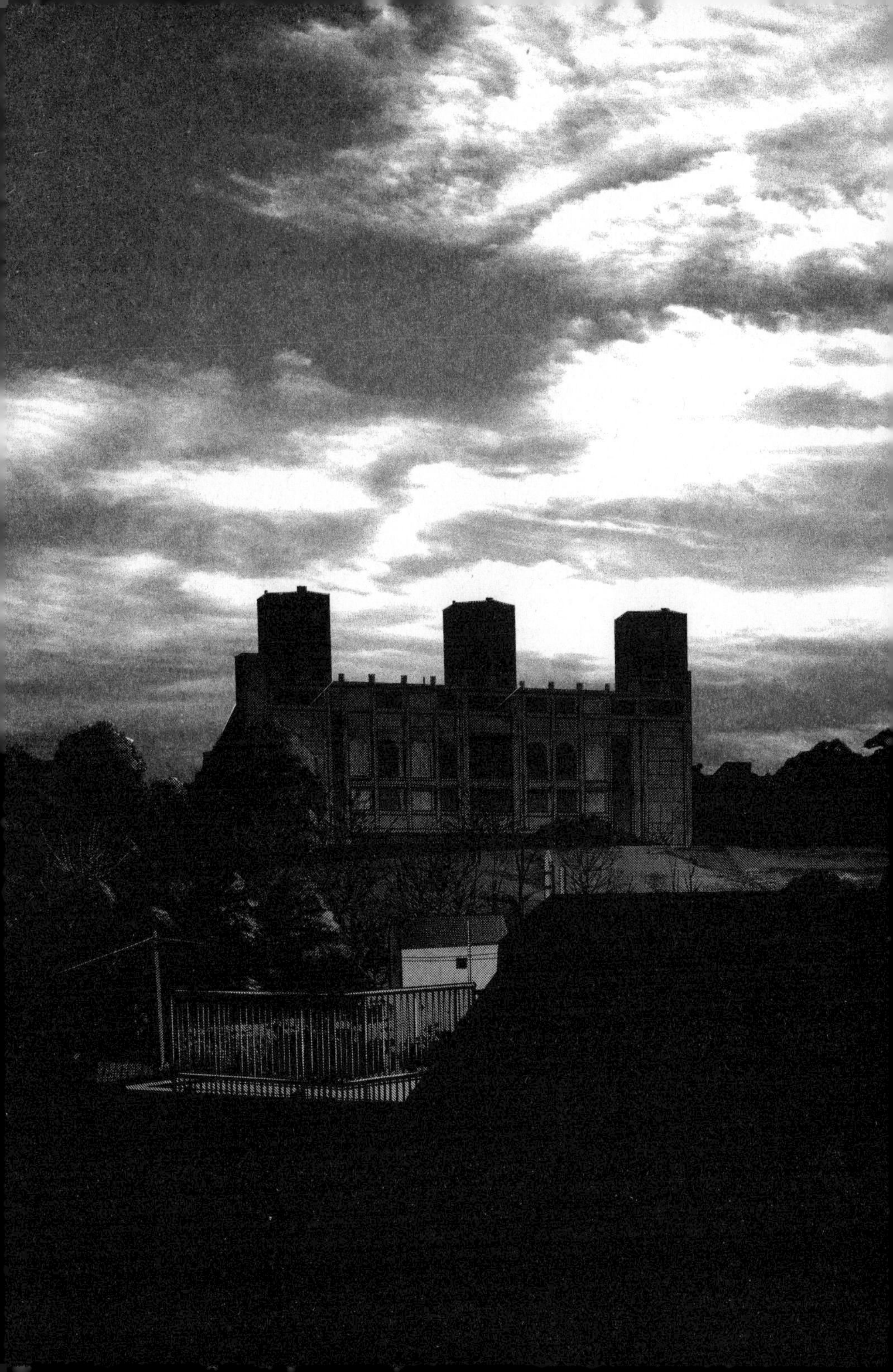

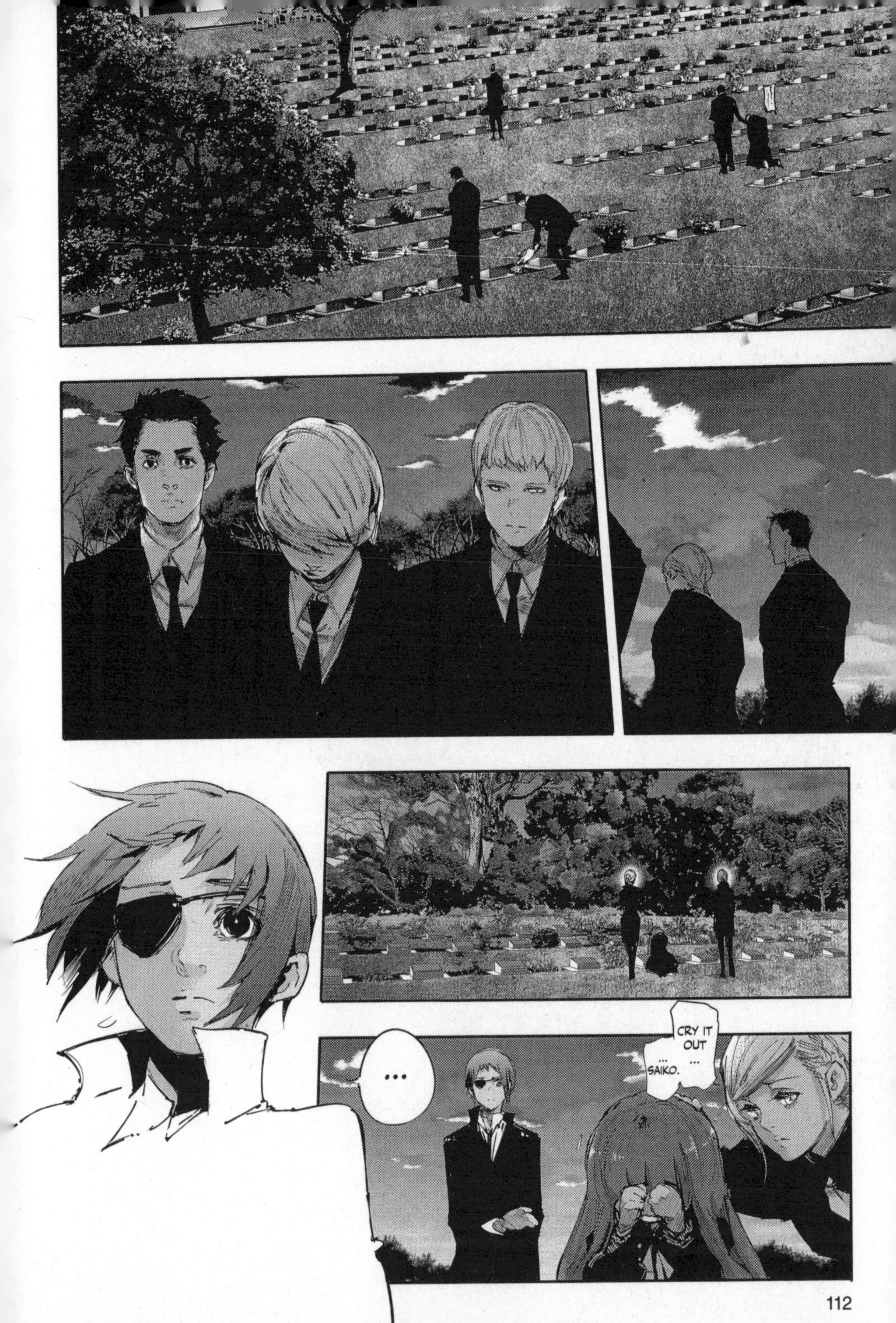
CRY IT OUT ... ... SAIKO.
...

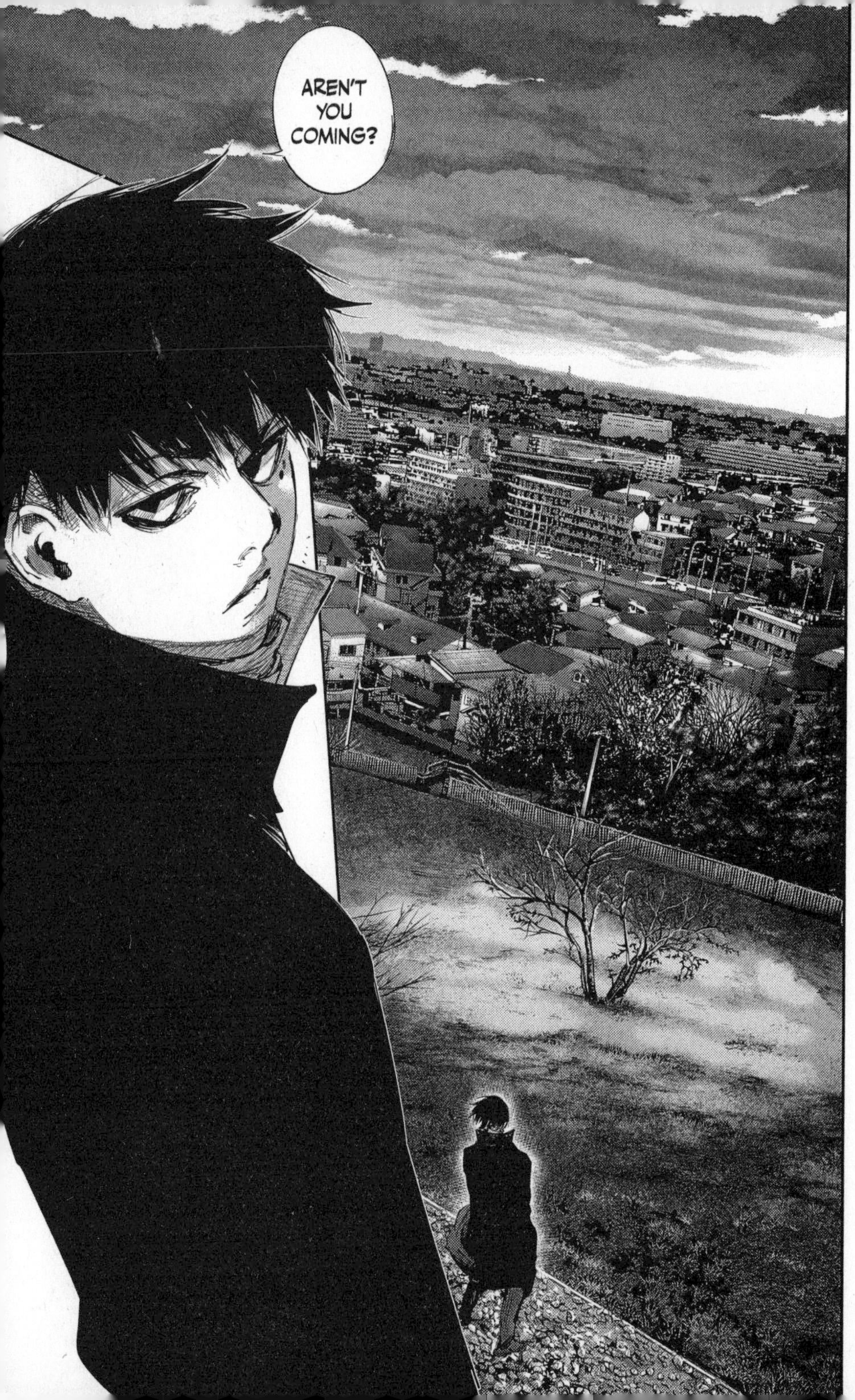
AREN'T YOU COMING?

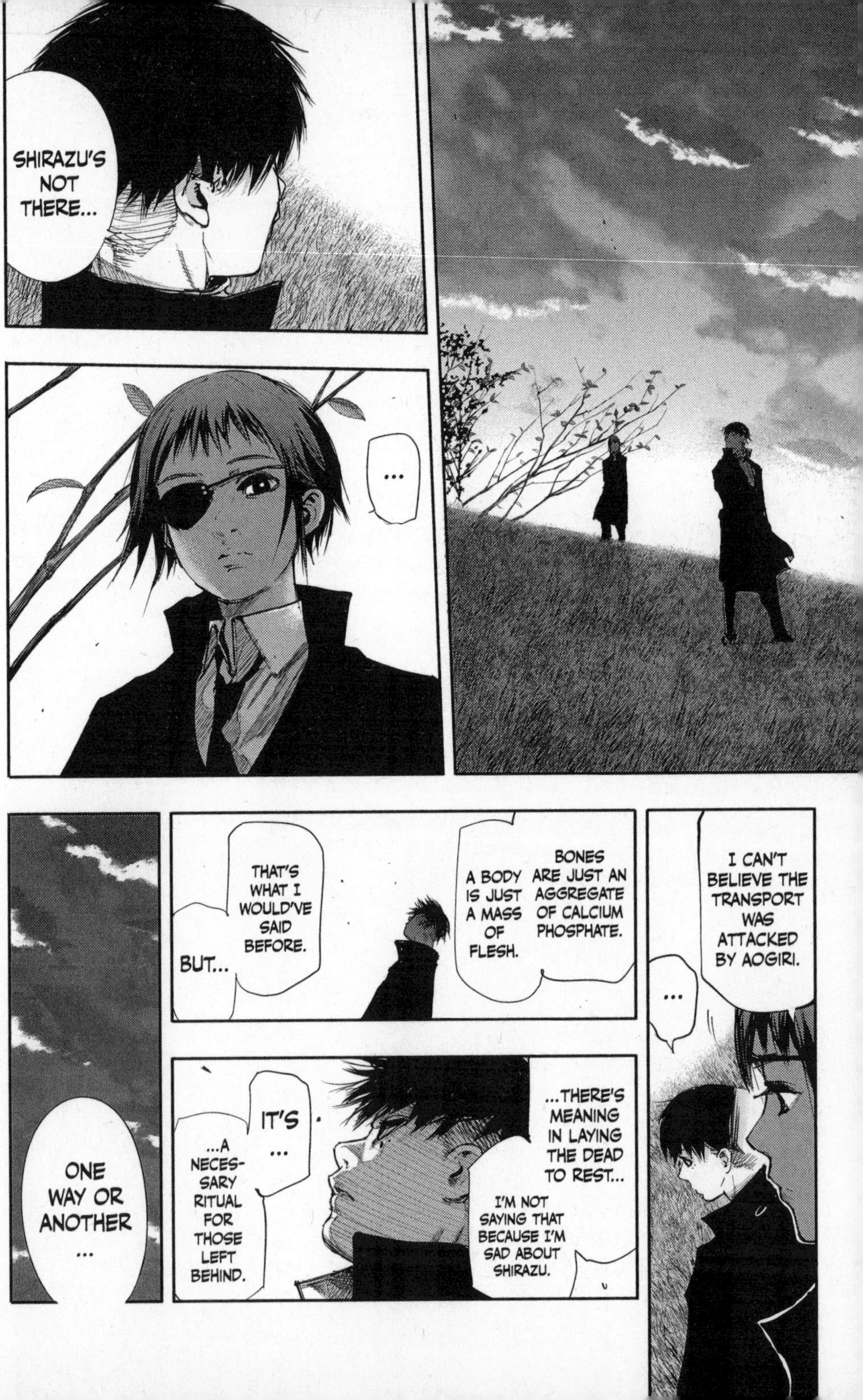
SHIRAZU'S NOT THERE...
...
I CAN'T BELIEVE THE TRANSPORT WAS ATTACKED BY AOGIRI.
...
A BODY IS JUST A MASS OF FLESH.
BONES ARE JUST AN AGGREGATE OF CALCIUM PHOSPHATE.
THAT'S WHAT I WOULD'VE SAID BEFORE.
BUT...
...THERE'S MEANING IN LAYING THE DEAD TO REST...
I'M NOT SAYING THAT BECAUSE I'M SAD ABOUT SHIRAZU.
IT'S...
...A NECES-SARY RITUAL FOR THOSE LEFT BEHIND.
ONE WAY OR ANOTHER...

...I WILL BRING SHIRAZU BACK.

WELL, KANO ...?

IT'S MAGNIFICENT.

THE STRUCTURE OF THIS FRAME IS EXCEPTIONAL.

GWM

GWM

THE IDEA OF FAMILIARIZING THE HUMAN BODY TO A GHOUL'S KAKUHO IN STAGES IS SIMPLE.

BUT THAT'S EXACTLY WHY IT'S SO EFFECTIVE.

THIS UNIQUE SUPPRESSION DEVICE THAT MAKES IT POSSIBLE ...

IT IS TRULY BRILLIANT!

IT PREVENTS THE ONSET OF REJECTION WHENEVER POSSIBLE.

WITH THIS QS TECHNOLOGY AND MY EXPERIENCE...

...WE SHOULD BE ABLE TO SUCCESSFULLY PERFORM OUR GHOULIFICATION PROCEDURE.

IMPRESSIVE, DR. CHIGYO.

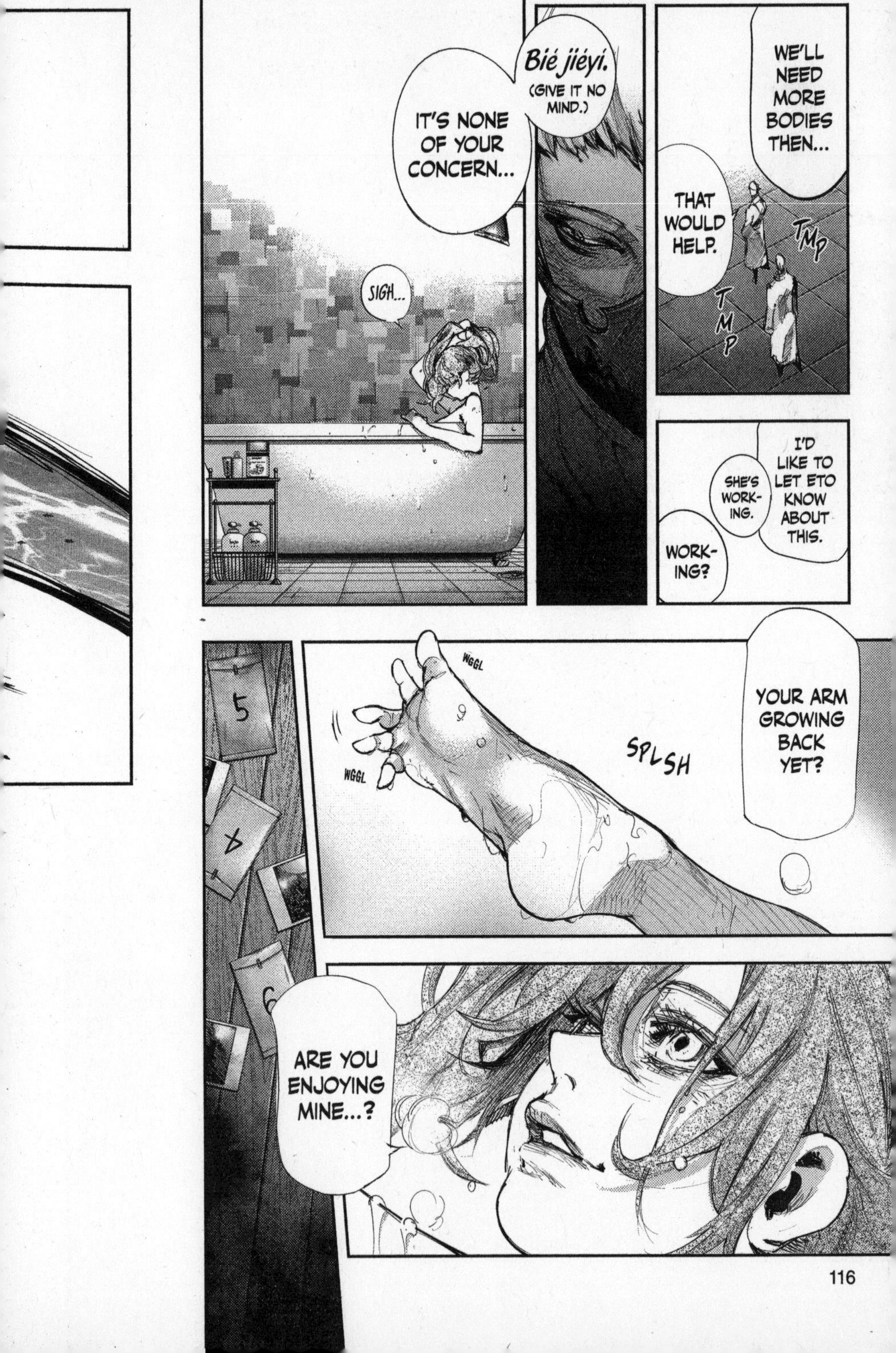
WE'LL NEED MORE BODIES THEN...
THAT WOULD HELP.
TMP
TMP
I'D LIKE TO LET ETO KNOW ABOUT THIS.
SHE'S WORKING.
WORKING?
Bié jiéyi.
(GIVE IT NO MIND.)
IT'S NONE OF YOUR CONCERN...
SIGH...
YOUR ARM GROWING BACK YET?
SPLSH
WGGL
WGGL
ARE YOU ENJOYING MINE...?

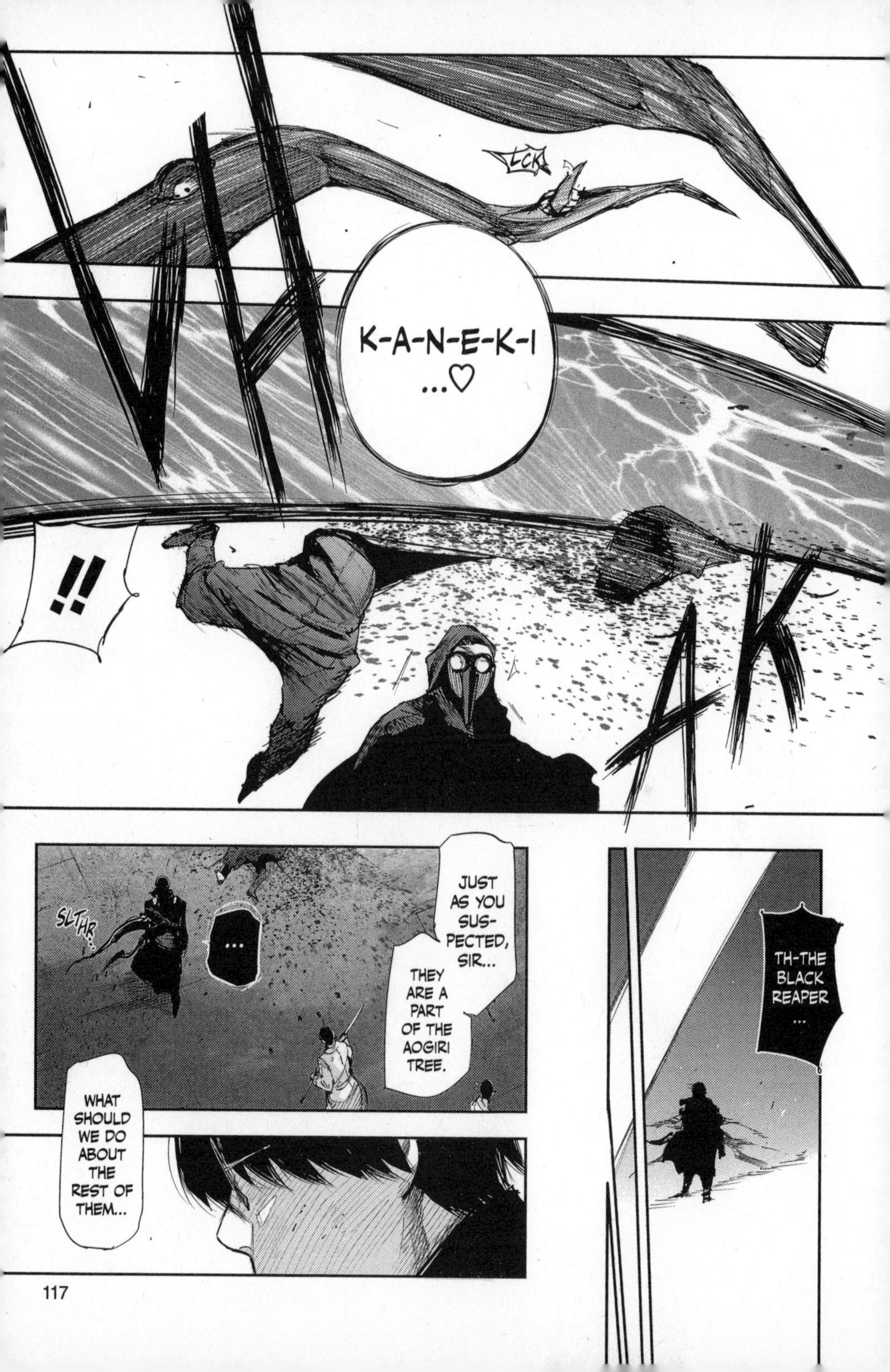
LCK
K-A-N-E-K-I ...♡
WHAK
!!
TH-THE BLACK REAPER ...
JUST AS YOU SUS-PECTED, SIR...
THEY ARE A PART OF THE AOGIRI TREE.
...
SLTHR...
WHAT SHOULD WE DO ABOUT THE REST OF THEM...

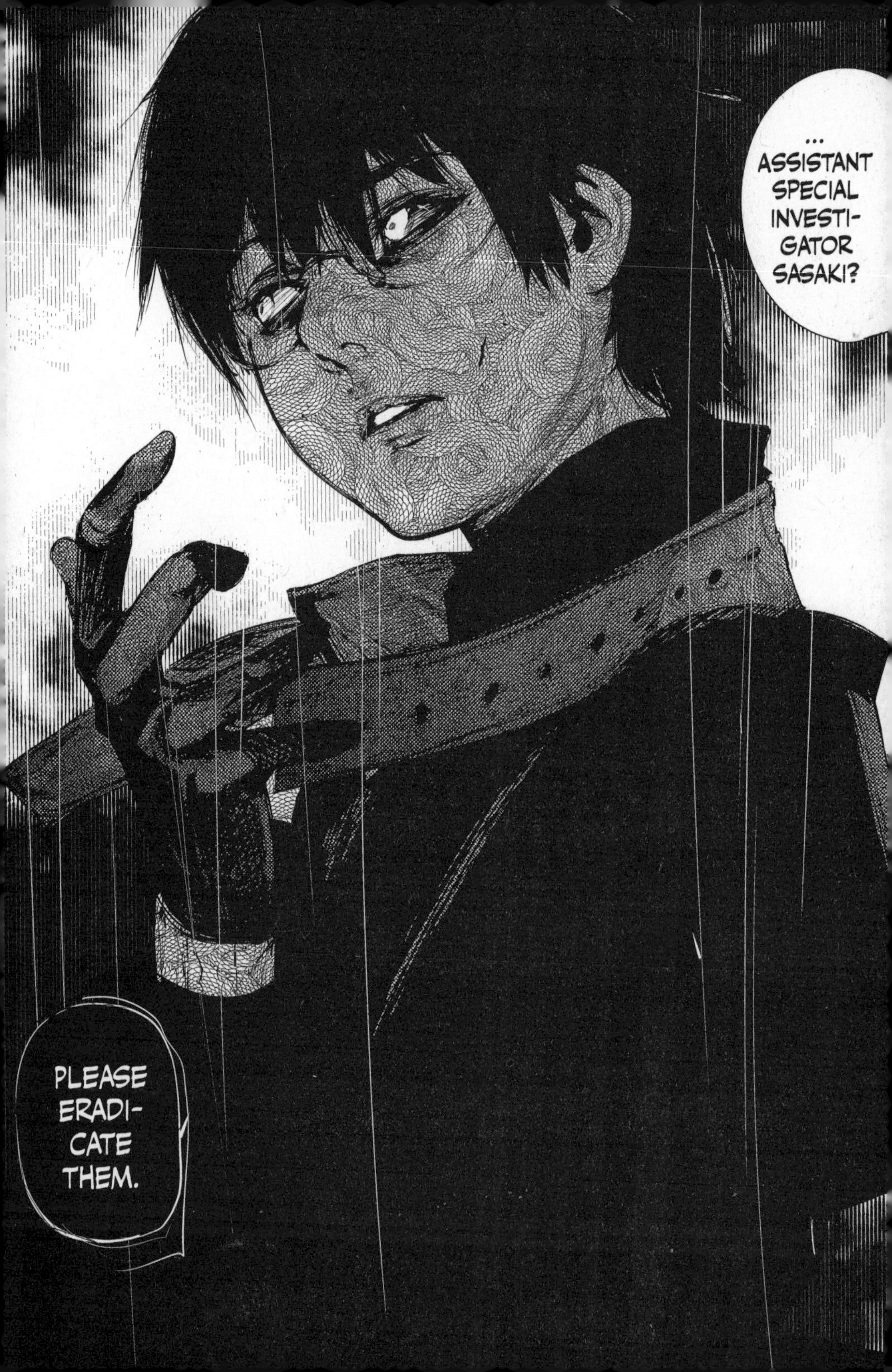
... ASSISTANT SPECIAL INVESTI-GATOR SASAKI?
PLEASE ERADI-CATE THEM.

Rank 1 Investigator Urie assumed the role of Qs Squad Leader in place of Ginshi Shirazu, who was killed in the line of duty.

Senior Investigator Haise Sasaki, in recognition for singlehandedly taking out the One-Eyed Owl, was given an early promotion to assistant special investigator.

At his request, he has resigned as mentor to the Qs.

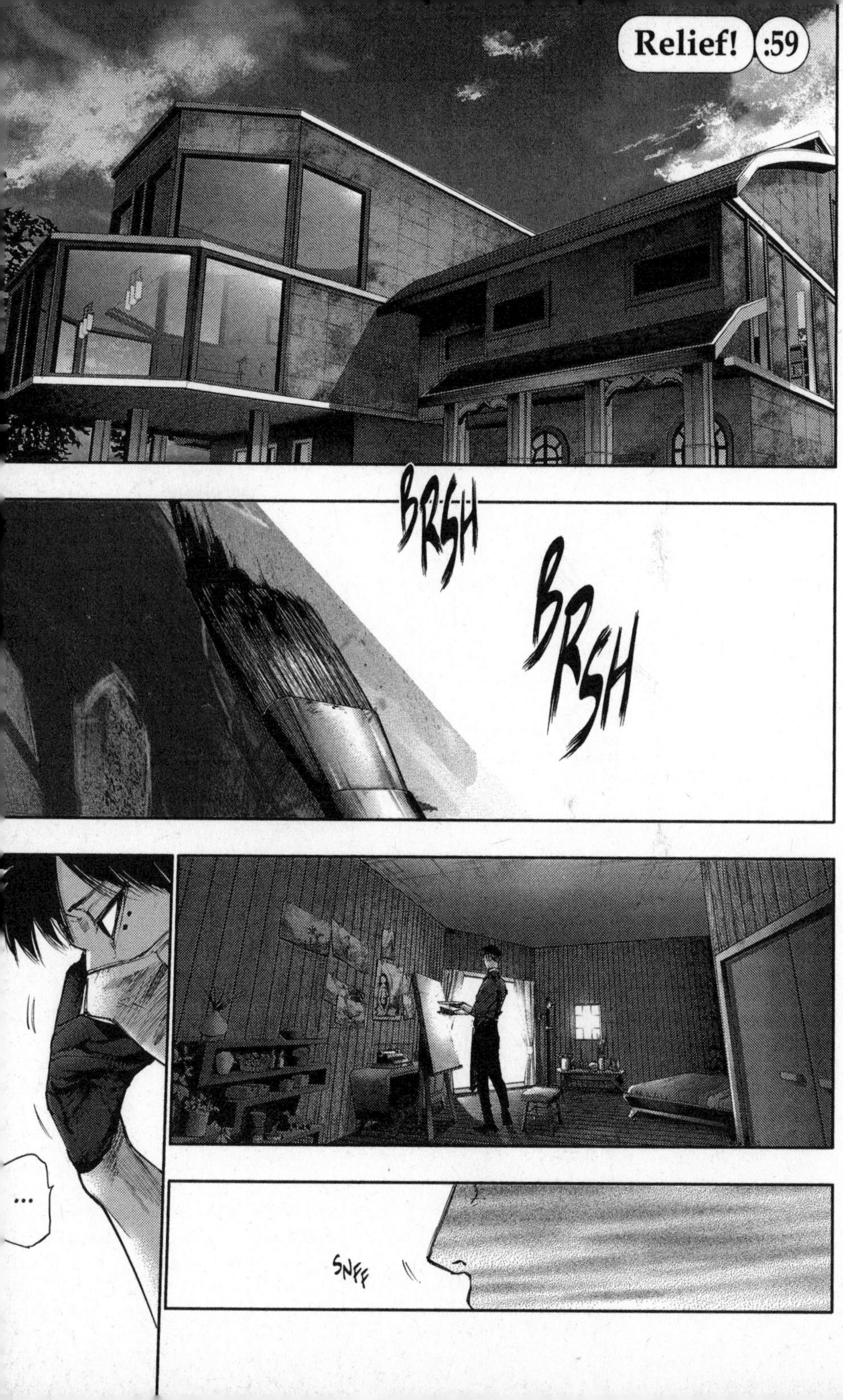
Relief! :59
BRSH
BRSH
SNFF
...

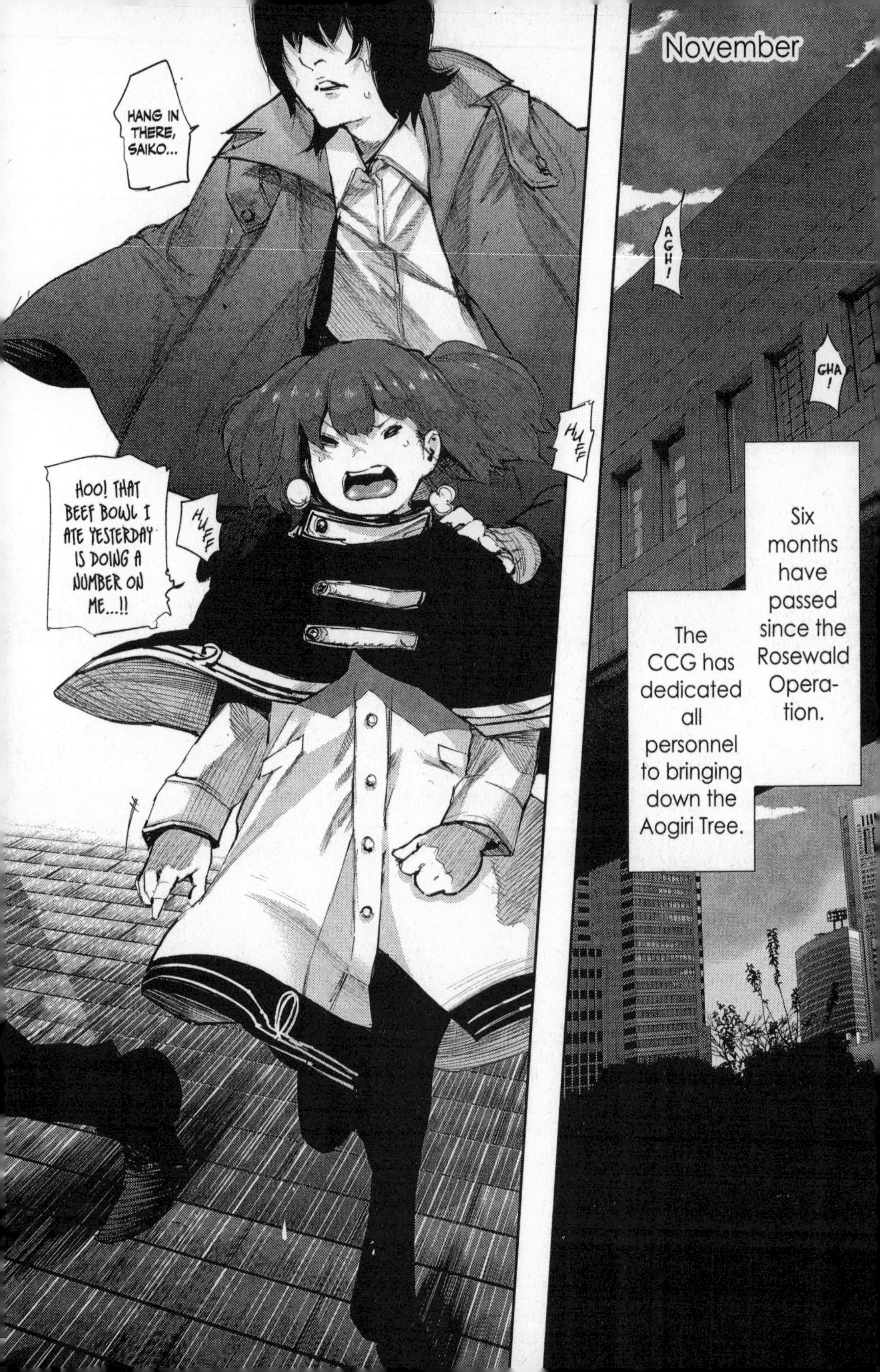
November
AGH!
GHA!
Six months have passed since the Rosewald Operation.
The CCG has dedicated all personnel to bringing down the Aogiri Tree.
HANG IN THERE, SAIKO...
HUFF
HUFF
HOO! THAT BEEF BOWL I ATE YESTERDAY IS DOING A NUMBER ON ME...!!

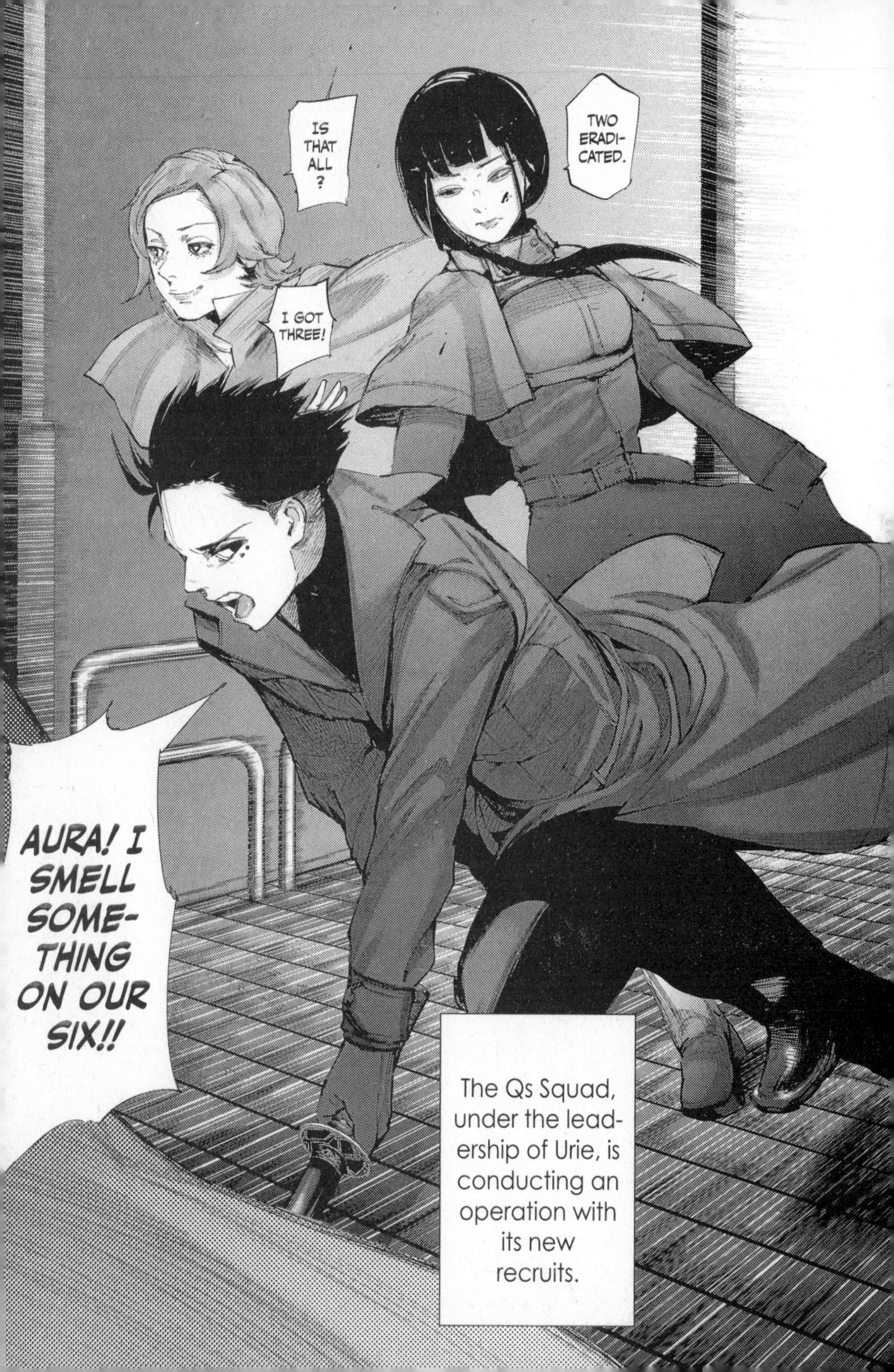
TWO ERADI-CATED.
IS THAT ALL?
I GOT THREE!
AURA! I SMELL SOME-THING ON OUR SIX!!
The Qs Squad, under the lead-ership of Urie, is conducting an operation with its new recruits.

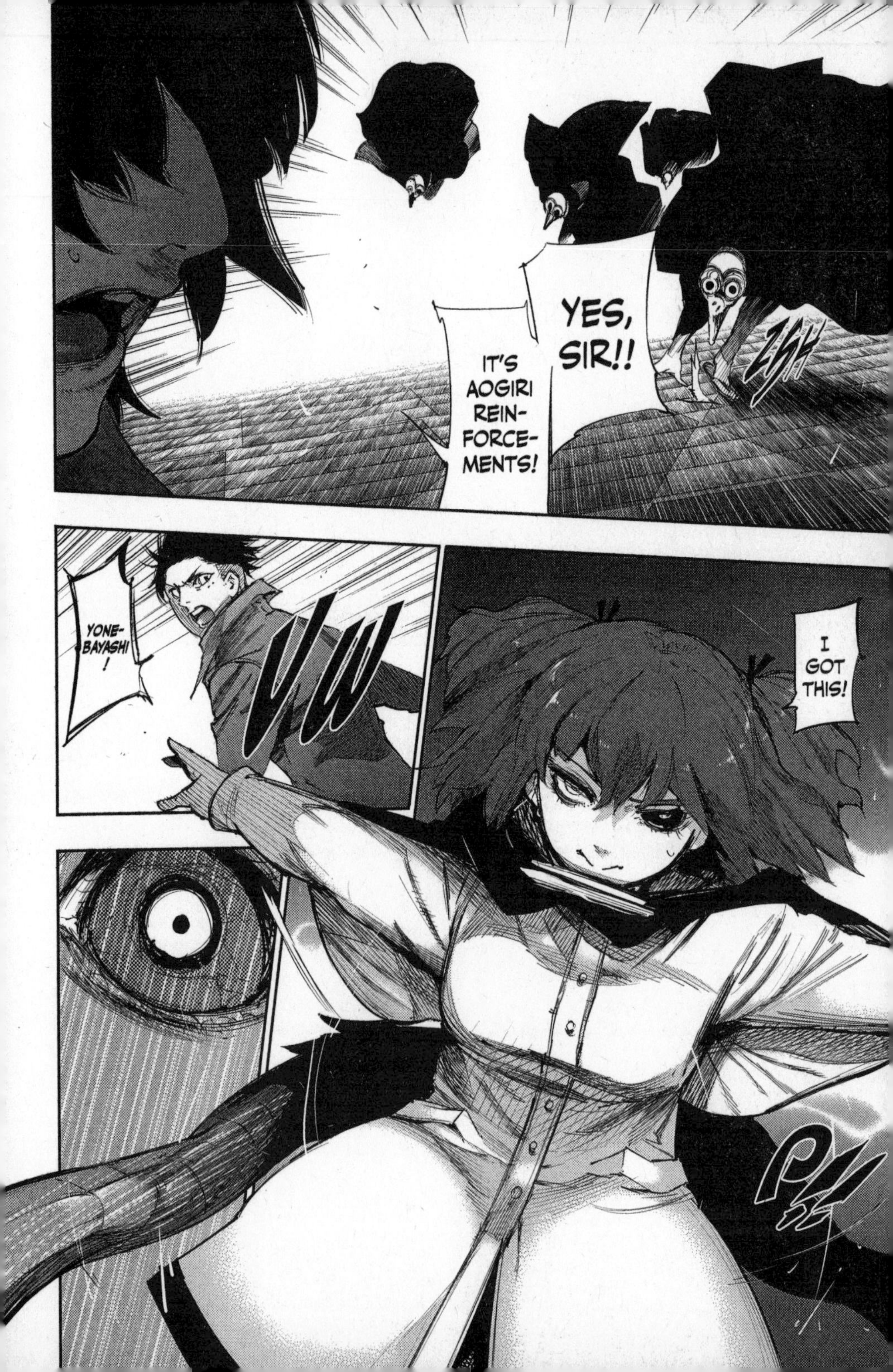
YES, SIR!!
IT'S AOGIRI REIN-FORCE-MENTS!
I GOT THIS!
YONE-BAYASHI!
VW

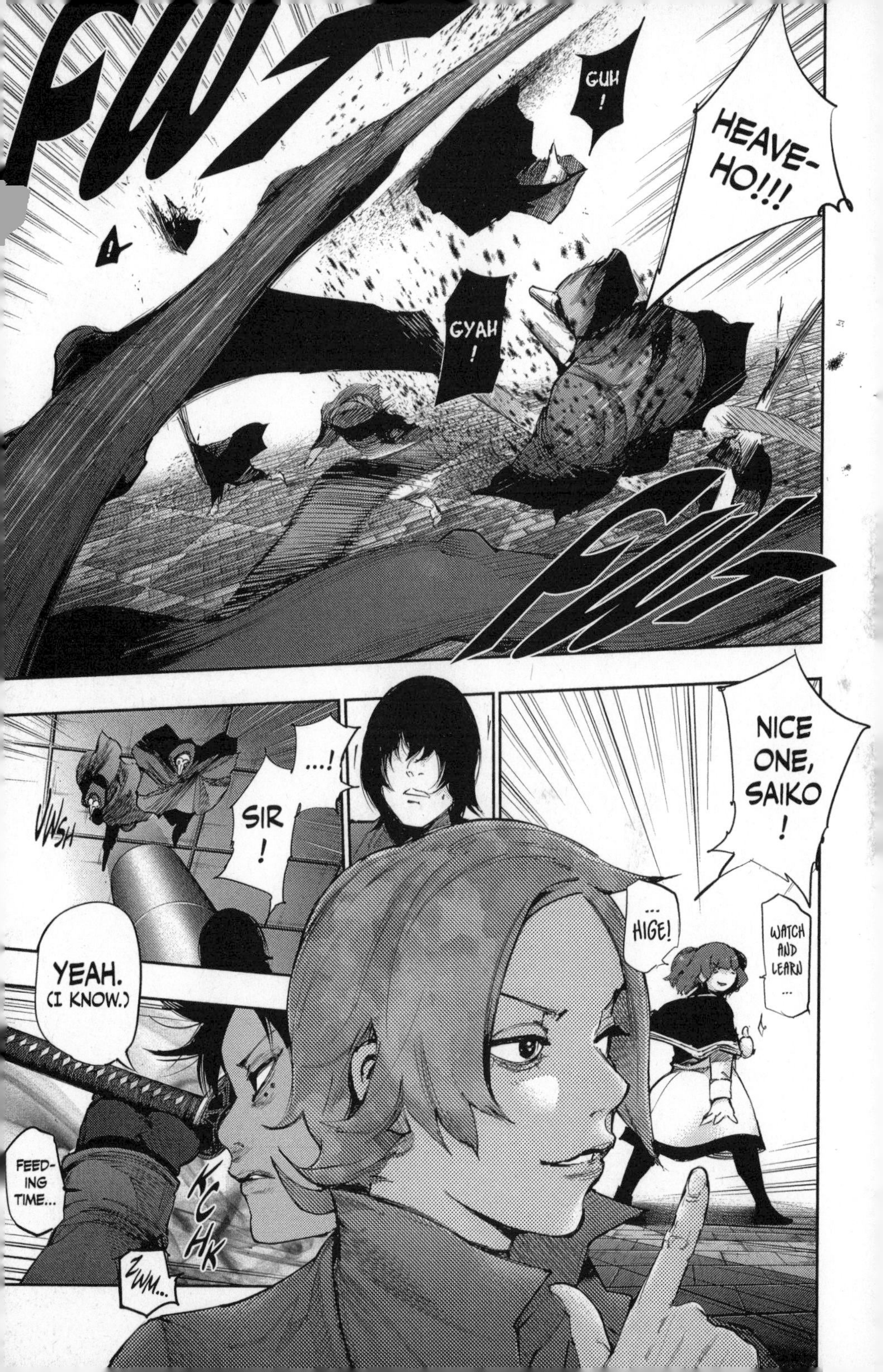
HEAVE-HO!!!
GUH!
FWT
GYAH!
!
FWT
NICE ONE, SAIKO!
...HIGE!
WATCH AND LEARN...
...!
SIR!
VNSH
YEAH. (I KNOW.)
FEEDING TIME...
KCHK
ZWM...

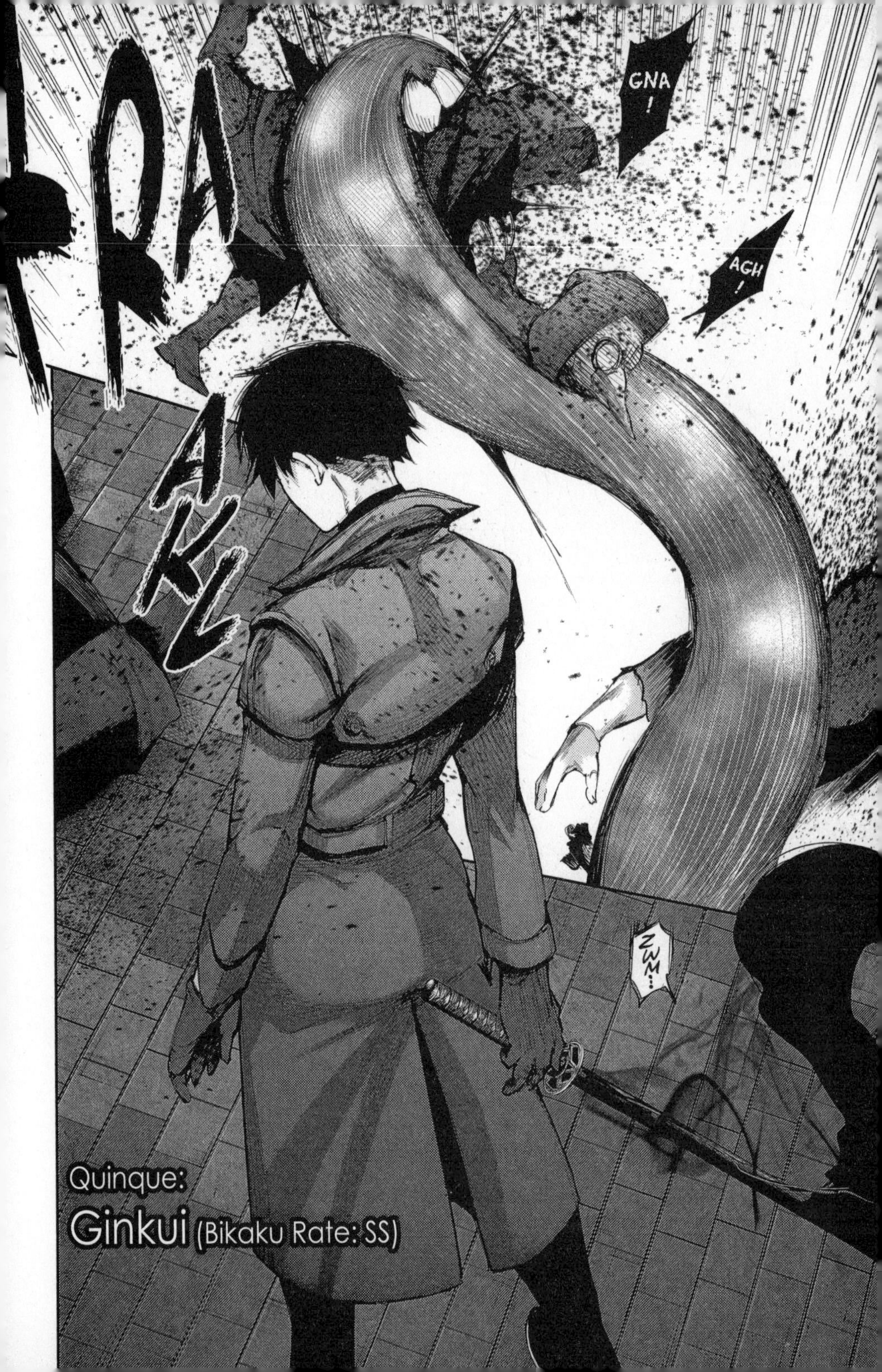
GNA!
AGH!
ZWM...
Quinque:
Ginkui (Bikaku Rate: SS)

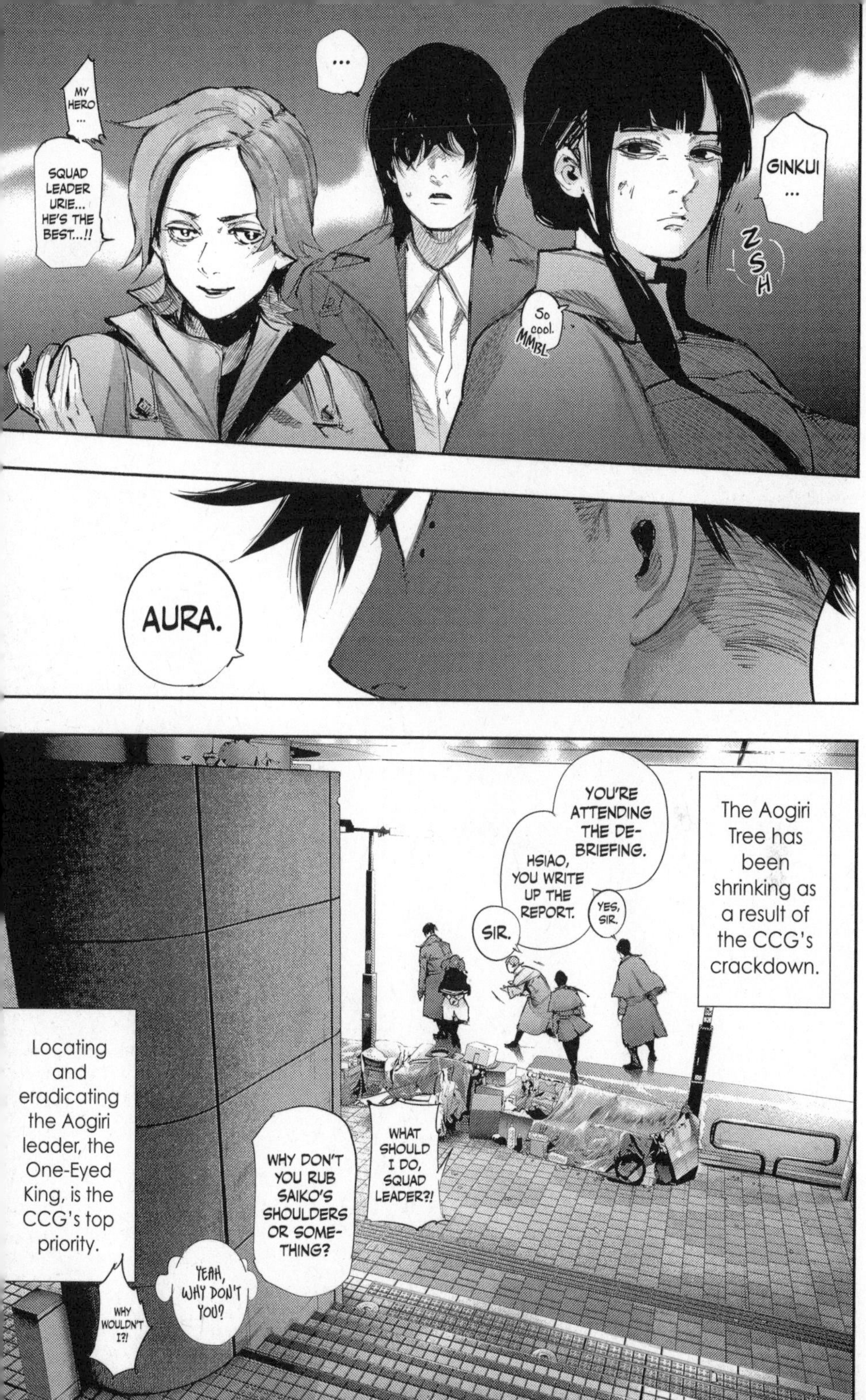
GINKUI ...
ZSH
So cool.
MMBL
...
MY HERO ...
SQUAD LEADER URIE... HE'S THE BEST...!!
AURA.
The Aogiri Tree has been shrinking as a result of the CCG's crackdown.
YOU'RE ATTENDING THE DE-BRIEFING.
HSIAO, YOU WRITE UP THE REPORT.
YES, SIR.
SIR.
WHAT SHOULD I DO, SQUAD LEADER?!
WHY DON'T YOU RUB SAIKO'S SHOULDERS OR SOME-THING?
Locating and eradicating the Aogiri leader, the One-Eyed King, is the CCG's top priority.
YEAH, WHY DON'T YOU?
WHY WOULDN'T I?!

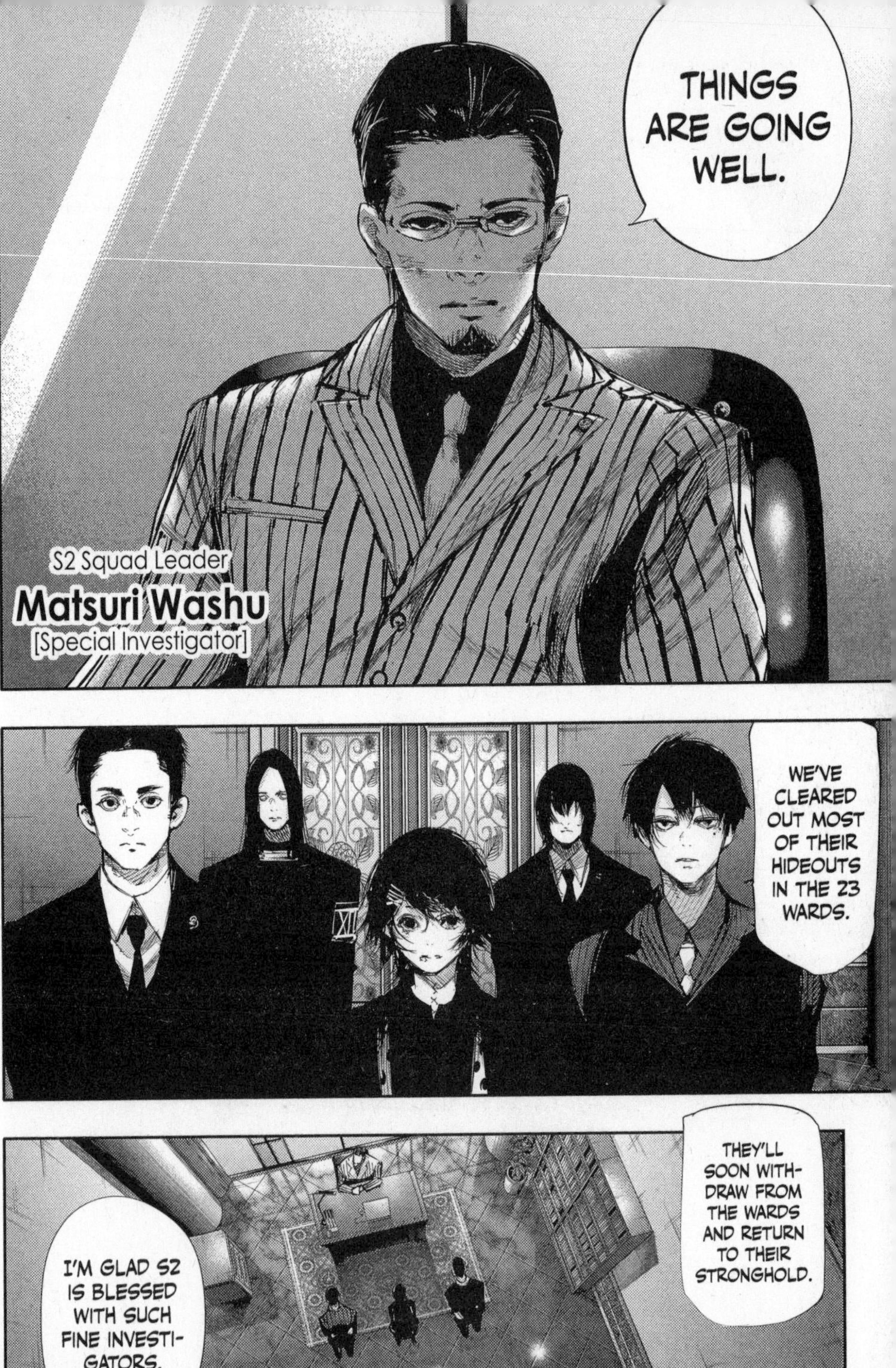
THINGS ARE GOING WELL.
S2 Squad Leader
Matsuri Washu
[Special Investigator]
WE'VE CLEARED OUT MOST OF THEIR HIDEOUTS IN THE 23 WARDS.
THEY'LL SOON WITH-DRAW FROM THE WARDS AND RETURN TO THEIR STRONGHOLD.
I'M GLAD S2 IS BLESSED WITH SUCH FINE INVESTI-GATORS.

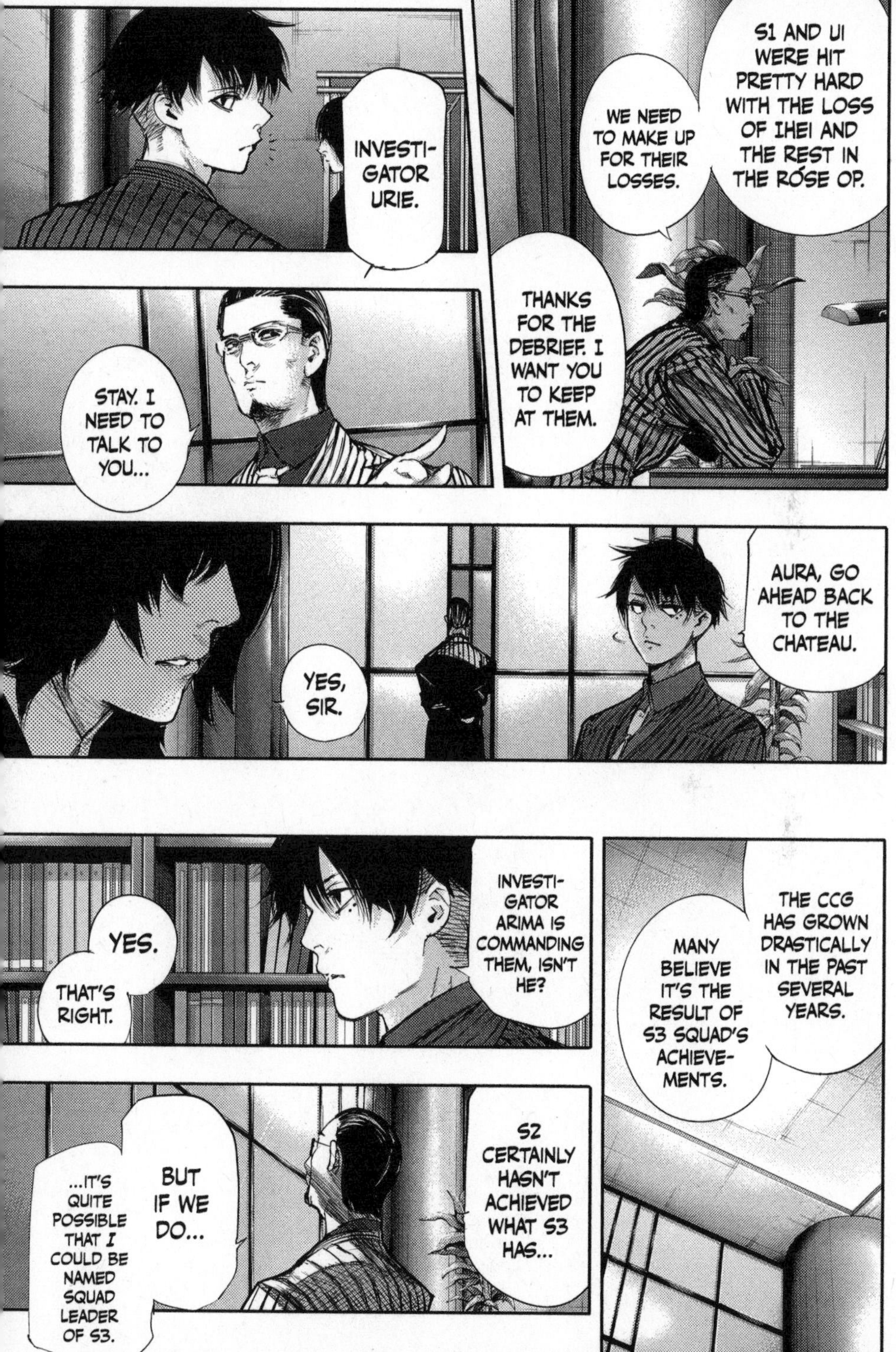
S1 AND UI WERE HIT PRETTY HARD WITH THE LOSS OF IHEI AND THE REST IN THE RÓSE OP.
WE NEED TO MAKE UP FOR THEIR LOSSES.
THANKS FOR THE DEBRIEF. I WANT YOU TO KEEP AT THEM.
INVESTI-GATOR URIE.
STAY. I NEED TO TALK TO YOU...
AURA, GO AHEAD BACK TO THE CHATEAU.
YES, SIR.
THE CCG HAS GROWN DRASTICALLY IN THE PAST SEVERAL YEARS.
MANY BELIEVE IT'S THE RESULT OF S3 SQUAD'S ACHIEVE-MENTS.
INVESTI-GATOR ARIMA IS COMMANDING THEM, ISN'T HE?
YES.
THAT'S RIGHT.
S2 CERTAINLY HASN'T ACHIEVED WHAT S3 HAS...
BUT IF WE DO...
...IT'S QUITE POSSIBLE THAT *I* COULD BE NAMED SQUAD LEADER OF S3.

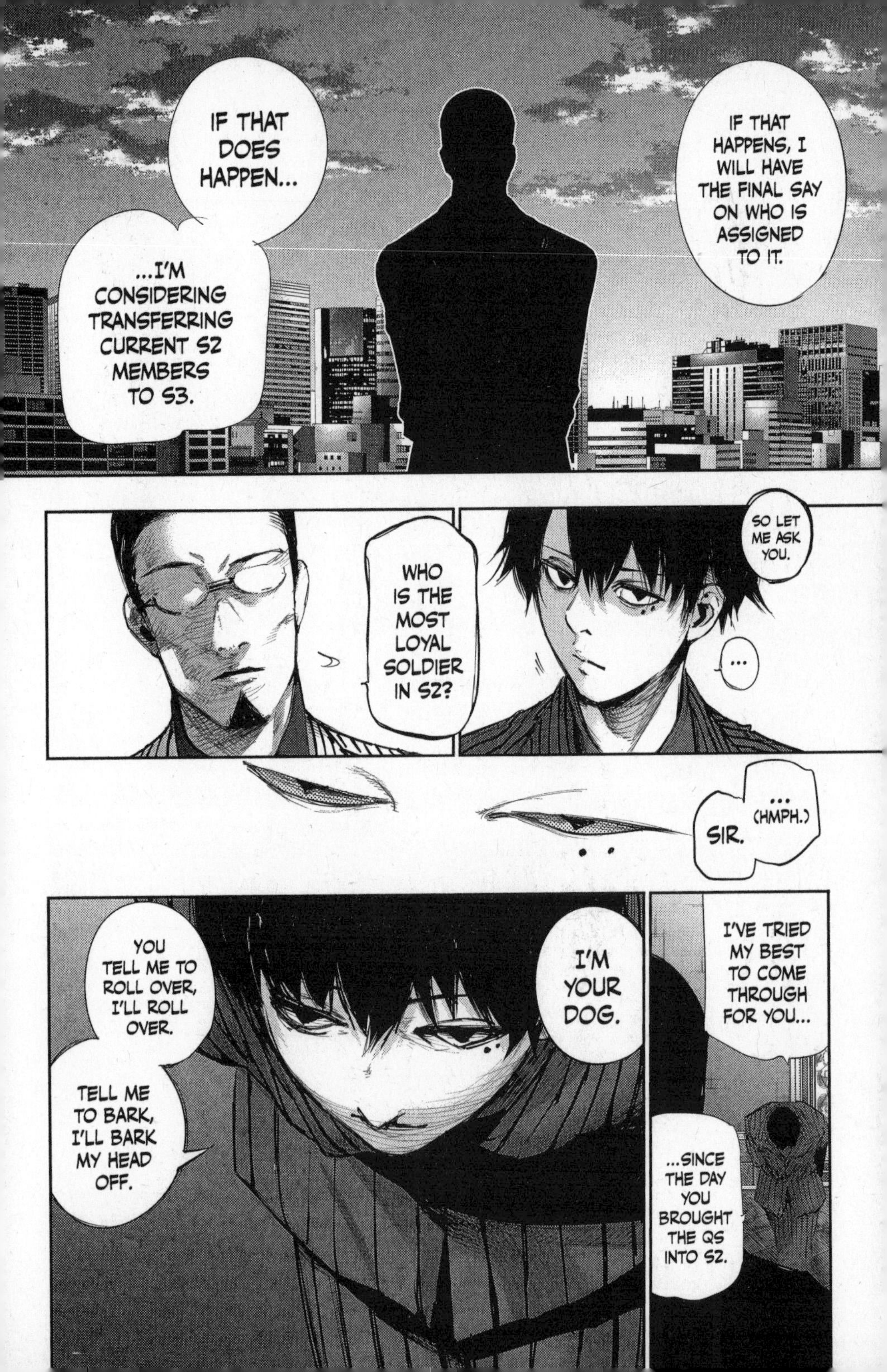
IF THAT HAPPENS, I WILL HAVE THE FINAL SAY ON WHO IS ASSIGNED TO IT.
IF THAT DOES HAPPEN...
...I'M CONSIDERING TRANSFERRING CURRENT S2 MEMBERS TO S3.
SO LET ME ASK YOU.
...
WHO IS THE MOST LOYAL SOLDIER IN S2?
... (HMPH.)
SIR.
I'VE TRIED MY BEST TO COME THROUGH FOR YOU...
...SINCE THE DAY YOU BROUGHT THE QS INTO S2.
I'M YOUR DOG.
YOU TELL ME TO ROLL OVER, I'LL ROLL OVER.
TELL ME TO BARK, I'LL BARK MY HEAD OFF.

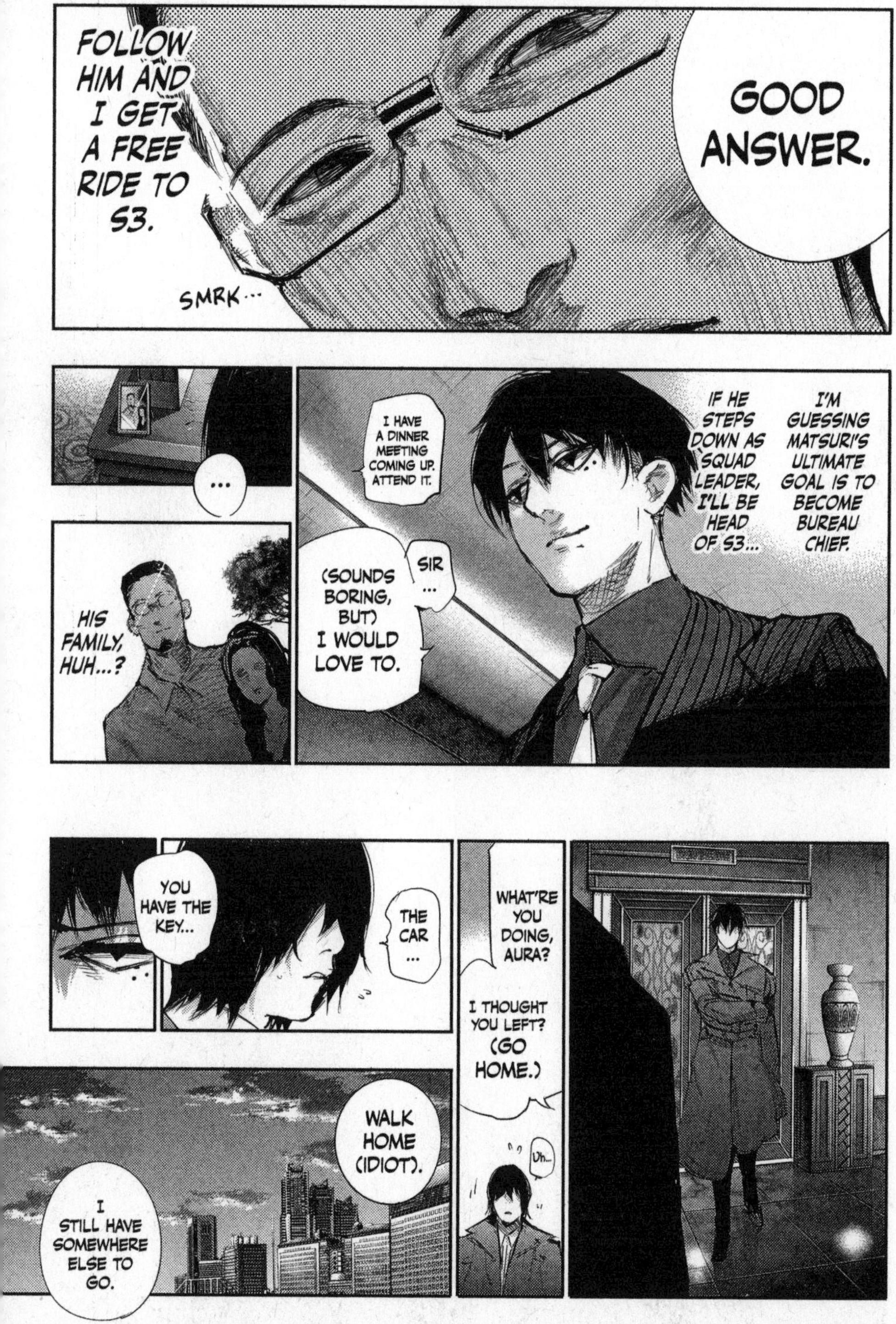
GOOD ANSWER.
FOLLOW HIM AND I GET A FREE RIDE TO S3.
SMRK...
I'M GUESSING MATSURI'S ULTIMATE GOAL IS TO BECOME BUREAU CHIEF.
IF HE STEPS DOWN AS SQUAD LEADER, I'LL BE HEAD OF S3...
I HAVE A DINNER MEETING COMING UP. ATTEND IT.
SIR...
(SOUNDS BORING, BUT) I WOULD LOVE TO.
...
HIS FAMILY, HUH...?
WHAT'RE YOU DOING, AURA?
I THOUGHT YOU LEFT? (GO HOME.)
Uh...
THE CAR...
YOU HAVE THE KEY...
WALK HOME (IDIOT).
I STILL HAVE SOMEWHERE ELSE TO GO.

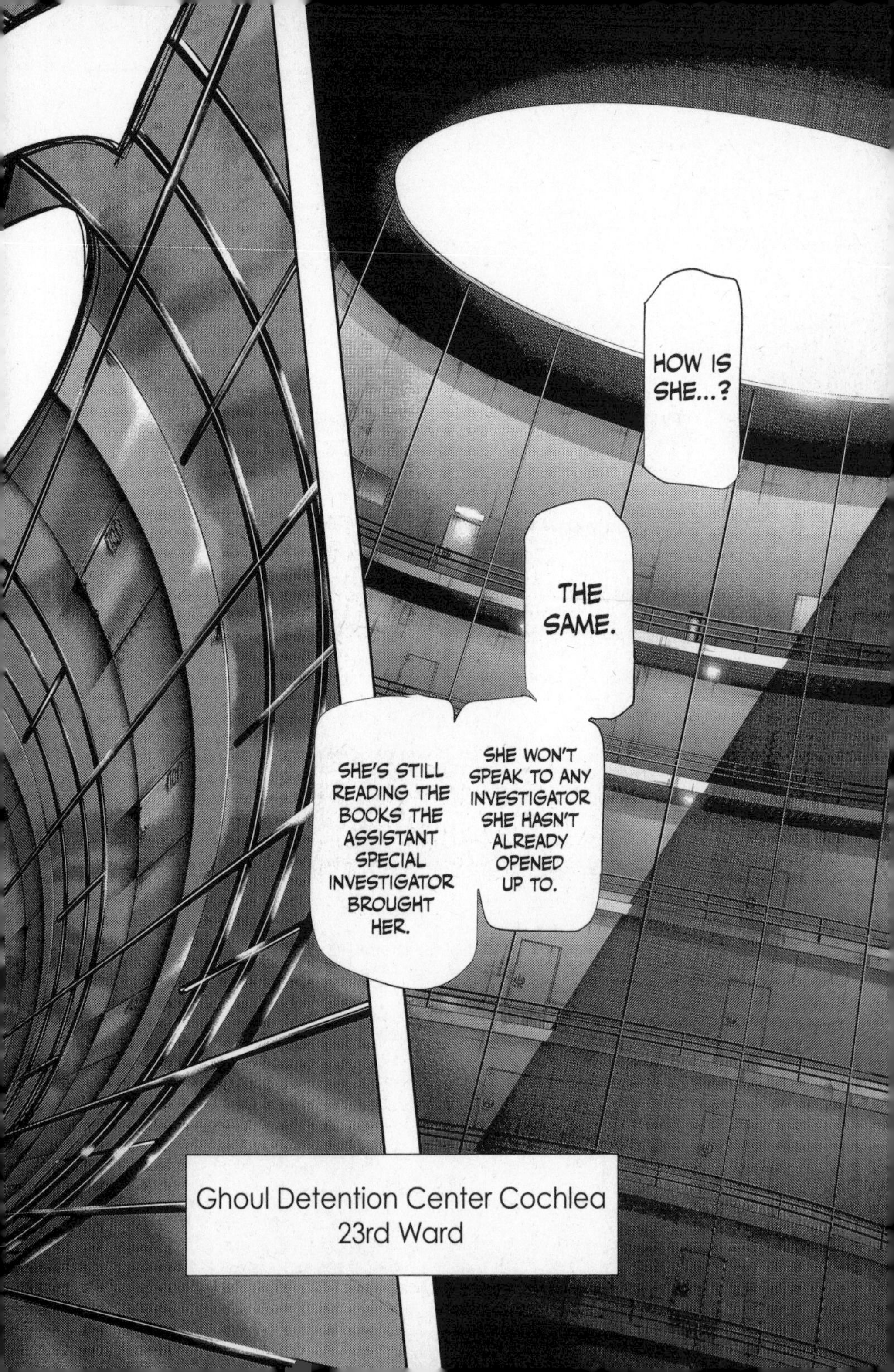
HOW IS SHE...?
THE SAME.
SHE WON'T SPEAK TO ANY INVESTIGATOR SHE HASN'T ALREADY OPENED UP TO.
SHE'S STILL READING THE BOOKS THE ASSISTANT SPECIAL INVESTIGATOR BROUGHT HER.
Ghoul Detention Center Cochlea
23rd Ward

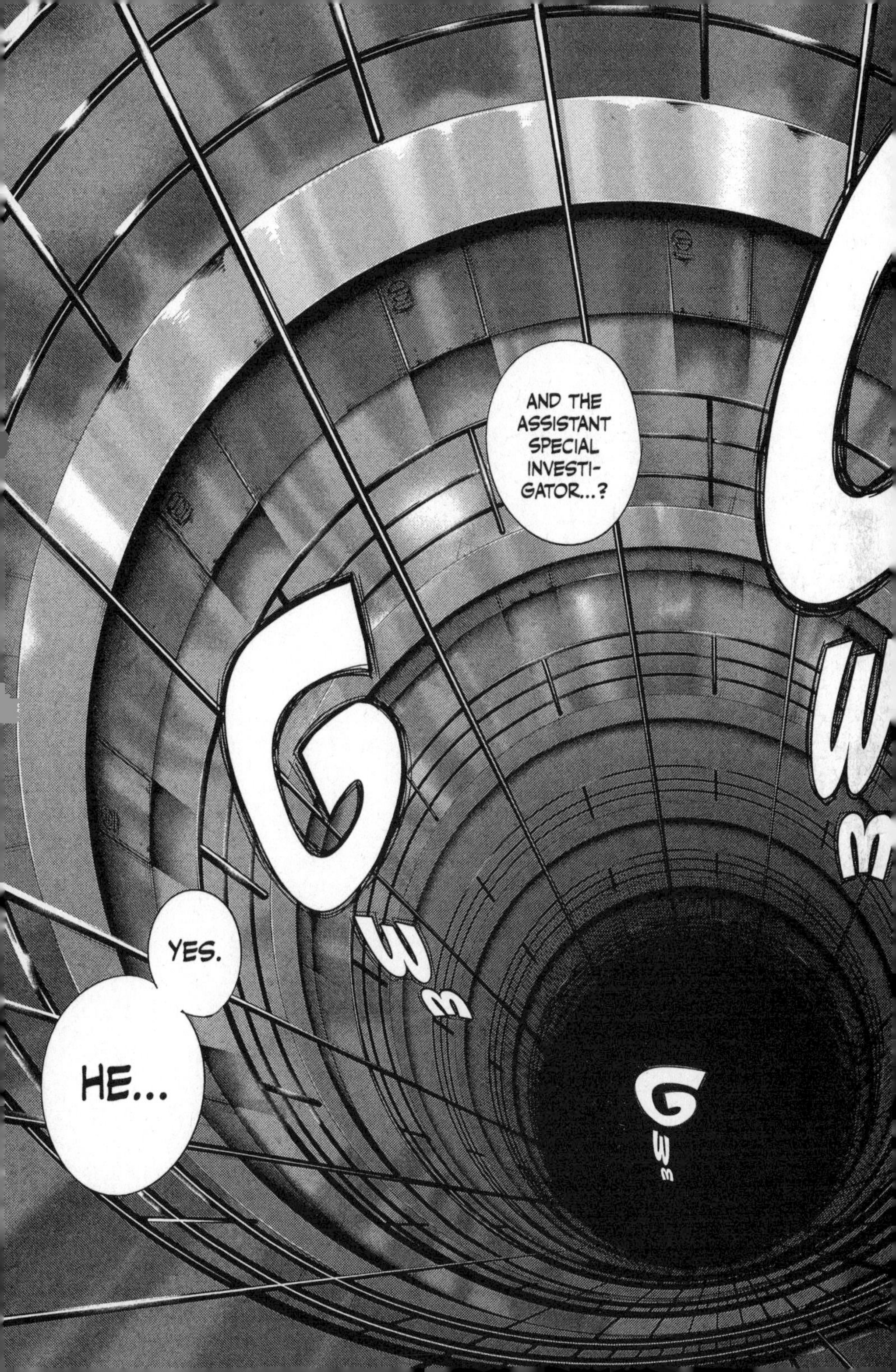
GWW
AND THE ASSISTANT SPECIAL INVESTIGATOR...?
GWW
YES.
HE...
GWW

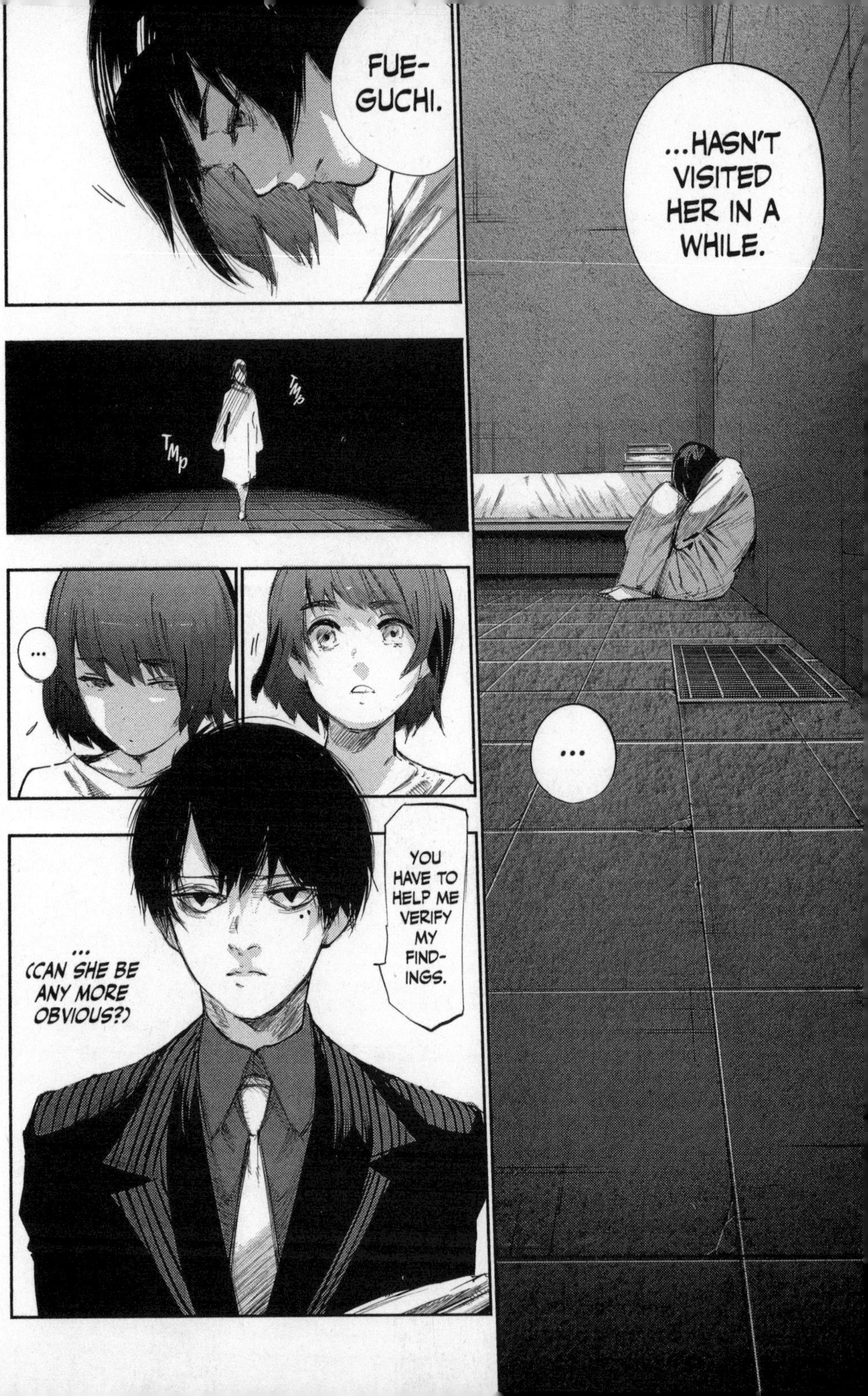
...HASN'T VISITED HER IN A WHILE.
...
FUE-GUCHI.
TMp
TMp
...
YOU HAVE TO HELP ME VERIFY MY FIND-INGS.
... (CAN SHE BE ANY MORE OBVIOUS?)

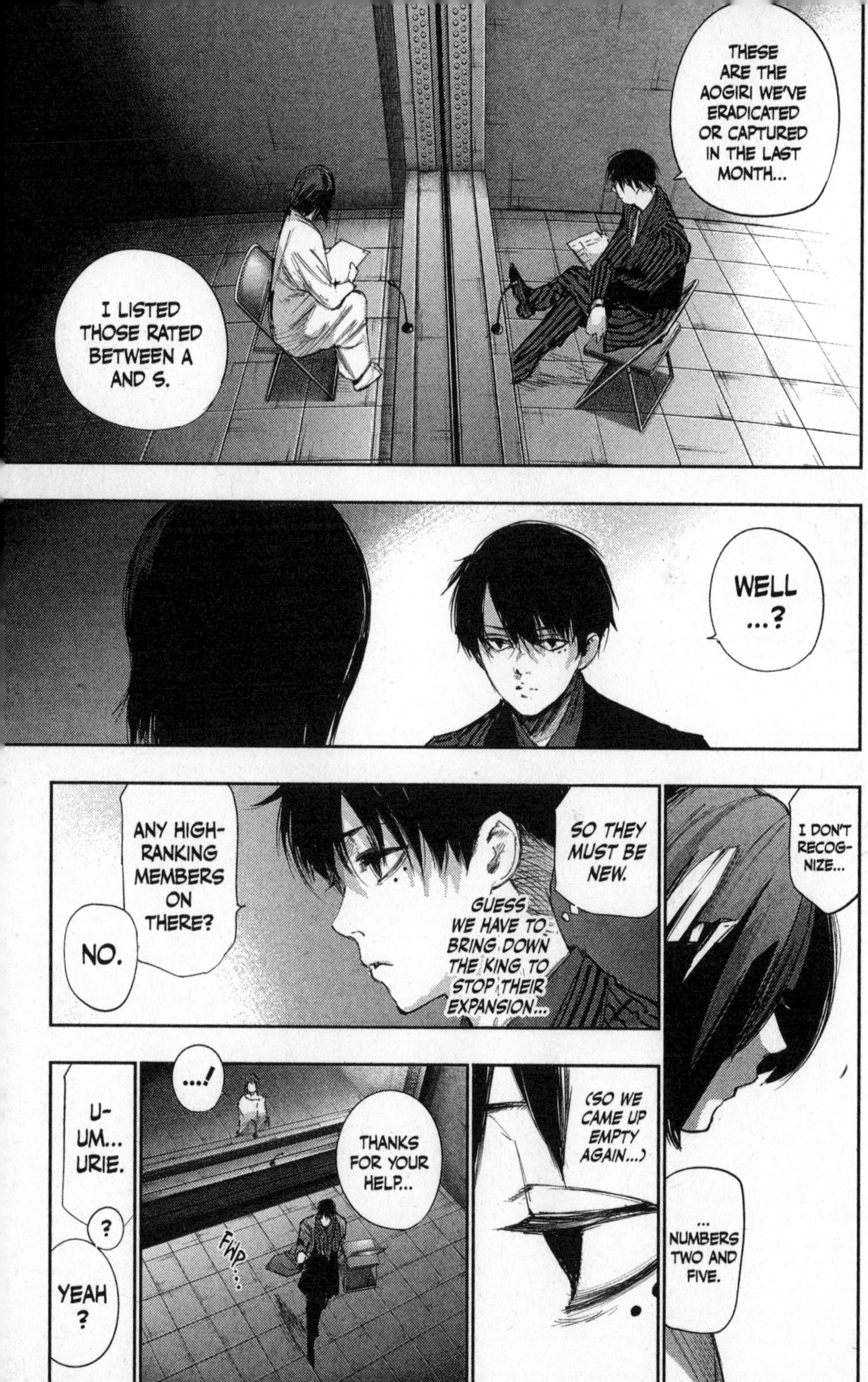
THESE ARE THE AOGIRI WE'VE ERADICATED OR CAPTURED IN THE LAST MONTH...
I LISTED THOSE RATED BETWEEN A AND S.
WELL ...?
I DON'T RECOG-NIZE...
... NUMBERS TWO AND FIVE.
SO THEY MUST BE NEW.
GUESS WE HAVE TO BRING DOWN THE KING TO STOP THEIR EXPANSION...
ANY HIGH-RANKING MEMBERS ON THERE?
NO.
(SO WE CAME UP EMPTY AGAIN...)
THANKS FOR YOUR HELP...
...!
FWP...
U-UM... URIE.
?
YEAH ?

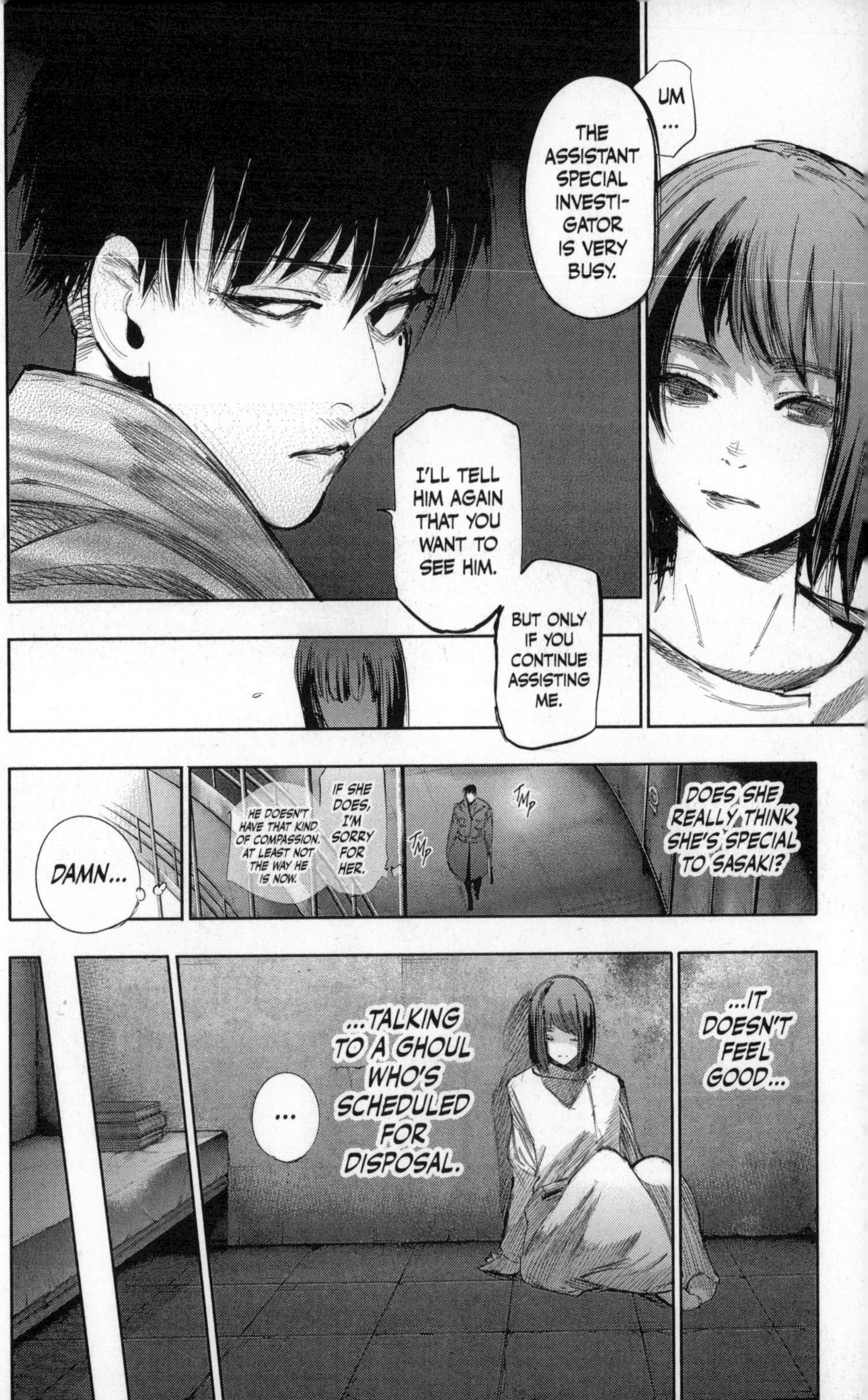
UM ...
THE ASSISTANT SPECIAL INVESTI-GATOR IS VERY BUSY.
I'LL TELL HIM AGAIN THAT YOU WANT TO SEE HIM.
BUT ONLY IF YOU CONTINUE ASSISTING ME.
DOES SHE REALLY THINK SHE'S SPECIAL TO SASAKI?
TMP
TMP
IF SHE DOES, I'M SORRY FOR HER.
HE DOESN'T HAVE THAT KIND OF COMPASSION. AT LEAST NOT THE WAY HE IS NOW.
DAMN...
...IT DOESN'T FEEL GOOD...
...TALKING TO A GHOUL WHO'S SCHEDULED FOR DISPOSAL.
...

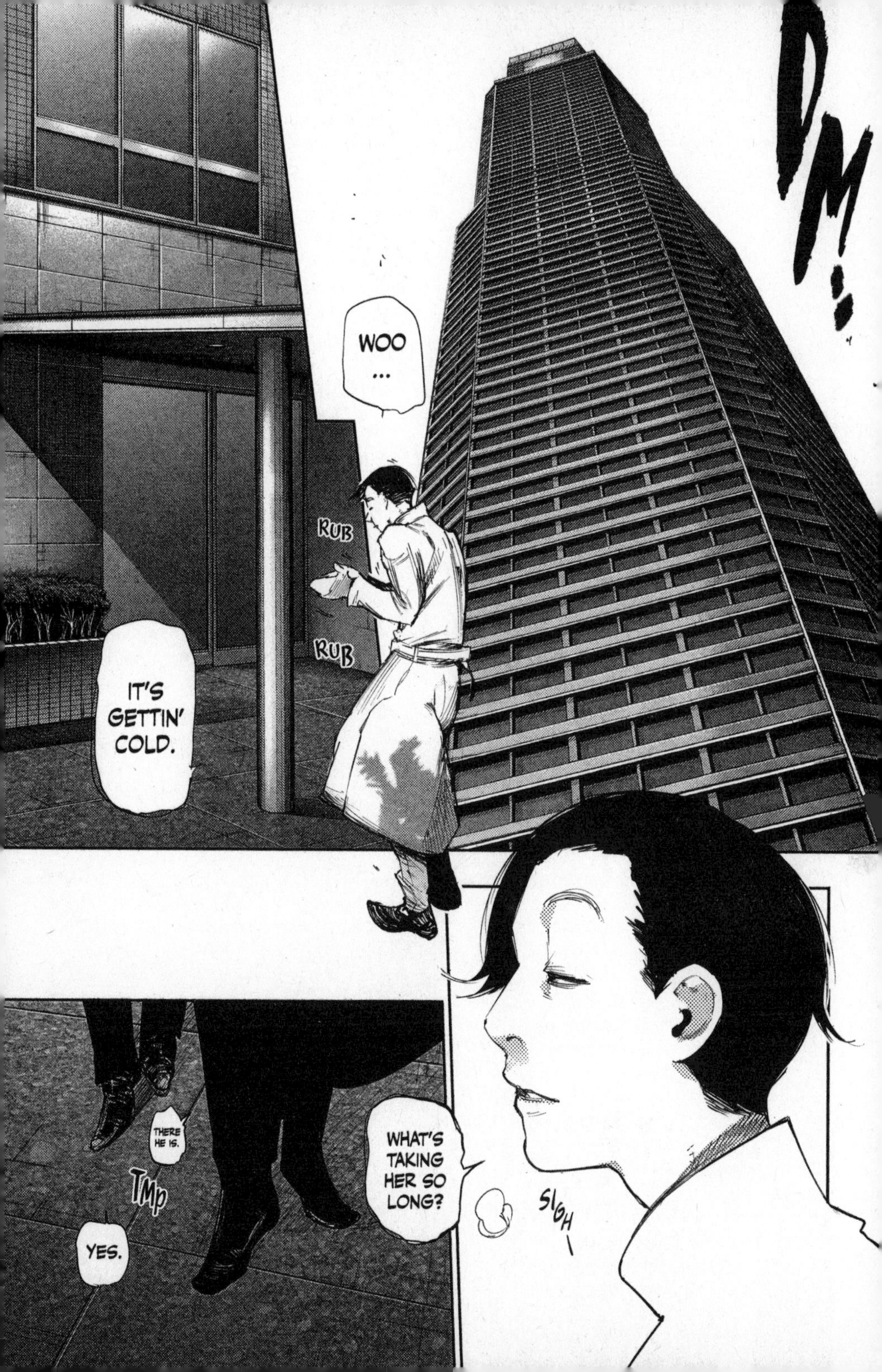
DM!!
WOO ...
RUB
RUB
IT'S GETTIN' COLD.
WHAT'S TAKING HER SO LONG?
SIGH
THERE HE IS.
TMP
YES.

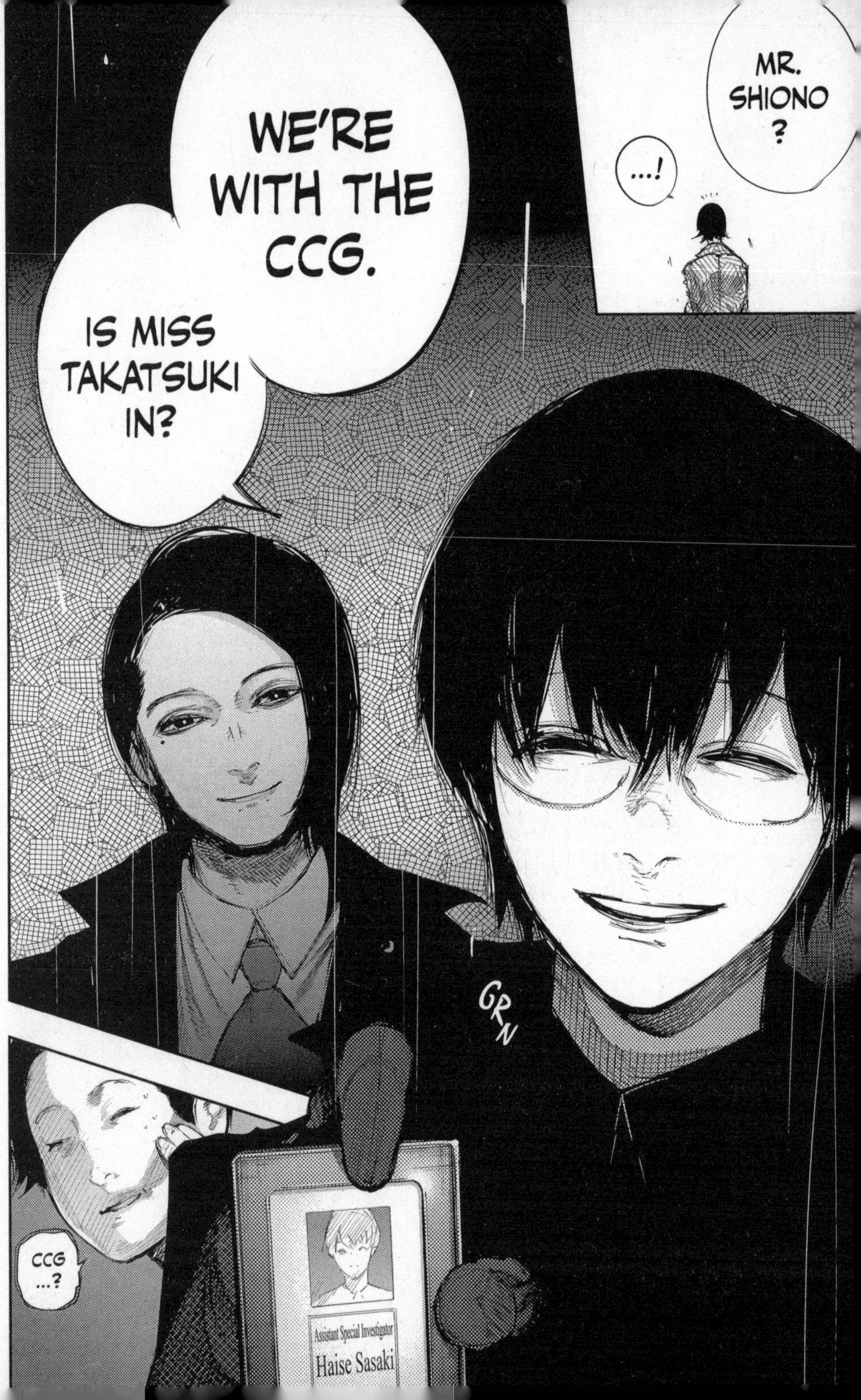
MR. SHIONO?
...!
WE'RE WITH THE CCG.
IS MISS TAKATSUKI IN?
GRN
Assistant Special Investigator
Haise Sasaki
CCG ...?

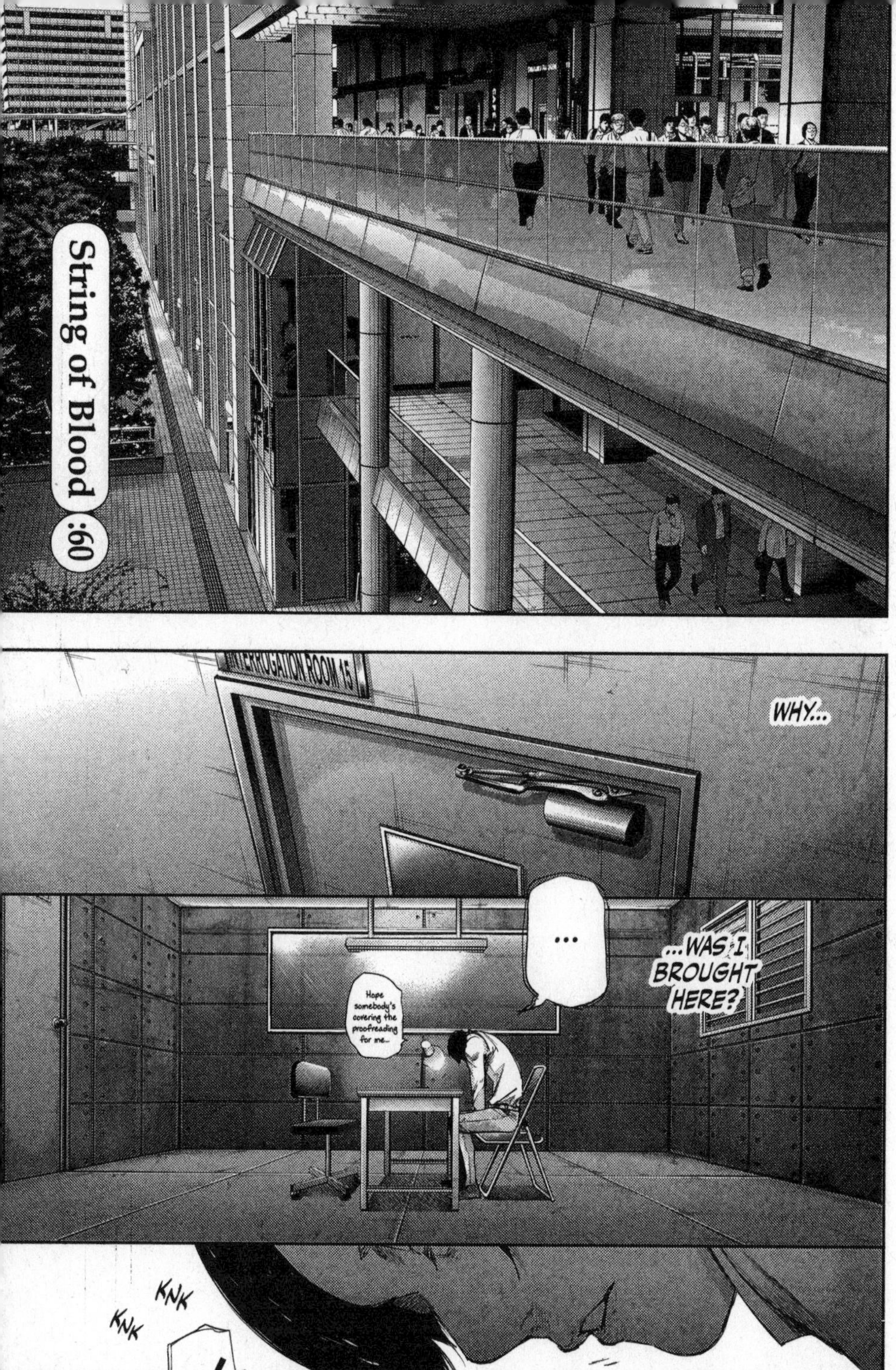
String of Blood :60
NTERROGATION ROOM 15
WHY...
...
...WAS I BROUGHT HERE?
Hope somebody's covering the proofreading for me...
KNK
KNK
...!

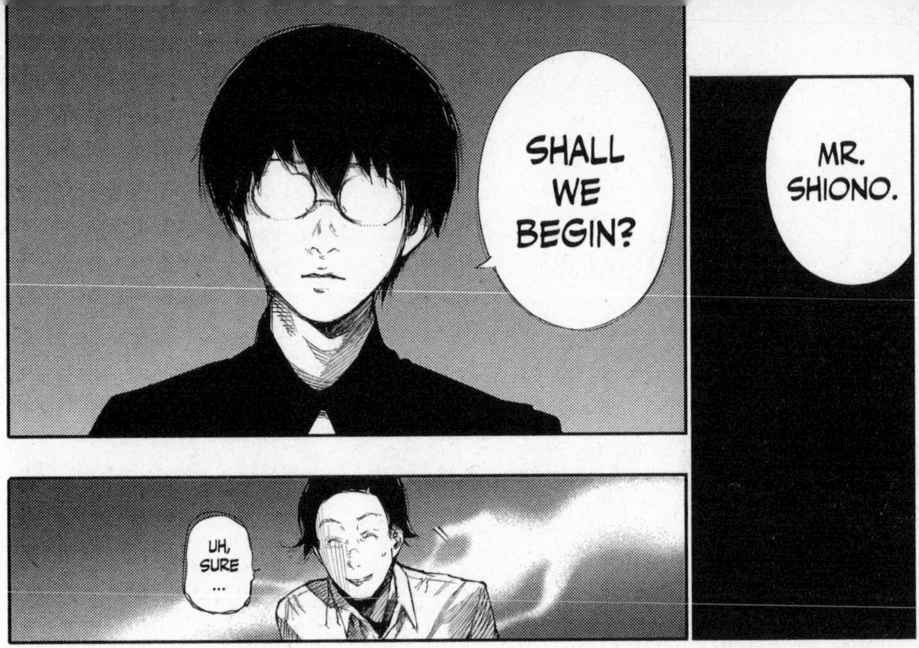
MR. SHIONO.
SHALL WE BEGIN?
UH, SURE ...

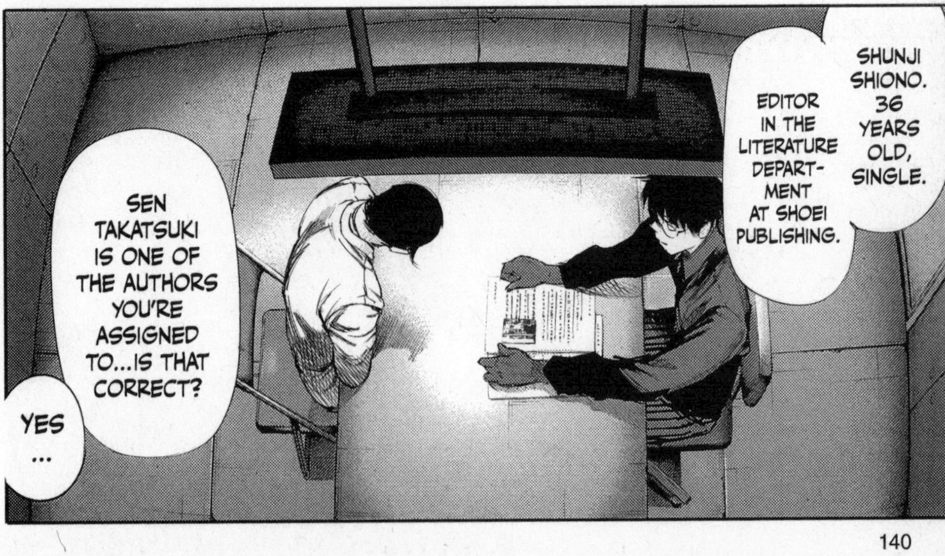
SHUNJI SHIONO. 36 YEARS OLD, SINGLE.
EDITOR IN THE LITERATURE DEPART-MENT AT SHOEI PUBLISHING.
SEN TAKATSUKI IS ONE OF THE AUTHORS YOU'RE ASSIGNED TO...IS THAT CORRECT?
YES ...

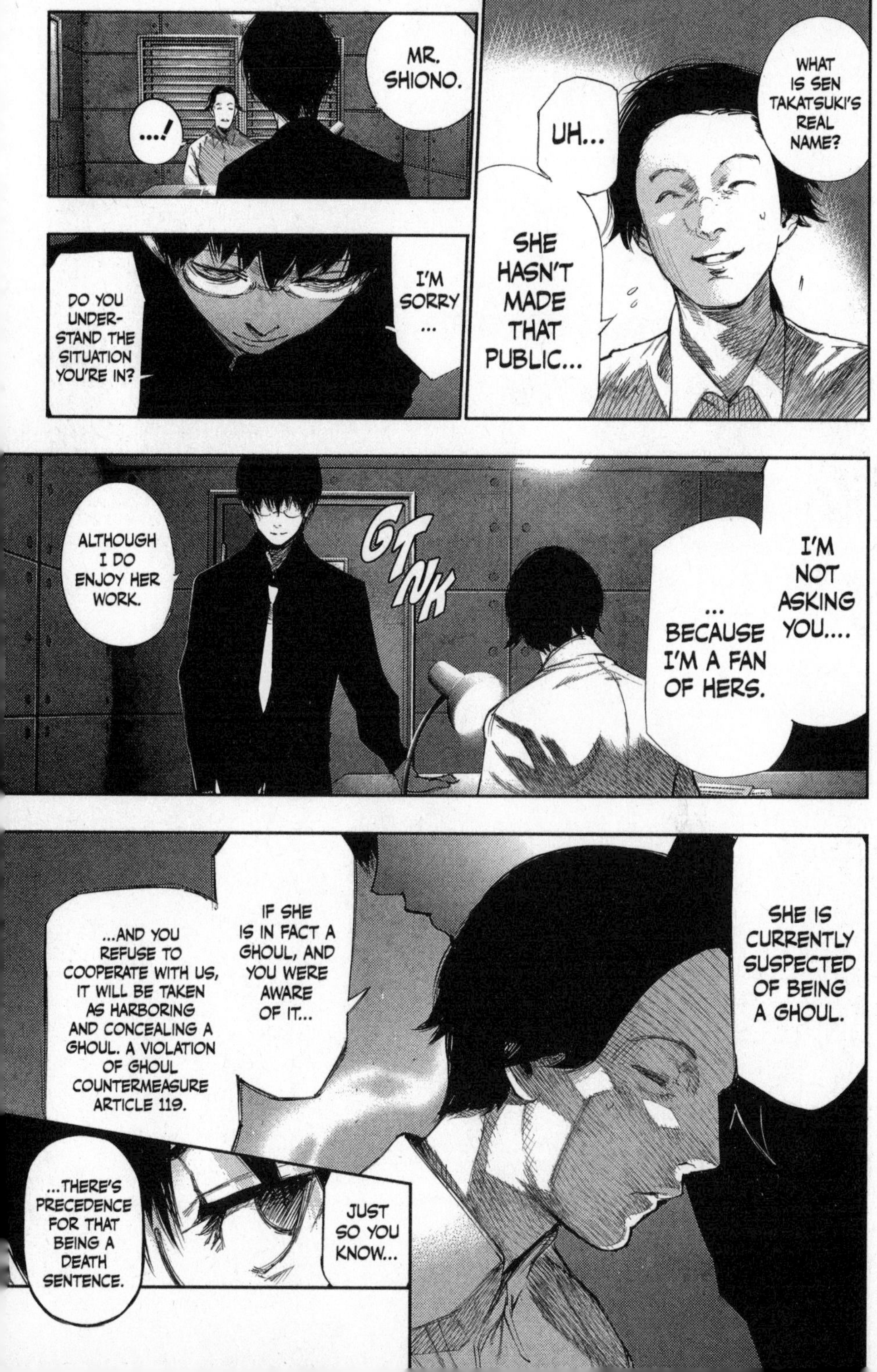
WHAT IS SEN TAKATSUKI'S REAL NAME?
UH...
SHE HASN'T MADE THAT PUBLIC...
MR. SHIONO.
...!
I'M SORRY ...
DO YOU UNDER-STAND THE SITUATION YOU'RE IN?
I'M NOT ASKING YOU....
... BECAUSE I'M A FAN OF HERS.
ALTHOUGH I DO ENJOY HER WORK.
GTNK
SHE IS CURRENTLY SUSPECTED OF BEING A GHOUL.
IF SHE IS IN FACT A GHOUL, AND YOU WERE AWARE OF IT...
...AND YOU REFUSE TO COOPERATE WITH US, IT WILL BE TAKEN AS HARBORING AND CONCEALING A GHOUL. A VIOLATION OF GHOUL COUNTERMEASURE ARTICLE 119.
JUST SO YOU KNOW...
...THERE'S PRECEDENCE FOR THAT BEING A DEATH SENTENCE.

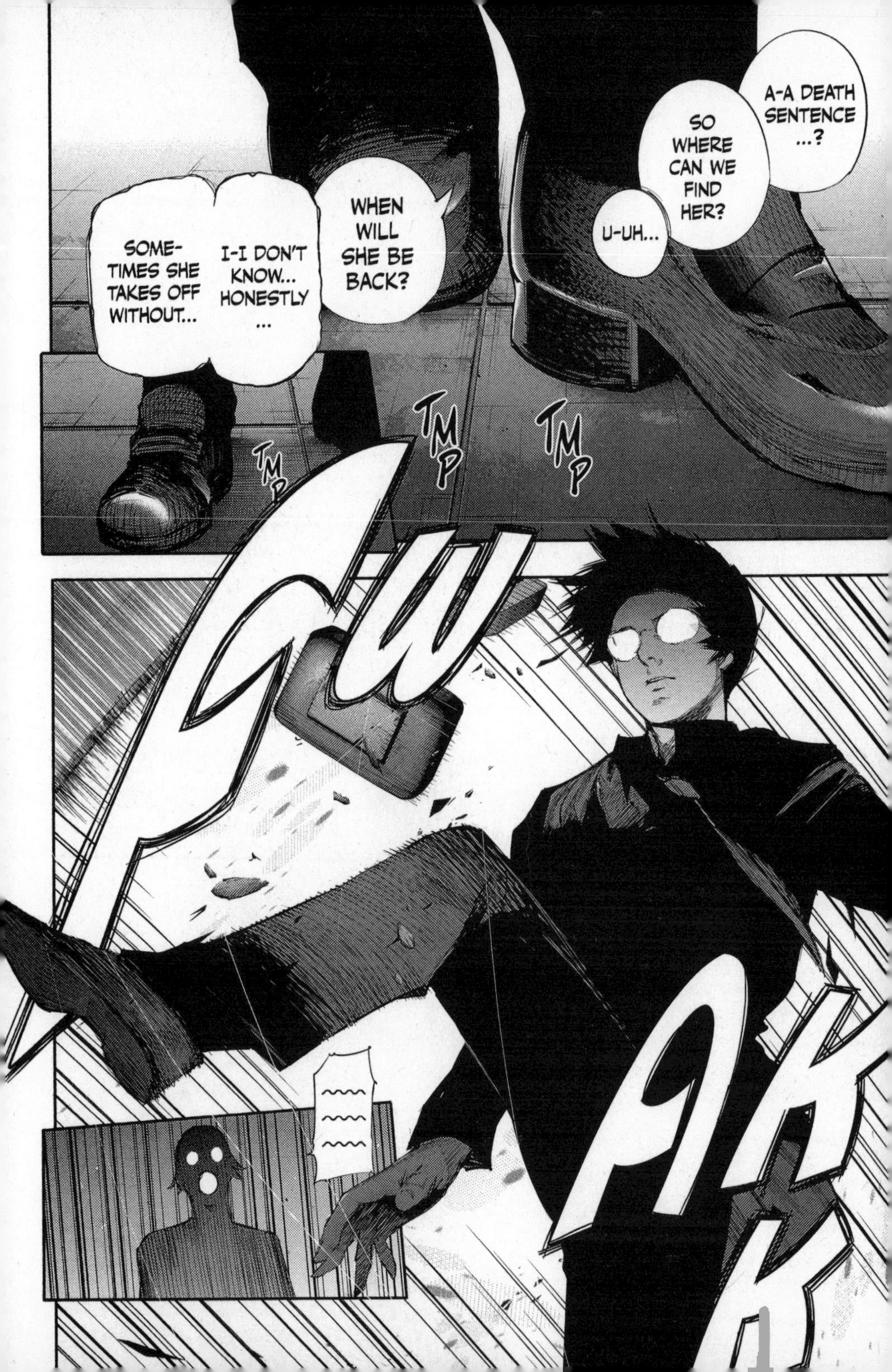
A-A DEATH SENTENCE ...?
SO WHERE CAN WE FIND HER?
U-UH...
WHEN WILL SHE BE BACK?
I-I DON'T KNOW... HONESTLY ...
SOME-TIMES SHE TAKES OFF WITHOUT...
TMP
TMP
TMP

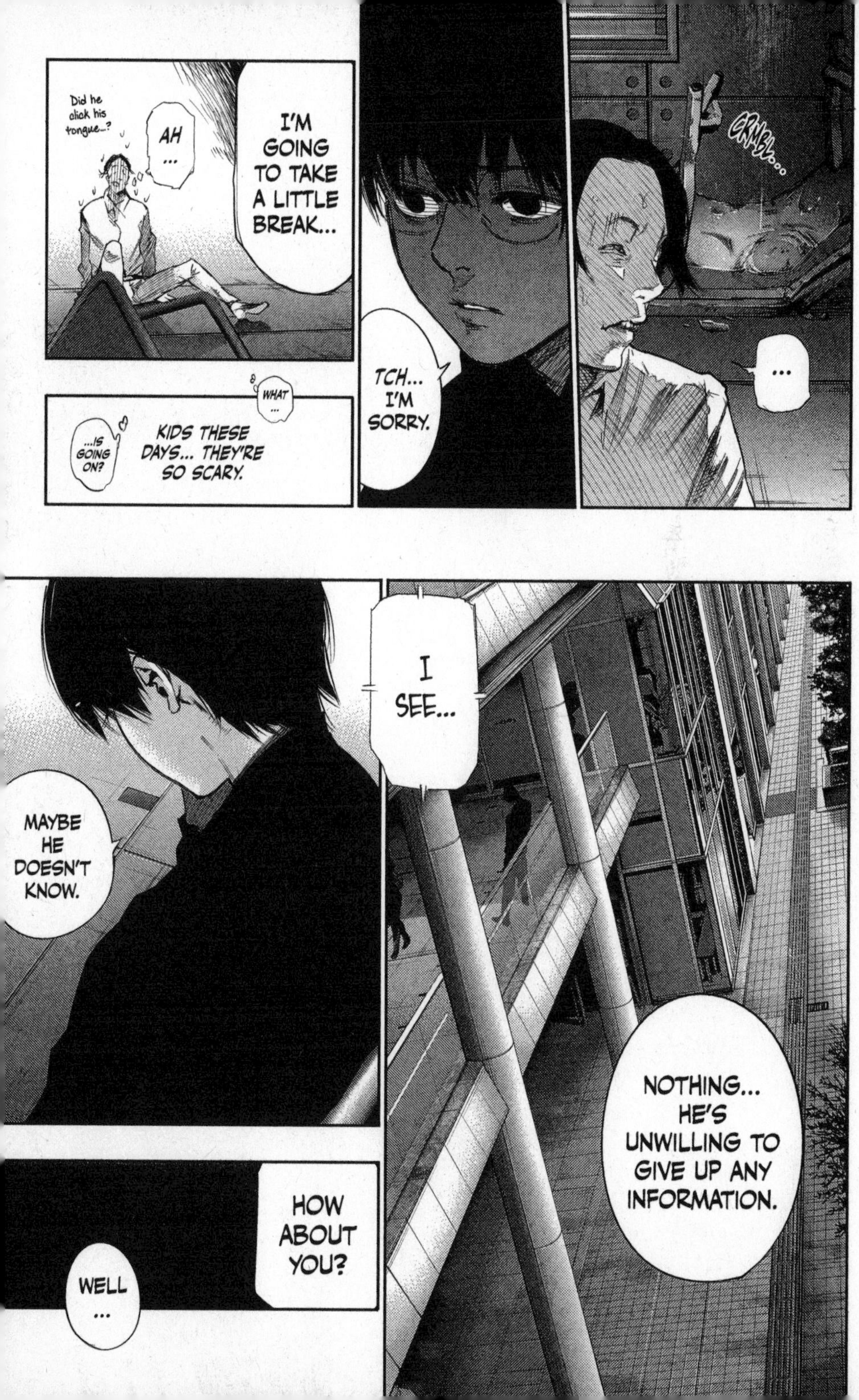
CRMBL...
...
TCH... I'M SORRY.
I'M GOING TO TAKE A LITTLE BREAK...
AH ...
Did he click his tongue...?
WHAT ...
KIDS THESE DAYS... THEY'RE SO SCARY.
...IS GOING ON?
I SEE...
NOTHING... HE'S UNWILLING TO GIVE UP ANY INFORMATION.
MAYBE HE DOESN'T KNOW.
HOW ABOUT YOU?
WELL ...

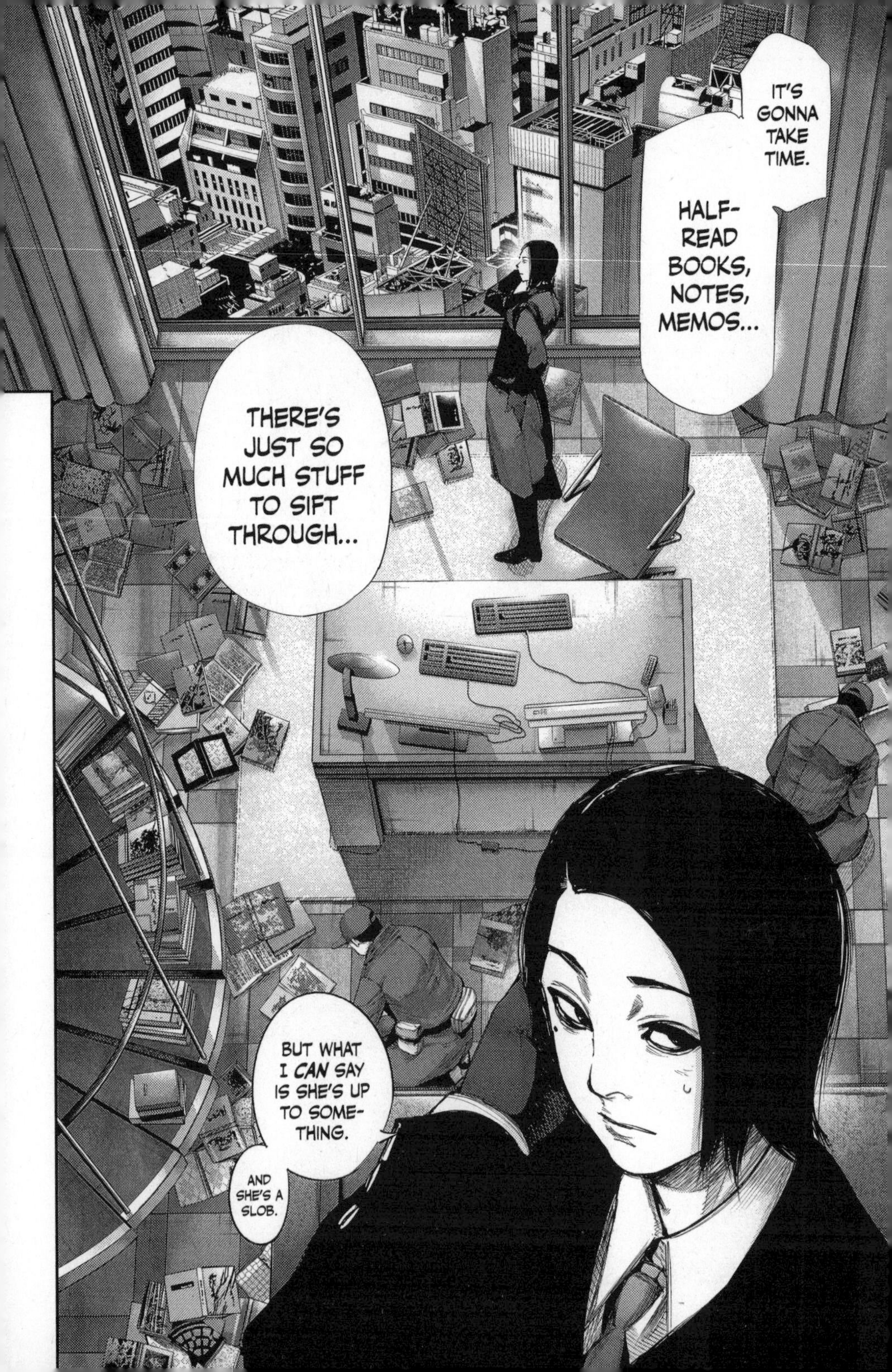
IT'S GONNA TAKE TIME.
HALF-READ BOOKS, NOTES, MEMOS...
THERE'S JUST SO MUCH STUFF TO SIFT THROUGH...
BUT WHAT I *CAN* SAY IS SHE'S UP TO SOME-THING.
AND SHE'S A SLOB.

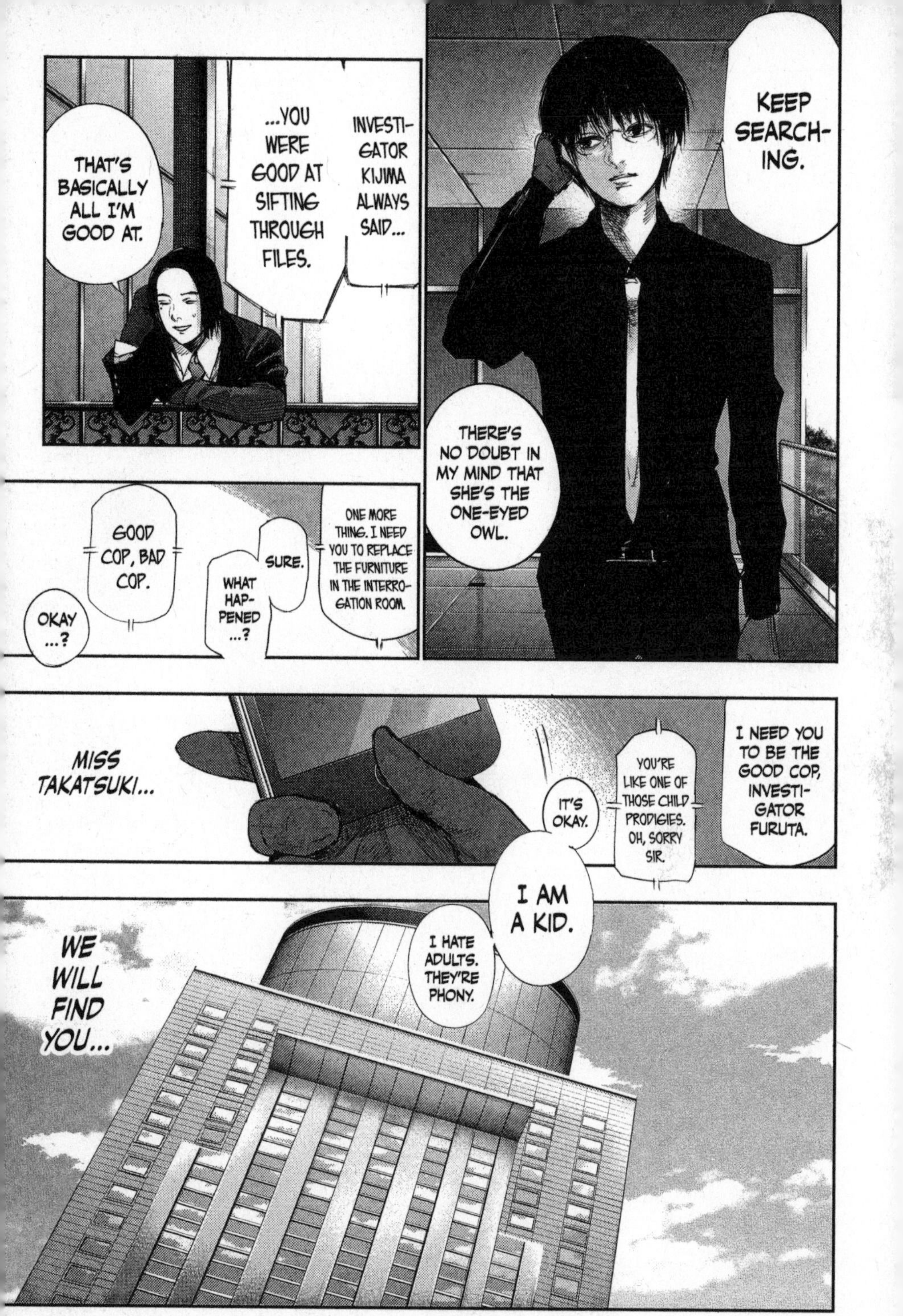
KEEP SEARCHING.
THERE'S NO DOUBT IN MY MIND THAT SHE'S THE ONE-EYED OWL.
INVESTIGATOR KIJIMA ALWAYS SAID...
...YOU WERE GOOD AT SIFTING THROUGH FILES.
THAT'S BASICALLY ALL I'M GOOD AT.
ONE MORE THING. I NEED YOU TO REPLACE THE FURNITURE IN THE INTERROGATION ROOM.
SURE.
WHAT HAPPENED ...?
GOOD COP, BAD COP.
OKAY ...?
I NEED YOU TO BE THE GOOD COP, INVESTIGATOR FURUTA.
YOU'RE LIKE ONE OF THOSE CHILD PRODIGIES. OH, SORRY SIR.
IT'S OKAY.
I AM A KID.
MISS TAKATSUKI...
I HATE ADULTS. THEY'RE PHONY.
WE WILL FIND YOU...

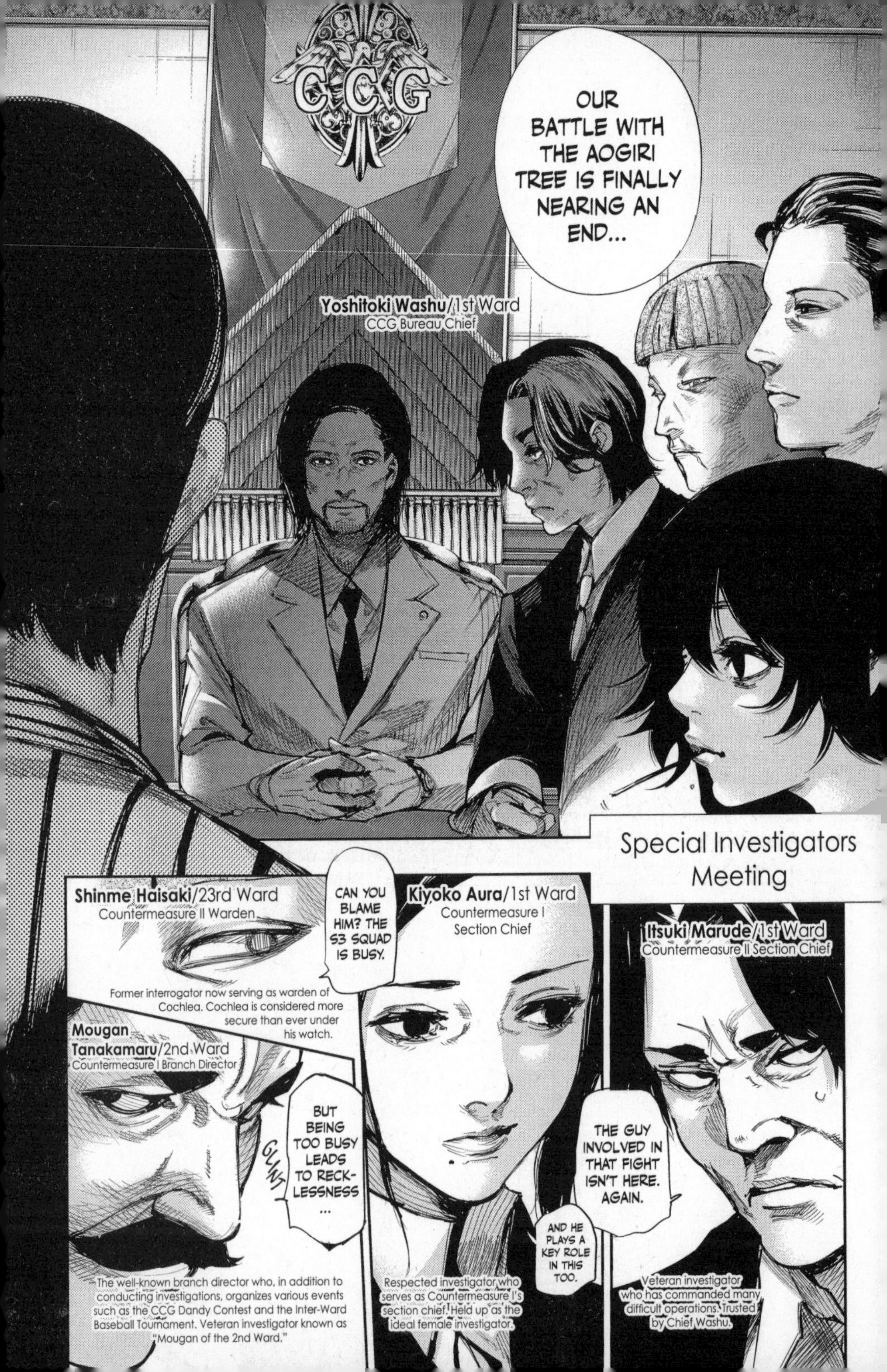
OUR BATTLE WITH THE AOGIRI TREE IS FINALLY NEARING AN END...
Yoshitoki Washu/1st Ward
CCG Bureau Chief
Special Investigators Meeting
Itsuki Marude/1st Ward
Countermeasure II Section Chief
THE GUY INVOLVED IN THAT FIGHT ISN'T HERE. AGAIN.
AND HE PLAYS A KEY ROLE IN THIS TOO.
Veteran investigator who has commanded many difficult operations. Trusted by Chief Washu.
Kiyoko Aura/1st Ward
Countermeasure I Section Chief
CAN YOU BLAME HIM? THE S3 SQUAD IS BUSY.
Respected investigator who serves as Countermeasure I's section chief. Held up as the ideal female investigator.
Shinme Haisaki/23rd Ward
Countermeasure II Warden
Former interrogator now serving as warden of Cochlea. Cochlea is considered more secure than ever under his watch.
Mougan Tanakamaru/2nd Ward
Countermeasure I Branch Director
BUT BEING TOO BUSY LEADS TO RECK-LESSNESS...
GLINT
The well-known branch director who, in addition to conducting investigations, organizes various events such as the CCG Dandy Contest and the Inter-Ward Baseball Tournament. Veteran investigator known as "Mougan of the 2nd Ward."

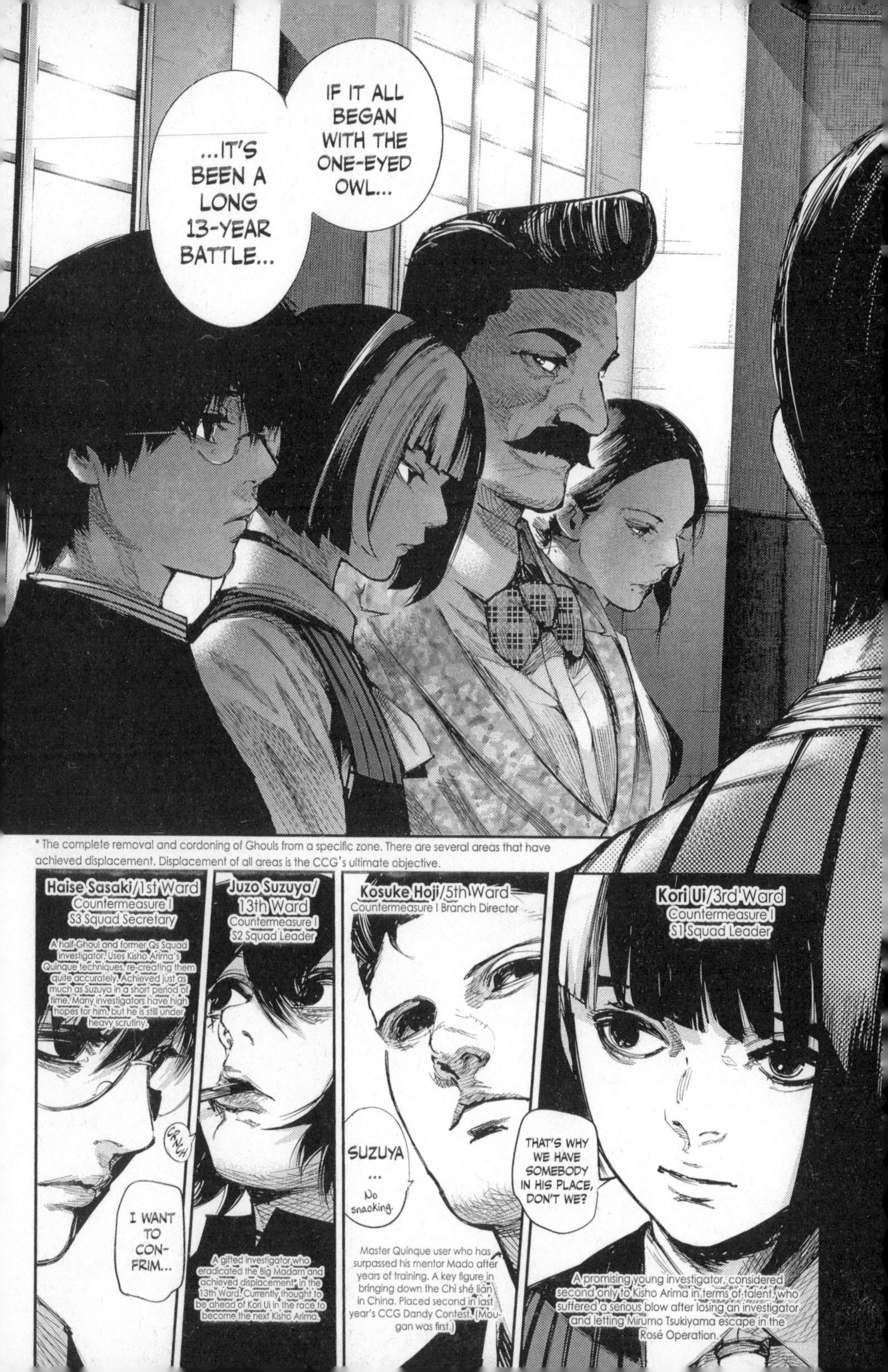
IF IT ALL BEGAN WITH THE ONE-EYED OWL...
...IT'S BEEN A LONG 13-YEAR BATTLE...
* The complete removal and cordoning of Ghouls from a specific zone. There are several areas that have achieved displacement. Displacement of all areas is the CCG's ultimate objective.
Kori Ui/3rd Ward
Countermeasure I
S1 Squad Leader
THAT'S WHY WE HAVE SOMEBODY IN HIS PLACE, DON'T WE?
A promising young investigator, considered second only to Kisho Arima in terms of talent, who suffered a serious blow after losing an investigator and letting Mirumo Tsukiyama escape in the Rosé Operation.
Kosuke Hoji/5th Ward
Countermeasure I Branch Director
SUZUYA ...
No snacking.
Master Quinque user who has surpassed his mentor Mado after years of training. A key figure in bringing down the Chì shé lián in China. Placed second in last year's CCG Dandy Contest. (Mou-gan was first.)
Juzo Suzuya/
13th Ward
Countermeasure I
S2 Squad Leader
CRNCH
A gifted investigator who eradicated the Big Madam and achieved displacement* in the 13th Ward. Currently thought to be ahead of Kori Ui in the race to become the next Kisho Arima.
Haise Sasaki/1st Ward
Countermeasure I
S3 Squad Secretary
A half-Ghoul and former Qs Squad investigator. Uses Kisho Arima's Quinque techniques, re-creating them quite accurately. Achieved just as much as Suzuya in a short period of time. Many investigators have high hopes for him, but he is still under heavy scrutiny.
I WANT TO CON-FRIM...

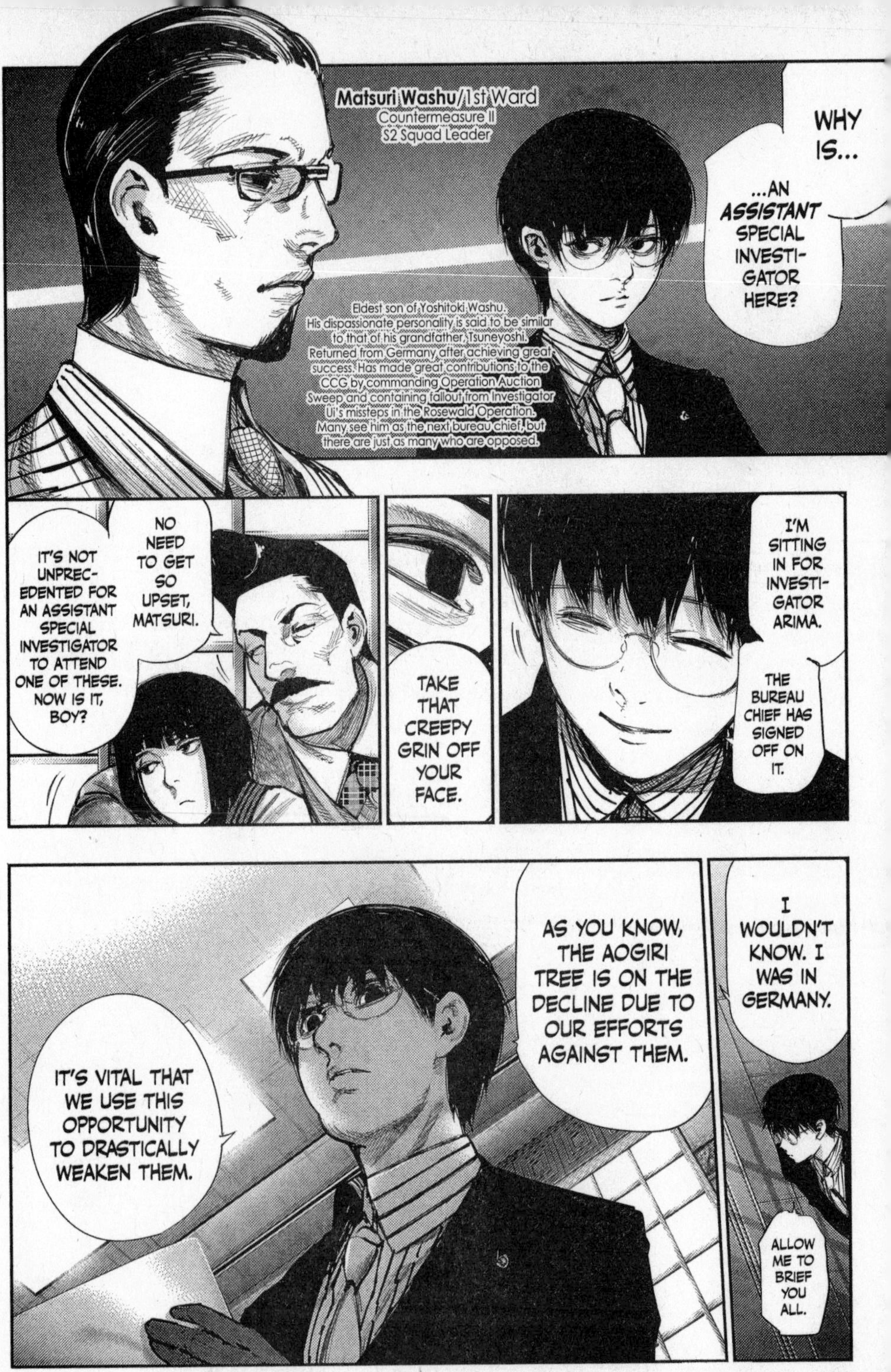
WHY IS...
...AN ASSISTANT SPECIAL INVESTIGATOR HERE?
Matsuri Washu/1st Ward
Countermeasure II
S2 Squad Leader
Eldest son of Yoshitoki Washu. His dispassionate personality is said to be similar to that of his grandfather, Tsuneyoshi. Returned from Germany after achieving great success. Has made great contributions to the CCG by commanding Operation Auction Sweep and containing fallout from Investigator Ui's missteps in the Rosewald Operation. Many see him as the next bureau chief, but there are just as many who are opposed.
I'M SITTING IN FOR INVESTIGATOR ARIMA.
THE BUREAU CHIEF HAS SIGNED OFF ON IT.
TAKE THAT CREEPY GRIN OFF YOUR FACE.
NO NEED TO GET SO UPSET, MATSURI.
IT'S NOT UNPRECEDENTED FOR AN ASSISTANT SPECIAL INVESTIGATOR TO ATTEND ONE OF THESE. NOW IS IT, BOY?
I WOULDN'T KNOW. I WAS IN GERMANY.
ALLOW ME TO BRIEF YOU ALL.
AS YOU KNOW, THE AOGIRI TREE IS ON THE DECLINE DUE TO OUR EFFORTS AGAINST THEM.
IT'S VITAL THAT WE USE THIS OPPORTUNITY TO DRASTICALLY WEAKEN THEM.

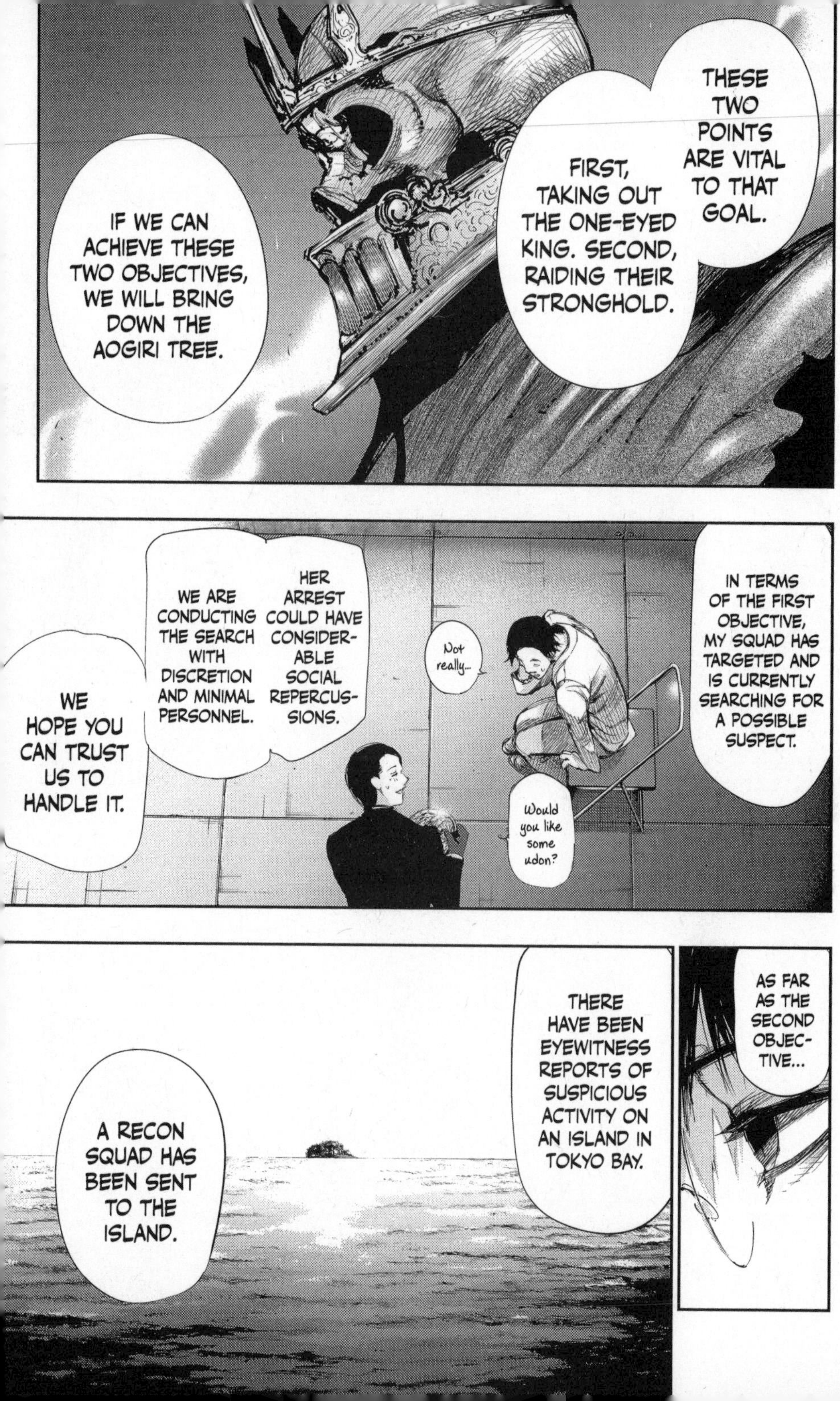
THESE TWO POINTS ARE VITAL TO THAT GOAL.
FIRST, TAKING OUT THE ONE-EYED KING. SECOND, RAIDING THEIR STRONGHOLD.
IF WE CAN ACHIEVE THESE TWO OBJECTIVES, WE WILL BRING DOWN THE AOGIRI TREE.
IN TERMS OF THE FIRST OBJECTIVE, MY SQUAD HAS TARGETED AND IS CURRENTLY SEARCHING FOR A POSSIBLE SUSPECT.
HER ARREST COULD HAVE CONSIDER-ABLE SOCIAL REPERCUS-SIONS.
WE ARE CONDUCTING THE SEARCH WITH DISCRETION AND MINIMAL PERSONNEL.
Not really...
WE HOPE YOU CAN TRUST US TO HANDLE IT.
Would you like some udon?
AS FAR AS THE SECOND OBJEC-TIVE...
THERE HAVE BEEN EYEWITNESS REPORTS OF SUSPICIOUS ACTIVITY ON AN ISLAND IN TOKYO BAY.
A RECON SQUAD HAS BEEN SENT TO THE ISLAND.

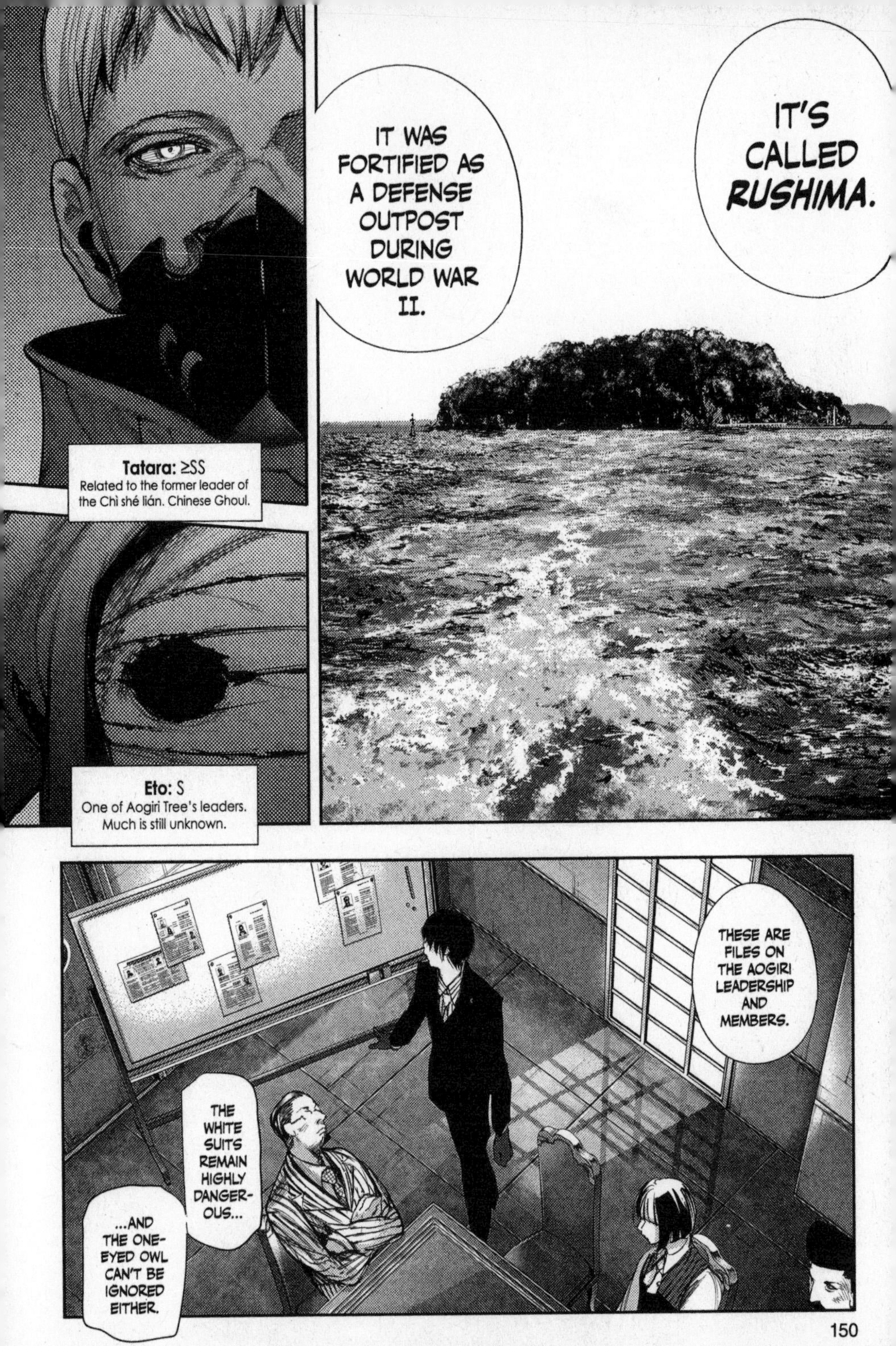
IT'S CALLED RUSHIMA.
IT WAS FORTIFIED AS A DEFENSE OUTPOST DURING WORLD WAR II.
Tatara: ≥SS
Related to the former leader of the Chì shé lián. Chinese Ghoul.
Eto: S
One of Aogiri Tree's leaders. Much is still unknown.
THESE ARE FILES ON THE AOGIRI LEADERSHIP AND MEMBERS.
THE WHITE SUITS REMAIN HIGHLY DANGER-OUS...
...AND THE ONE-EYED OWL CAN'T BE IGNORED EITHER.

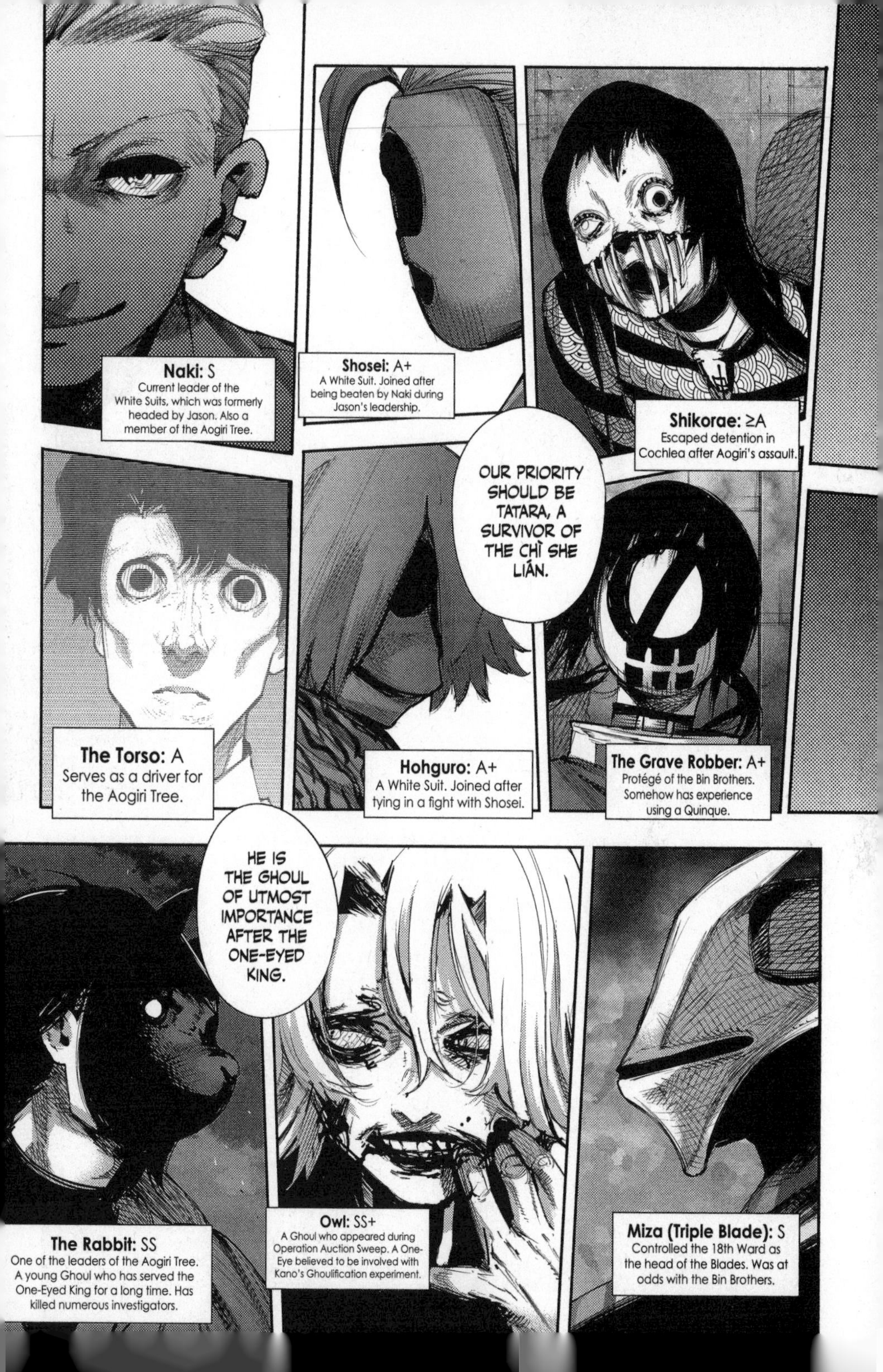
Shikorae: ≥A Escaped detention in Cochlea after Aogiri's assault.
Shosei: A+ A White Suit. Joined after being beaten by Naki during Jason's leadership.
Naki: S Current leader of the White Suits, which was formerly headed by Jason. Also a member of the Aogiri Tree.
OUR PRIORITY SHOULD BE TATARA, A SURVIVOR OF THE CHÌ SHE LIÁN.
The Grave Robber: A+ Protégé of the Bin Brothers. Somehow has experience using a Quinque.
Hohguro: A+ A White Suit. Joined after tying in a fight with Shosei.
The Torso: A Serves as a driver for the Aogiri Tree.
Miza (Triple Blade): S Controlled the 18th Ward as the head of the Blades. Was at odds with the Bin Brothers.
HE IS THE GHOUL OF UTMOST IMPORTANCE AFTER THE ONE-EYED KING.
Owl: SS+ A Ghoul who appeared during Operation Auction Sweep. A One-Eye believed to be involved with Kano's Ghoulification experiment.
The Rabbit: SS One of the leaders of the Aogiri Tree. A young Ghoul who has served the One-Eyed King for a long time. Has killed numerous investigators.

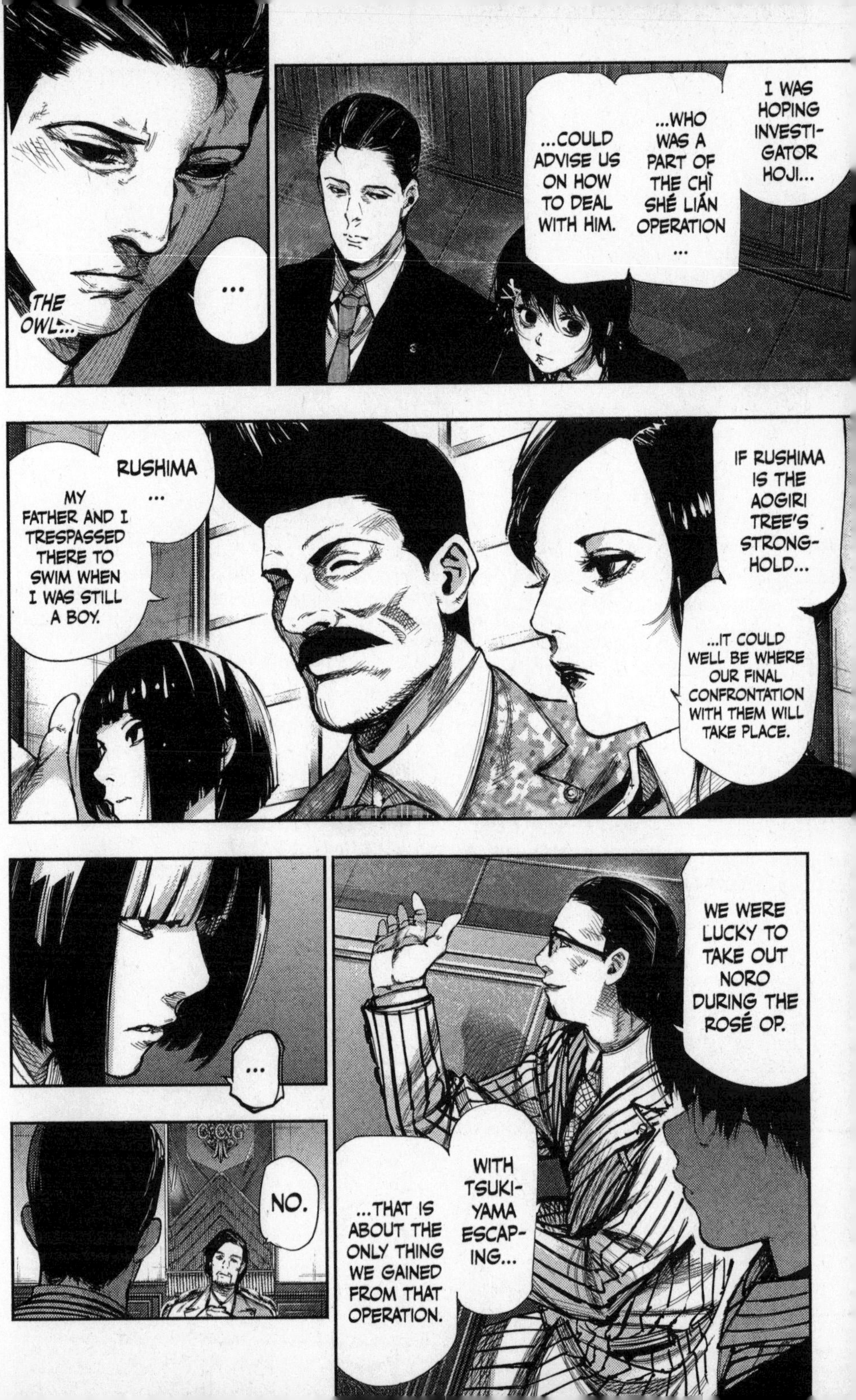
I WAS HOPING INVESTIGATOR HOJI...
...WHO WAS A PART OF THE CHÌ SHÉ LIÁN OPERATION...
...COULD ADVISE US ON HOW TO DEAL WITH HIM.
...
THE OWL...
IF RUSHIMA IS THE AOGIRI TREE'S STRONGHOLD...
...IT COULD WELL BE WHERE OUR FINAL CONFRONTATION WITH THEM WILL TAKE PLACE.
RUSHIMA...
MY FATHER AND I TRESPASSED THERE TO SWIM WHEN I WAS STILL A BOY.
WE WERE LUCKY TO TAKE OUT NORO DURING THE ROSÉ OP.
WITH TSUKIYAMA ESCAPING...
...THAT IS ABOUT THE ONLY THING WE GAINED FROM THAT OPERATION.
...
NO.

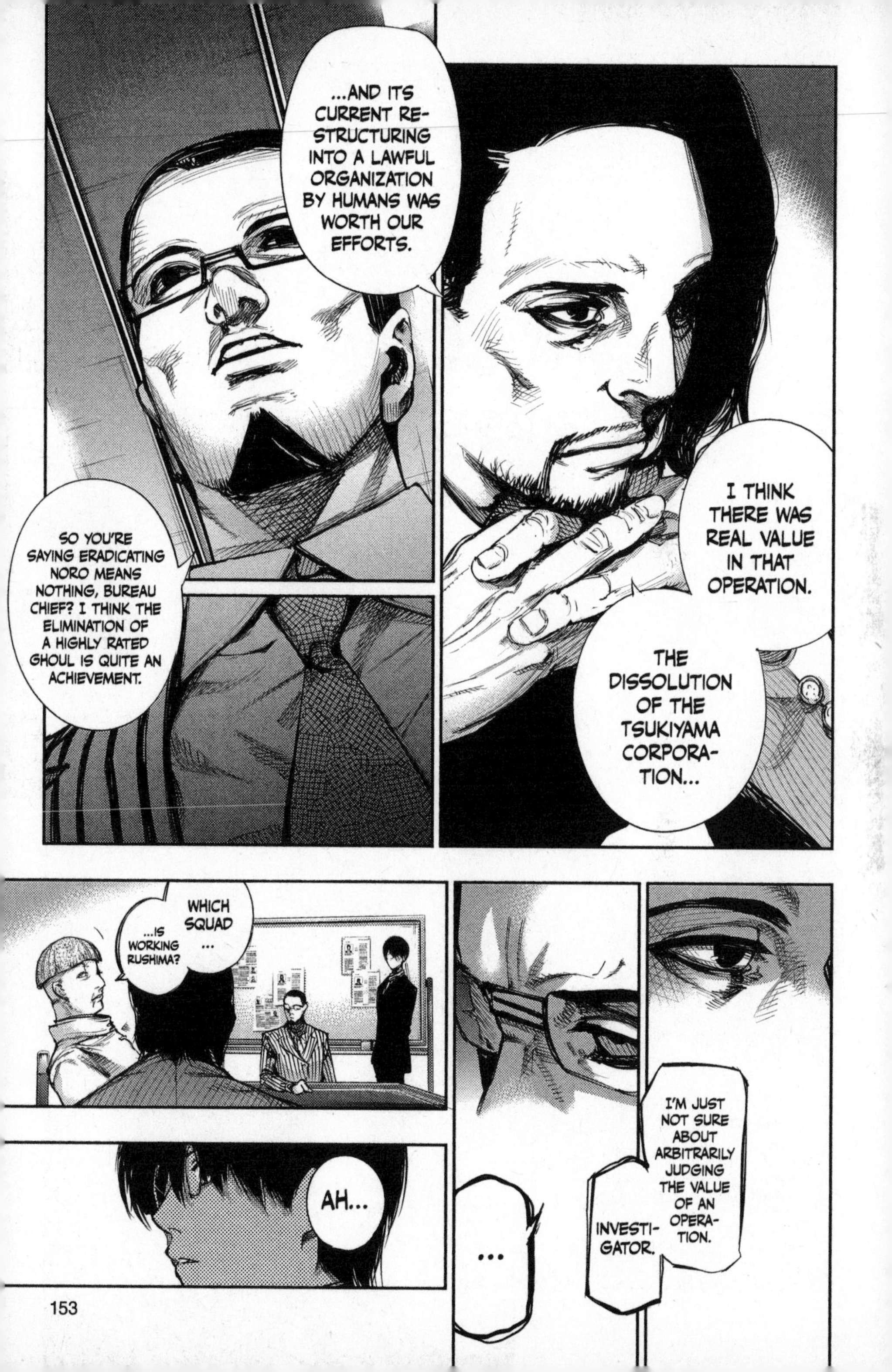
I THINK THERE WAS REAL VALUE IN THAT OPERATION.
THE DISSOLUTION OF THE TSUKIYAMA CORPORATION...
...AND ITS CURRENT RESTRUCTURING INTO A LAWFUL ORGANIZATION BY HUMANS WAS WORTH OUR EFFORTS.
SO YOU'RE SAYING ERADICATING NORO MEANS NOTHING, BUREAU CHIEF? I THINK THE ELIMINATION OF A HIGHLY RATED GHOUL IS QUITE AN ACHIEVEMENT.
I'M JUST NOT SURE ABOUT ARBITRARILY JUDGING THE VALUE OF AN OPERATION.
INVESTIGATOR.
...
WHICH SQUAD ...
...IS WORKING RUSHIMA?
AH...

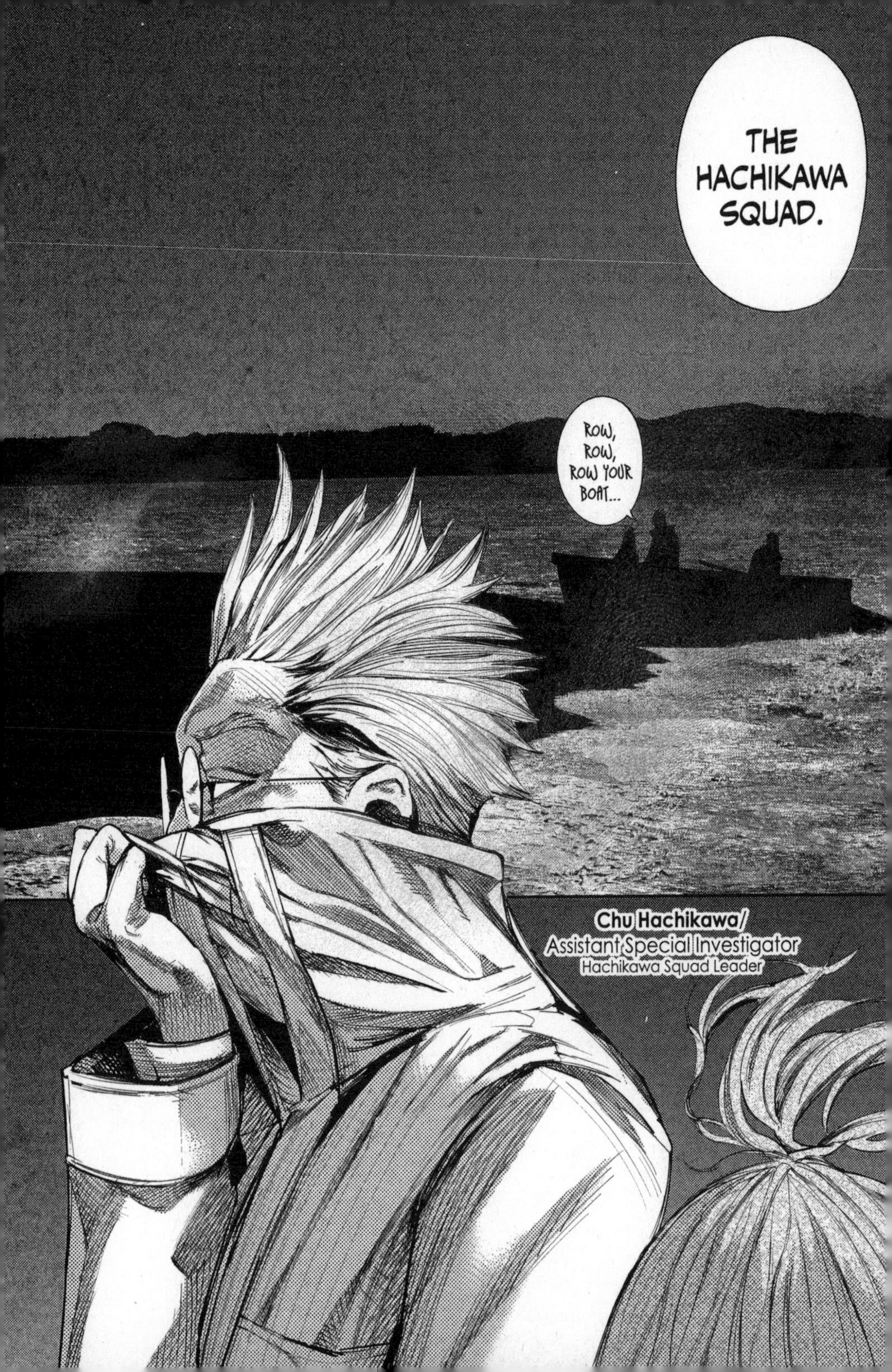
THE HACHIKAWA SQUAD.
ROW, ROW, ROW YOUR BOAT...
Chu Hachikawa/
Assistant Special Investigator
Hachikawa Squad Leader

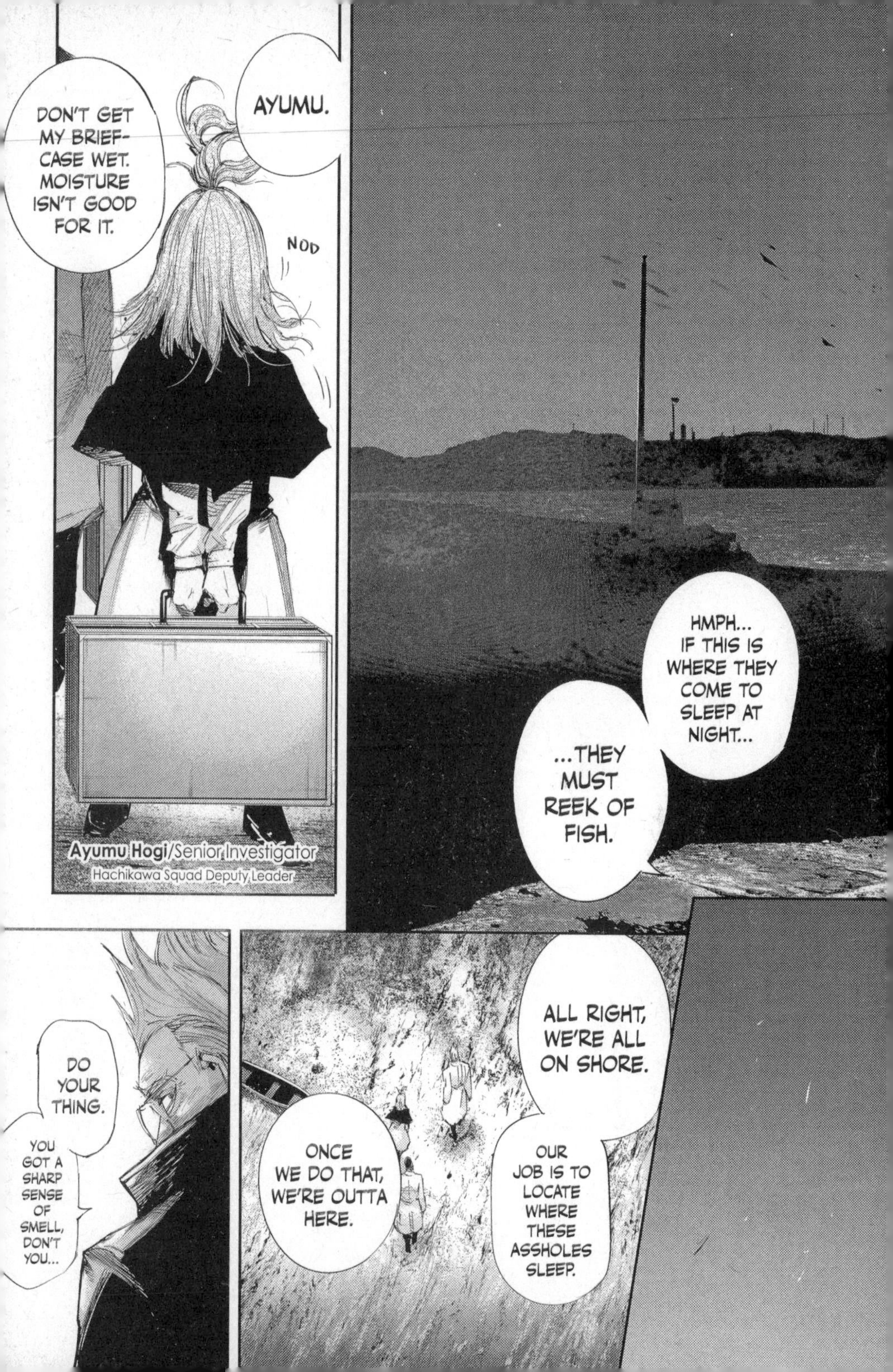
HMPH... IF THIS IS WHERE THEY COME TO SLEEP AT NIGHT...
...THEY MUST REEK OF FISH.
AYUMU.
DON'T GET MY BRIEF-CASE WET. MOISTURE ISN'T GOOD FOR IT.
NOD
Ayumu Hogi/Senior Investigator
Hachikawa Squad Deputy Leader
ALL RIGHT, WE'RE ALL ON SHORE.
OUR JOB IS TO LOCATE WHERE THESE ASSHOLES SLEEP.
ONCE WE DO THAT, WE'RE OUTTA HERE.
DO YOUR THING.
YOU GOT A SHARP SENSE OF SMELL, DON'T YOU...

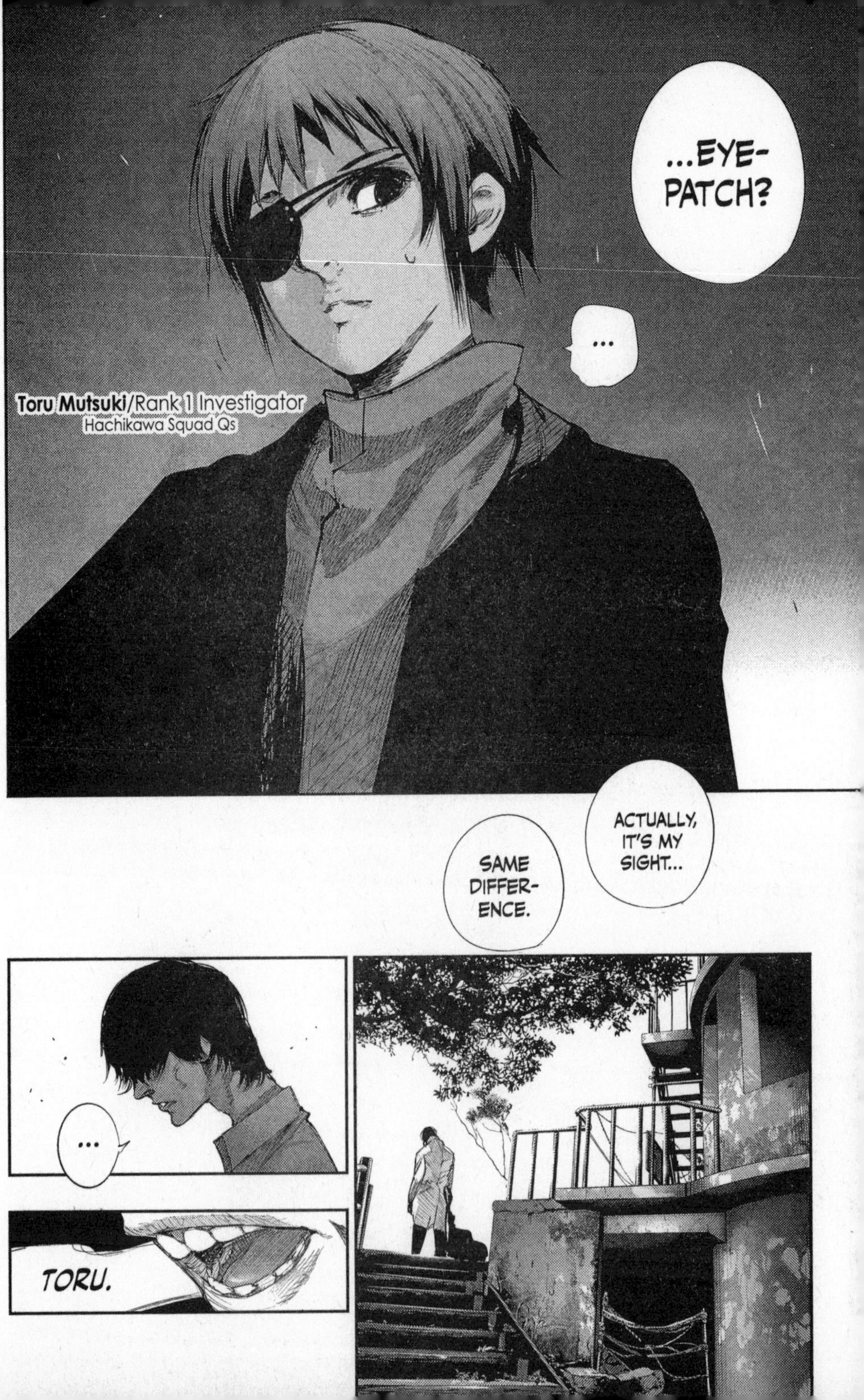
...EYE-PATCH?
...
Toru Mutsuki/Rank 1 Investigator
Hachikawa Squad Qs
ACTUALLY, IT'S MY SIGHT...
SAME DIFFERENCE.
...
TORU.

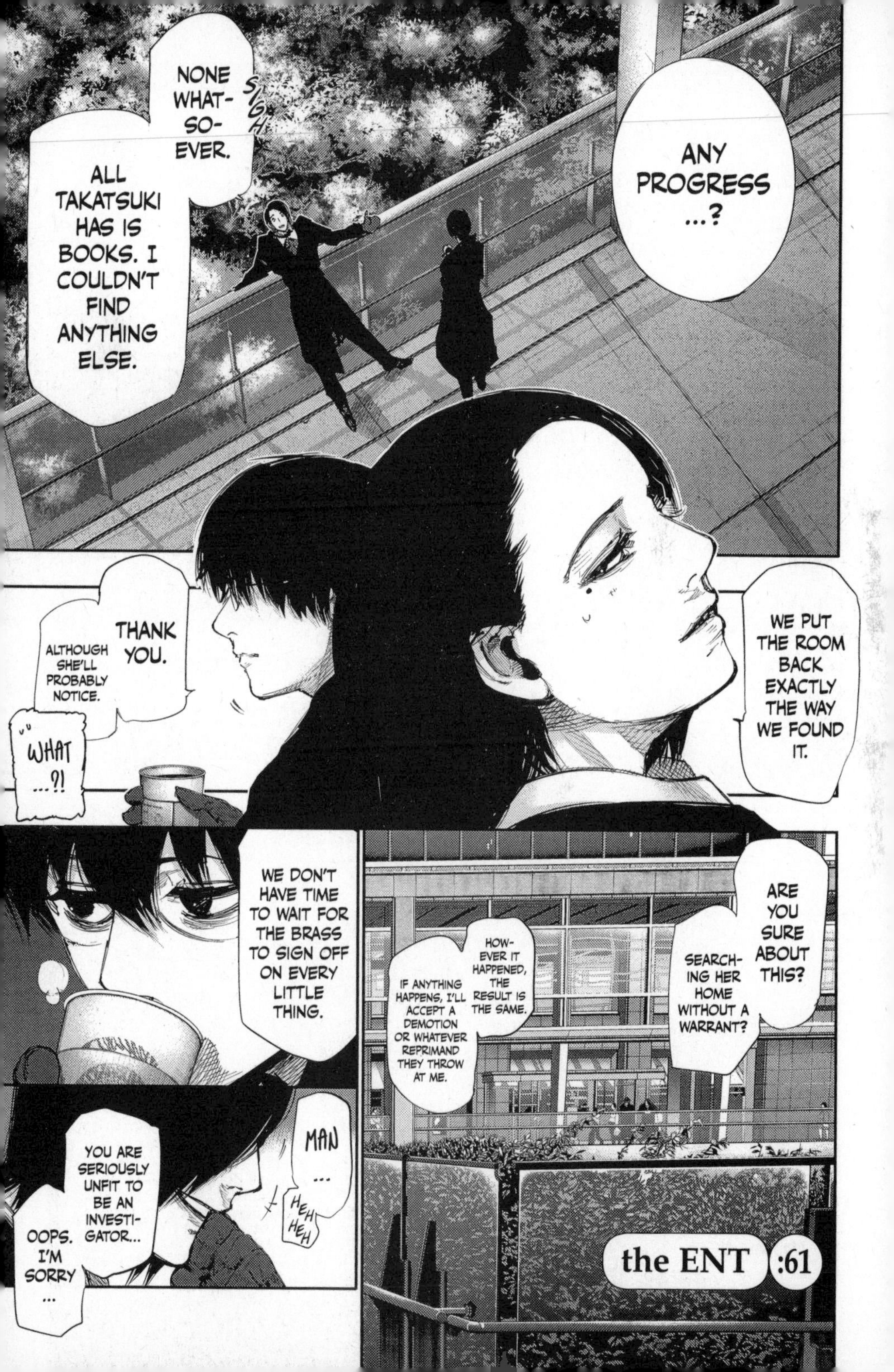
ANY PROGRESS ...?
SIGH
NONE WHAT-SO-EVER.
ALL TAKATSUKI HAS IS BOOKS. I COULDN'T FIND ANYTHING ELSE.
WE PUT THE ROOM BACK EXACTLY THE WAY WE FOUND IT.
THANK YOU.
ALTHOUGH SHE'LL PROBABLY NOTICE.
WHAT ...?!
ARE YOU SURE ABOUT THIS?
SEARCHING HER HOME WITHOUT A WARRANT?
HOWEVER IT HAPPENED, THE RESULT IS THE SAME.
IF ANYTHING HAPPENS, I'LL ACCEPT A DEMOTION OR WHATEVER REPRIMAND THEY THROW AT ME.
the ENT :61
WE DON'T HAVE TIME TO WAIT FOR THE BRASS TO SIGN OFF ON EVERY LITTLE THING.
MAN ...
HEH HEH
YOU ARE SERIOUSLY UNFIT TO BE AN INVESTIGATOR...
OOPS. I'M SORRY ...

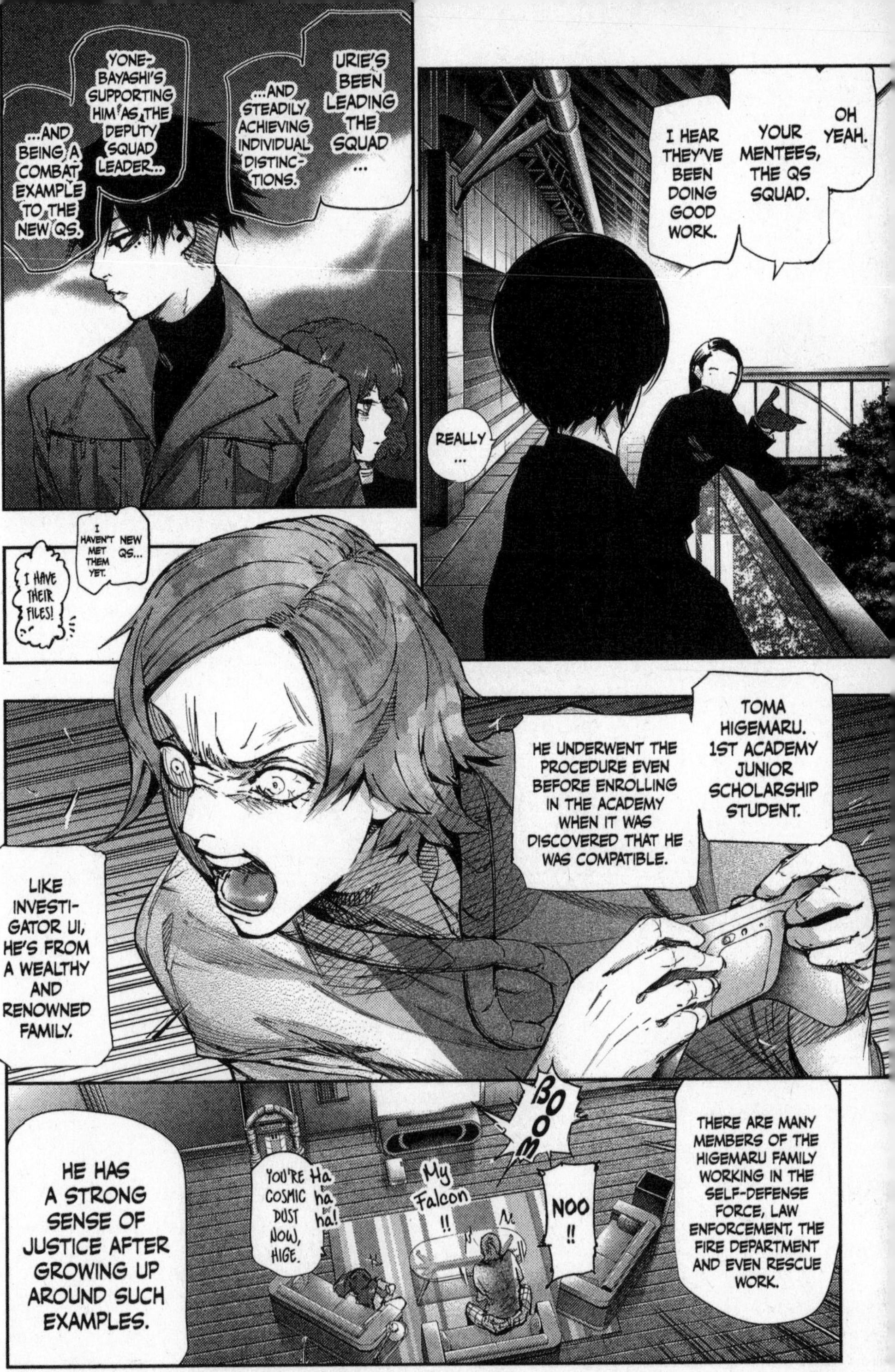

OH YEAH.
YOUR MENTEES, THE QS SQUAD.
I HEAR THEY'VE BEEN DOING GOOD WORK.
REALLY...
URIE'S BEEN LEADING THE SQUAD...
...AND STEADILY ACHIEVING INDIVIDUAL DISTINCTIONS.
YONE-BAYASHI'S SUPPORTING HIM AS THE DEPUTY SQUAD LEADER...
...AND BEING A COMBAT EXAMPLE TO THE NEW QS.
NEW QS...
I HAVEN'T MET THEM YET.
...AND I HAVE THEIR FILES!
TOMA HIGEMARU. 1ST ACADEMY JUNIOR SCHOLARSHIP STUDENT.
HE UNDERWENT THE PROCEDURE EVEN BEFORE ENROLLING IN THE ACADEMY WHEN IT WAS DISCOVERED THAT HE WAS COMPATIBLE.
LIKE INVESTI-GATOR UI, HE'S FROM A WEALTHY AND RENOWNED FAMILY.
THERE ARE MANY MEMBERS OF THE HIGEMARU FAMILY WORKING IN THE SELF-DEFENSE FORCE, LAW ENFORCEMENT, THE FIRE DEPARTMENT AND EVEN RESCUE WORK.
BOOOM
NOO !!
My Falcon !!
Ha ha ha!
YOU'RE COSMIC DUST NOW, HIGE.
HE HAS A STRONG SENSE OF JUSTICE AFTER GROWING UP AROUND SUCH EXAMPLES.

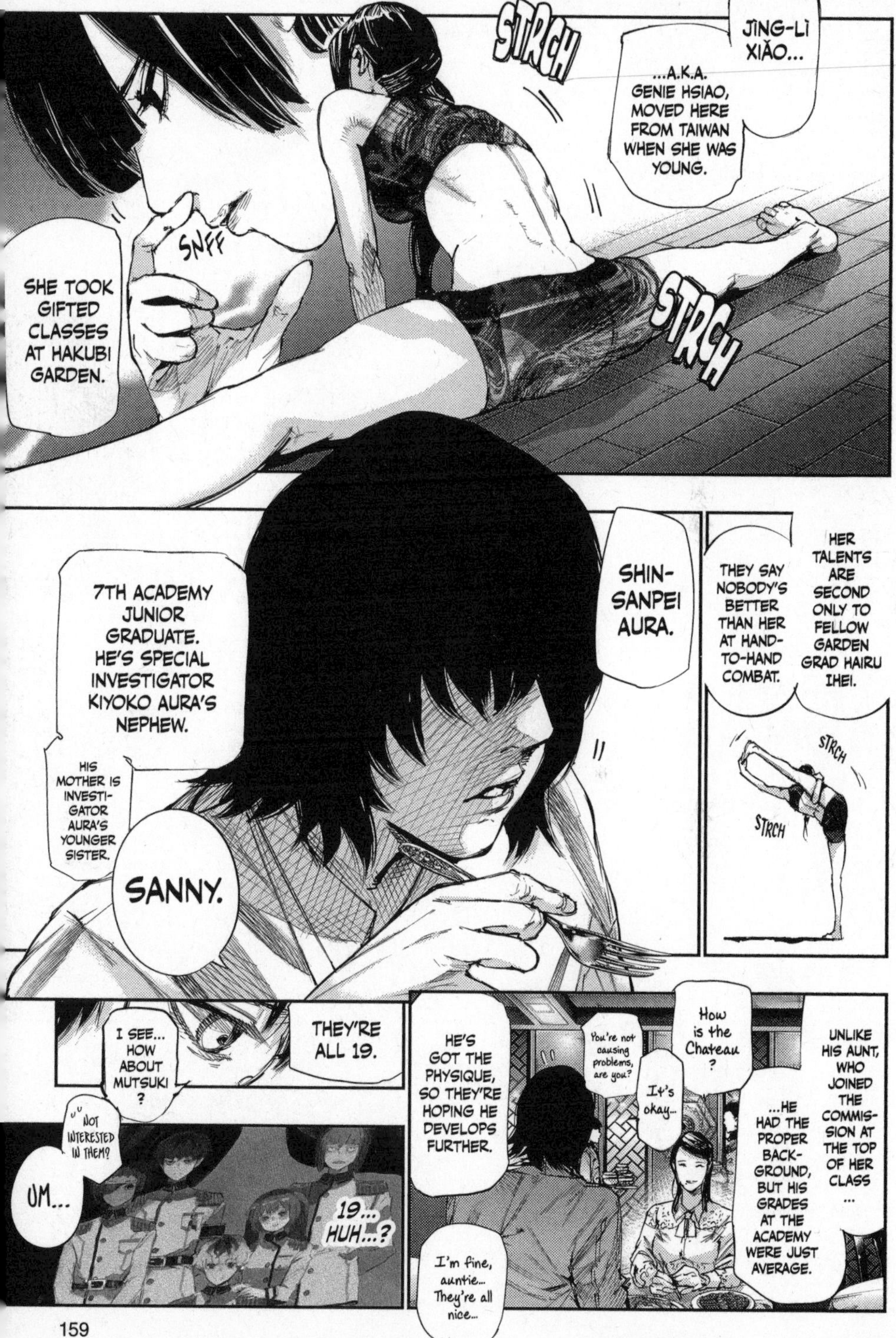
STRCH
JĪNG-LÌ XIĀO...
...A.K.A. GENIE HSIAO, MOVED HERE FROM TAIWAN WHEN SHE WAS YOUNG.
SNFF
SHE TOOK GIFTED CLASSES AT HAKUBI GARDEN.
STRCH
HER TALENTS ARE SECOND ONLY TO FELLOW GARDEN GRAD HAIRU IHEI.
THEY SAY NOBODY'S BETTER THAN HER AT HAND-TO-HAND COMBAT.
STRCH
STRCH
SHIN-SANPEI AURA.
7TH ACADEMY JUNIOR GRADUATE. HE'S SPECIAL INVESTIGATOR KIYOKO AURA'S NEPHEW.
HIS MOTHER IS INVESTI-GATOR AURA'S YOUNGER SISTER.
SANNY.
UNLIKE HIS AUNT, WHO JOINED THE COMMIS-SION AT THE TOP OF HER CLASS...
...HE HAD THE PROPER BACK-GROUND, BUT HIS GRADES AT THE ACADEMY WERE JUST AVERAGE.
How is the Chateau?
You're not causing problems, are you?
It's okay...
HE'S GOT THE PHYSIQUE, SO THEY'RE HOPING HE DEVELOPS FURTHER.
I'm fine, auntie... They're all nice...
THEY'RE ALL 19.
I SEE... HOW ABOUT MUTSUKI?
19... HUH...?
Not interested in them?
UM...

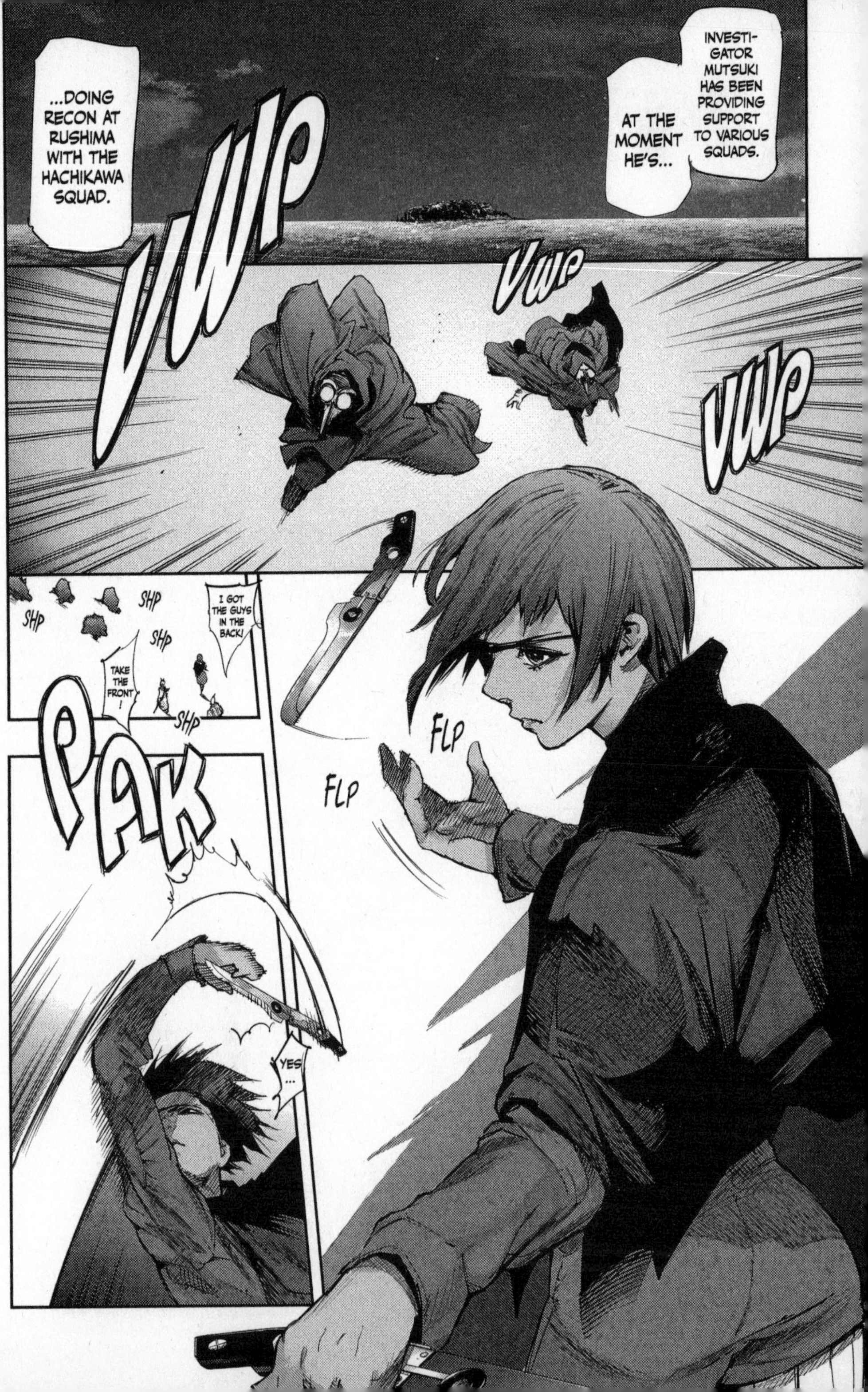

INVESTIGATOR MUTSUKI HAS BEEN PROVIDING SUPPORT TO VARIOUS SQUADS.
AT THE MOMENT HE'S...
...DOING RECON AT RUSHIMA WITH THE HACHIKAWA SQUAD.
VWP
VWP
VWP
FLP
FLP
I GOT THE GUYS IN THE BACK!
TAKE THE FRONT!
SHP
SHP
SHP
SHP
PAK
YES...

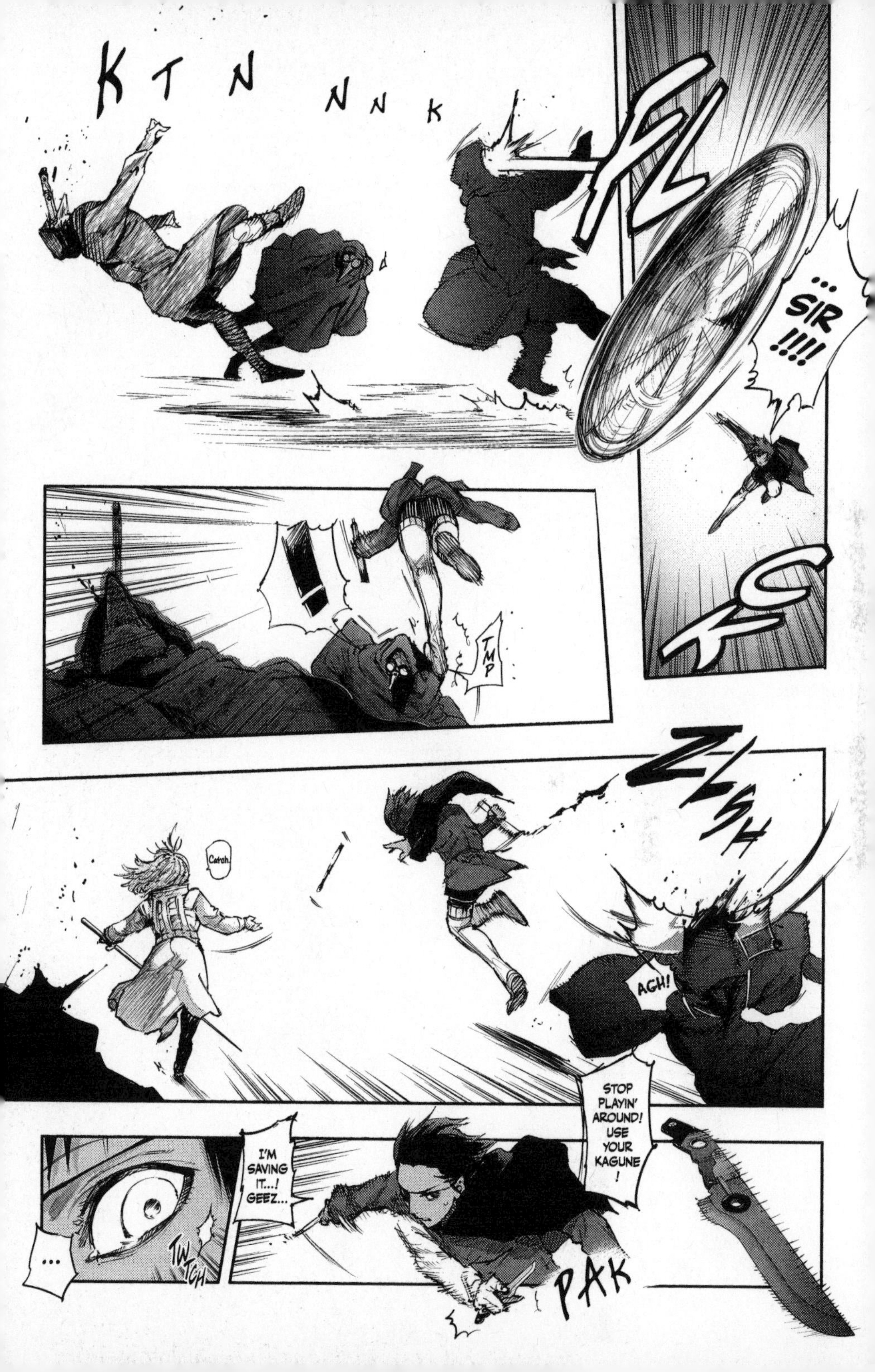

...SIR!!!!
KTN
NNK
TMP
ZLSH
AGH!
Catch.
STOP PLAYIN' AROUND! USE YOUR KAGUNE!
PAK
I'M SAVING IT...! GEEZ...
TWTCH
...

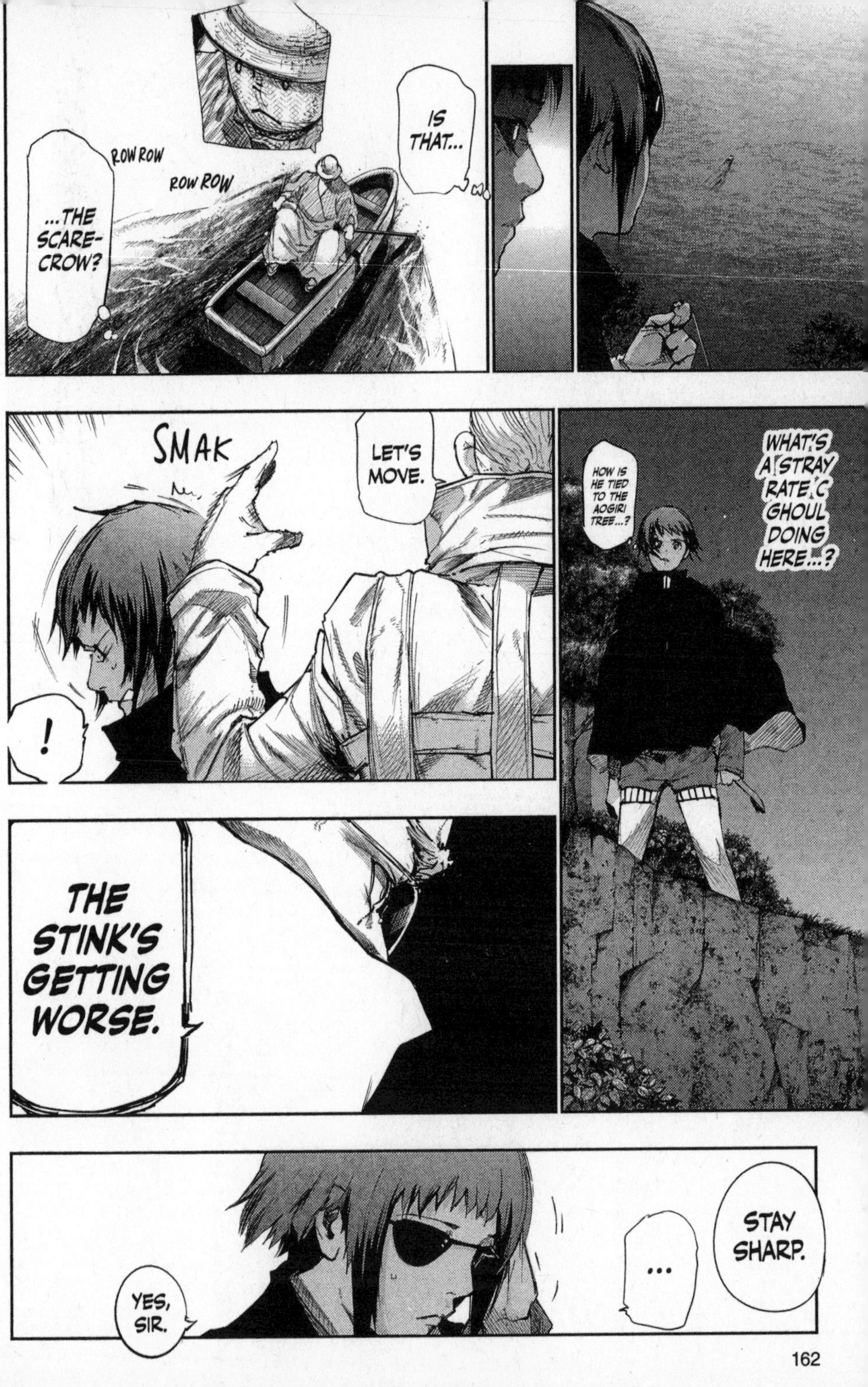
IS THAT...
ROW ROW
ROW ROW
...THE SCARE-CROW?
WHAT'S A STRAY RATE C GHOUL DOING HERE...?
HOW IS HE TIED TO THE AOGIRI TREE...?
LET'S MOVE.
SMAK
!
THE STINK'S GETTING WORSE.
STAY SHARP.
...
YES, SIR.

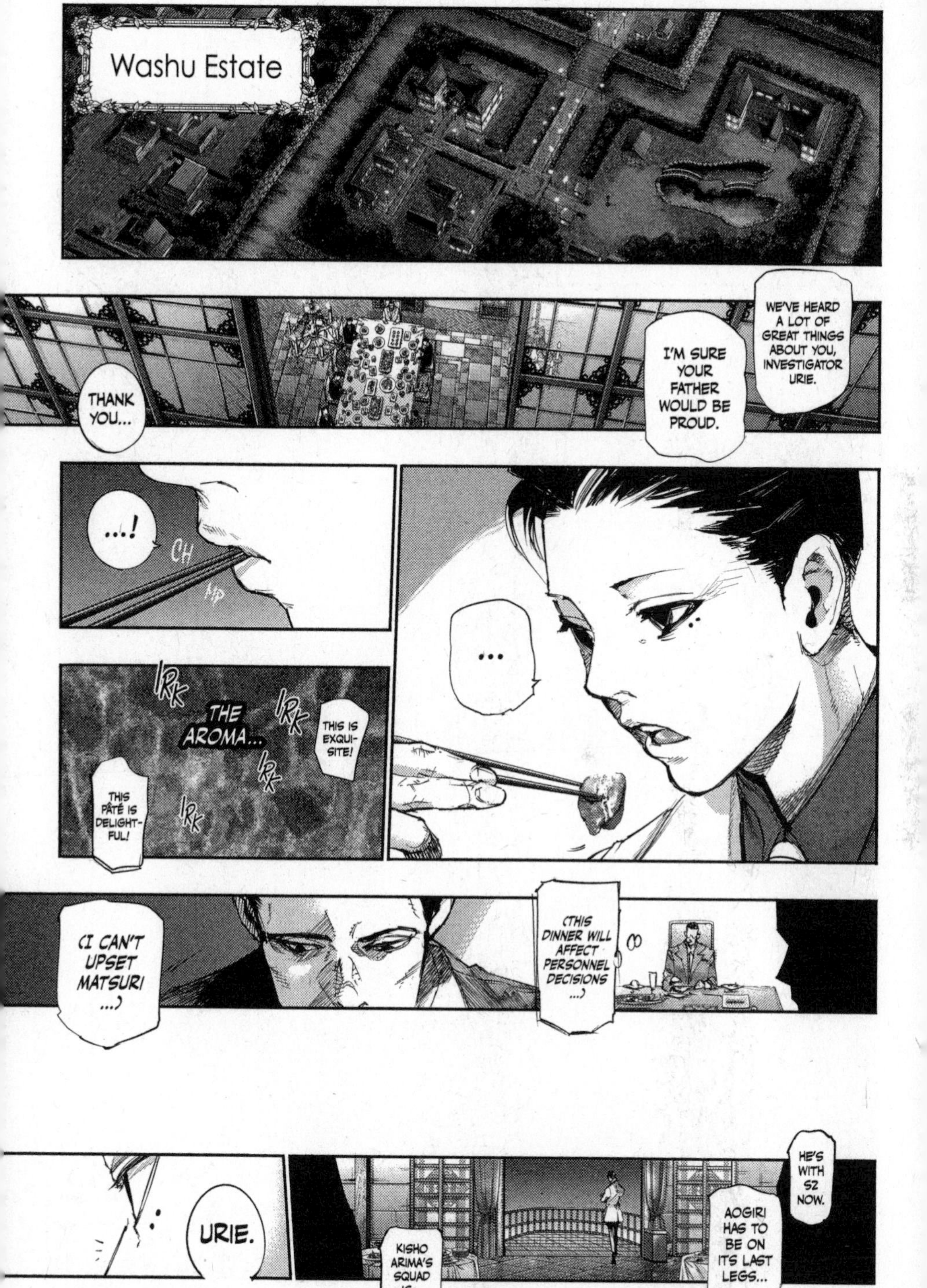
Washu Estate
WE'VE HEARD A LOT OF GREAT THINGS ABOUT YOU, INVESTIGATOR URIE.
I'M SURE YOUR FATHER WOULD BE PROUD.
THANK YOU...
...
...!
CH
MP
IRK
THIS IS EXQUISITE!
IRK
THE AROMA...
IRK
IRK
THIS PÂTÉ IS DELIGHTFUL!
(THIS DINNER WILL AFFECT PERSONNEL DECISIONS...)
(I CAN'T UPSET MATSURI...)
HE'S WITH S2 NOW.
AOGIRI HAS TO BE ON ITS LAST LEGS...
KISHO ARIMA'S SQUAD IS...
URIE.

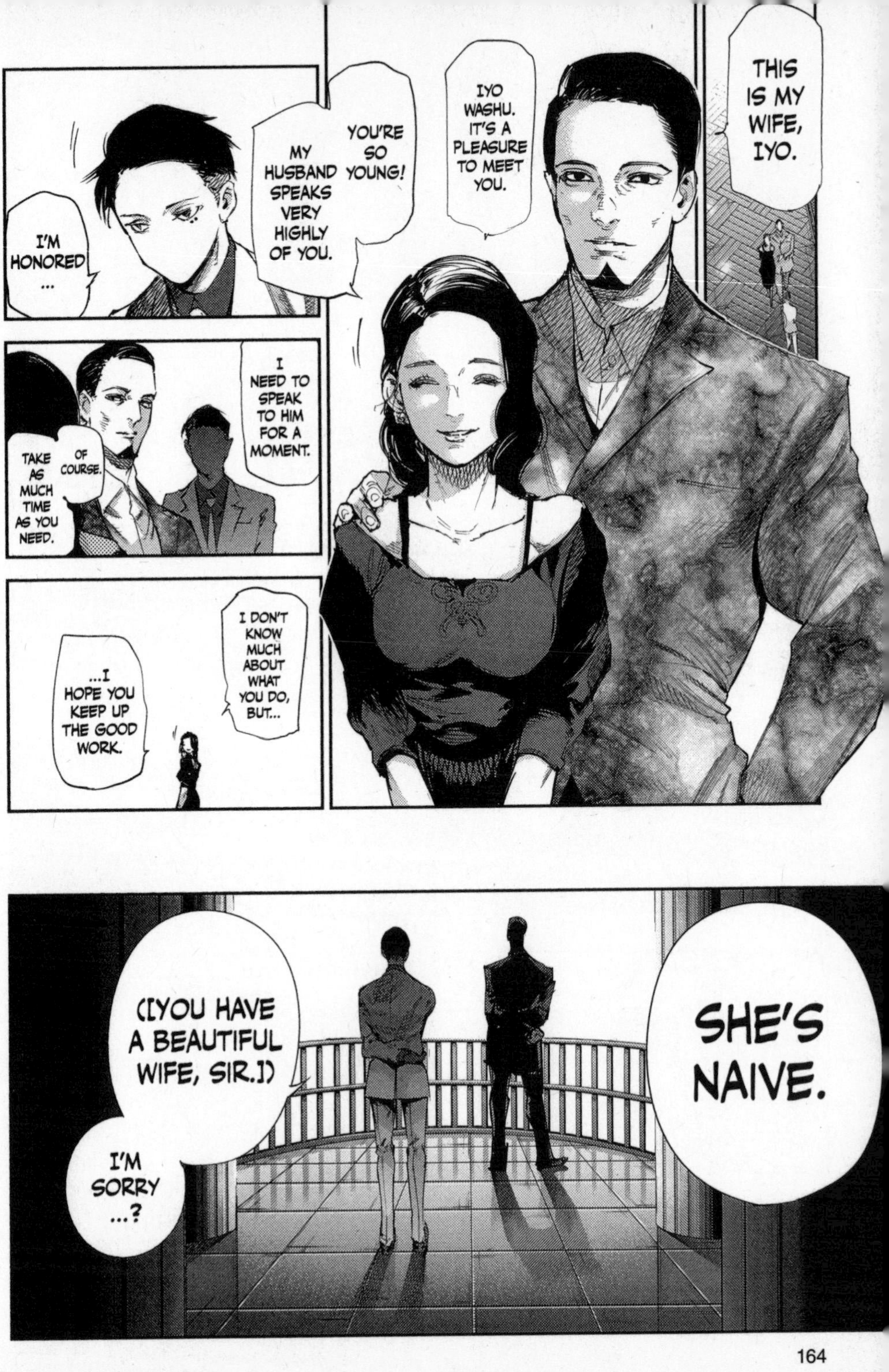
THIS IS MY WIFE, IYO.
IYO WASHU. IT'S A PLEASURE TO MEET YOU.
YOU'RE SO YOUNG!
MY HUSBAND SPEAKS VERY HIGHLY OF YOU.
I'M HONORED...
I NEED TO SPEAK TO HIM FOR A MOMENT.
OF COURSE.
TAKE AS MUCH TIME AS YOU NEED.
I DON'T KNOW MUCH ABOUT WHAT YOU DO, BUT...
...I HOPE YOU KEEP UP THE GOOD WORK.
SHE'S NAIVE.
([YOU HAVE A BEAUTIFUL WIFE, SIR.])
I'M SORRY...?

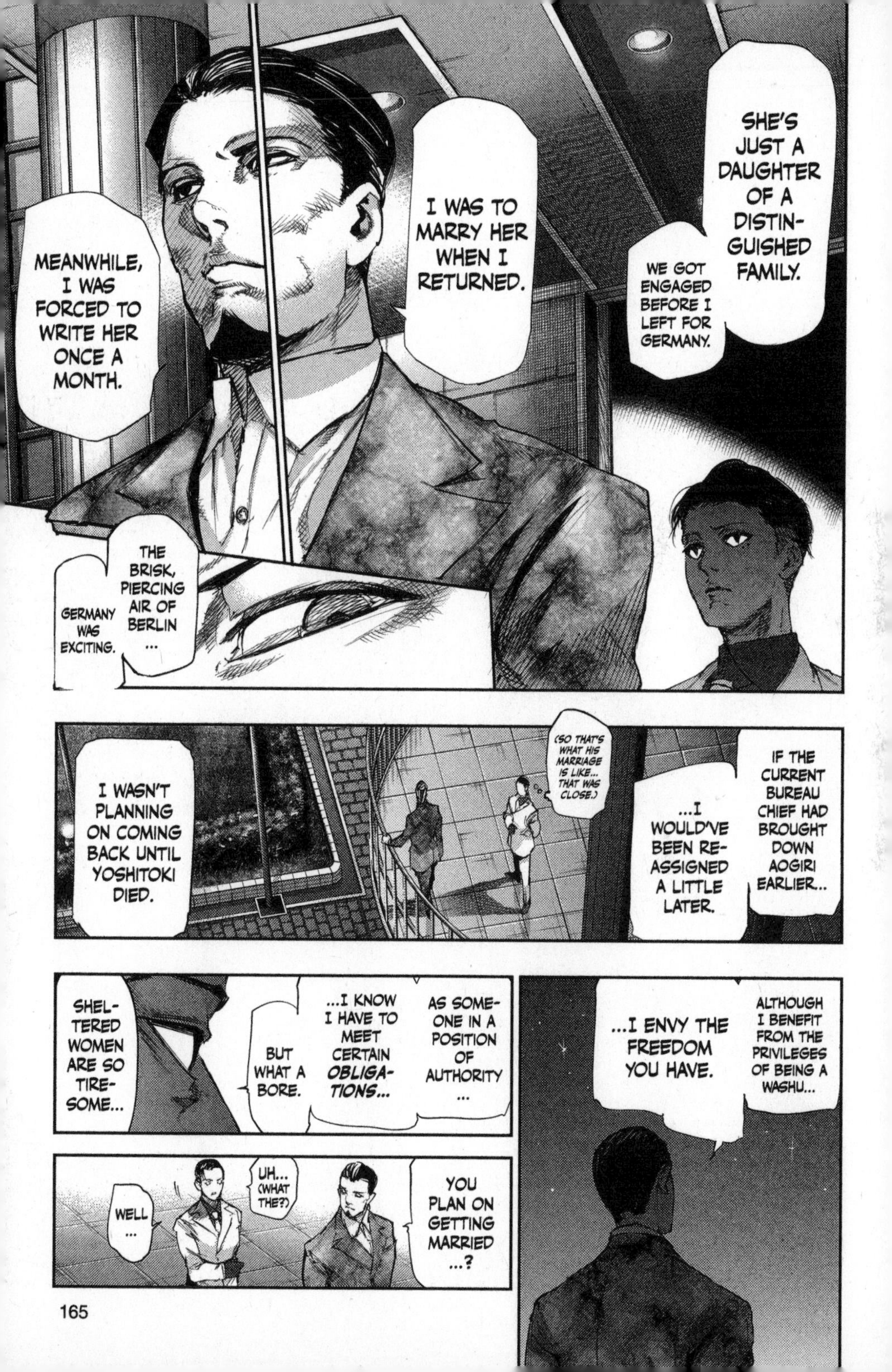

SHE'S JUST A DAUGHTER OF A DISTIN-GUISHED FAMILY.
WE GOT ENGAGED BEFORE I LEFT FOR GERMANY.
I WAS TO MARRY HER WHEN I RETURNED.
MEANWHILE, I WAS FORCED TO WRITE HER ONCE A MONTH.
THE BRISK, PIERCING AIR OF BERLIN ...
GERMANY WAS EXCITING.
IF THE CURRENT BUREAU CHIEF HAD BROUGHT DOWN AOGIRI EARLIER...
...I WOULD'VE BEEN RE-ASSIGNED A LITTLE LATER.
(SO THAT'S WHAT HIS MARRIAGE IS LIKE... THAT WAS CLOSE.)
I WASN'T PLANNING ON COMING BACK UNTIL YOSHITOKI DIED.
ALTHOUGH I BENEFIT FROM THE PRIVILEGES OF BEING A WASHU...
...I ENVY THE FREEDOM YOU HAVE.
AS SOME-ONE IN A POSITION OF AUTHORITY ...
...I KNOW I HAVE TO MEET CERTAIN *OBLIGA-TIONS*...
BUT WHAT A BORE.
SHEL-TERED WOMEN ARE SO TIRE-SOME...
YOU PLAN ON GETTING MARRIED ...?
UH... (WHAT THE?)
WELL ...

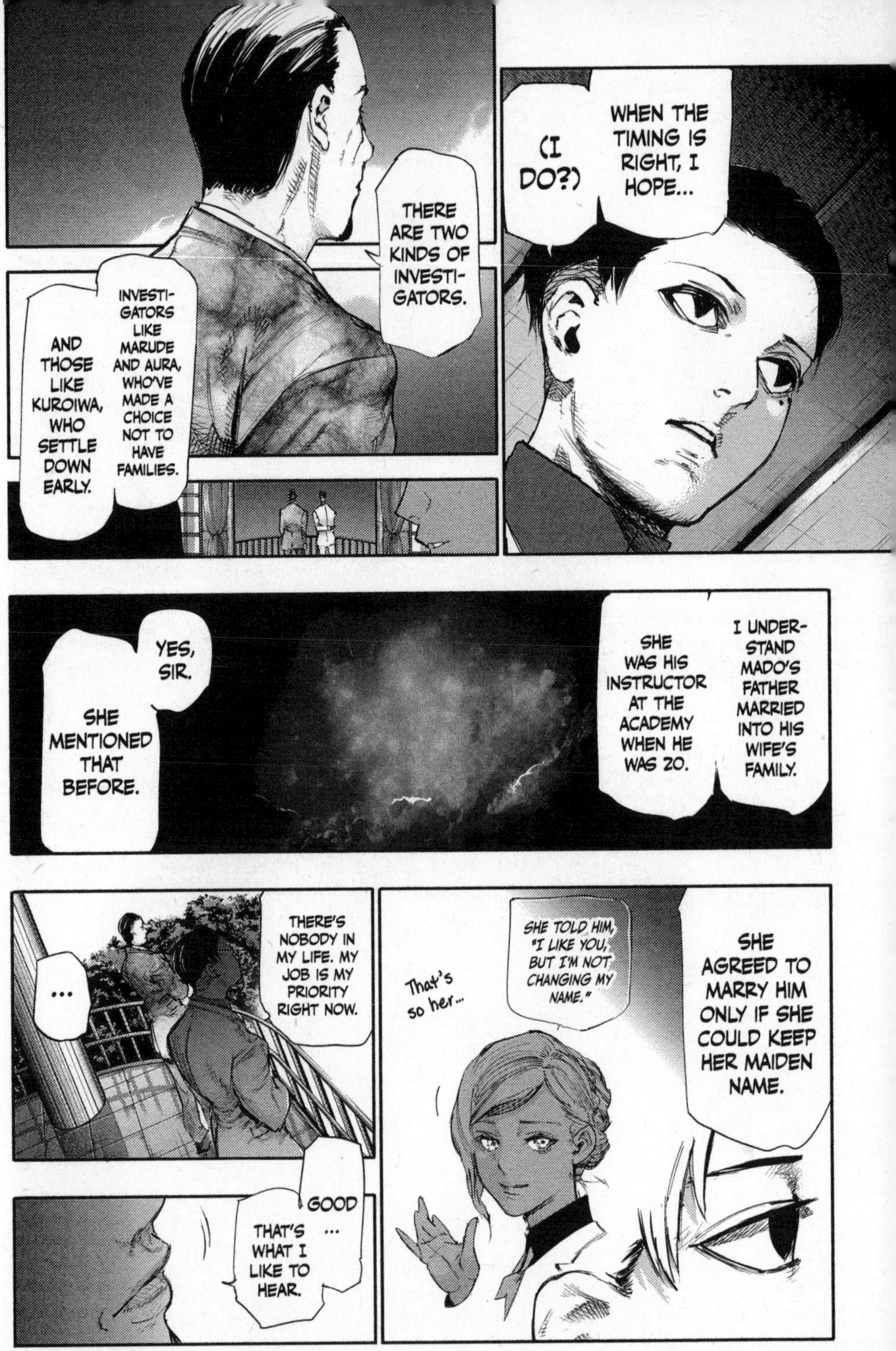
WHEN THE TIMING IS RIGHT, I HOPE...
(I DO?)
THERE ARE TWO KINDS OF INVESTIGATORS.
INVESTIGATORS LIKE MARUDE AND AURA, WHO'VE MADE A CHOICE NOT TO HAVE FAMILIES.
AND THOSE LIKE KUROIWA, WHO SETTLE DOWN EARLY.
I UNDERSTAND MADO'S FATHER MARRIED INTO HIS WIFE'S FAMILY.
SHE WAS HIS INSTRUCTOR AT THE ACADEMY WHEN HE WAS 20.
YES, SIR.
SHE MENTIONED THAT BEFORE.
SHE AGREED TO MARRY HIM ONLY IF SHE COULD KEEP HER MAIDEN NAME.
SHE TOLD HIM, "I LIKE YOU, BUT I'M NOT CHANGING MY NAME."
That's so her...
THERE'S NOBODY IN MY LIFE. MY JOB IS MY PRIORITY RIGHT NOW.
...
GOOD...
THAT'S WHAT I LIKE TO HEAR.

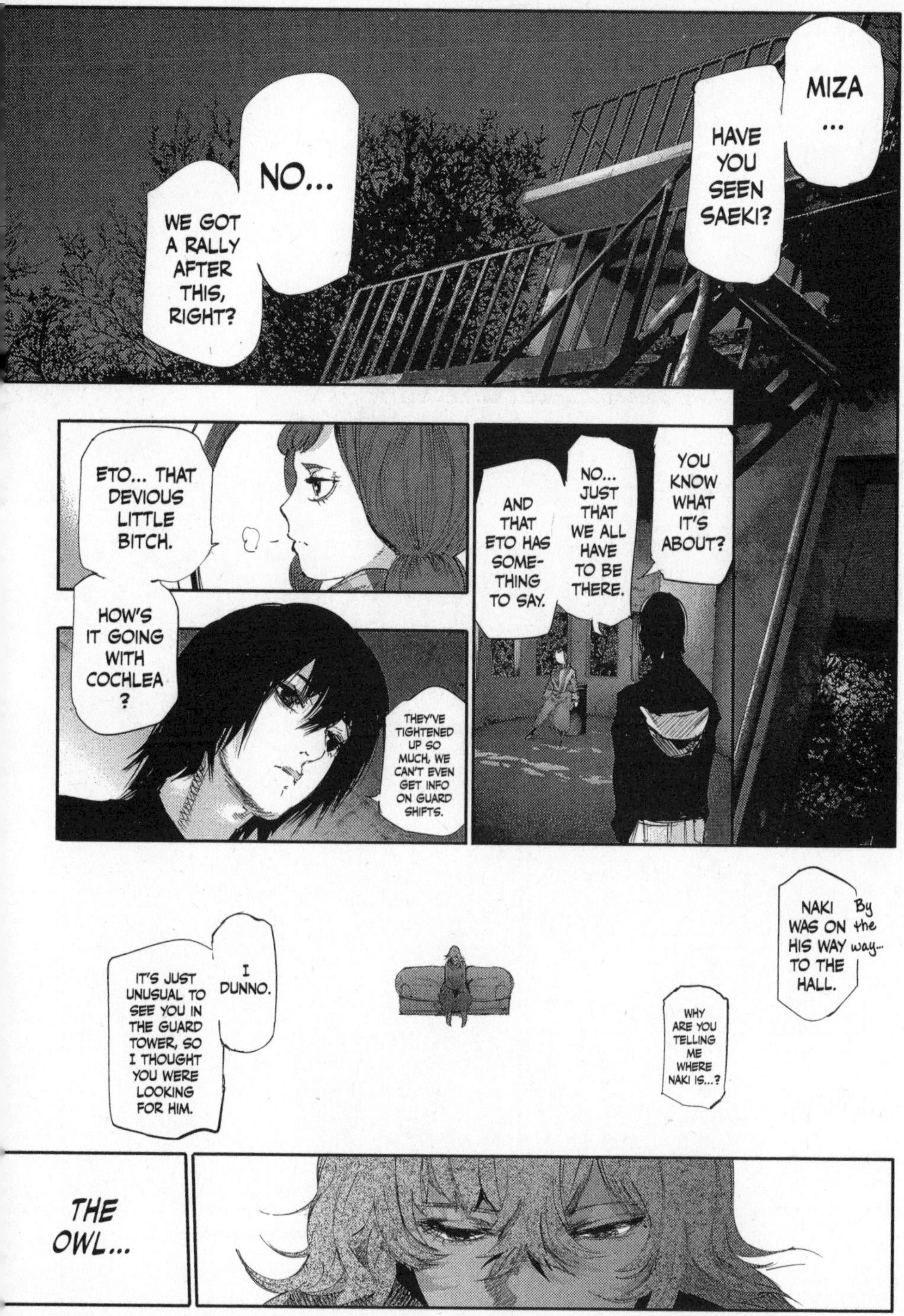
MIZA ...
HAVE YOU SEEN SAEKI?
NO...
WE GOT A RALLY AFTER THIS, RIGHT?
YOU KNOW WHAT IT'S ABOUT?
NO... JUST THAT WE ALL HAVE TO BE THERE.
AND THAT ETO HAS SOME-THING TO SAY.
ETO... THAT DEVIOUS LITTLE BITCH.
HOW'S IT GOING WITH COCHLEA?
THEY'VE TIGHTENED UP SO MUCH, WE CAN'T EVEN GET INFO ON GUARD SHIFTS.
By the way...
NAKI WAS ON HIS WAY TO THE HALL.
WHY ARE YOU TELLING ME WHERE NAKI IS...?
I DUNNO.
IT'S JUST UNUSUAL TO SEE YOU IN THE GUARD TOWER, SO I THOUGHT YOU WERE LOOKING FOR HIM.
THE OWL...

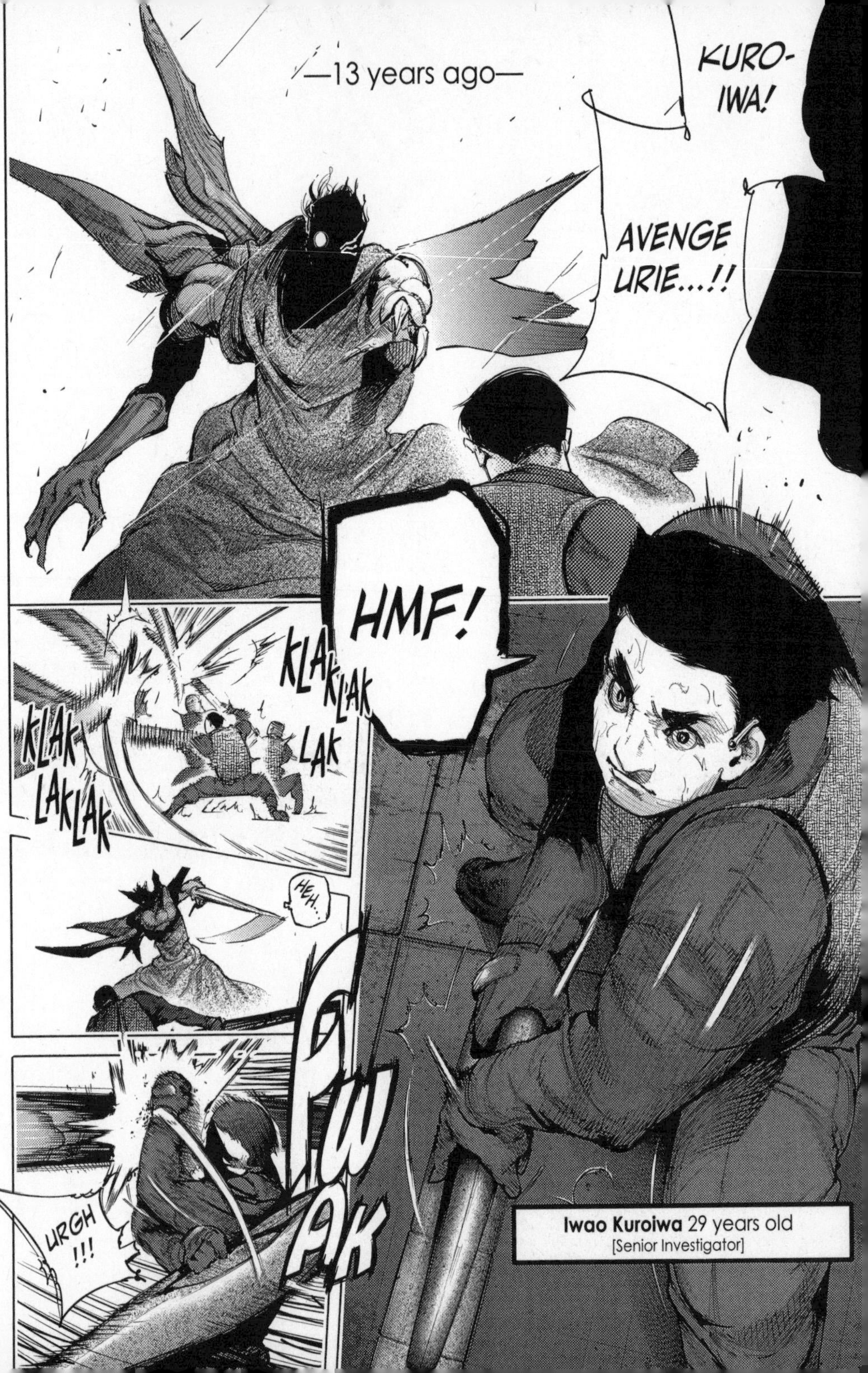
—13 years ago—
KURO-IWA!
AVENGE URIE...!!
HMF!
Iwao Kuroiwa 29 years old
[Senior Investigator]
KLAKKLAK LAK
KLAK-LAKLAK
HEH...
THWAK
URGH!!!

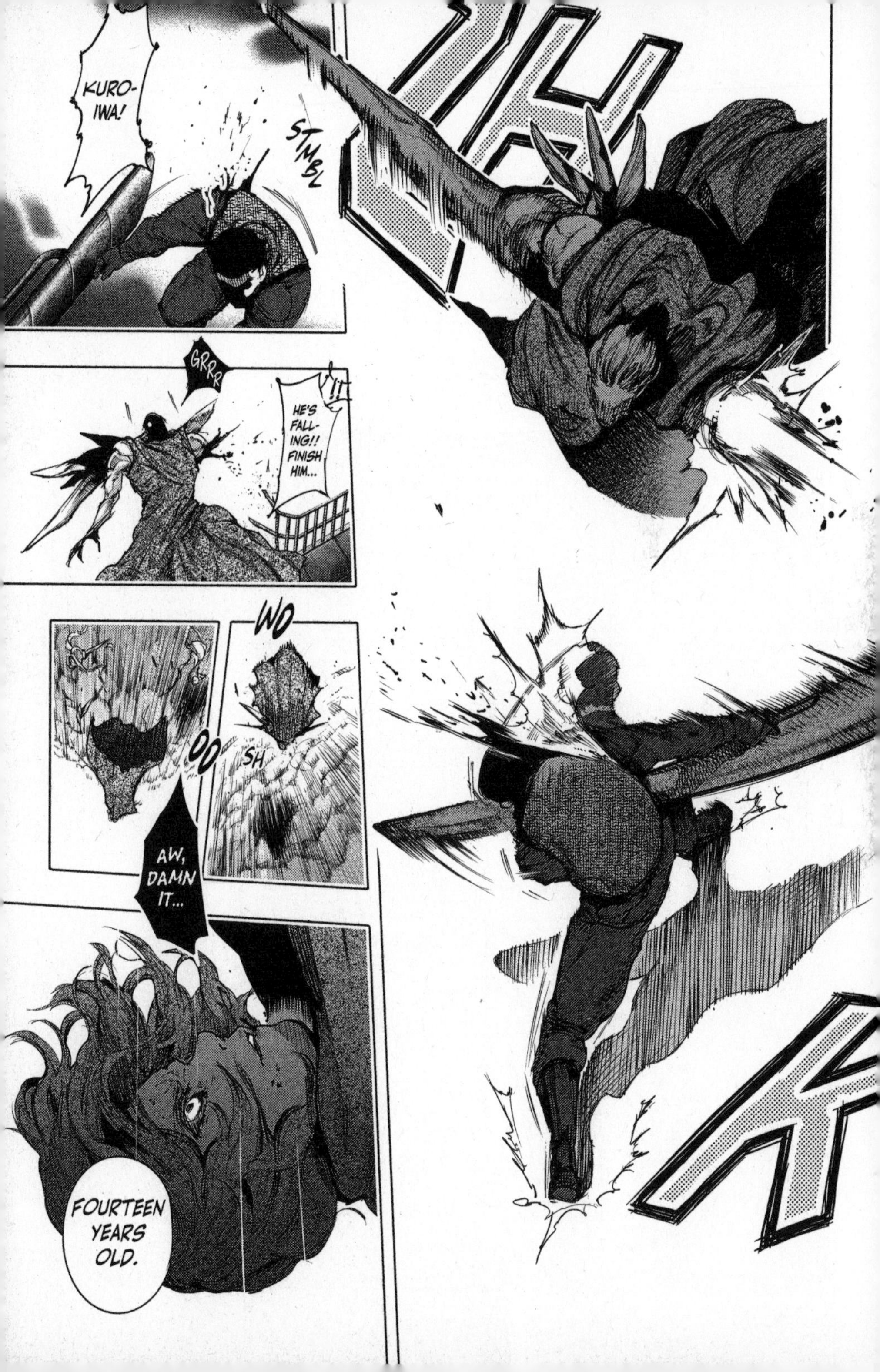
KURO-IWA!
STMBL
GRRR
!!
HE'S FALLING!! FINISH HIM...
WO
SH
OO
AW, DAMN IT...
FOURTEEN YEARS OLD.

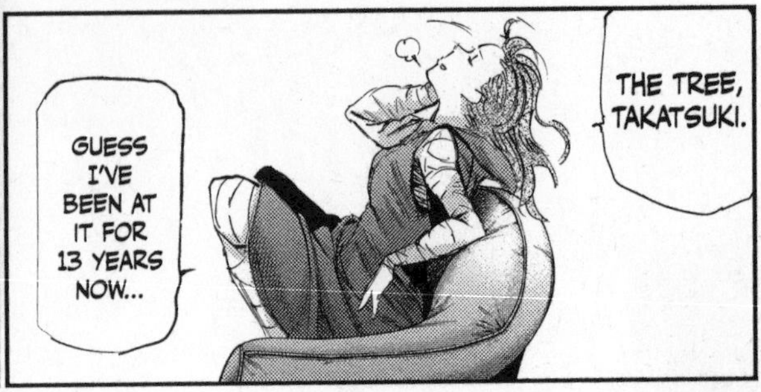
THE TREE, TAKATSUKI.
GUESS I'VE BEEN AT IT FOR 13 YEARS NOW...

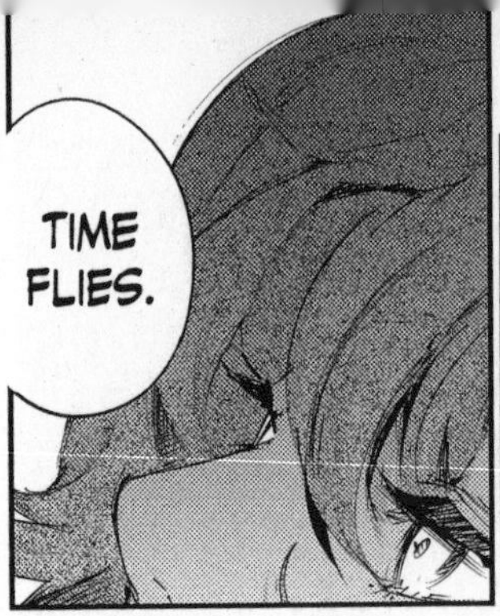
TIME FLIES.

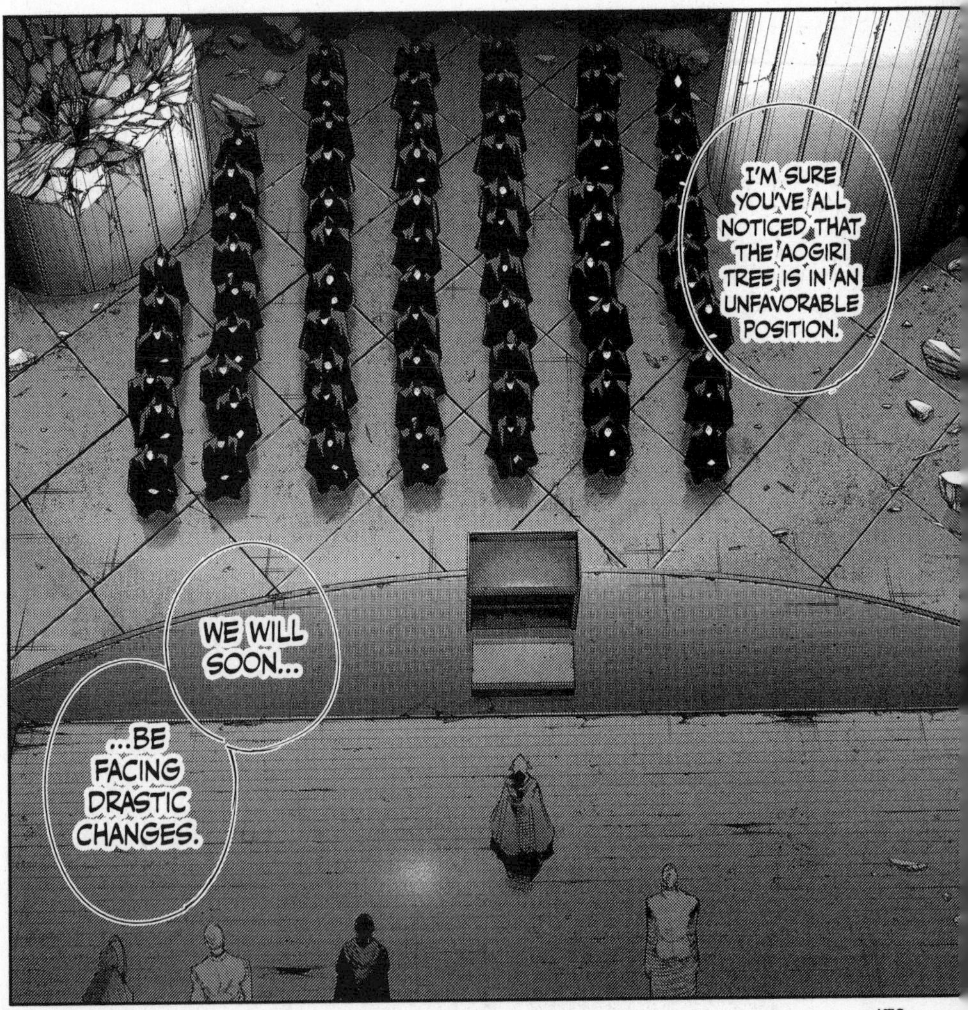
I'M SURE YOU'VE ALL NOTICED THAT THE AOGIRI TREE IS IN AN UNFAVORABLE POSITION.
WE WILL SOON...
...BE FACING DRASTIC CHANGES.

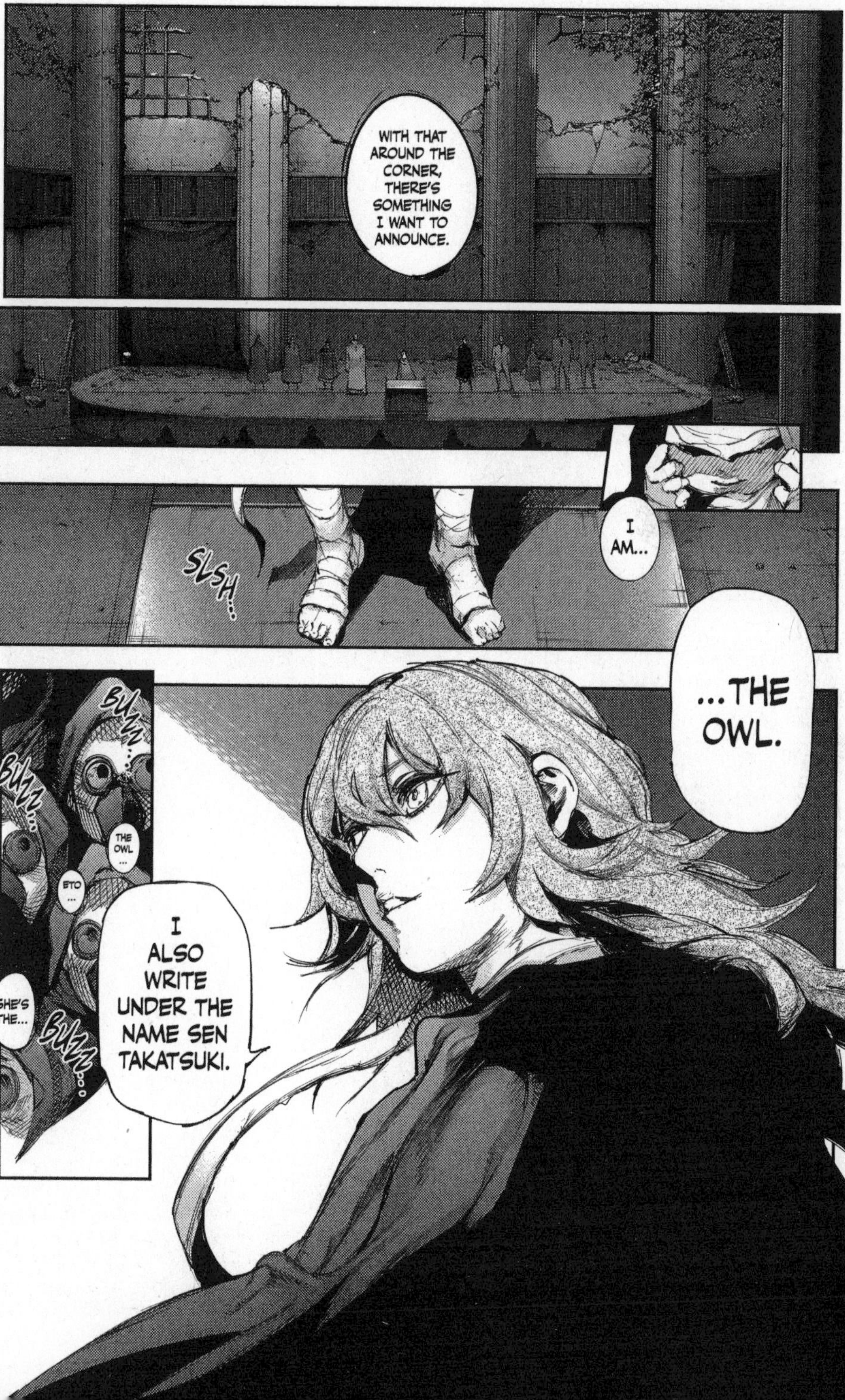
WITH THAT AROUND THE CORNER, THERE'S SOMETHING I WANT TO ANNOUNCE.
I AM...
SLSH...
...THE OWL.
I ALSO WRITE UNDER THE NAME SEN TAKATSUKI.
BUZZ...
BUZZ...
THE OWL...
ETO...
SHE'S THE...
BUZZ...

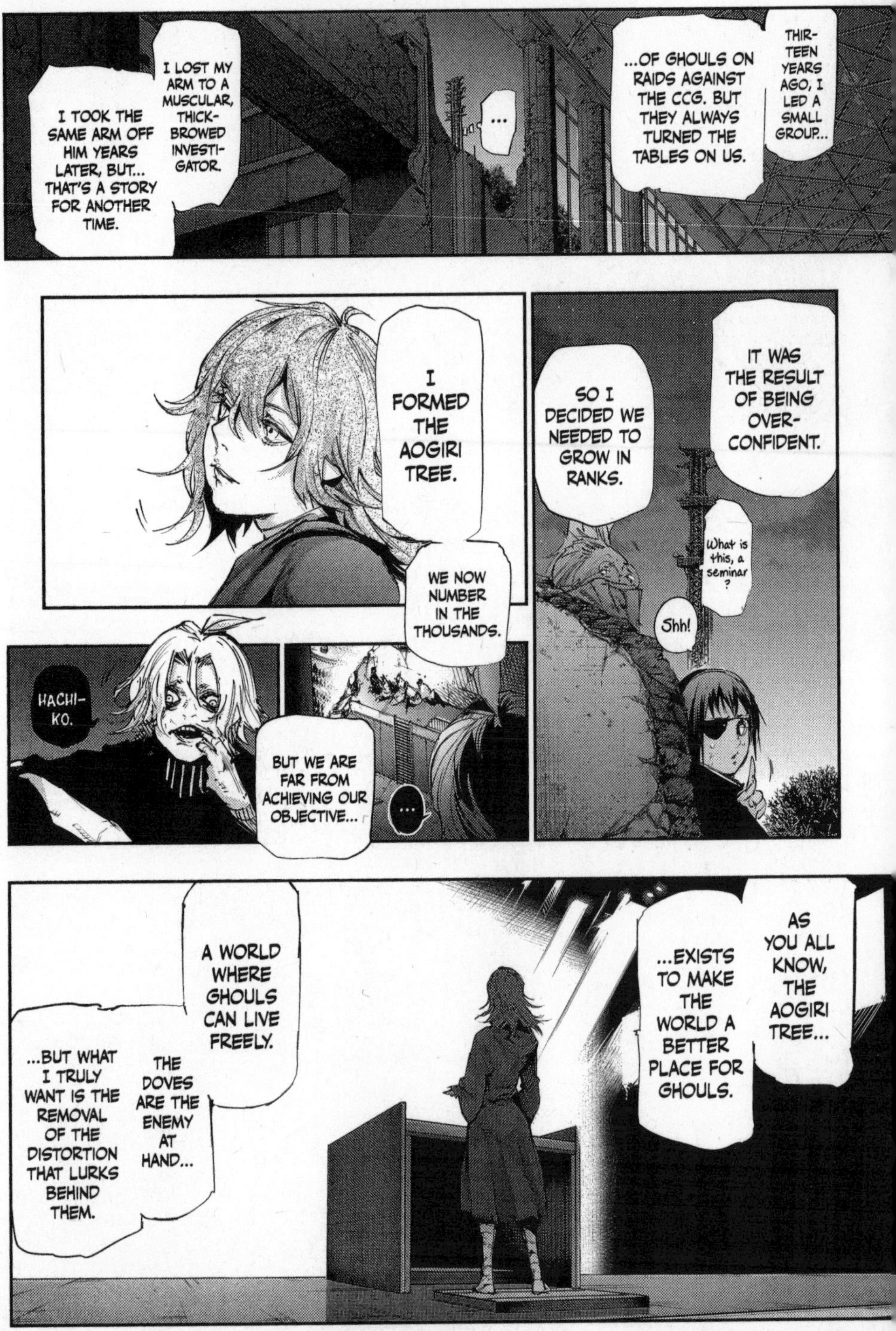
THIRTEEN YEARS AGO, I LED A SMALL GROUP...
...OF GHOULS ON RAIDS AGAINST THE CCG. BUT THEY ALWAYS TURNED THE TABLES ON US.
...
I LOST MY ARM TO A MUSCULAR, THICK-BROWED INVESTIGATOR.
I TOOK THE SAME ARM OFF HIM YEARS LATER, BUT... THAT'S A STORY FOR ANOTHER TIME.
IT WAS THE RESULT OF BEING OVER-CONFIDENT.
SO I DECIDED WE NEEDED TO GROW IN RANKS.
What is this, a seminar?
Shh!
I FORMED THE AOGIRI TREE.
WE NOW NUMBER IN THE THOUSANDS.
BUT WE ARE FAR FROM ACHIEVING OUR OBJECTIVE...
...
HACHIKO.
AS YOU ALL KNOW, THE AOGIRI TREE...
...EXISTS TO MAKE THE WORLD A BETTER PLACE FOR GHOULS.
A WORLD WHERE GHOULS CAN LIVE FREELY.
THE DOVES ARE THE ENEMY AT HAND...
...BUT WHAT I TRULY WANT IS THE REMOVAL OF THE DISTORTION THAT LURKS BEHIND THEM.

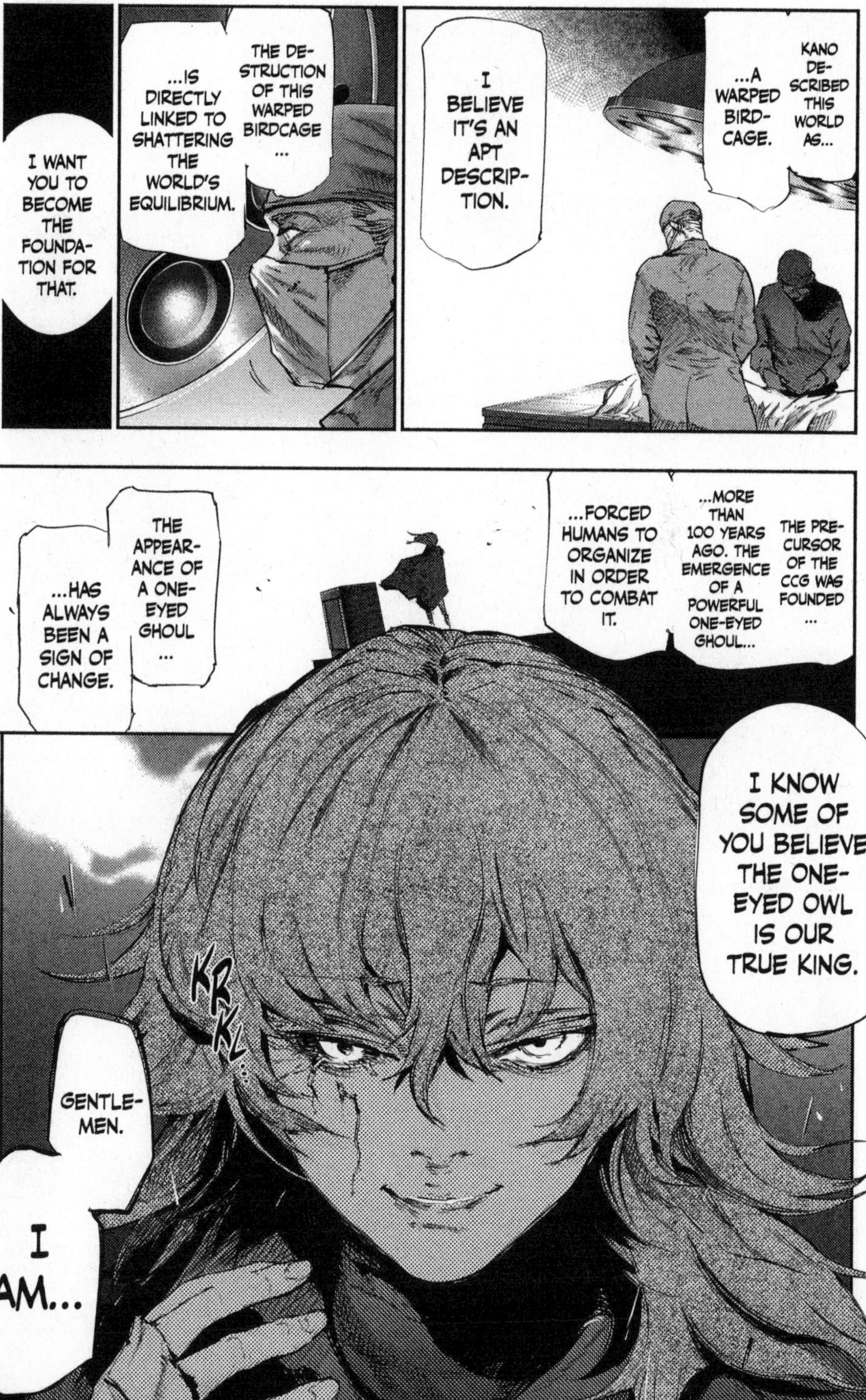
KANO DESCRIBED THIS WORLD AS...
...A WARPED BIRDCAGE.
I BELIEVE IT'S AN APT DESCRIPTION.
THE DESTRUCTION OF THIS WARPED BIRDCAGE...
...IS DIRECTLY LINKED TO SHATTERING THE WORLD'S EQUILIBRIUM.
I WANT YOU TO BECOME THE FOUNDATION FOR THAT.
THE PRECURSOR OF THE CCG WAS FOUNDED...
...MORE THAN 100 YEARS AGO. THE EMERGENCE OF A POWERFUL ONE-EYED GHOUL...
...FORCED HUMANS TO ORGANIZE IN ORDER TO COMBAT IT.
THE APPEARANCE OF A ONE-EYED GHOUL...
...HAS ALWAYS BEEN A SIGN OF CHANGE.
I KNOW SOME OF YOU BELIEVE THE ONE-EYED OWL IS OUR TRUE KING.
KRKL...
GENTLEMEN.
I AM...

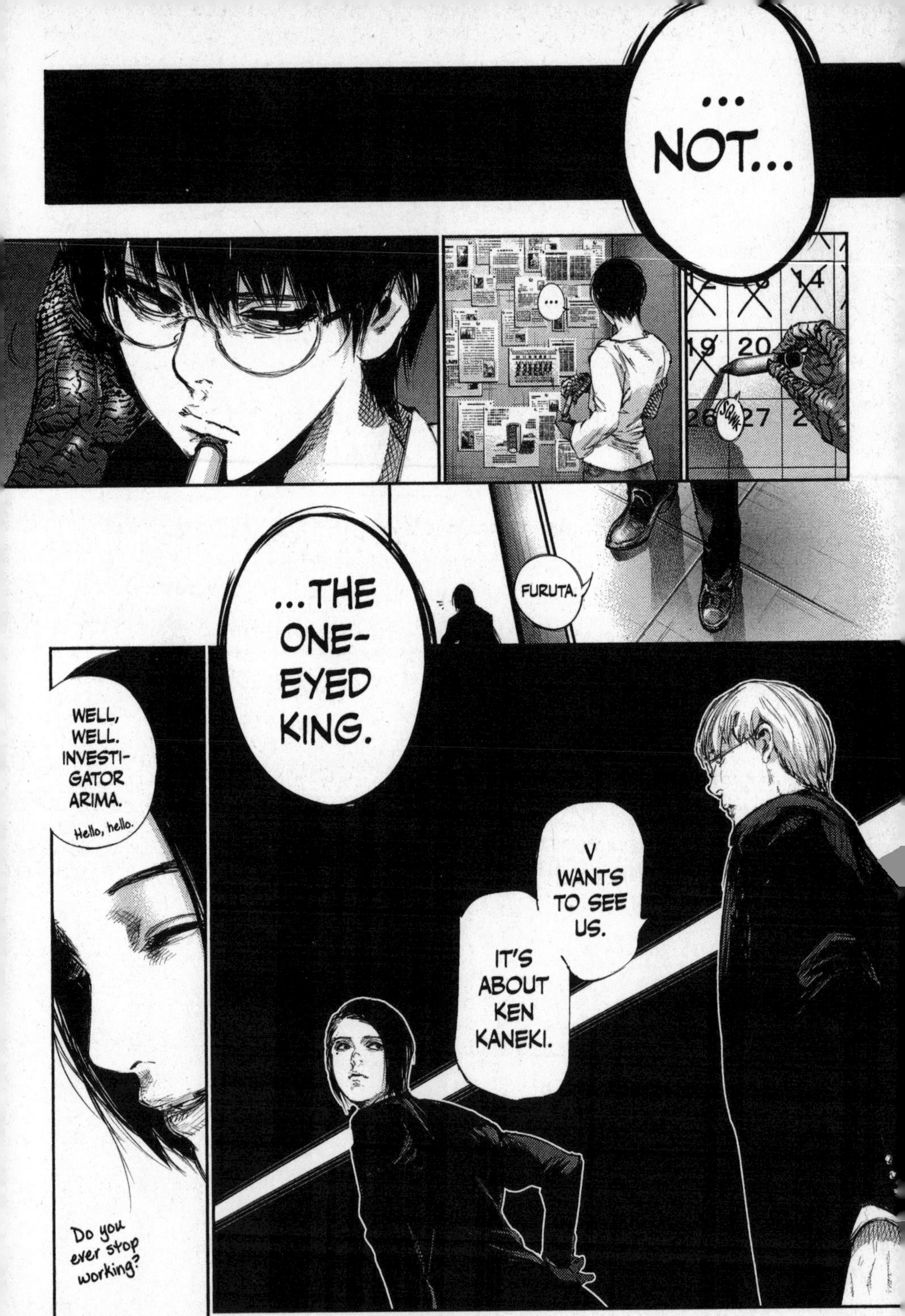
... NOT...
SQUNK
...
...THE ONE-EYED KING.
FURUTA.
V WANTS TO SEE US.
IT'S ABOUT KEN KANEKI.
WELL, WELL. INVESTIGATOR ARIMA.
Hello, hello.
Do you ever stop working?

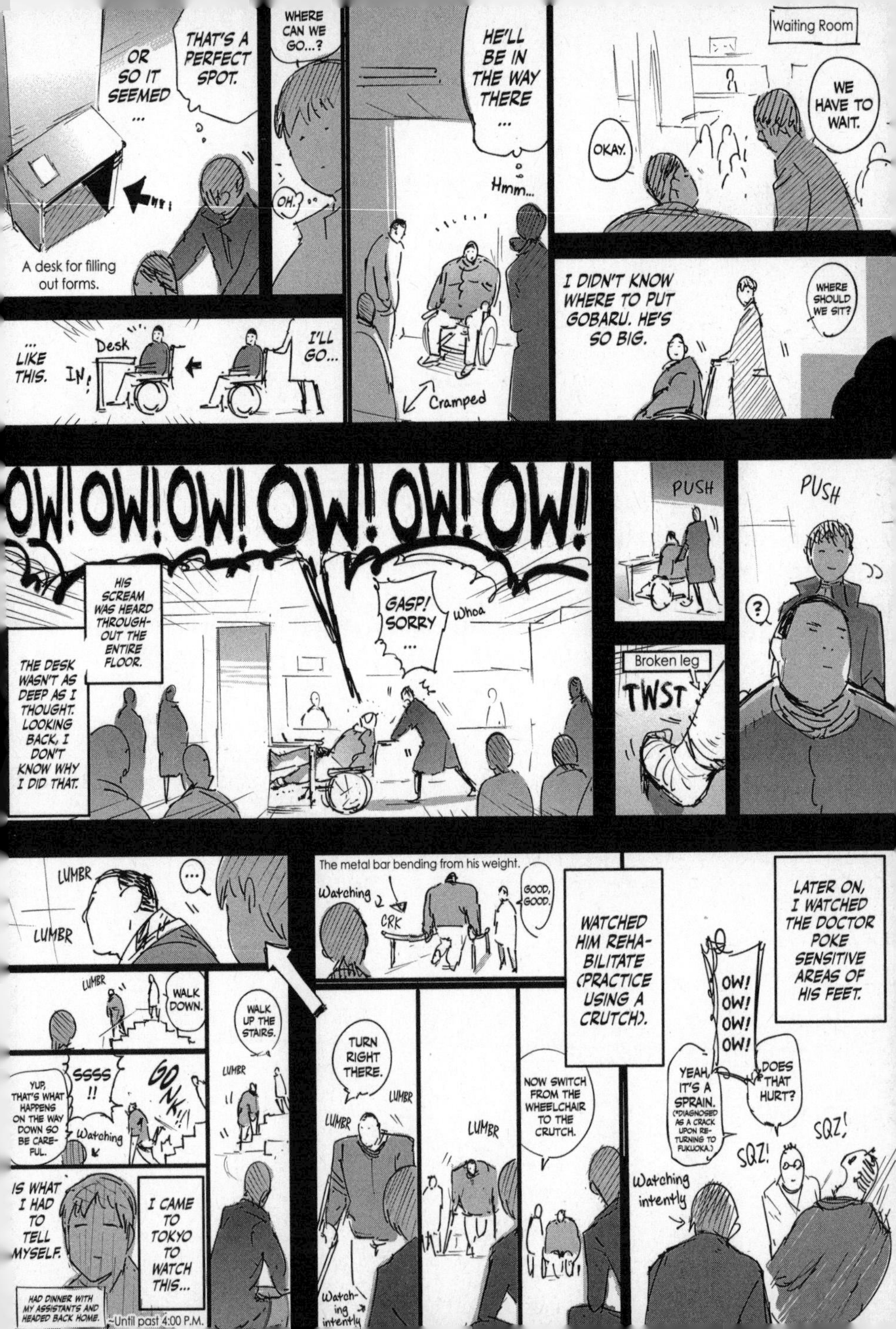

Waiting Room
WE HAVE TO WAIT.
OKAY.
I DIDN'T KNOW WHERE TO PUT GOBARU. HE'S SO BIG.
WHERE SHOULD WE SIT?
HE'LL BE IN THE WAY THERE ...
Hmm...
Cramped
WHERE CAN WE GO...?
OH.
THAT'S A PERFECT SPOT.
OR SO IT SEEMED ...
A desk for filling out forms.
I'LL GO...
... LIKE THIS.
Desk
IN
PUSH
?
PUSH
Broken leg
TWST
OW! OW! OW! OW! OW! OW! OW!
HIS SCREAM WAS HEARD THROUGH-OUT THE ENTIRE FLOOR.
GASP! SORRY ...
Whoa
THE DESK WASN'T AS DEEP AS I THOUGHT. LOOKING BACK, I DON'T KNOW WHY I DID THAT.
LATER ON, I WATCHED THE DOCTOR POKE SENSITIVE AREAS OF HIS FEET.
OW! OW! OW! OW!
DOES THAT HURT?
SQZ!
SQZ!
YEAH, IT'S A SPRAIN.
(*DIAGNOSED AS A CRACK UPON RE-TURNING TO FUKUOKA.)
Watching intently
WATCHED HIM REHA-BILITATE (PRACTICE USING A CRUTCH).
NOW SWITCH FROM THE WHEELCHAIR TO THE CRUTCH.
LUMBR
The metal bar bending from his weight.
GOOD, GOOD.
Watching
CRK
TURN RIGHT THERE.
LUMBR
LUMBR
Watch-ing intently
...
LUMBR
LUMBR
WALK UP THE STAIRS.
LUMBR
LUMBR
WALK DOWN.
GONK
SSSS !!
YUP, THAT'S WHAT HAPPENS ON THE WAY DOWN SO BE CARE-FUL.
Watching
I CAME TO TOKYO TO WATCH THIS...
IS WHAT I HAD TO TELL MYSELF.
HAD DINNER WITH MY ASSISTANTS AND HEADED BACK HOME.
~Until past 4:00 P.M.

Holding the City :62

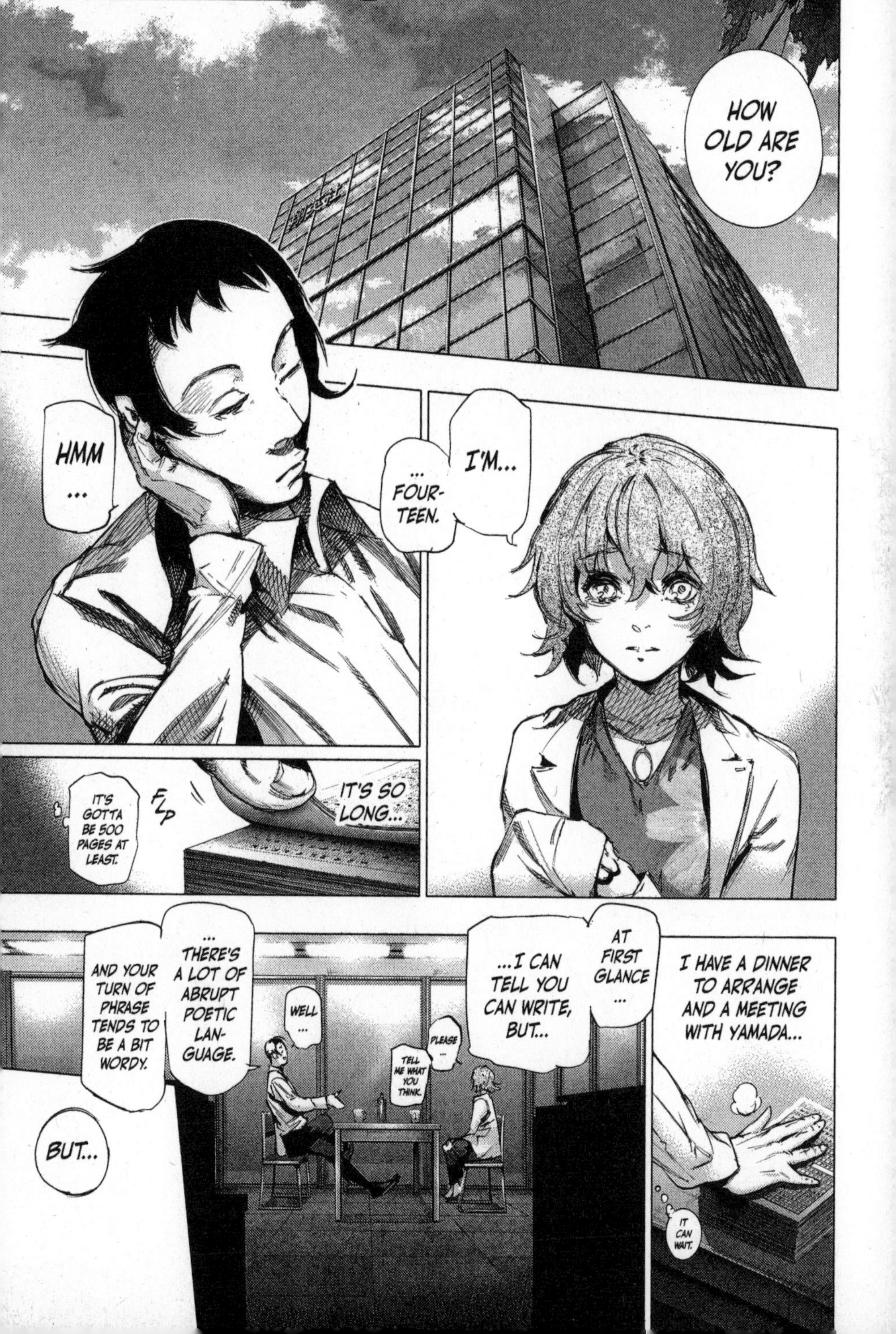
HOW OLD ARE YOU?
I'M...
... FOUR-TEEN.
HMM ...
IT'S SO LONG...
FLP
IT'S GOTTA BE 500 PAGES AT LEAST.
I HAVE A DINNER TO ARRANGE AND A MEETING WITH YAMADA...
IT CAN WAIT.
AT FIRST GLANCE ...
...I CAN TELL YOU CAN WRITE, BUT...
PLEASE ...
TELL ME WHAT YOU THINK.
WELL ...
... THERE'S A LOT OF ABRUPT POETIC LAN-GUAGE.
AND YOUR TURN OF PHRASE TENDS TO BE A BIT WORDY.
BUT...

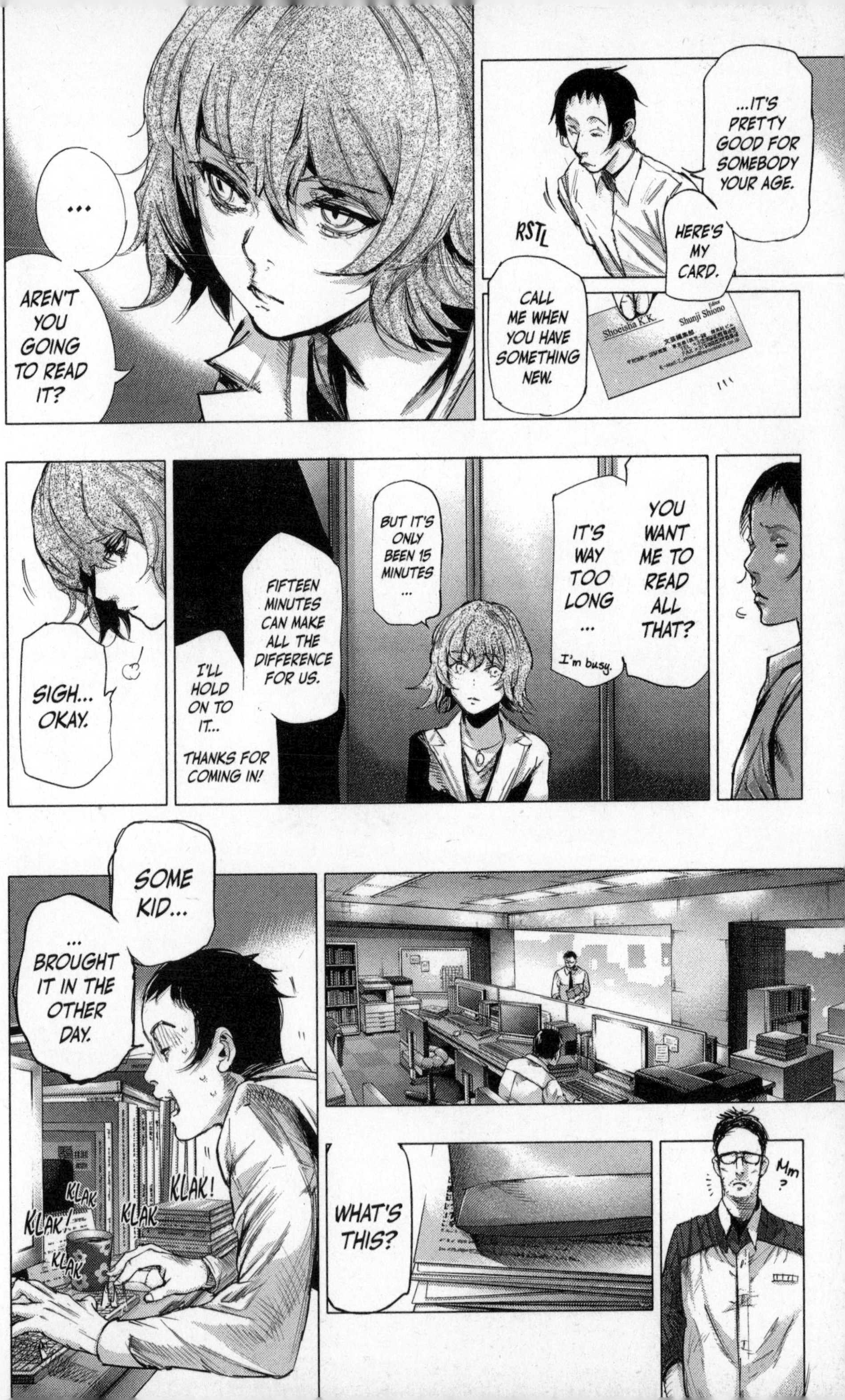
...IT'S PRETTY GOOD FOR SOMEBODY YOUR AGE.
RSTL
HERE'S MY CARD.
CALL ME WHEN YOU HAVE SOMETHING NEW.
Shoeisha K.K.
Editor
Shunji Shiono
...
AREN'T YOU GOING TO READ IT?
YOU WANT ME TO READ ALL THAT?
IT'S WAY TOO LONG...
I'm busy.
BUT IT'S ONLY BEEN 15 MINUTES...
FIFTEEN MINUTES CAN MAKE ALL THE DIFFERENCE FOR US.
I'LL HOLD ON TO IT...
THANKS FOR COMING IN!
SIGH... OKAY.
Mm?
WHAT'S THIS?
SOME KID...
...BROUGHT IT IN THE OTHER DAY.
KLAK!
KLAK
KLAK
KLAK!
KLAK

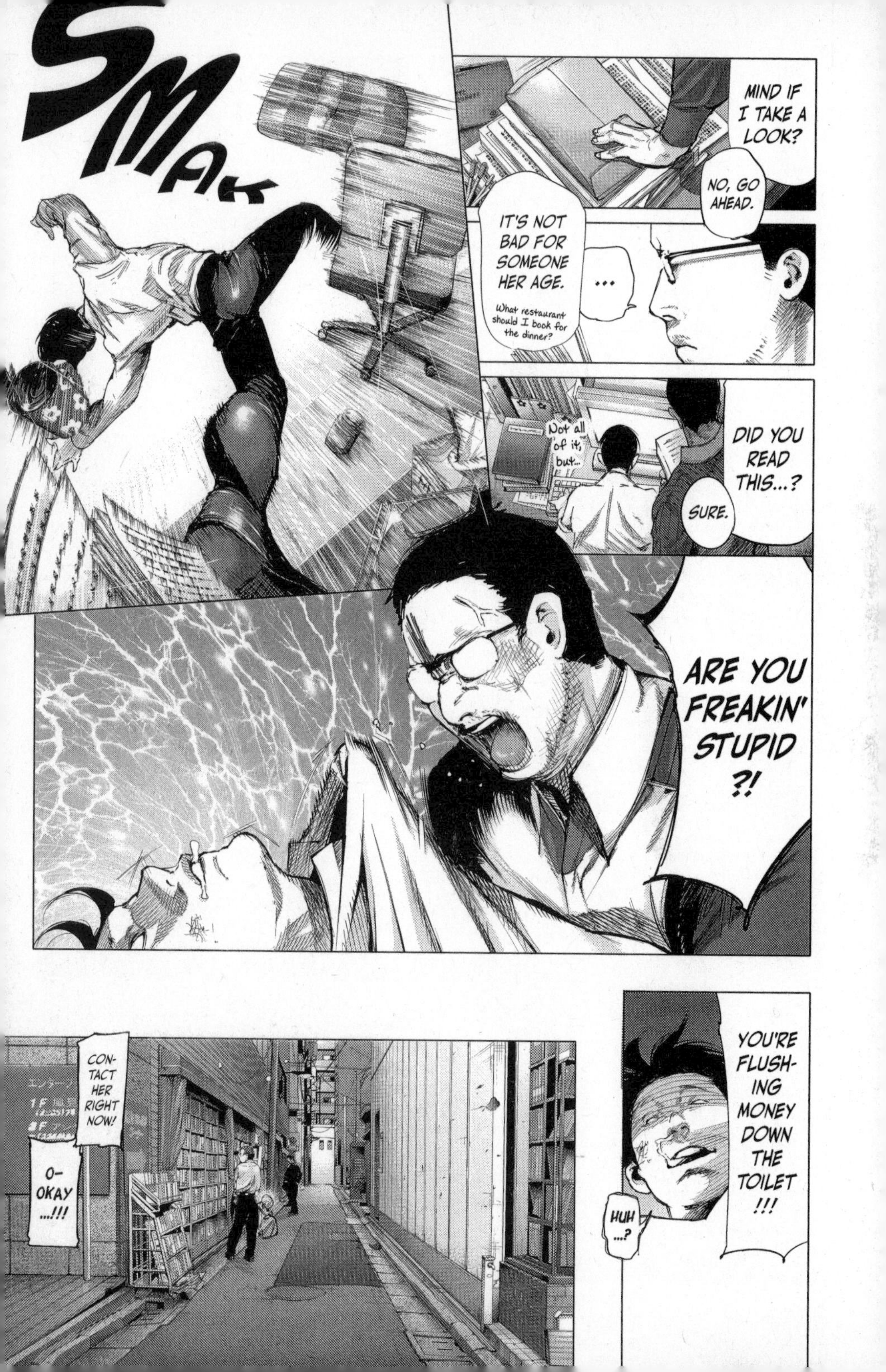
MIND IF I TAKE A LOOK?
NO, GO AHEAD.
...
IT'S NOT BAD FOR SOMEONE HER AGE.
What restaurant should I book for the dinner?
DID YOU READ THIS...?
SURE.
Not all of it, but...
ARE YOU FREAKIN' STUPID ?!
SMAK
YOU'RE FLUSH-ING MONEY DOWN THE TOILET !!!
HUH ...?
CON-TACT HER RIGHT NOW!
O-OKAY ...!!!

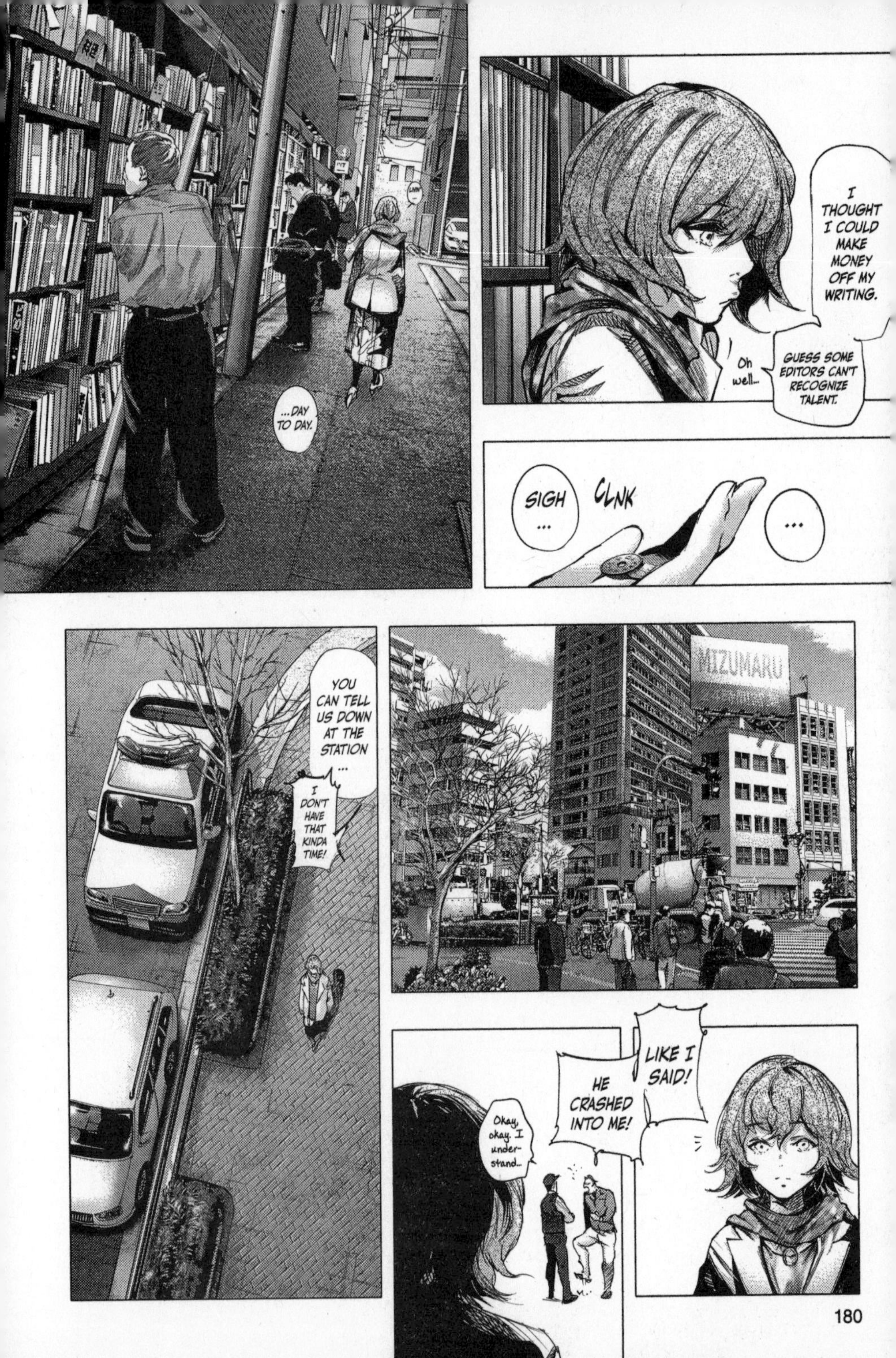
I THOUGHT I COULD MAKE MONEY OFF MY WRITING.
GUESS SOME EDITORS CAN'T RECOGNIZE TALENT.
Oh well...
...
CLNK
SIGH...
...DAY TO DAY.
MIZUMARU
LIKE I SAID!
HE CRASHED INTO ME!
Okay, okay. I under-stand...
YOU CAN TELL US DOWN AT THE STATION...
I DON'T HAVE THAT KINDA TIME!

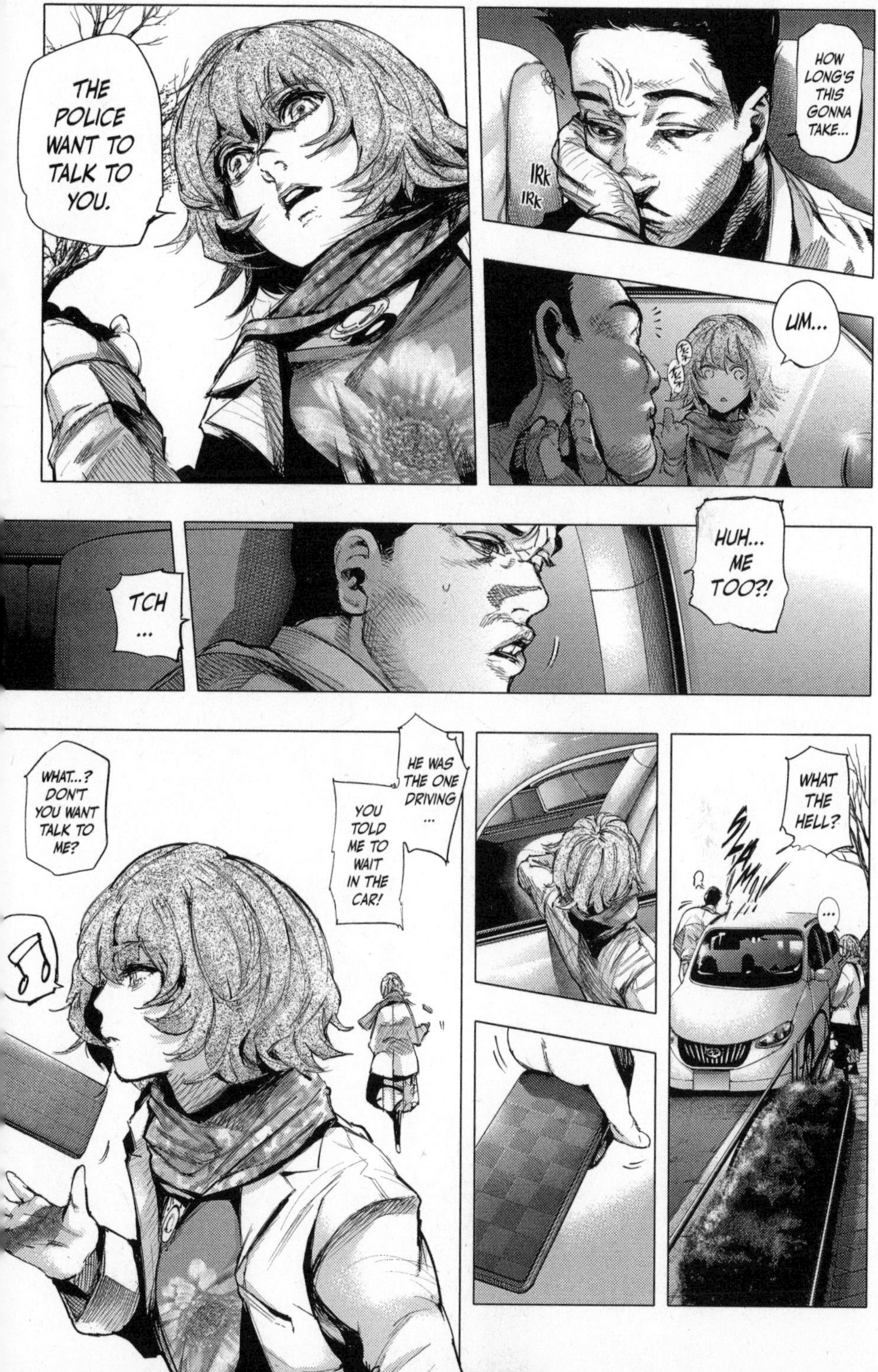
HOW LONG'S THIS GONNA TAKE...
IRK IRK
UM...
THE POLICE WANT TO TALK TO YOU.
HUH... ME TOO?!
TCH ...
WHAT THE HELL?
...
HE WAS THE ONE DRIVING ...
YOU TOLD ME TO WAIT IN THE CAR!
WHAT...? DON'T YOU WANT TALK TO ME?

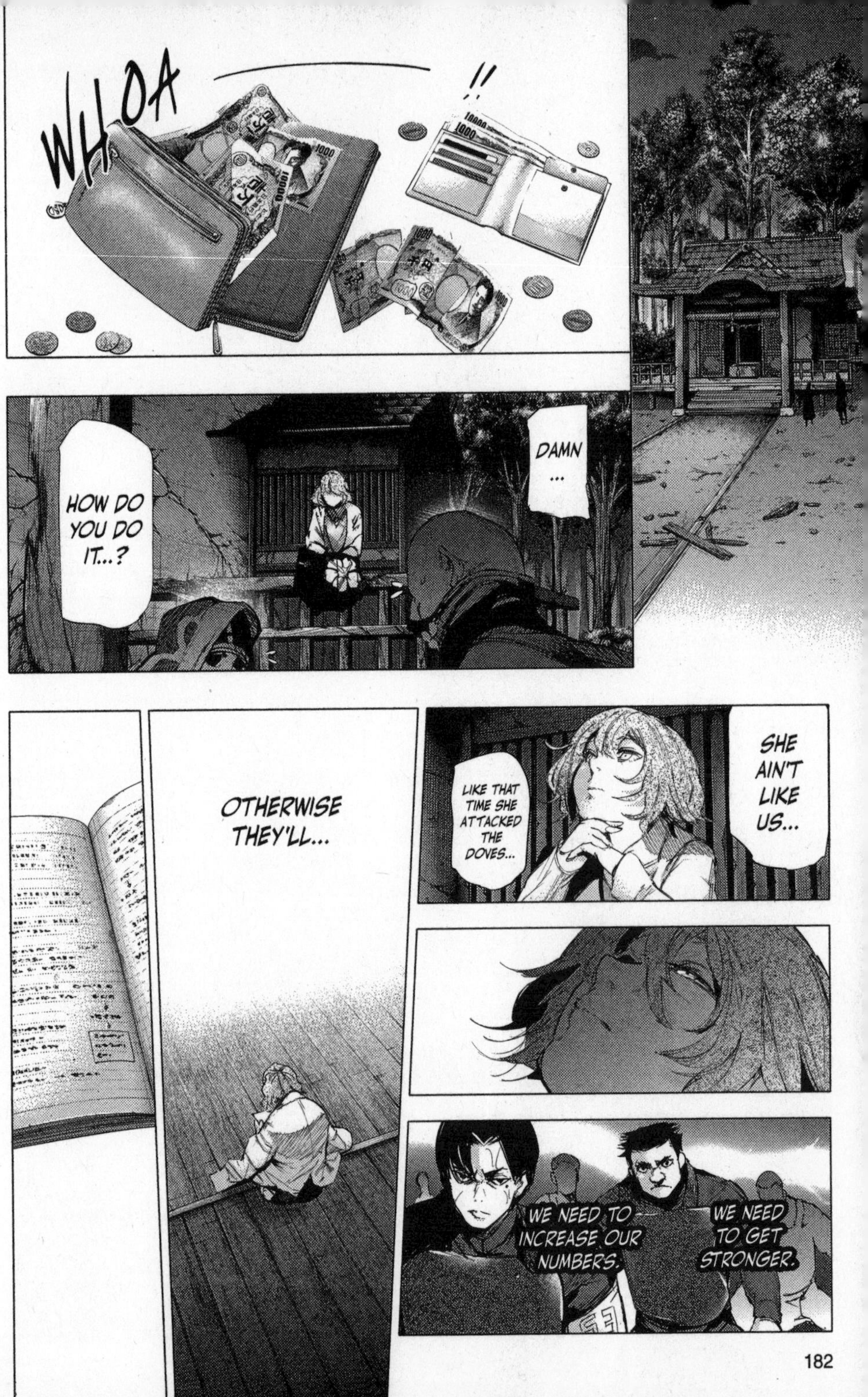
WHOA
!!
DAMN...
HOW DO YOU DO IT...?
SHE AIN'T LIKE US...
LIKE THAT TIME SHE ATTACKED THE DOVES...
WE NEED TO GET STRONGER.
WE NEED TO INCREASE OUR NUMBERS.
OTHERWISE THEY'LL...

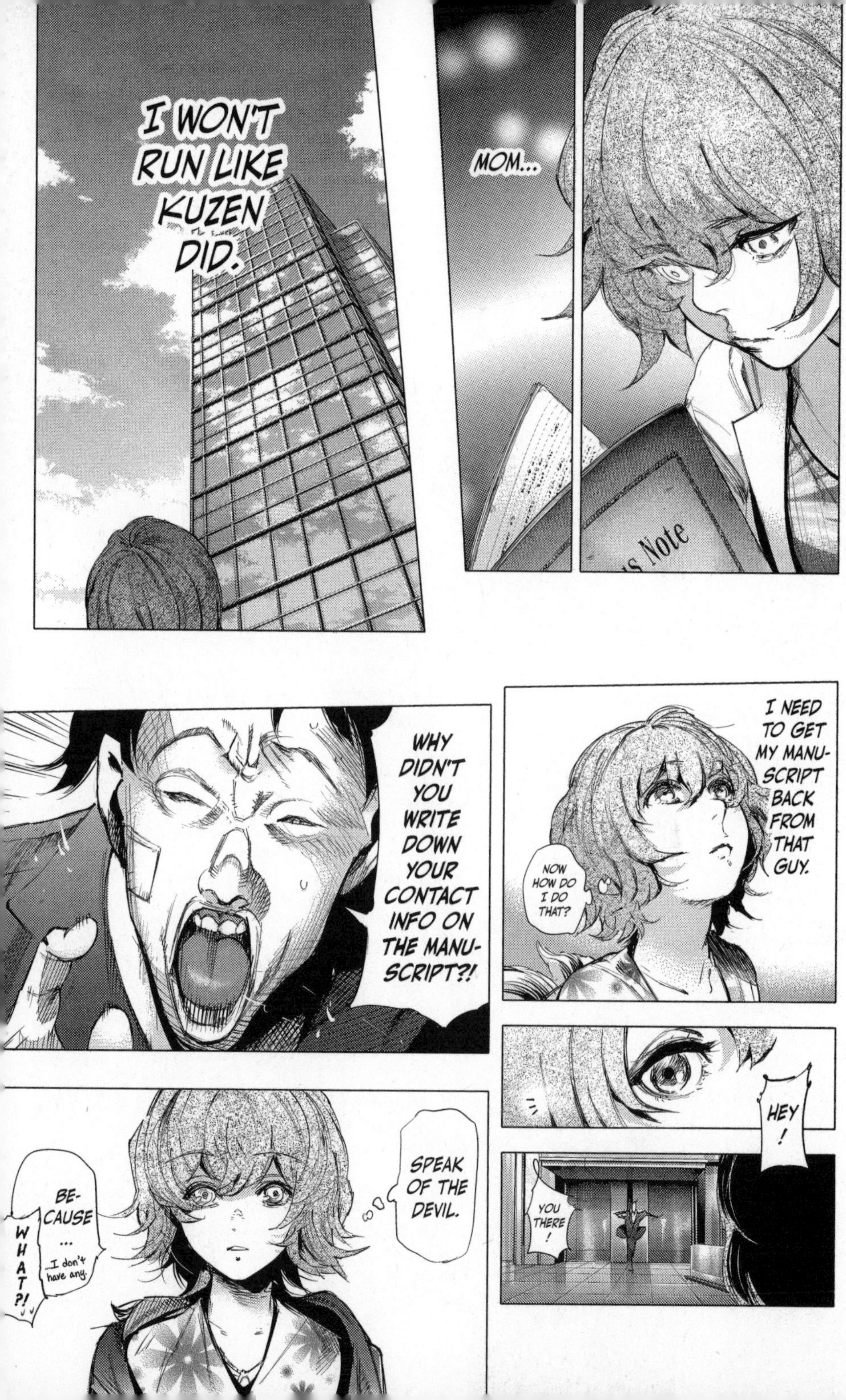

MOM...
I WON'T RUN LIKE KUZEN DID.
I NEED TO GET MY MANU-SCRIPT BACK FROM THAT GUY.
NOW HOW DO I DO THAT?
WHY DIDN'T YOU WRITE DOWN YOUR CONTACT INFO ON THE MANU-SCRIPT?!
HEY!
YOU THERE!
SPEAK OF THE DEVIL.
BE-CAUSE...
...I don't have any.
WHAT?!

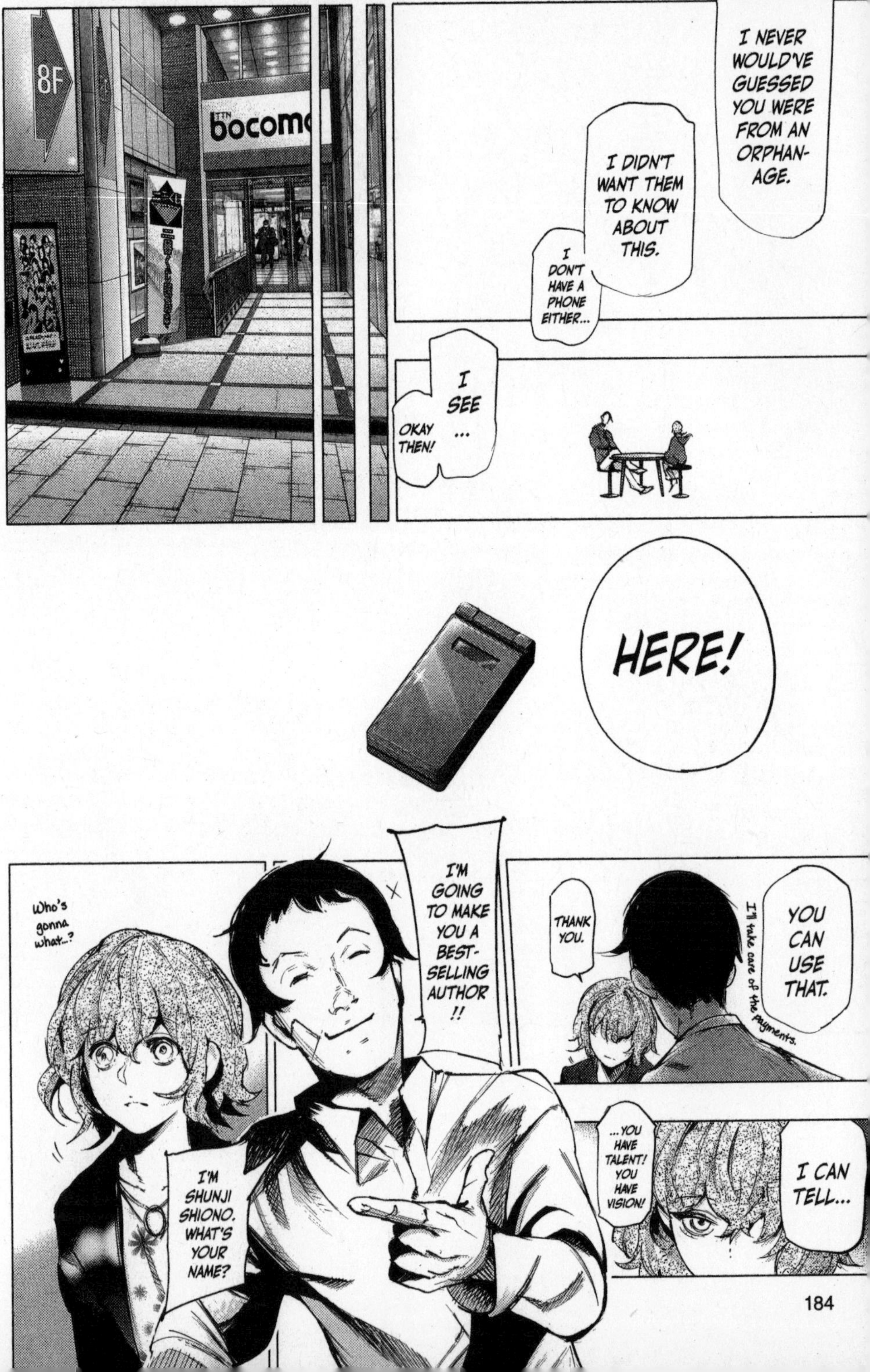
I NEVER WOULD'VE GUESSED YOU WERE FROM AN ORPHAN-AGE.
I DIDN'T WANT THEM TO KNOW ABOUT THIS.
I DON'T HAVE A PHONE EITHER...
I SEE ...
OKAY THEN!
8F
bocomo
HERE!
YOU CAN USE THAT.
I'll take care of the payments.
THANK YOU.
I CAN TELL...
...YOU HAVE TALENT! YOU HAVE VISION!
I'M GOING TO MAKE YOU A BEST-SELLING AUTHOR !!
I'M SHUNJI SHIONO. WHAT'S YOUR NAME?
Who's gonna what...?

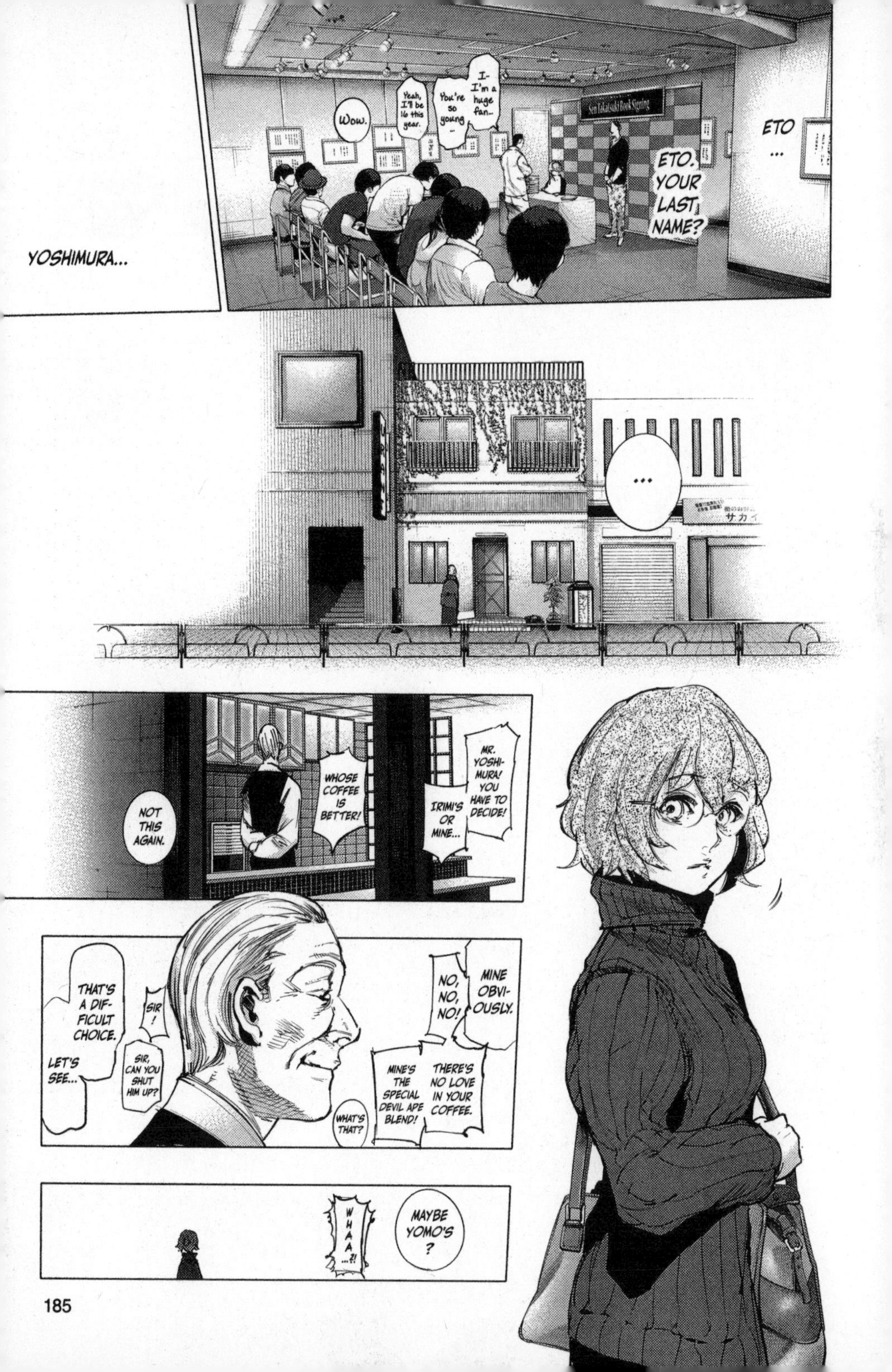
ETO ...
ETO. YOUR LAST NAME?
I- I'm a huge fan...
You're so young ...
Yeah, I'll be 16 this year.
Wow.
YOSHIMURA...
...
MR. YOSHIMURA! YOU HAVE TO DECIDE!
IRIMI'S OR MINE...
WHOSE COFFEE IS BETTER!
NOT THIS AGAIN.
MINE OBVIOUSLY.
NO, NO, NO!
THERE'S NO LOVE IN YOUR COFFEE.
MINE'S THE SPECIAL DEVIL APE BLEND!
WHAT'S THAT?
THAT'S A DIFFICULT CHOICE.
SIR!
SIR, CAN YOU SHUT HIM UP?
LET'S SEE...
MAYBE YOMO'S?
WHAAA...?!

CR   NKL...

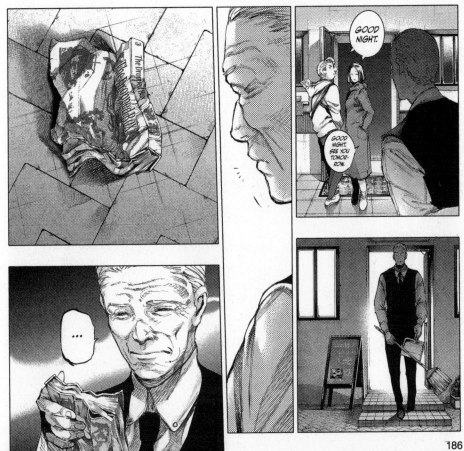

GOOD
NIGHT.

GOOD
NIGHT.
SEE YOU
TOMOR-
ROW.

...

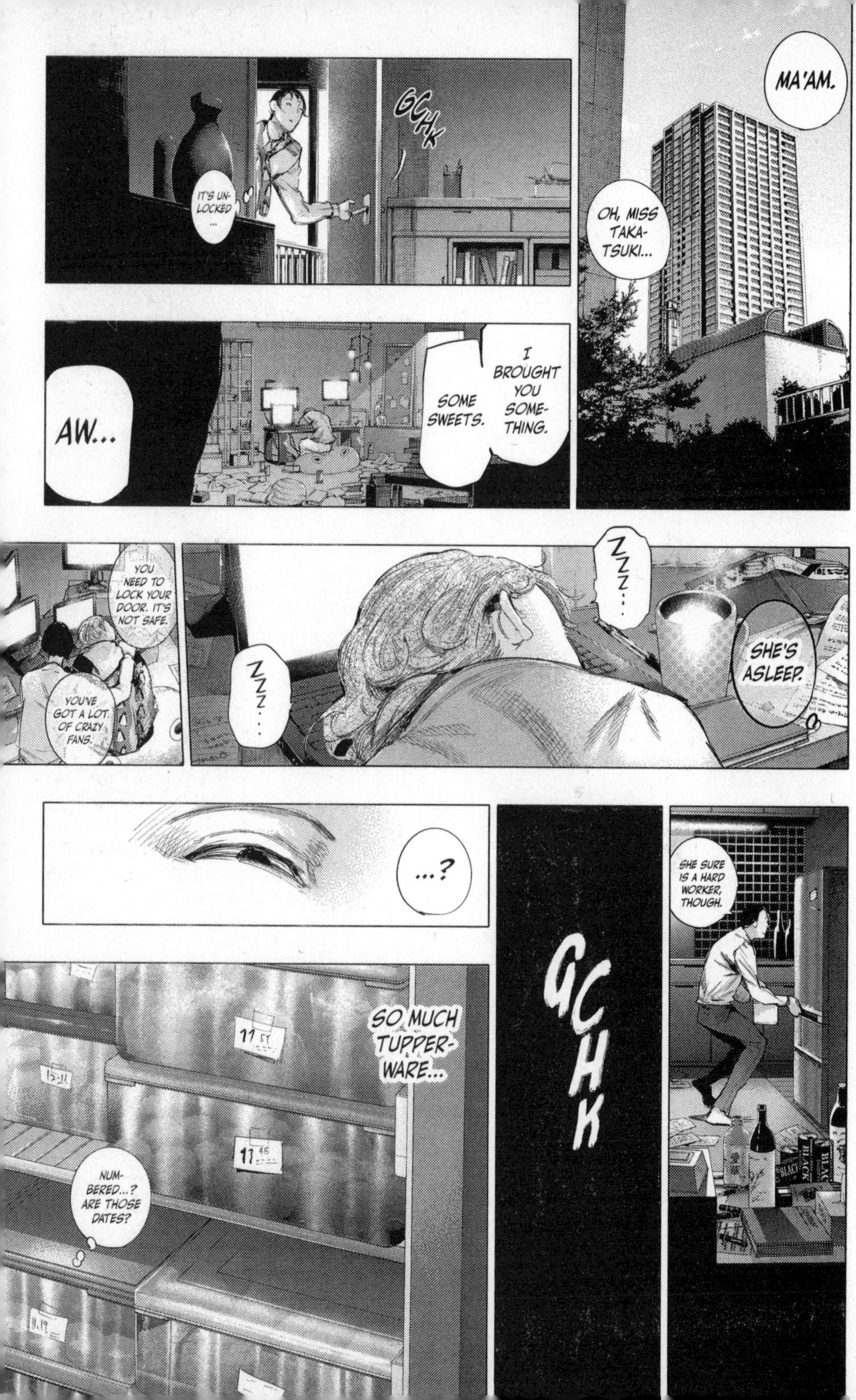
MA'AM.
OH, MISS TAKA-TSUKI...
GCHK
IT'S UN-LOCKED ...
I BROUGHT YOU SOME-THING.
SOME SWEETS.
AW...
ZZZ...
SHE'S ASLEEP.
ZZZ...
YOU NEED TO LOCK YOUR DOOR. IT'S NOT SAFE.
YOU'VE GOT A LOT OF CRAZY FANS.
SHE SURE IS A HARD WORKER, THOUGH.
GCHK
...?
SO MUCH TUPPER-WARE...
NUM-BERED...? ARE THOSE DATES?

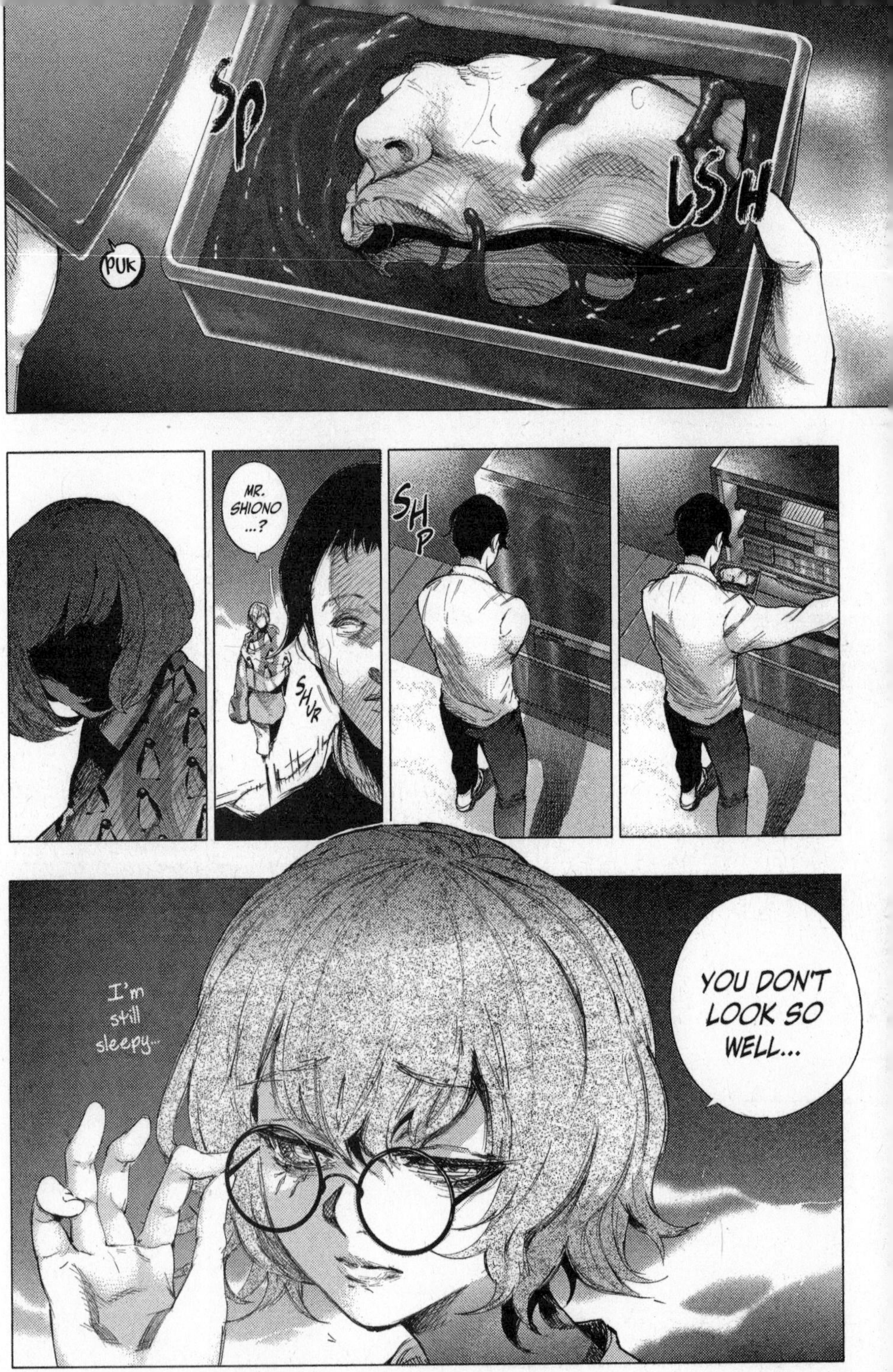
SP
LSH
PUK
SHP
MR. SHIONO ...?
SHJR
YOU DON'T LOOK SO WELL...
I'm still sleepy...

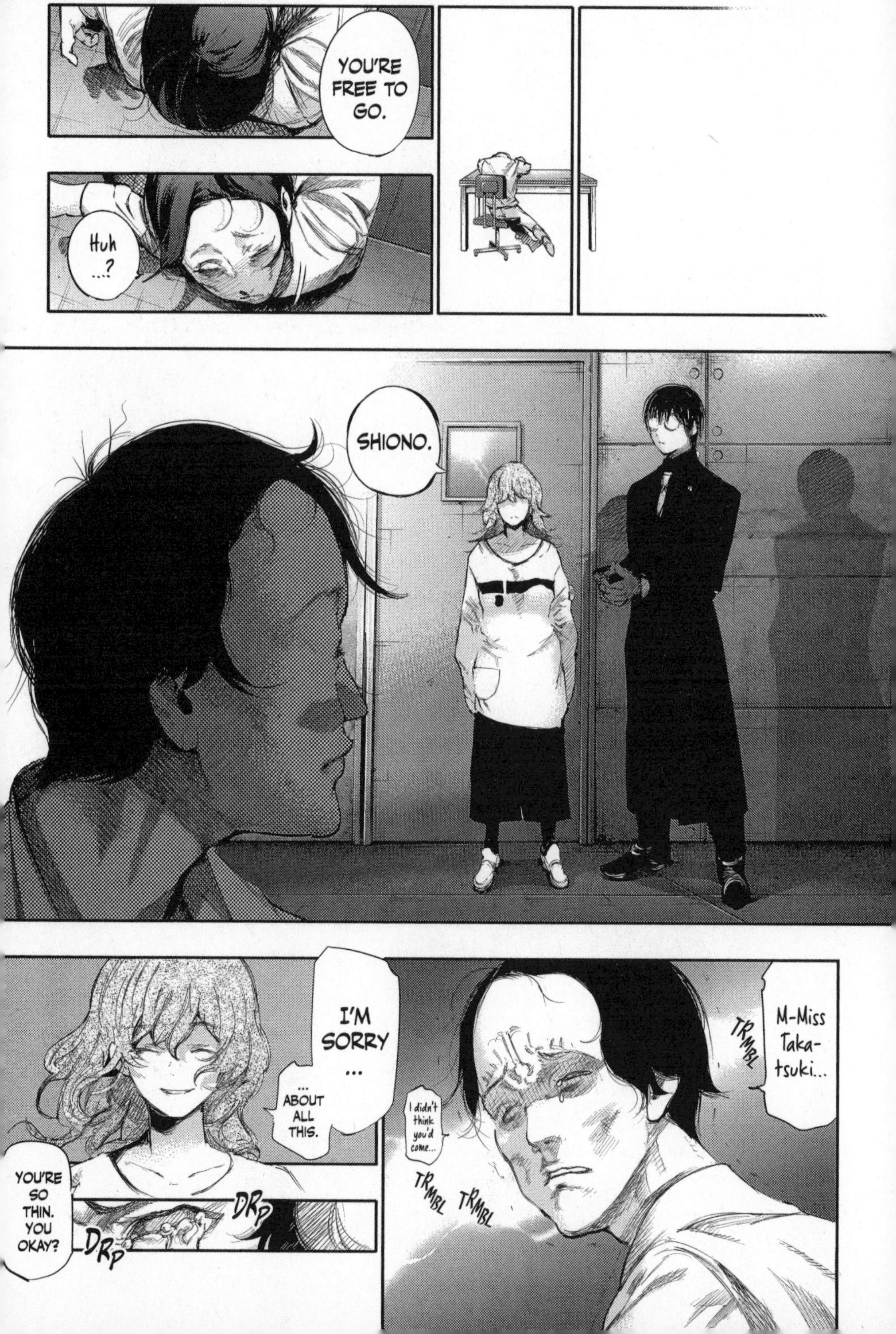
YOU'RE FREE TO GO.
Huh ...?
SHIONO.
M-Miss Taka-tsuki...
TRMBL
I didn't think you'd come...
TRMBL
TRMBL
I'M SORRY ...
... ABOUT ALL THIS.
DRP
DRP
YOU'RE SO THIN. YOU OKAY?

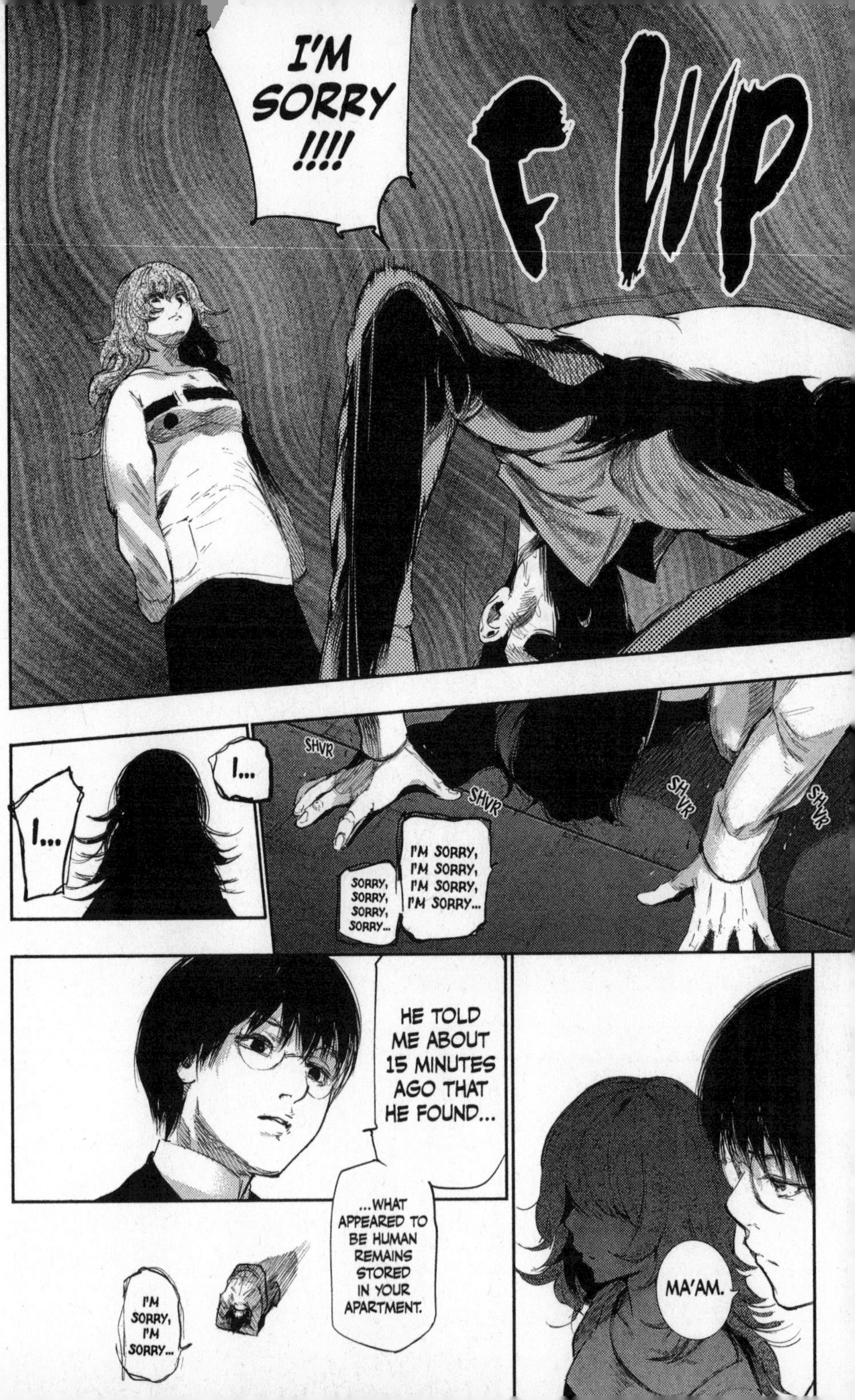
FWP
I'M SORRY !!!!
SHVR
SHVR
SHVR
SHVR
I'M SORRY, I'M SORRY, I'M SORRY, I'M SORRY...
SORRY, SORRY, SORRY, SORRY...
I...
I...
MA'AM.
HE TOLD ME ABOUT 15 MINUTES AGO THAT HE FOUND...
...WHAT APPEARED TO BE HUMAN REMAINS STORED IN YOUR APARTMENT.
I'M SORRY, I'M SORRY...

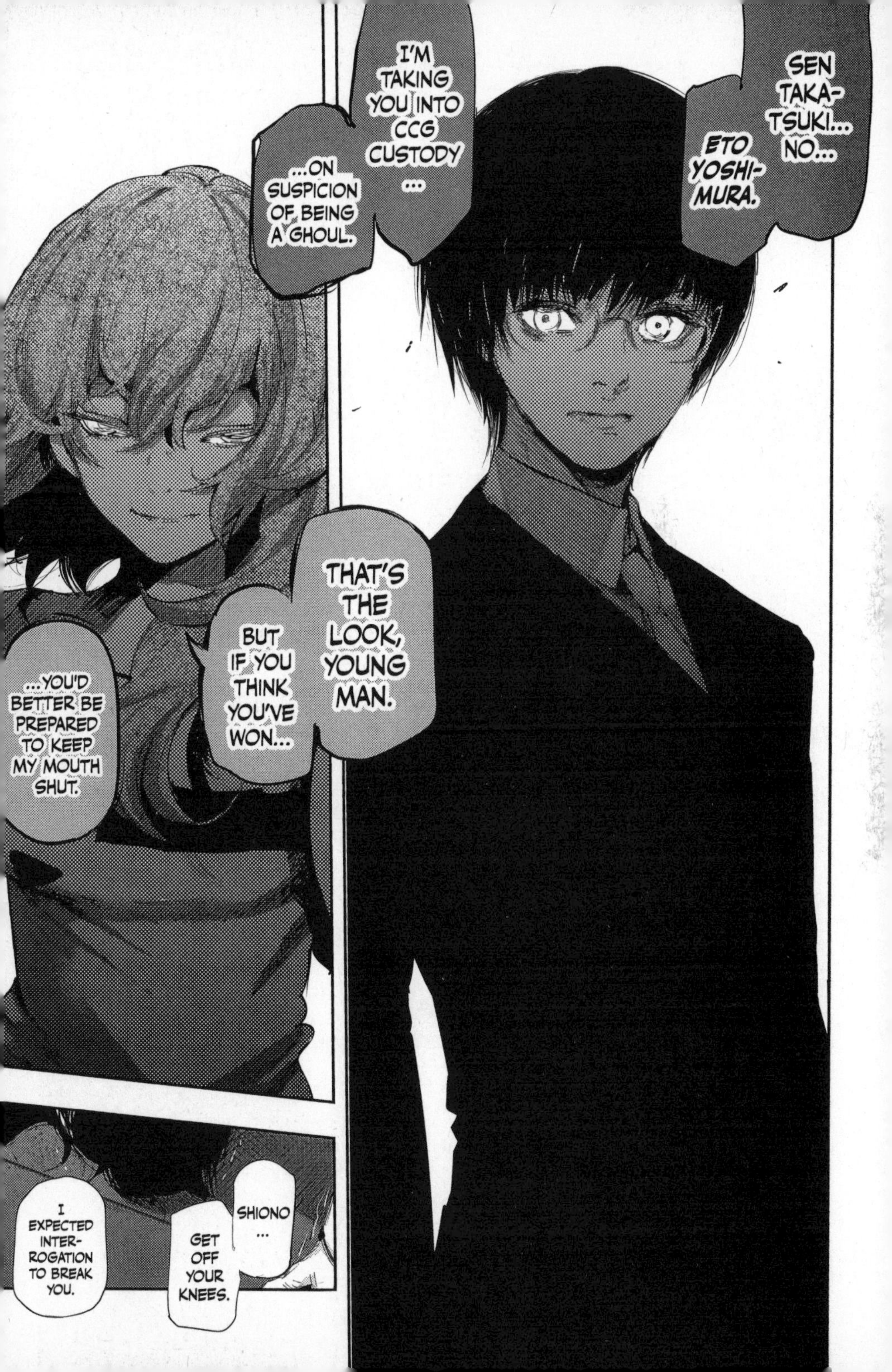
SEN TAKA-TSUKI... NO...
ETO YOSHI-MURA.
I'M TAKING YOU INTO CCG CUSTODY...
...ON SUSPICION OF BEING A GHOUL.
THAT'S THE LOOK, YOUNG MAN.
BUT IF YOU THINK YOU'VE WON...
...YOU'D BETTER BE PREPARED TO KEEP MY MOUTH SHUT.
SHIONO...
GET OFF YOUR KNEES.
I EXPECTED INTER-ROGATION TO BREAK YOU.

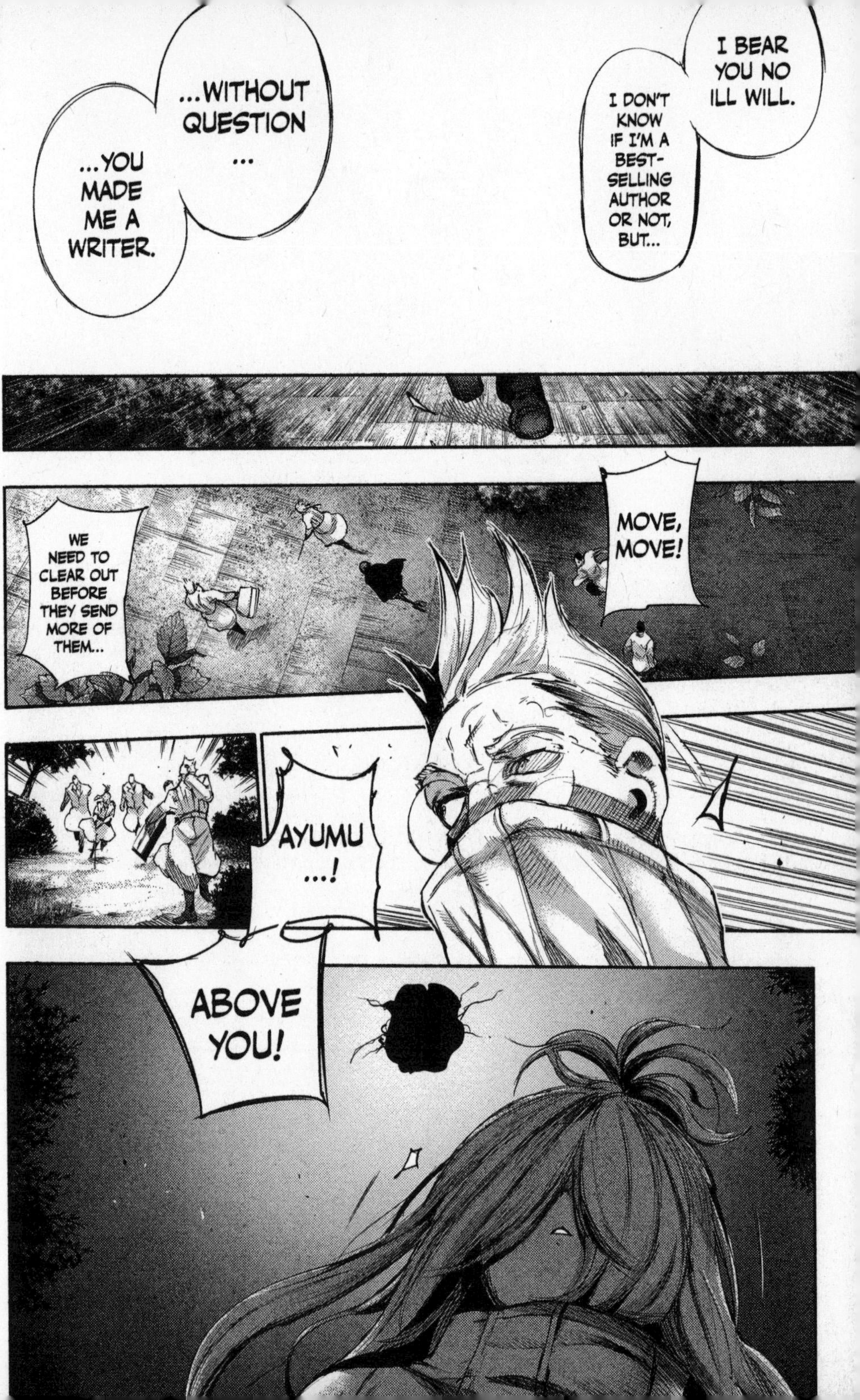
I BEAR YOU NO ILL WILL.
I DON'T KNOW IF I'M A BEST-SELLING AUTHOR OR NOT, BUT...
...WITHOUT QUESTION ...
...YOU MADE ME A WRITER.
MOVE, MOVE!
WE NEED TO CLEAR OUT BEFORE THEY SEND MORE OF THEM...
AYUMU ...!
ABOVE YOU!

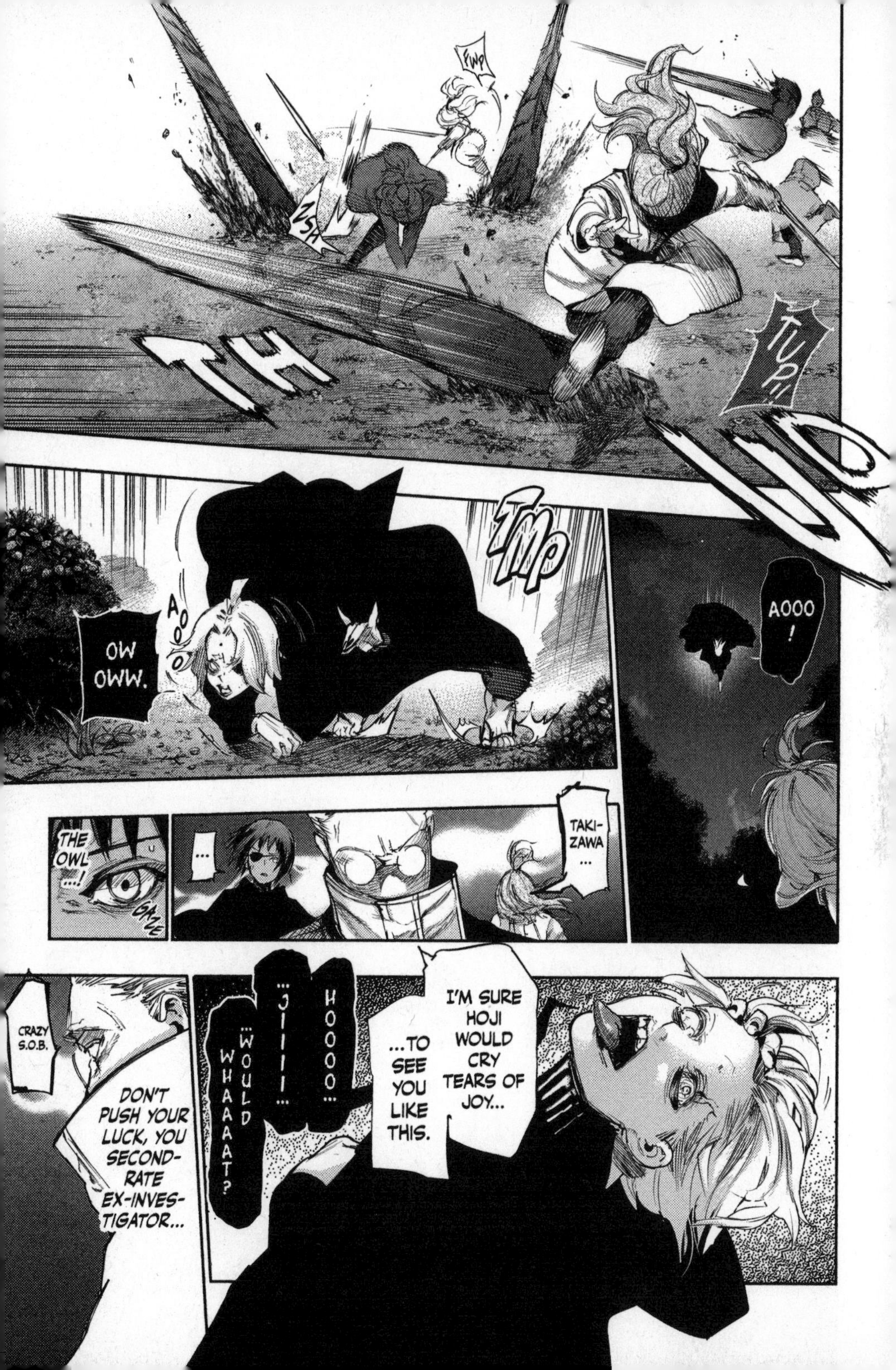
TUP!!
FWP
ZSH
THUD
AOOO!
TMP
AOOO
OW OWW.
TAKIZAWA...
...
THE OWL...!
GAZE
I'M SURE HOJI WOULD CRY TEARS OF JOY...
...TO SEE YOU LIKE THIS.
HOOOO...
...JIIII...
...WOULD WHAAAAT?
DON'T PUSH YOUR LUCK, YOU SECOND-RATE EX-INVESTIGATOR...
CRAZY S.O.B.

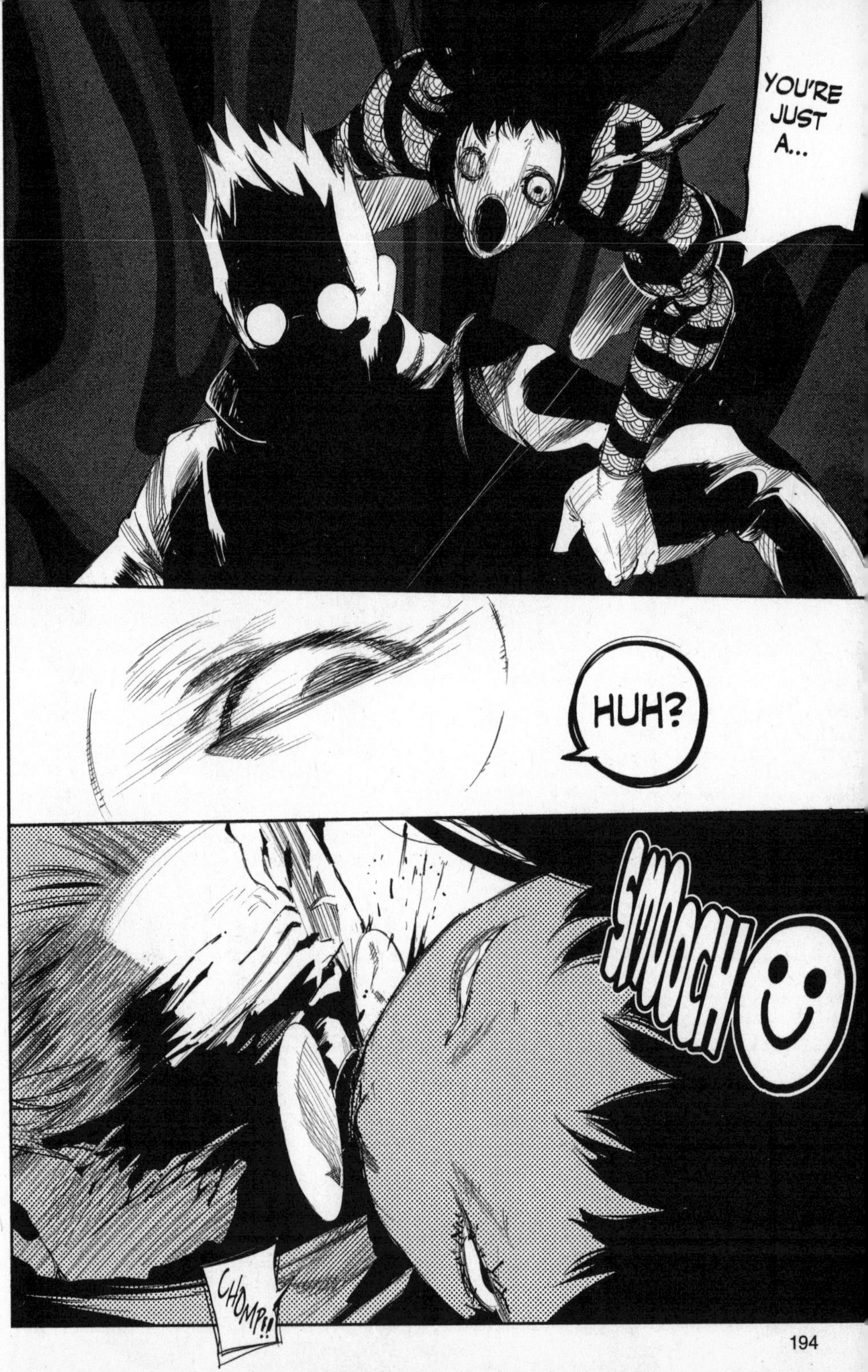
YOU'RE JUST A...
HUH?
SMOOCH
CHOMP!!

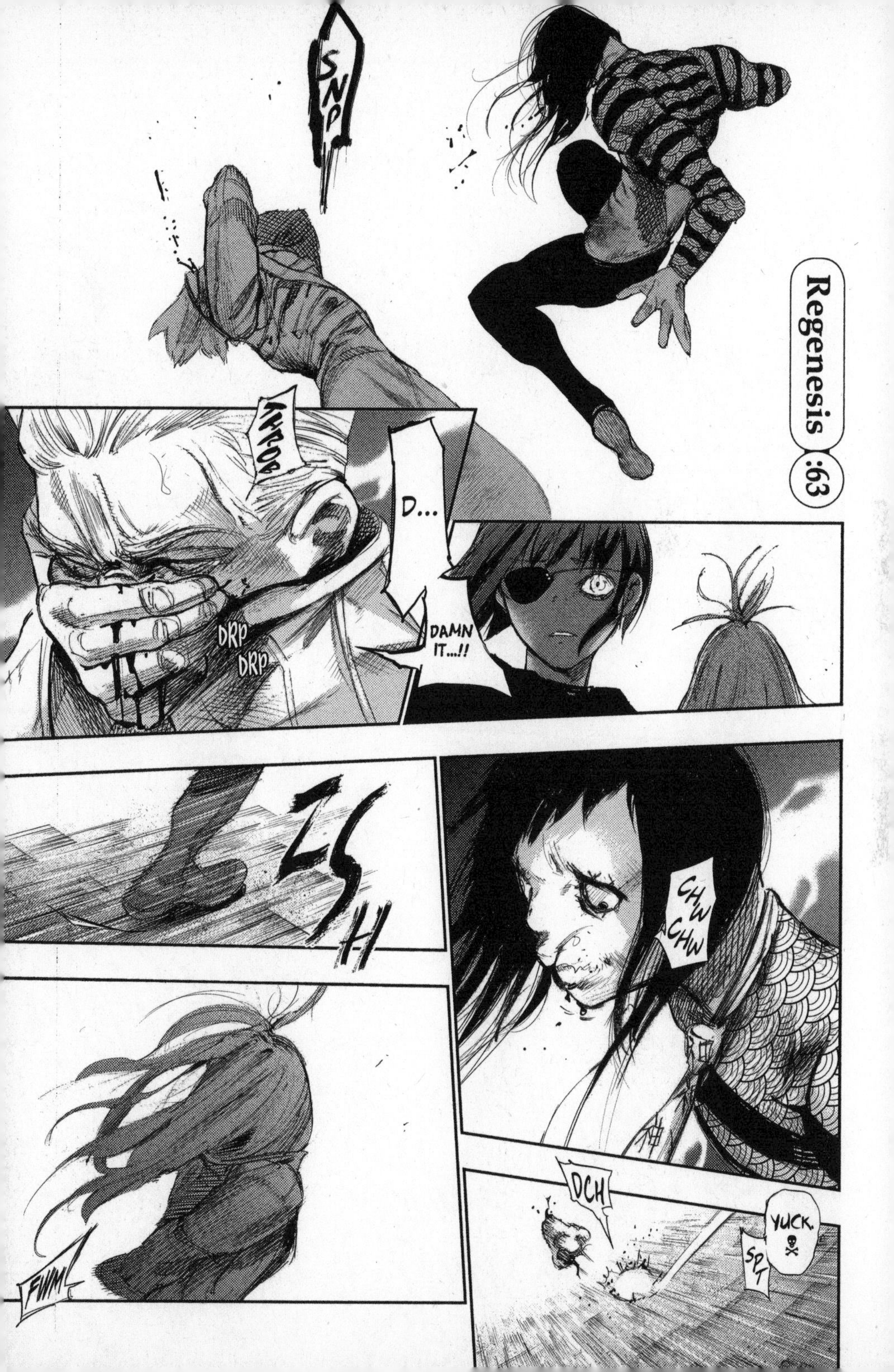
Regenesis :63
SNP
D...
DAMN IT...!!
DRP
DRP
CHW CHW
ZSH
FWM
YUCK.
SPT
DCH

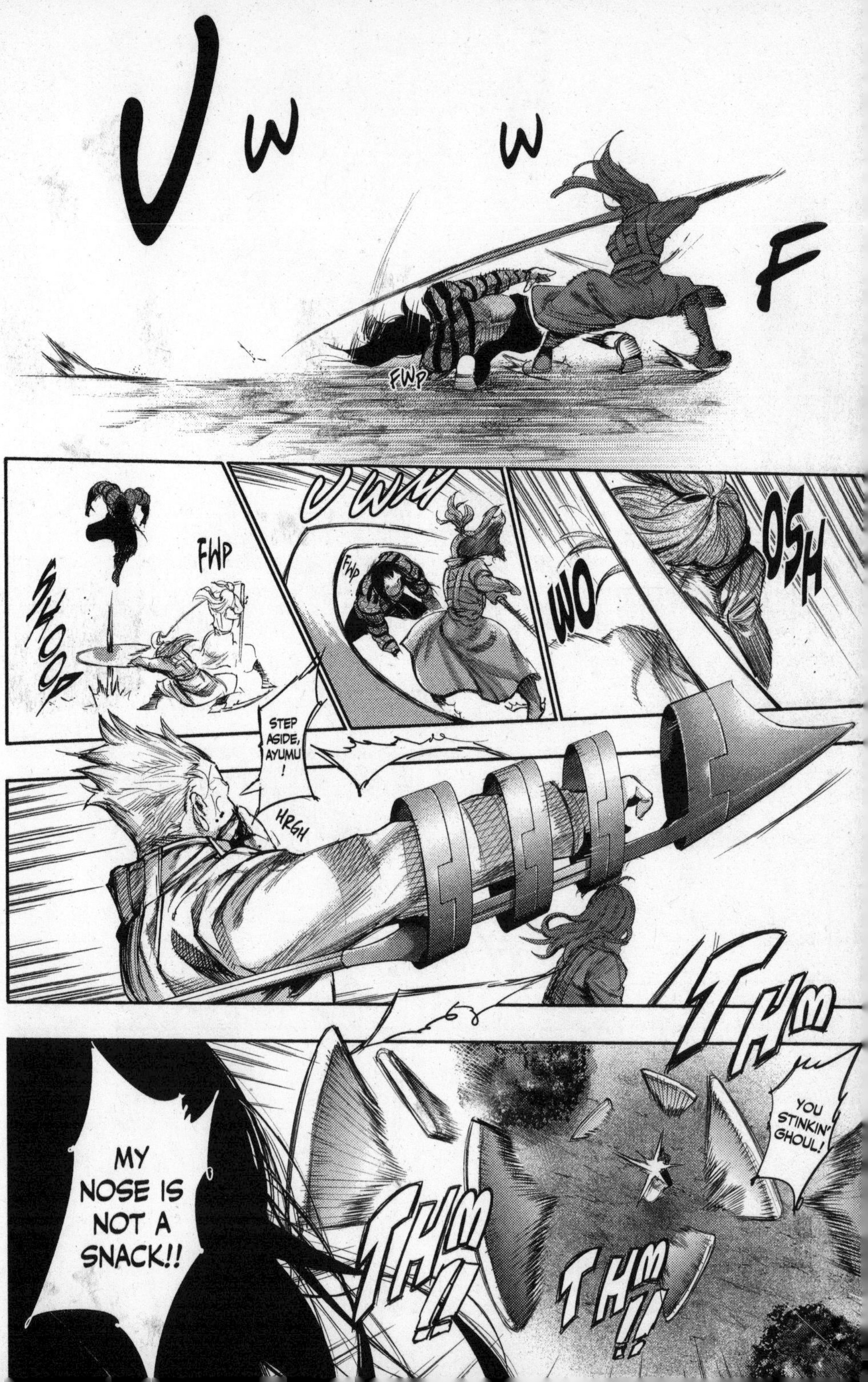

FWP
WOOSH
FWP
FWP
STEP ASIDE, AYUMU!
HRGH
THM
YOU STINKIN' GHOUL!
MY NOSE IS NOT A SNACK!!
THM
THM!!

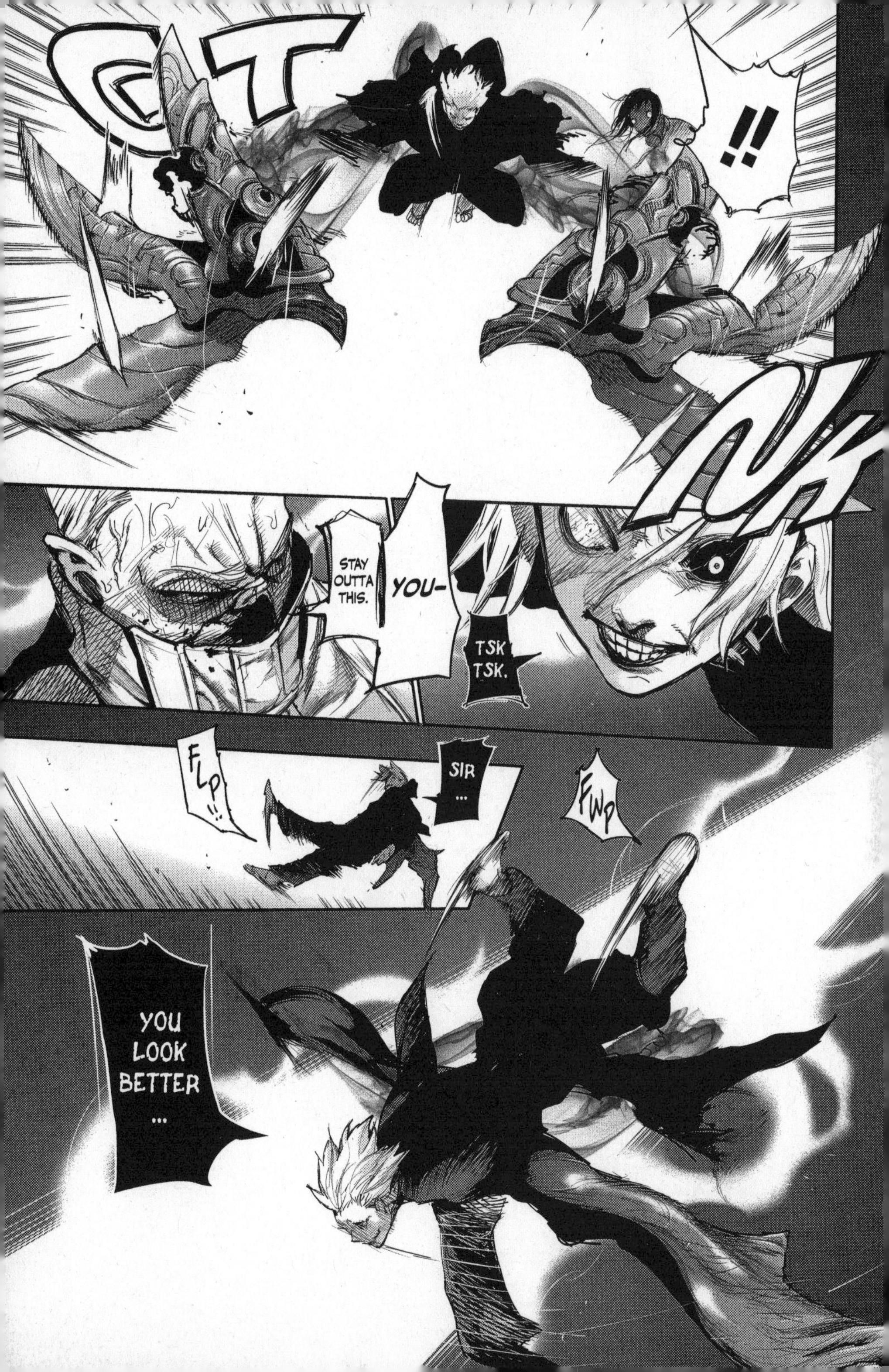

!!
TSK TSK.
YOU-
STAY OUTTA THIS.
FWP
SIR ...
FLP!!
YOU LOOK BETTER ...

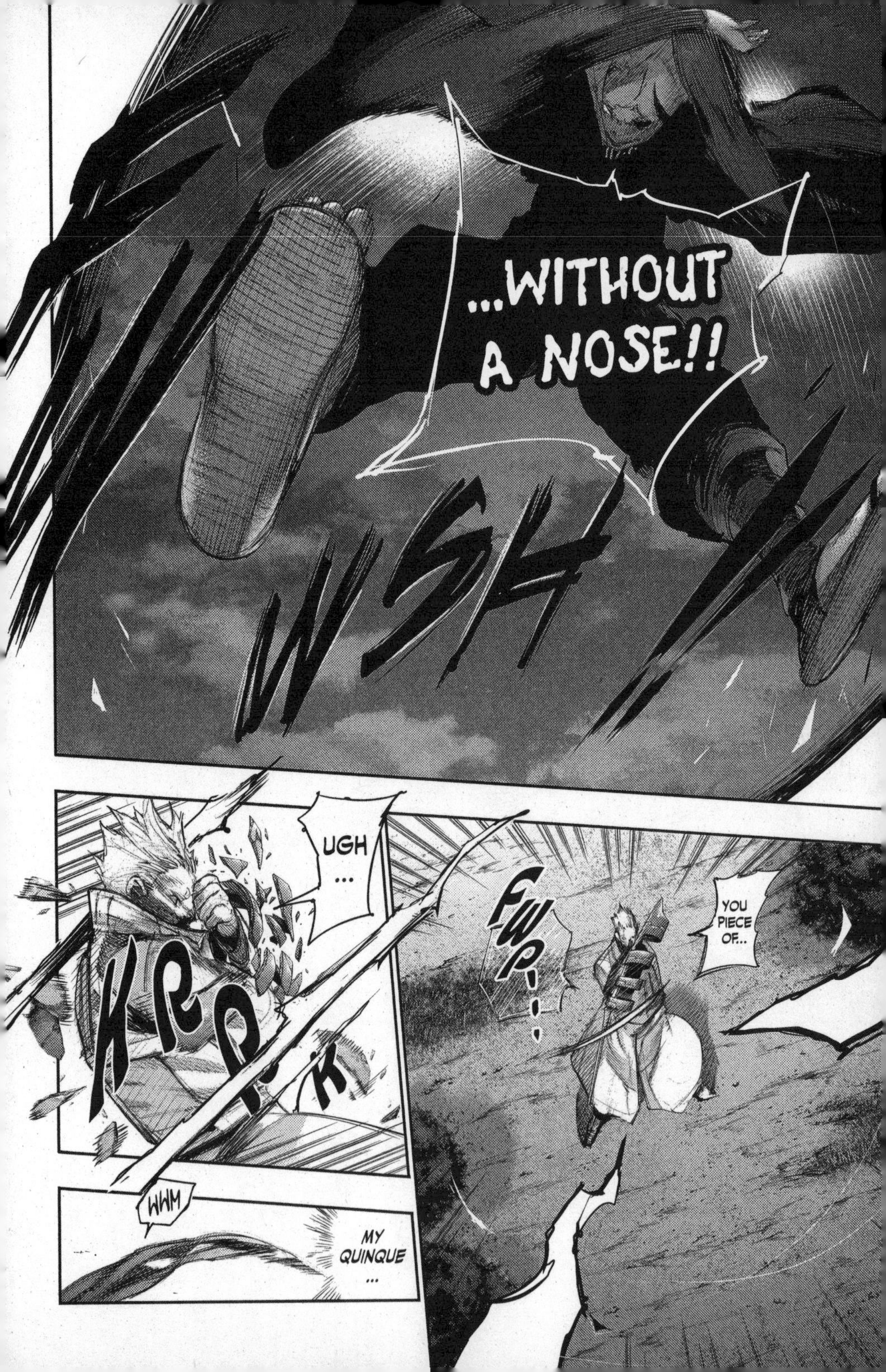
...WITHOUT A NOSE!!
WSH
YOU PIECE OF...
FWP...
UGH ...
KRRK
WWM
MY QUINQUE ...

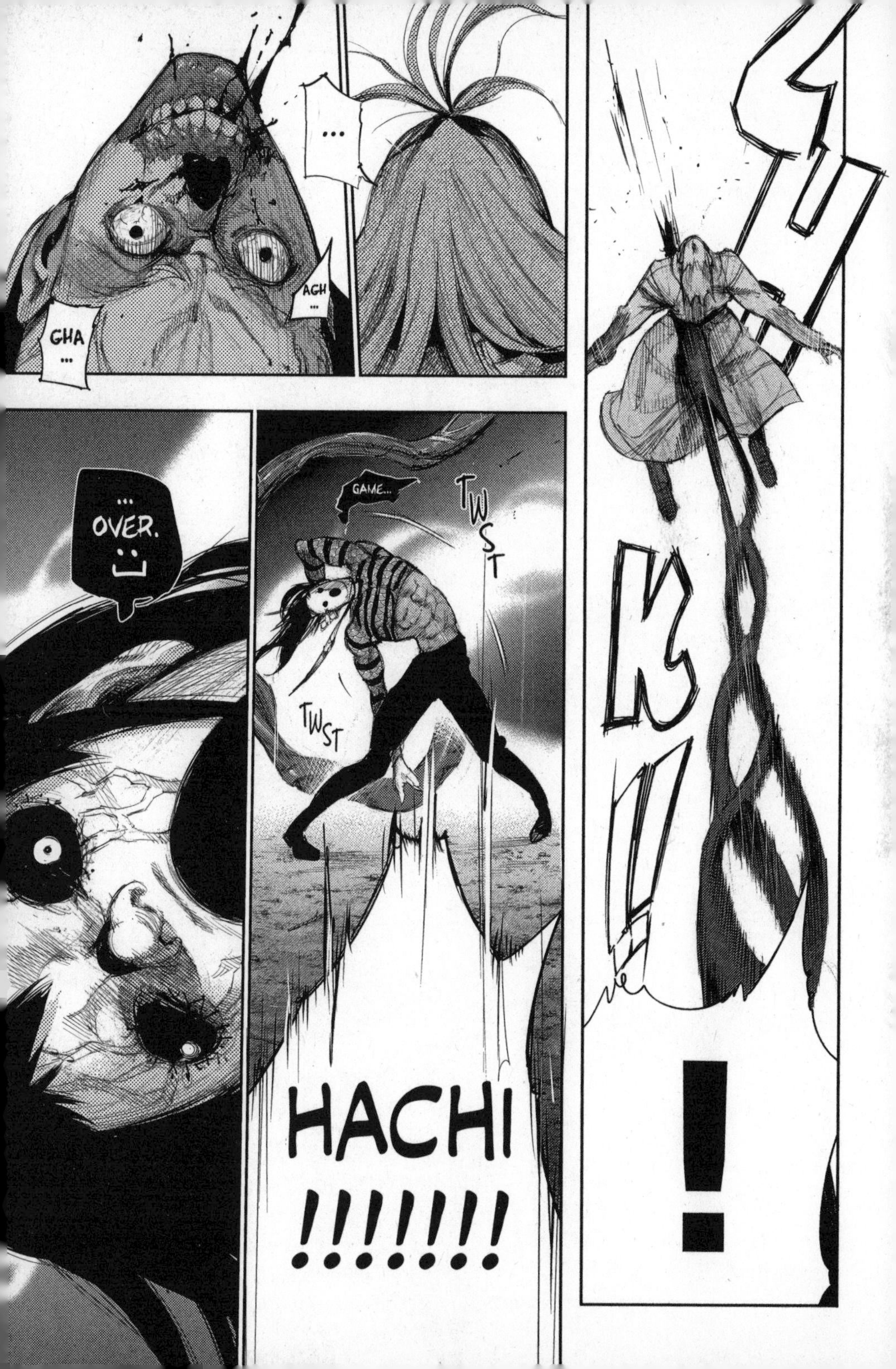
!
...
AGH ...
GHA ...
GAME...
TWST
TWST
HACHI !!!!!!!
... OVER.
:)

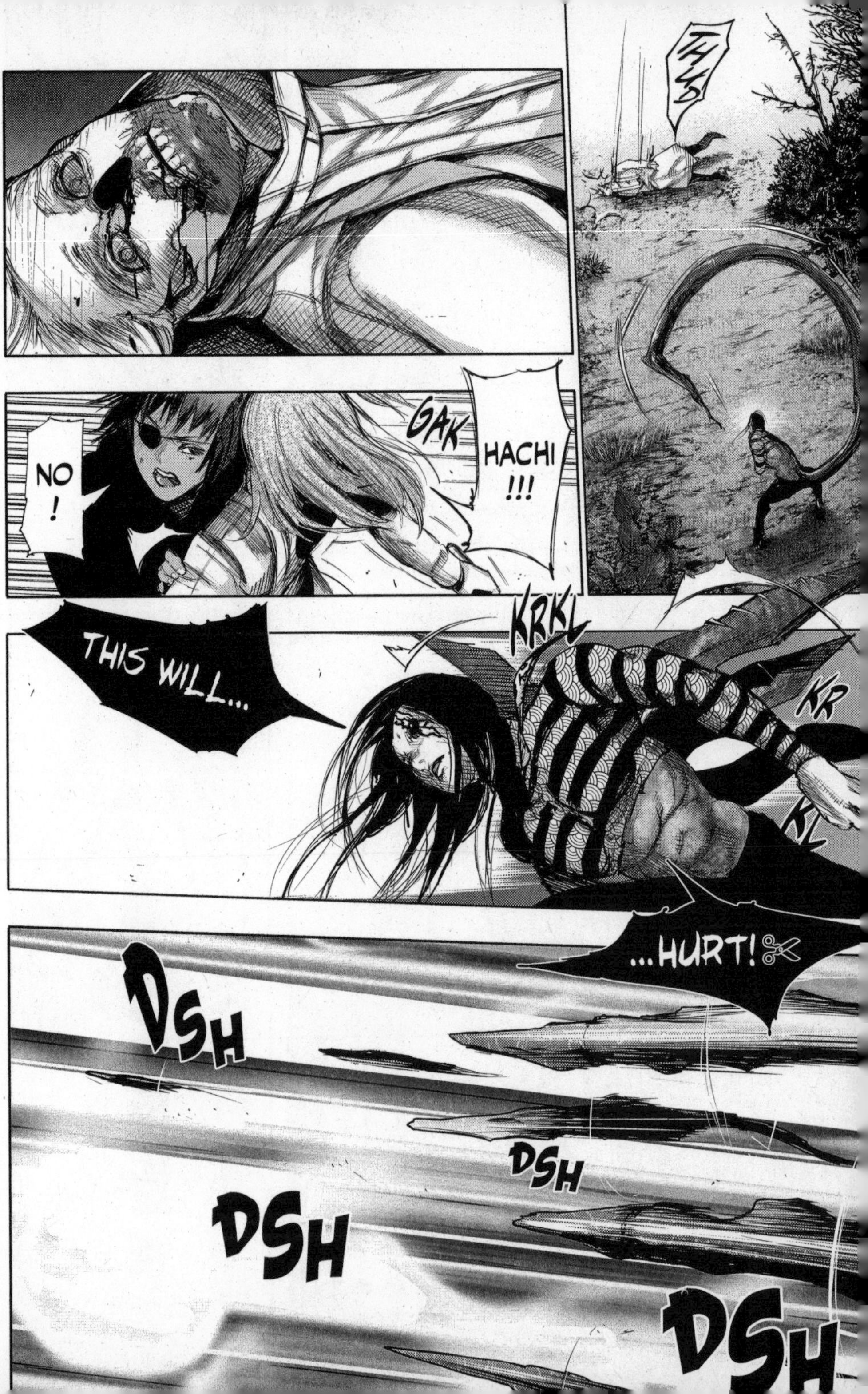
THUD
HACHI !!!
GAK
NO !
KRKL
KR
KL
THIS WILL...
...HURT!
DSH
DSH
DSH
DSH

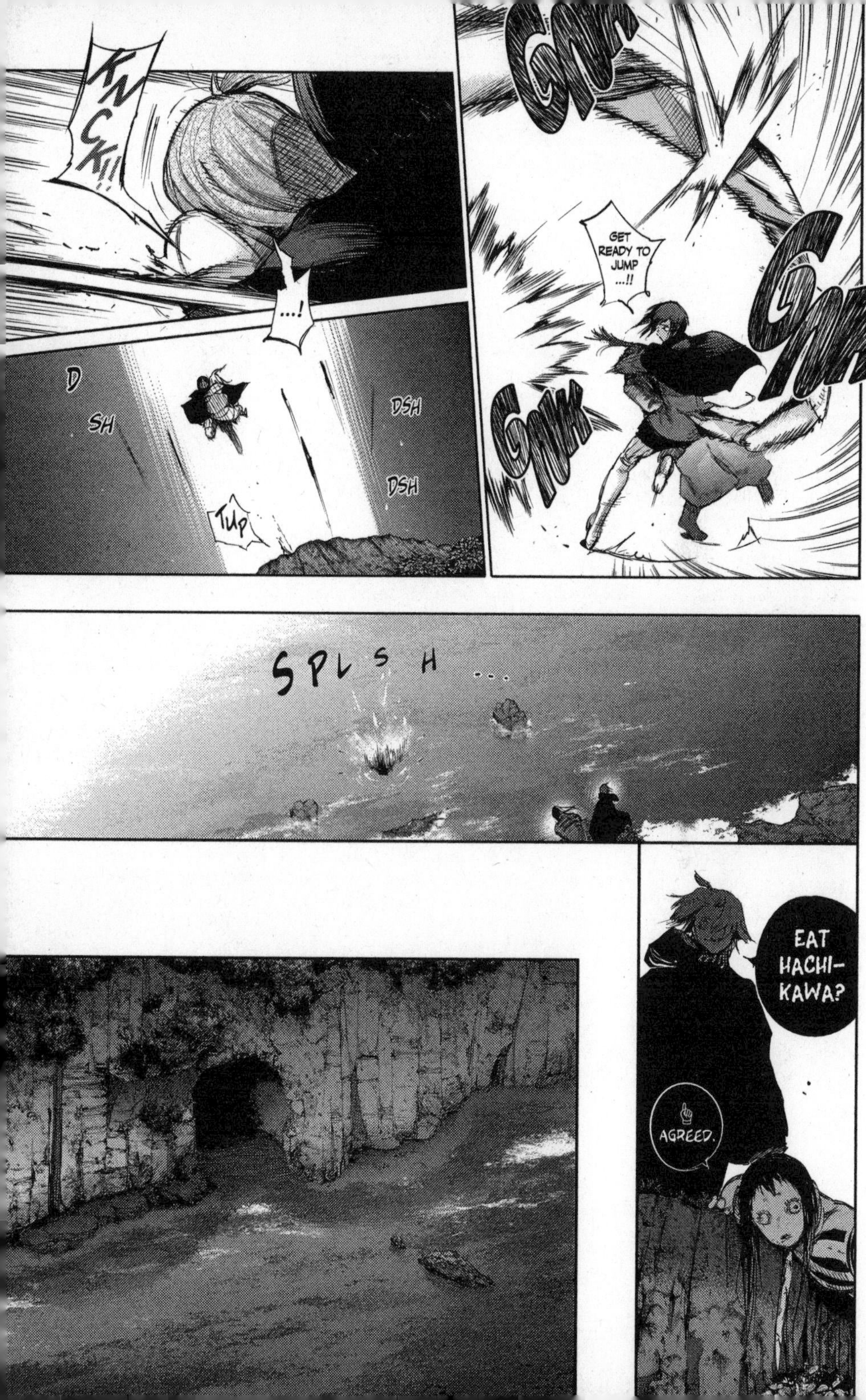
GNK
GET READY TO JUMP ...!!
GNK
GNK
KNCK!!
...!
D SH
DSH
DSH
TUP
SPLSH ...
EAT HACHI-KAWA?
AGREED.

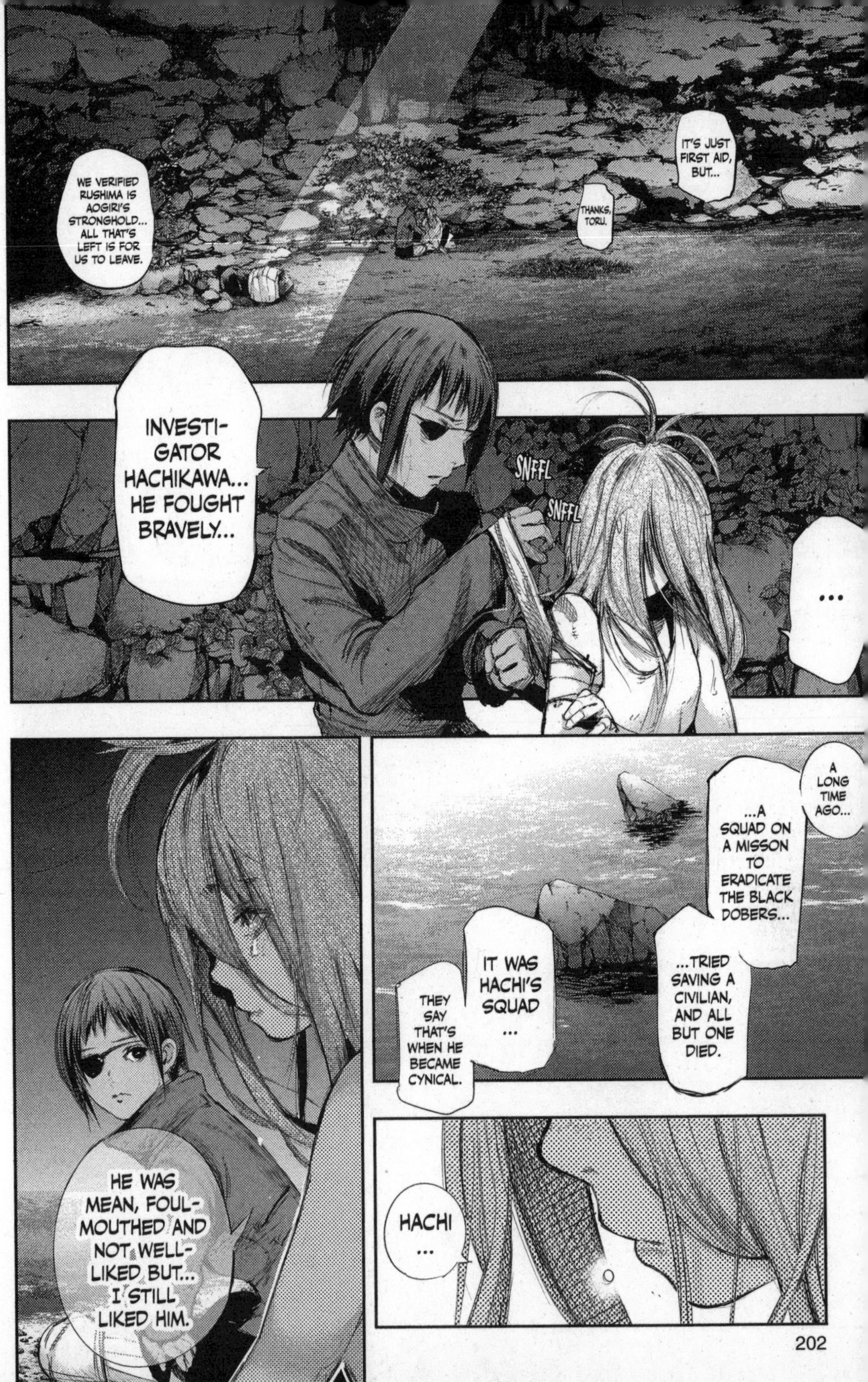
IT'S JUST FIRST AID, BUT...
THANKS, TORU.
WE VERIFIED RUSHIMA IS AOGIRI'S STRONGHOLD... ALL THAT'S LEFT IS FOR US TO LEAVE.
...
SNFFL
SNFFL
INVESTI-GATOR HACHIKAWA... HE FOUGHT BRAVELY...
A LONG TIME AGO...
...A SQUAD ON A MISSON TO ERADICATE THE BLACK DOBERS...
...TRIED SAVING A CIVILIAN, AND ALL BUT ONE DIED.
IT WAS HACHI'S SQUAD...
THEY SAY THAT'S WHEN HE BECAME CYNICAL.
HACHI...
HE WAS MEAN, FOUL-MOUTHED AND NOT WELL-LIKED BUT... I STILL LIKED HIM.

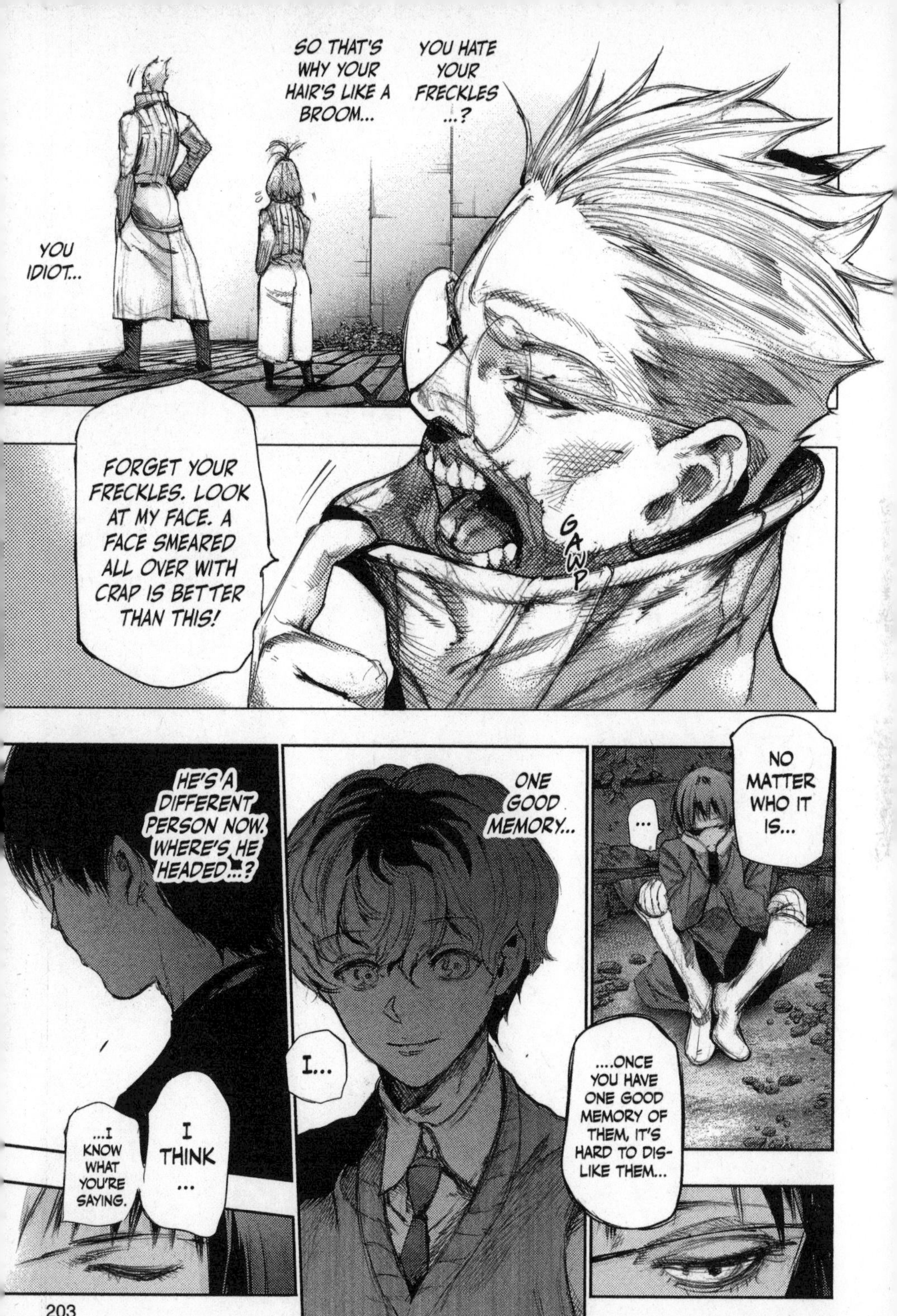
YOU HATE YOUR FRECKLES ...?
SO THAT'S WHY YOUR HAIR'S LIKE A BROOM...
YOU IDIOT...
FORGET YOUR FRECKLES. LOOK AT MY FACE. A FACE SMEARED ALL OVER WITH CRAP IS BETTER THAN THIS!
GAWP
NO MATTER WHO IT IS...
...
....ONCE YOU HAVE ONE GOOD MEMORY OF THEM, IT'S HARD TO DIS-LIKE THEM...
ONE GOOD MEMORY...
I...
HE'S A DIFFERENT PERSON NOW. WHERE'S HE HEADED...?
I THINK ...
...I KNOW WHAT YOU'RE SAYING.

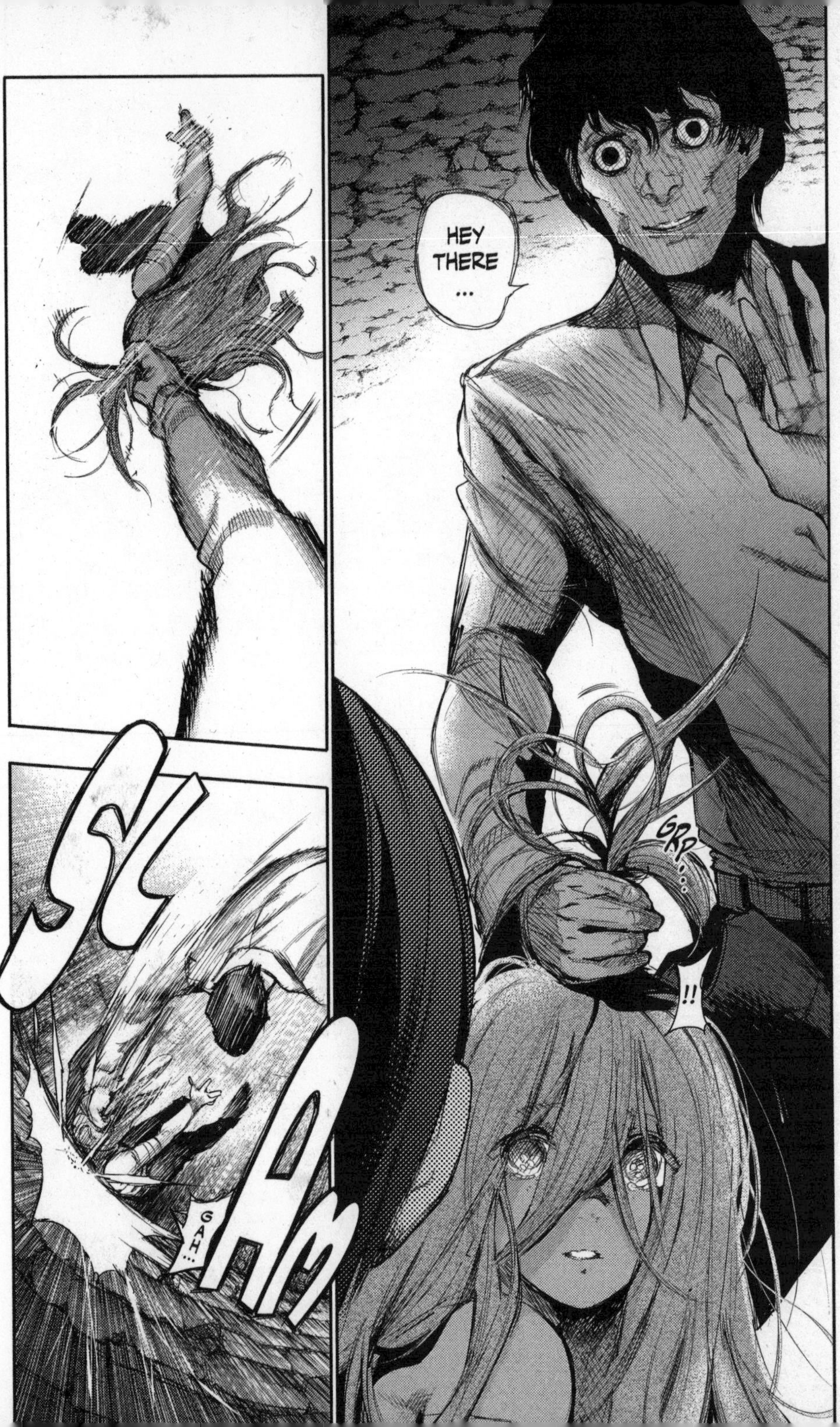
HEY THERE ...
GRP...
!!
SLAM
GAH...

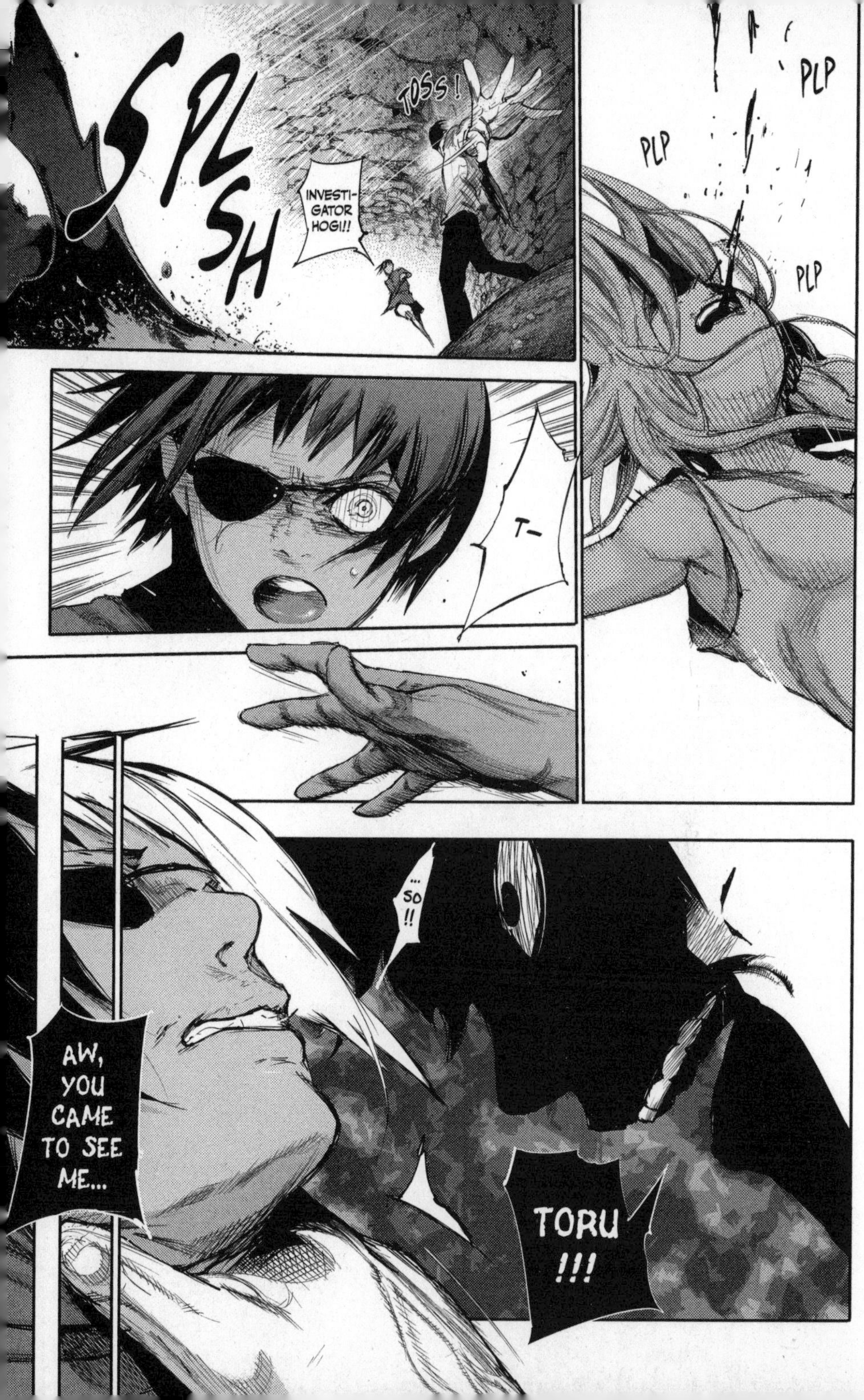
PLP
PLP
PLP
SPLSH
TOSS!
INVESTI-GATOR HOGI!!
T—
...SO!!
TORU!!!
AW, YOU CAME TO SEE ME...

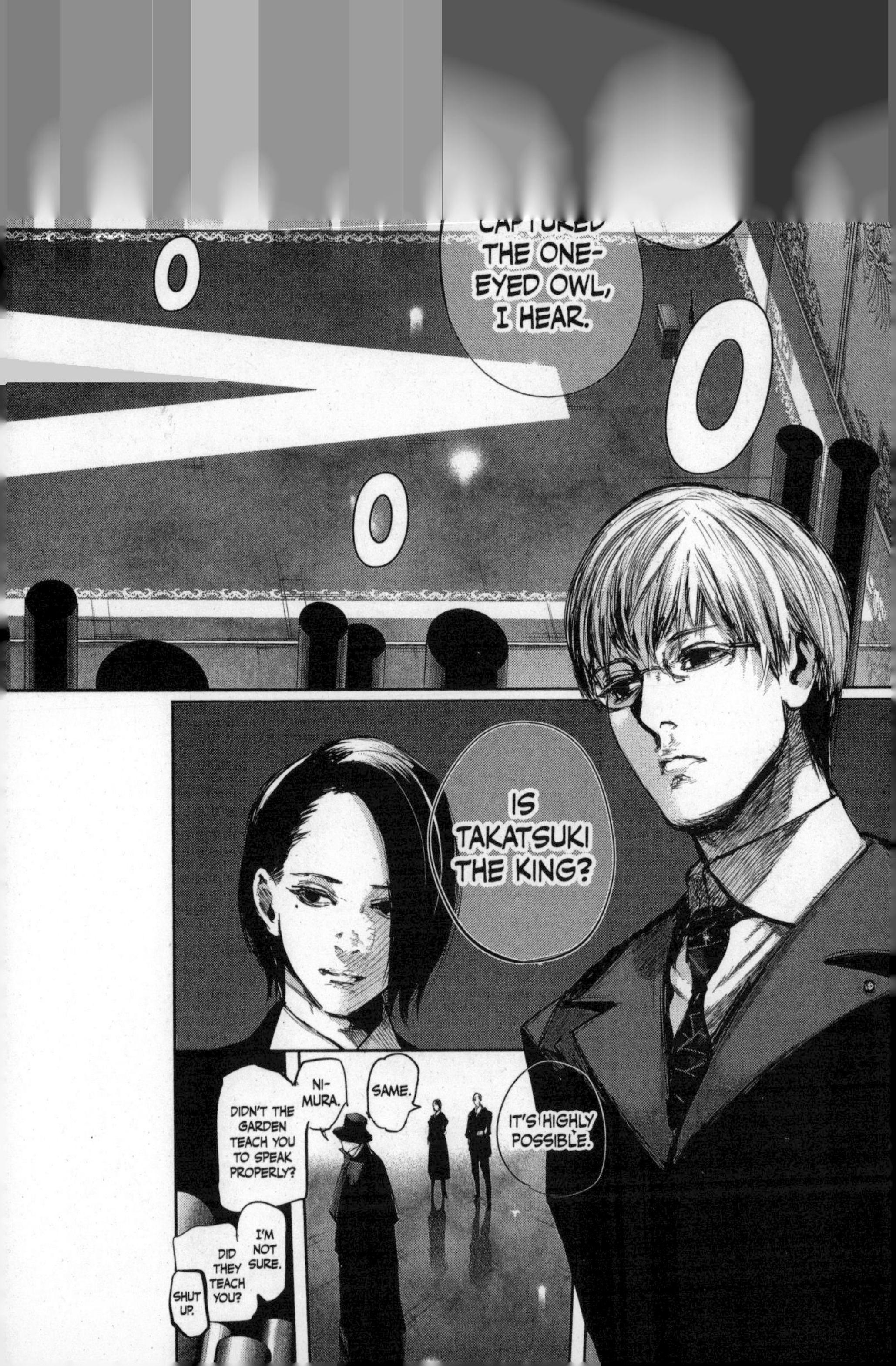
CAPTURED THE ONE-EYED OWL, I HEAR.
IS TAKATSUKI THE KING?
IT'S HIGHLY POSSIBLE.
SAME.
NI-MURA.
DIDN'T THE GARDEN TEACH YOU TO SPEAK PROPERLY?
I'M NOT SURE.
DID THEY TEACH YOU?
SHUT UP.

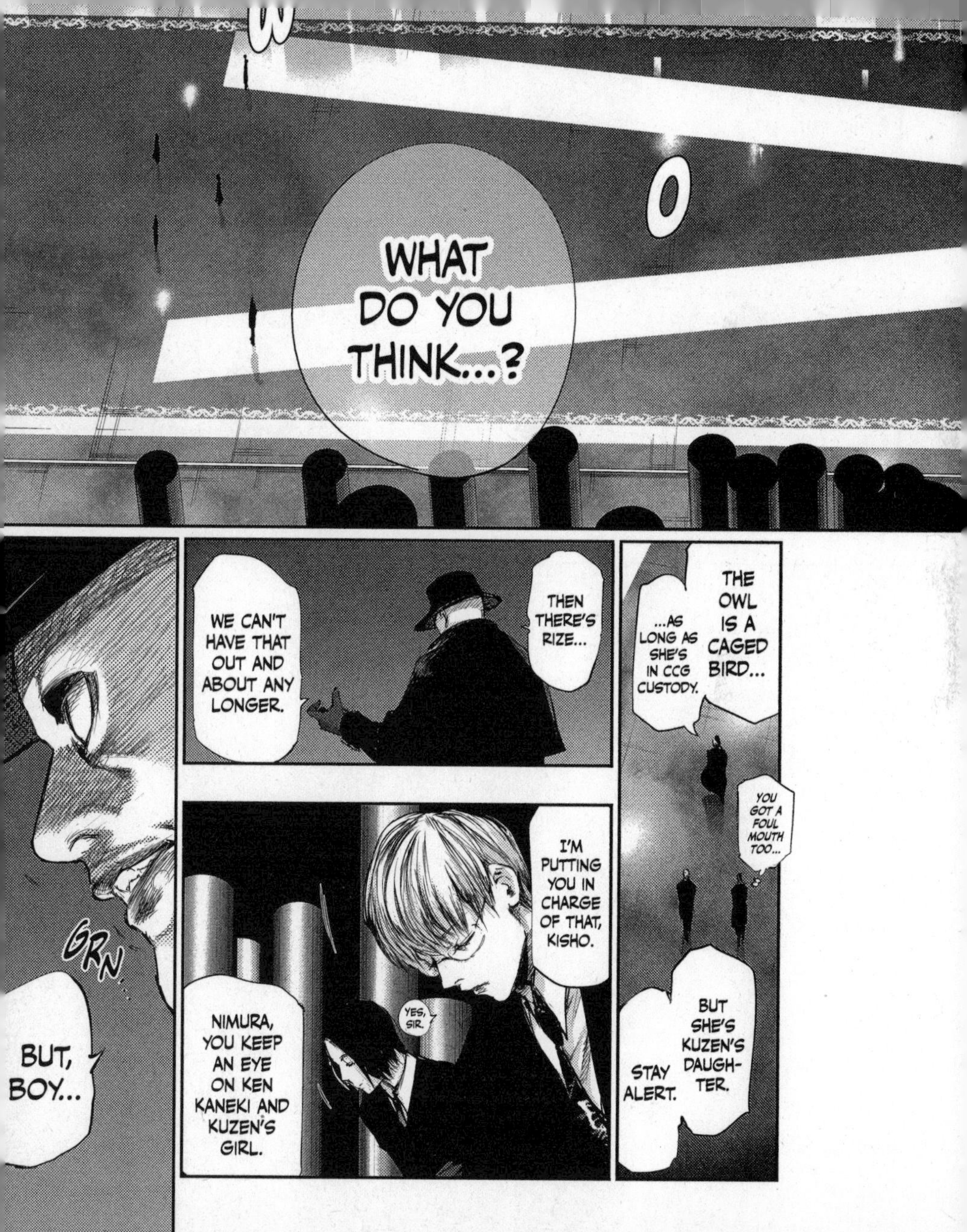
WHAT DO YOU THINK...?
THE OWL IS A CAGED BIRD...
...AS LONG AS SHE'S IN CCG CUSTODY.
YOU GOT A FOUL MOUTH TOO...
BUT SHE'S KUZEN'S DAUGH-TER.
STAY ALERT.
THEN THERE'S RIZE...
WE CAN'T HAVE THAT OUT AND ABOUT ANY LONGER.
I'M PUTTING YOU IN CHARGE OF THAT, KISHO.
YES, SIR.
NIMURA, YOU KEEP AN EYE ON KEN KANEKI AND KUZEN'S GIRL.
GRN
BUT, BOY...

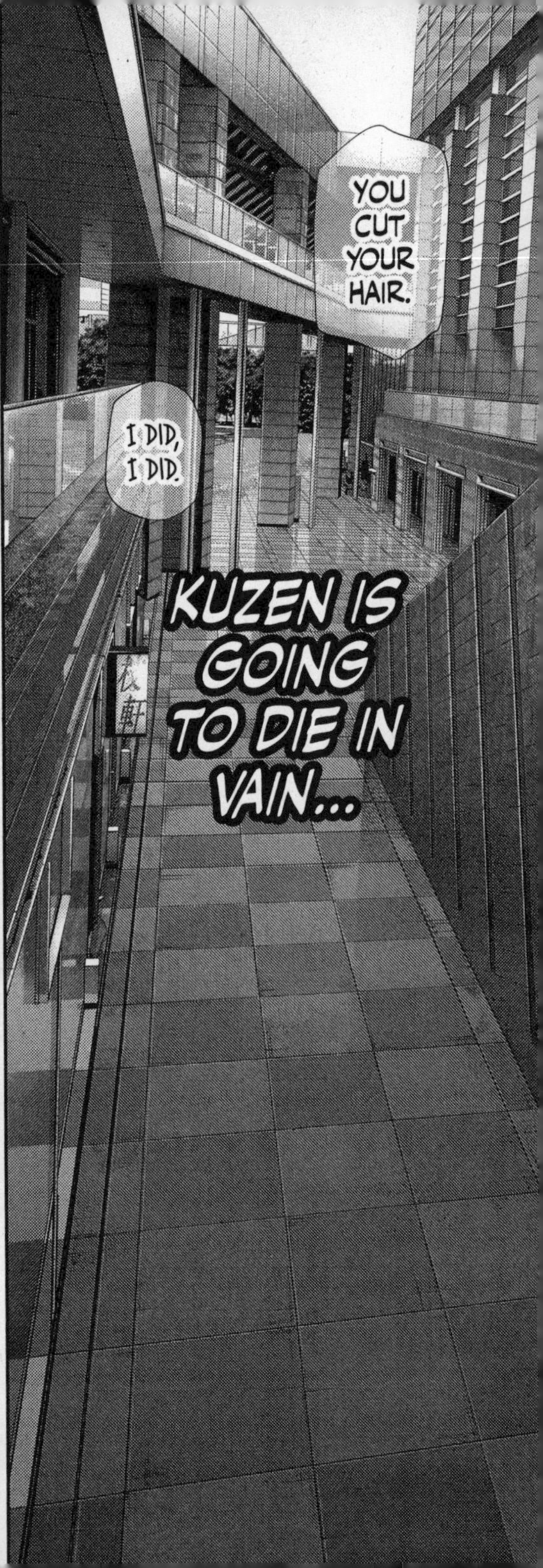
YOU CUT YOUR HAIR.
I DID, I DID.
KUZEN IS GOING TO DIE IN VAIN...

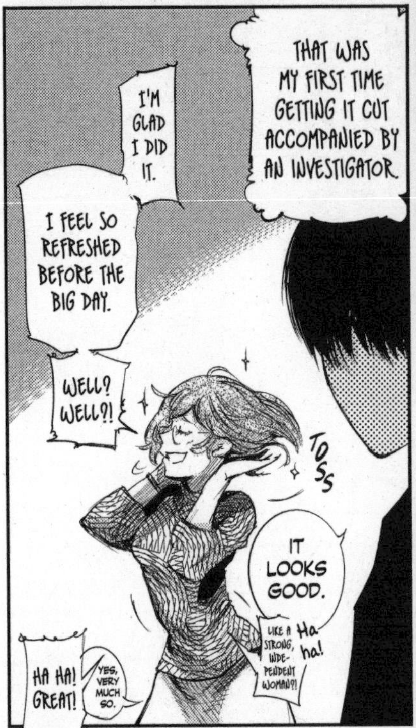
THAT WAS MY FIRST TIME GETTING IT CUT ACCOMPANIED BY AN INVESTIGATOR.
I'M GLAD I DID IT.
I FEEL SO REFRESHED BEFORE THE BIG DAY.
WELL? WELL?!
TOSS
IT LOOKS GOOD.
Ha ha!
LIKE A STRONG, INDE-PENDENT WOMAN?!
YES, VERY MUCH SO.
HA HA! GREAT!

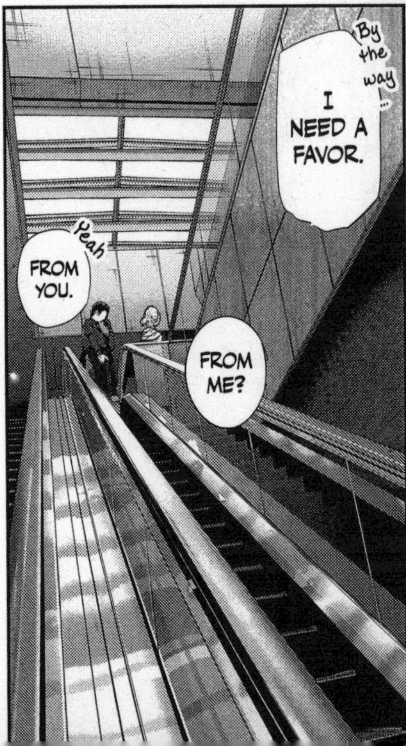
By the way...
I NEED A FAVOR.
FROM ME?
Yeah
FROM YOU.

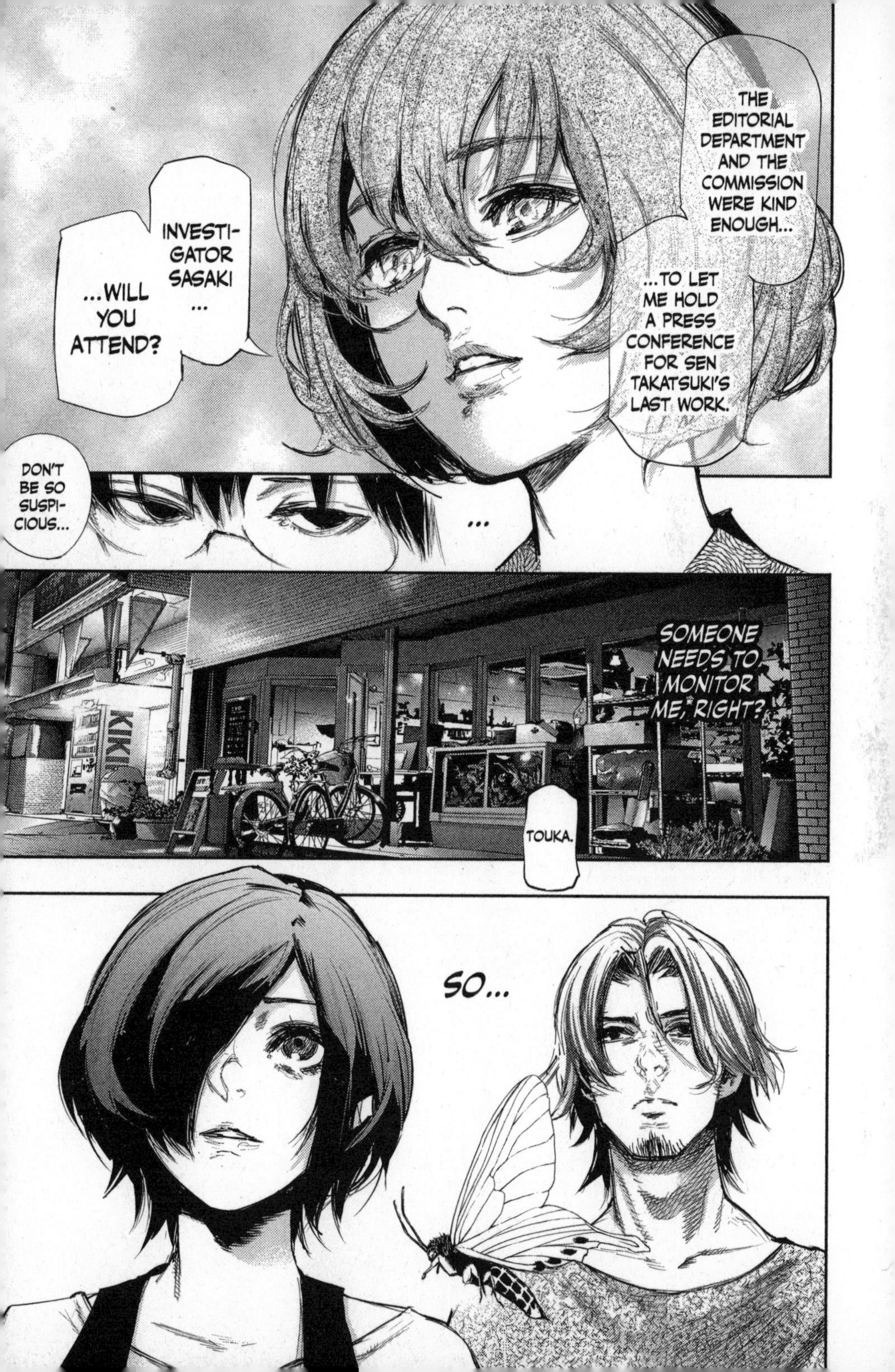
THE EDITORIAL DEPARTMENT AND THE COMMISSION WERE KIND ENOUGH...
...TO LET ME HOLD A PRESS CONFERENCE FOR SEN TAKATSUKI'S LAST WORK.
INVESTI-GATOR SASAKI ...
...WILL YOU ATTEND?
...
DON'T BE SO SUSPI-CIOUS...
SOMEONE NEEDS TO MONITOR ME, RIGHT?
KIKI
TOUKA.
SO...

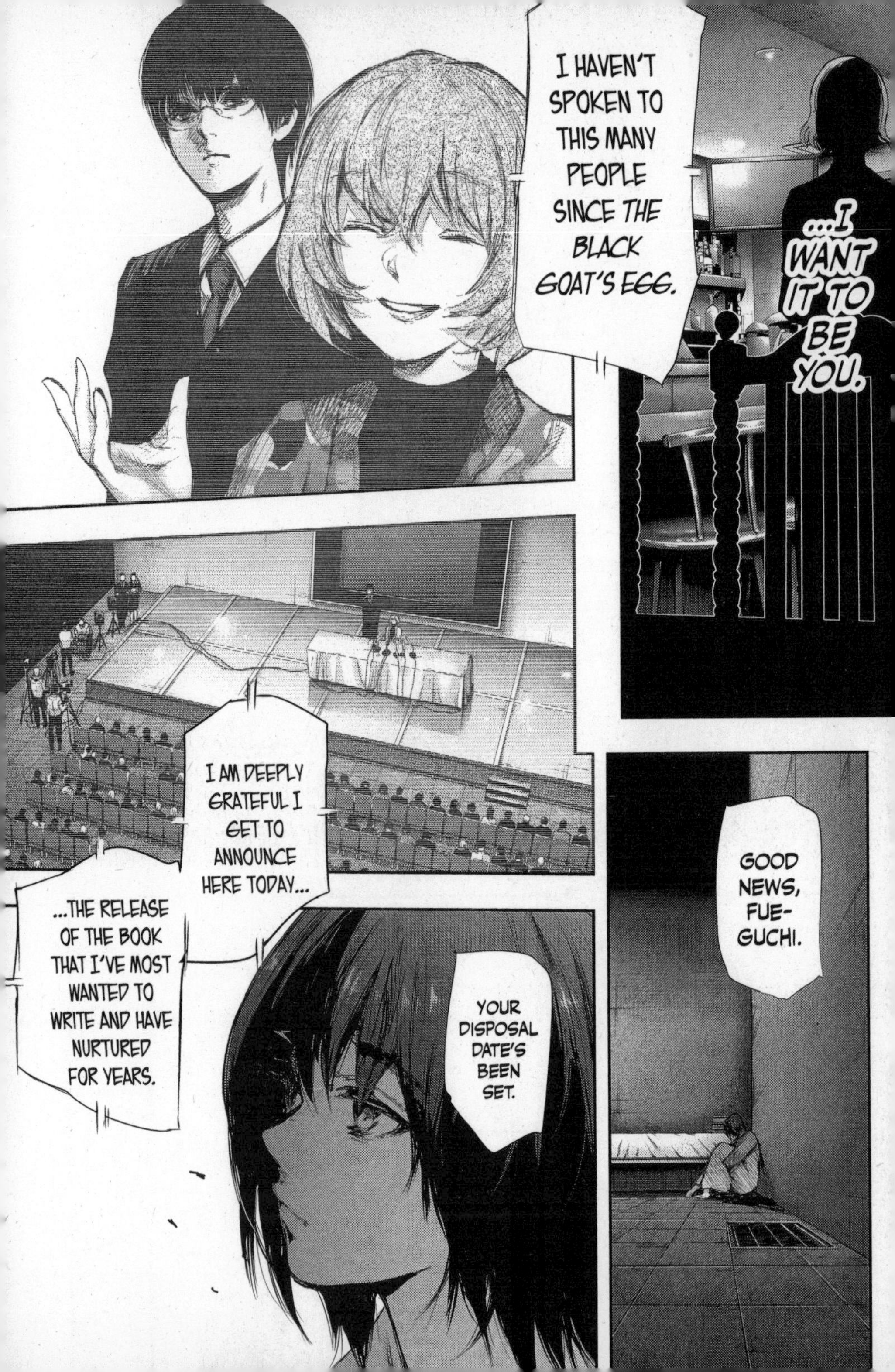
...I WANT IT TO BE YOU.
I HAVEN'T SPOKEN TO THIS MANY PEOPLE SINCE THE BLACK GOAT'S EGG.
I AM DEEPLY GRATEFUL I GET TO ANNOUNCE HERE TODAY...
GOOD NEWS, FUE-GUCHI.
...THE RELEASE OF THE BOOK THAT I'VE MOST WANTED TO WRITE AND HAVE NURTURED FOR YEARS.
YOUR DISPOSAL DATE'S BEEN SET.

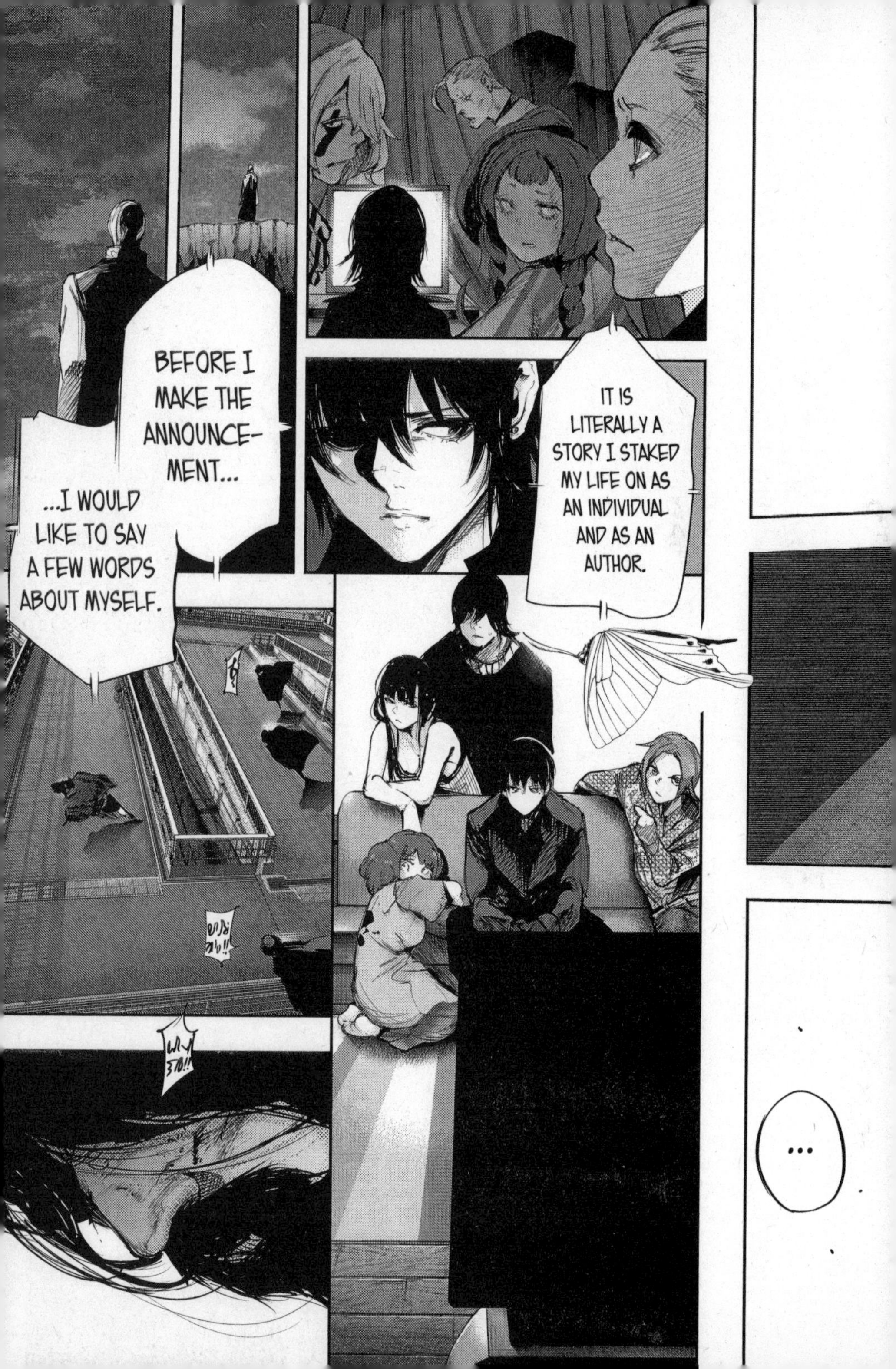
BEFORE I MAKE THE ANNOUNCEMENT...
...I WOULD LIKE TO SAY A FEW WORDS ABOUT MYSELF.
IT IS LITERALLY A STORY I STAKED MY LIFE ON AS AN INDIVIDUAL AND AS AN AUTHOR.
...

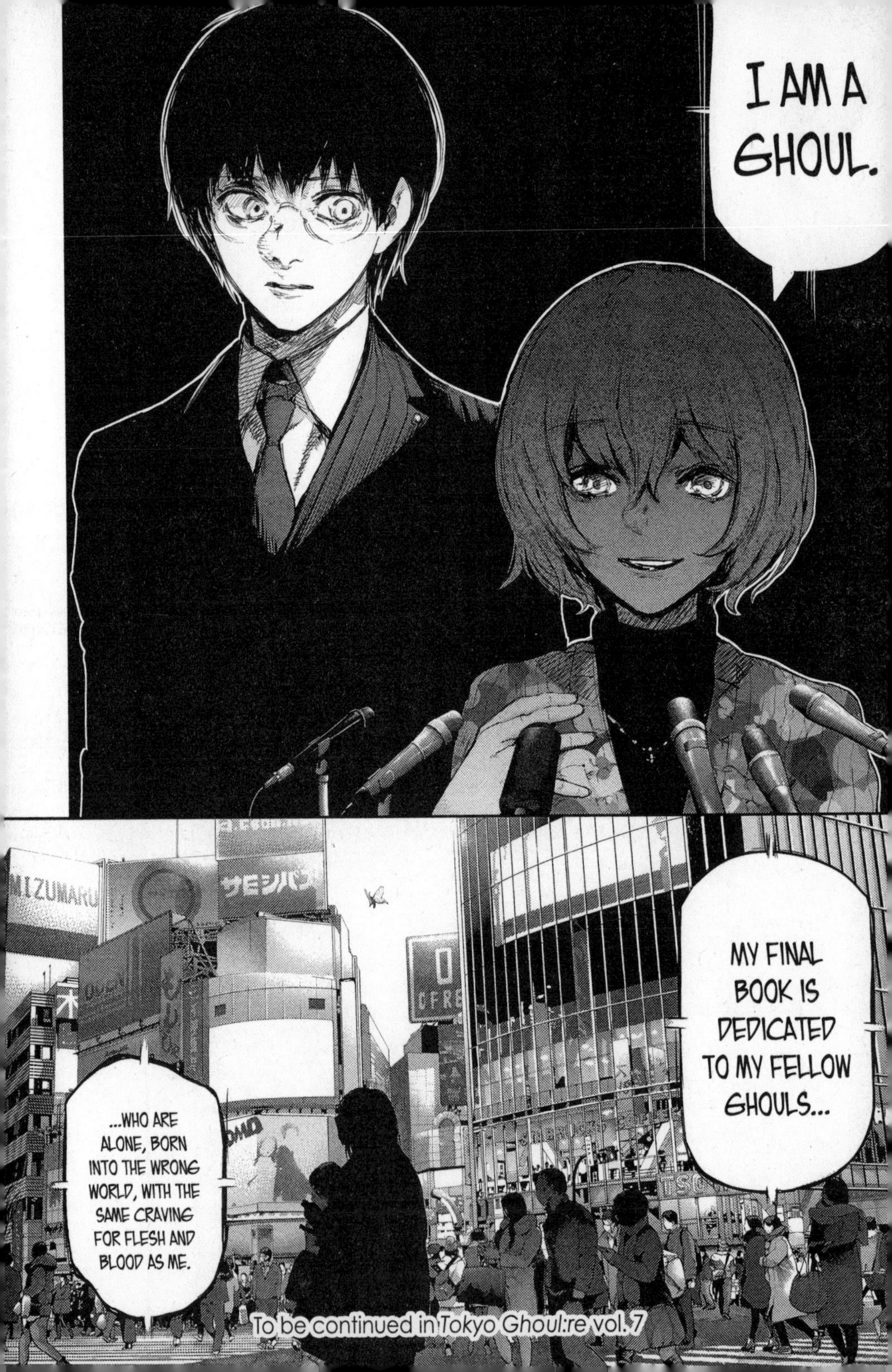
I AM A GHOUL.
MY FINAL BOOK IS DEDICATED TO MY FELLOW GHOULS...
...WHO ARE ALONE, BORN INTO THE WRONG WORLD, WITH THE SAME CRAVING FOR FLESH AND BLOOD AS ME.
To be continued in *Tokyo Ghoul:re* vol. 7

Staff

Mizuki Ide
Kota Shugyo (~58)
Hashimoto
Kiyotaka Aihara (out 3 months)
Rikako Miura
Niina (67~)

Comic design   Hideaki Shimada (L.S.D.)
Magazine design   Akie Demachi (POCKET)
Photography   Wataru Tanaka
Editor   Junpei Matsuo

Helpers   Ryuji Matusmoto (#62)
                    Matsuzaki (#62)
                    Kota Shugyo (#62)

Special thanks   Kaze Germany

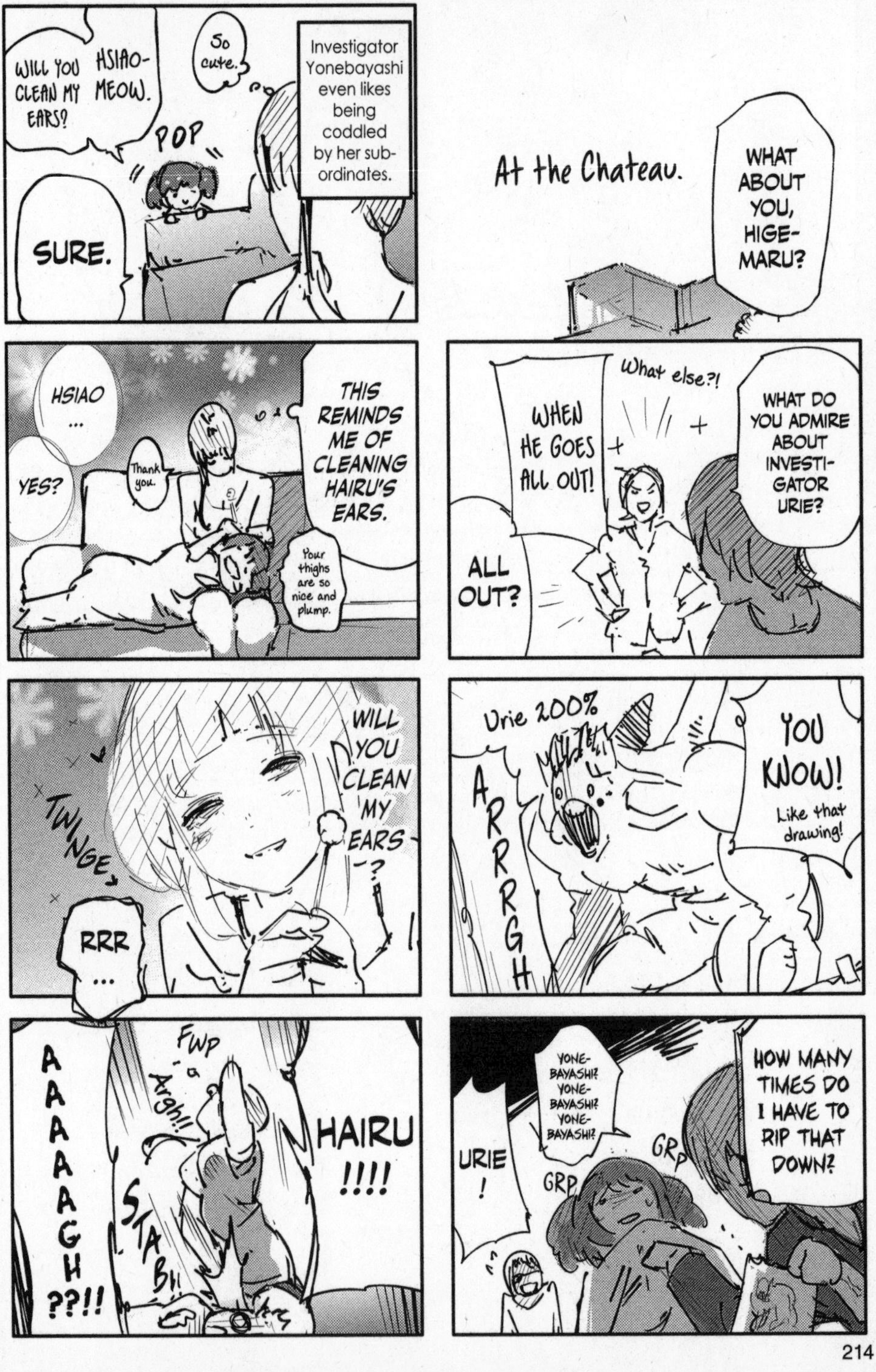
At the Chateau.
WHAT ABOUT YOU, HIGE-MARU?
WHAT DO YOU ADMIRE ABOUT INVESTI-GATOR URIE?
What else?!
WHEN HE GOES ALL OUT!
ALL OUT?
YOU KNOW!
Like that drawing!
Urie 200%
ARRRGH
HOW MANY TIMES DO I HAVE TO RIP THAT DOWN?
GRP
GRP
YONE-BAYASHI? YONE-BAYASHI? YONE-BAYASHI?
URIE!
Investigator Yonebayashi even likes being coddled by her sub-ordinates.
So cute.
HSIAO-MEOW.
WILL YOU CLEAN MY EARS?
POP
SURE.
THIS REMINDS ME OF CLEANING HAIRU'S EARS.
Your thighs are so nice and plump.
Thank you.
HSIAO...
YES?
WILL YOU CLEAN MY EARS?
TWINGE
RRR...
HAIRU!!!!
FWP
Argh!!
STAB!!
AAAAAAAGH??!!

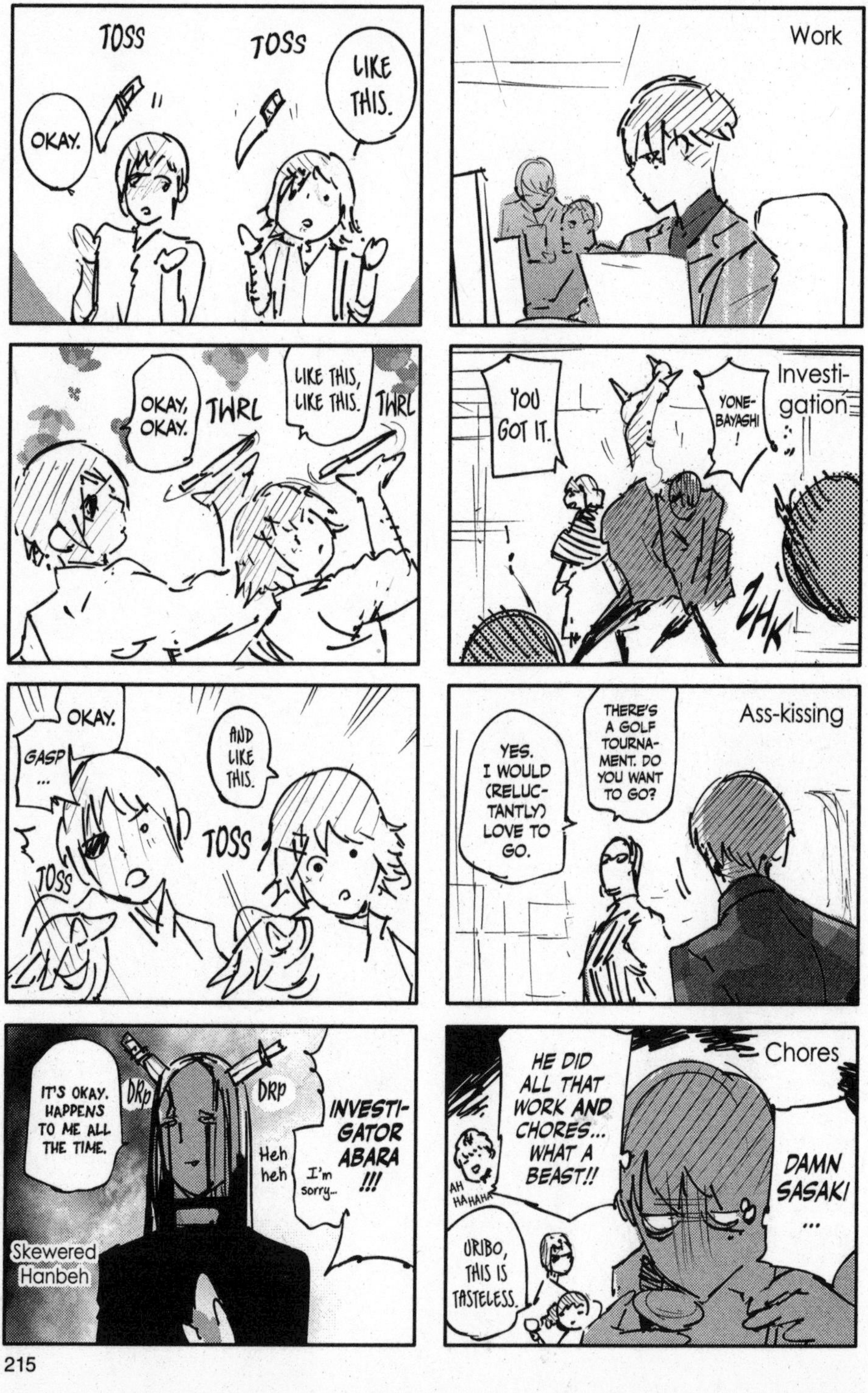
Work
Investigation
YONE-BAYASHI!
YOU GOT IT.
ZHK
Ass-kissing
THERE'S A GOLF TOURNAMENT. DO YOU WANT TO GO?
YES. I WOULD (RELUCTANTLY) LOVE TO GO.
Chores
DAMN SASAKI...
HE DID ALL THAT WORK AND CHORES... WHAT A BEAST!!
AH HA HAHA
URIBO, THIS IS TASTELESS.
LIKE THIS.
TOSS
TOSS
OKAY.
LIKE THIS, LIKE THIS.
TWRL
TWRL
OKAY, OKAY.
AND LIKE THIS.
TOSS
OKAY.
GASP...
TOSS
INVESTIGATOR ABARA!!!
I'm sorry...
DRP
Heh heh
DRP
IT'S OKAY. HAPPENS TO ME ALL THE TIME.
Skewered Hanbeh

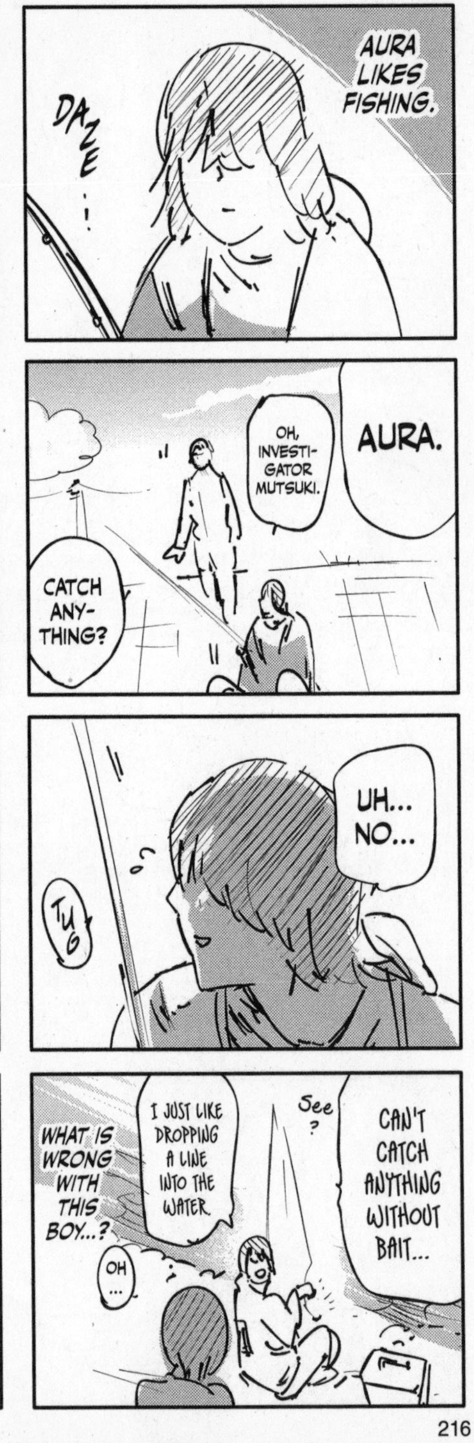
AURA LIKES FISHING.
DAZE!
AURA.
OH, INVESTIGATOR MUTSUKI.
CATCH ANYTHING?
UH... NO...
TUG
CAN'T CATCH ANYTHING WITHOUT BAIT...
See?
I JUST LIKE DROPPING A LINE INTO THE WATER.
WHAT IS WRONG WITH THIS BOY...?
OH...

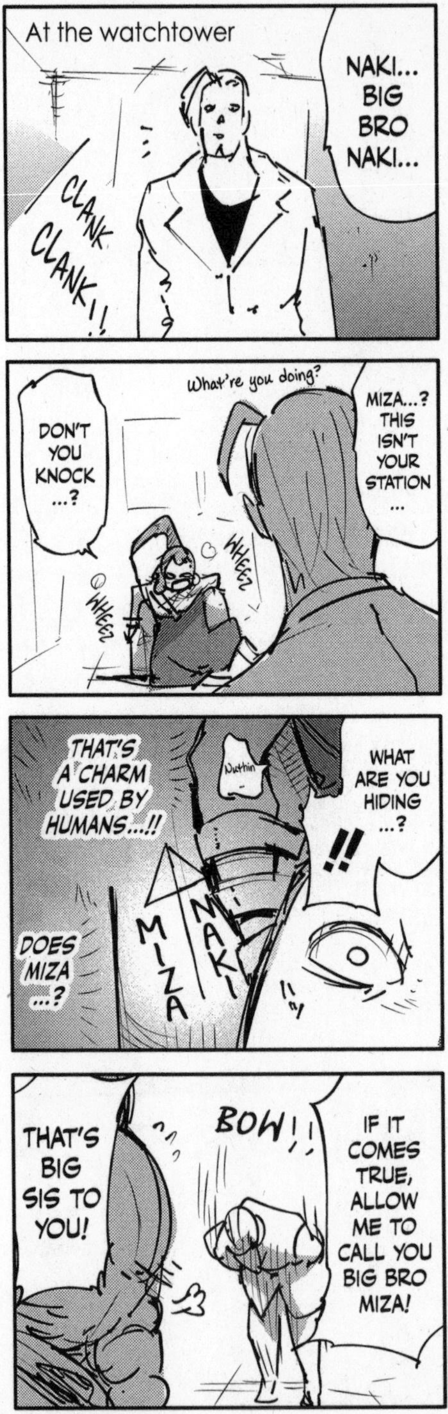
At the watchtower
NAKI... BIG BRO NAKI...
CLANK CLANK!!
MIZA...? THIS ISN'T YOUR STATION...
What're you doing?
DON'T YOU KNOCK...?
WHEEZ
WHEEZ
WHAT ARE YOU HIDING...?
Nuthin...
!!
THAT'S A CHARM USED BY HUMANS...!!
NAKI
MIZA
DOES MIZA...?
IF IT COMES TRUE, ALLOW ME TO CALL YOU BIG BRO MIZA!
BOW!!
THAT'S BIG SIS TO YOU!

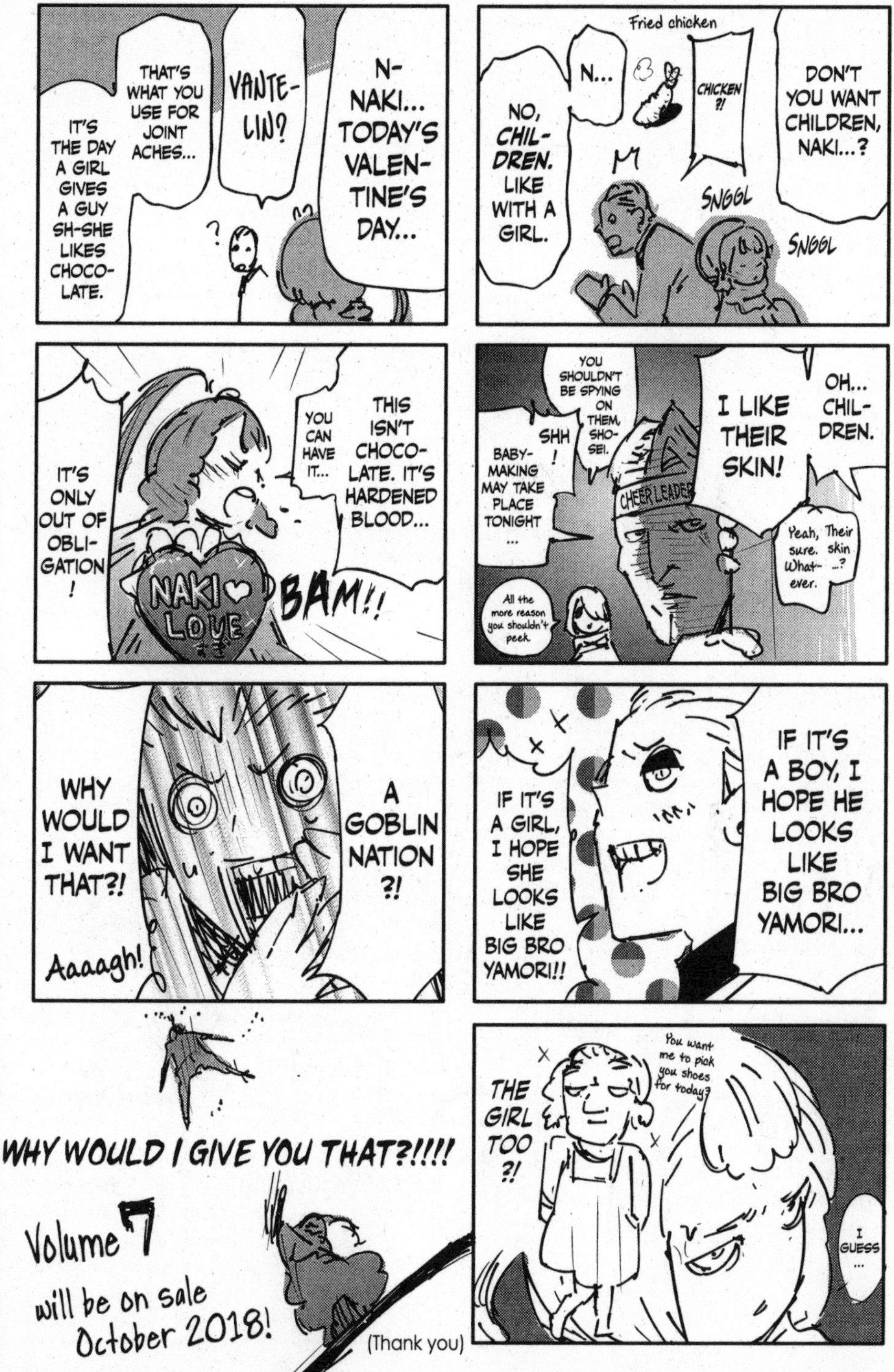
DON'T YOU WANT CHILDREN, NAKI...?
CHICKEN?!
N...
Fried chicken
NO, CHILDREN. LIKE WITH A GIRL.
SNGGL
SNGGL
N-NAKI... TODAY'S VALENTINE'S DAY...
VANTELIN?
THAT'S WHAT YOU USE FOR JOINT ACHES...
IT'S THE DAY A GIRL GIVES A GUY SH-SHE LIKES CHOCOLATE.
OH... CHILDREN.
I LIKE THEIR SKIN!
Their skin ...?
Yeah, sure. Whatever.
YOU SHOULDN'T BE SPYING ON THEM, SHOSEI.
SHH!
BABY-MAKING MAY TAKE PLACE TONIGHT...
CHEER LEADER
All the more reason you shouldn't peek.
THIS ISN'T CHOCOLATE. IT'S HARDENED BLOOD...
YOU CAN HAVE IT...
IT'S ONLY OUT OF OBLIGATION!
NAKI LOVE
BAM!!
IF IT'S A BOY, I HOPE HE LOOKS LIKE BIG BRO YAMORI...
IF IT'S A GIRL, I HOPE SHE LOOKS LIKE BIG BRO YAMORI!!
A GOBLIN NATION?!
WHY WOULD I WANT THAT?!
Aaaagh!
You want me to pick you shoes for today?
THE GIRL TOO?!
I GUESS...
WHY WOULD I GIVE YOU THAT?!!!!
Volume 7 will be on sale October 2018!
(Thank you)

(Leader of the Blades)

Miza Kusakari / Triple Blade
草刈 ミザ（くさかり みざ）/ 三枚刃

- Age: 31 (DOB 11/4) ♀ • Blood type: O • Height/weight: 145cm/43kg
- RC Type: Bikaku • Rate: S • R&R: Getting drunk and griping to her henchmen
- Ambition: Having children • Likes: Blood wine, cigarettes, Naki?

(A leader of the White Suits)

Hohguro
ホオグロ

- Age: 25 (DOB 10/8) ♂ • Blood type: B • Height/weight: 184cm/57kg
- RC Type: Rinkaku • Rate: A+ • Hobbies: Coordinating outfits, picking
  up human women • Ambition: Increasing the number of White Suits to
  match their heyday • Respects: Yamori, Naki

(A leader of the White Suits)

Shosei Idera
井寺 承生（いでら しょせい）

- Age: 25 (DOB 11/5) ♂ • Blood type: B • Height/weight: 201cm/120kg
- RC Type: Ukaku • Rate: A+ • Hobbies: Studying kanji, doing math drills
  (now at a 4th grade level) • Ambition: Studying and supporting Naki
- Respects: Yamori, Naki

(Aogiri Tree, Tatara's direct subordinate)

Yumitsu Tomoe / The Grave Robber
巴 ユミツ（ともえ ゆみつ）/ 墓盗り（はかとり）

- Age: 16 (DOB 8/12) ♀ • Blood type: A • Height/weight: 150cm/46kg
- RC Type: Bikaku • Rate: A+ • Respects: Bin Brothers, Tatara
- Hobbies: Collecting beautiful bottles, looking at books about plants and flowers
- Ambition: Avenging the Bin Brothers • Hates: Kotaro Amon

*Ages are from the start of the year.

Quinxes Squad Organizational Chart

(Squad Leader)

● Kuki Urie
瓜江 久生 (うりえ くき)

Rank 1 Investigator (Class 77)
Matsuri Washu, S2 Squad Member (Mentor)

- Age: 20 (DOB 2/12) ♂ • Blood type: O • Height/weight: 175cm/72kg
- RC Type: Kokaku • Quinque: Ginkui (Bikaku – Rate SS) • Honors: Double White Wing Badge, Gold Osmanthus Badge • Currently: Getting ripped...

(Deputy Squad Leader)

● Saiko Yonebayashi
米林 才子 (よねばやし さいこ)

Rank 2 Investigator (Class 77)

- Age: 20 (DOB 9/4) ♀ • Blood type: B • Height/weight: 143cm/?2kg
- RC Type: Rinkaku • Quinque: Bokusatsu (Kokaku – Rate B)
- Currently: Developing into a fine woman

● Toma Higemaru
トウマ髯丸 (ひげまる とうま)

Rank 3 Investigator (Class 79)
1st Academy Junior

- Age: 18 (DOB 8/20) ♂ • Blood type: O • Height/weight: 167cm/59kg
- RC Type: Bikaku • Quinque: Higeonimaru (Bikaku – Rate A) • Honors: Awarded scholarship to CCG Academy • Hobbies: Collecting pins, researching CCG history, thinking about kaiju

● Xiǎo Jìng-Lì
小静麗 （シャオ・ジンリ）

Rank 1 Investigator (Class 76)
Hakubi Garden

- Age: 18 (DOB 6/20) ♀ • Blood type: B • Height/weight: 167cm/58kg
- RC Type: Kokaku • Quinque: Kuai ¼ (Rinkaku – Rate A) • Honors: Single White Wing Badge • Hobbies: Ear cleaning (Yonebayashi's)

● Shinsanpei Aura
安浦 晋三平(あうら しんさんぺい)

Rank 2 Investigator (Class 79)
7th Academy Junior

- Age: 18 (DOB 11/18) ♂ • Blood type: AB • Height/weight: 185cm/85kg
- RC Type: Ukaku • Quinque: Tsunagi Hard (Bikaku – Rate C) • Honors: Awarded scholarship to CCG Academy • Hobbies: Magic, reading, fishing

TOKYO G

GHOUL:re

SUI ISHIDA is the author of the immensely popular *Tokyo Ghoul* and several *Tokyo Ghoul* one-shots, including one that won second place in the *Weekly Young Jump* 113th Grand Prix award in 2010. *Tokyo Ghoul:re* is the sequel to *Tokyo Ghoul*.

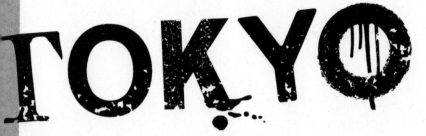

TOKYO G

Story and art by
SUI ISHIDA

First published in Japan in 2014 by SHUEISHA Inc., Tokyo.
English translation rights arranged by SHUEISHA Inc.

Translation Joe Yamazaki
Touch-Up Art & Lettering Vanessa Satone
Design Shawn Carrico
Editor Pancha Diaz

Printed in the U.S.A.

Published by VIZ Media, LLC
P.O. Box 77010
San Francisco, CA 94107

10 9 8 7 6 5 4 3 2 1
First printing, August 2018

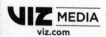

VIZ MEDIA
viz.com

VIZ SIGNATURE
vizsignature.com

ratings.viz.com
RATED T+ OLDER TEEN

PARENTAL ADVISORY
TOKYO GHOUL: RE is rated T+ for Older Teen and is recommended for ages 16 and up. This volume contains violence and gore.

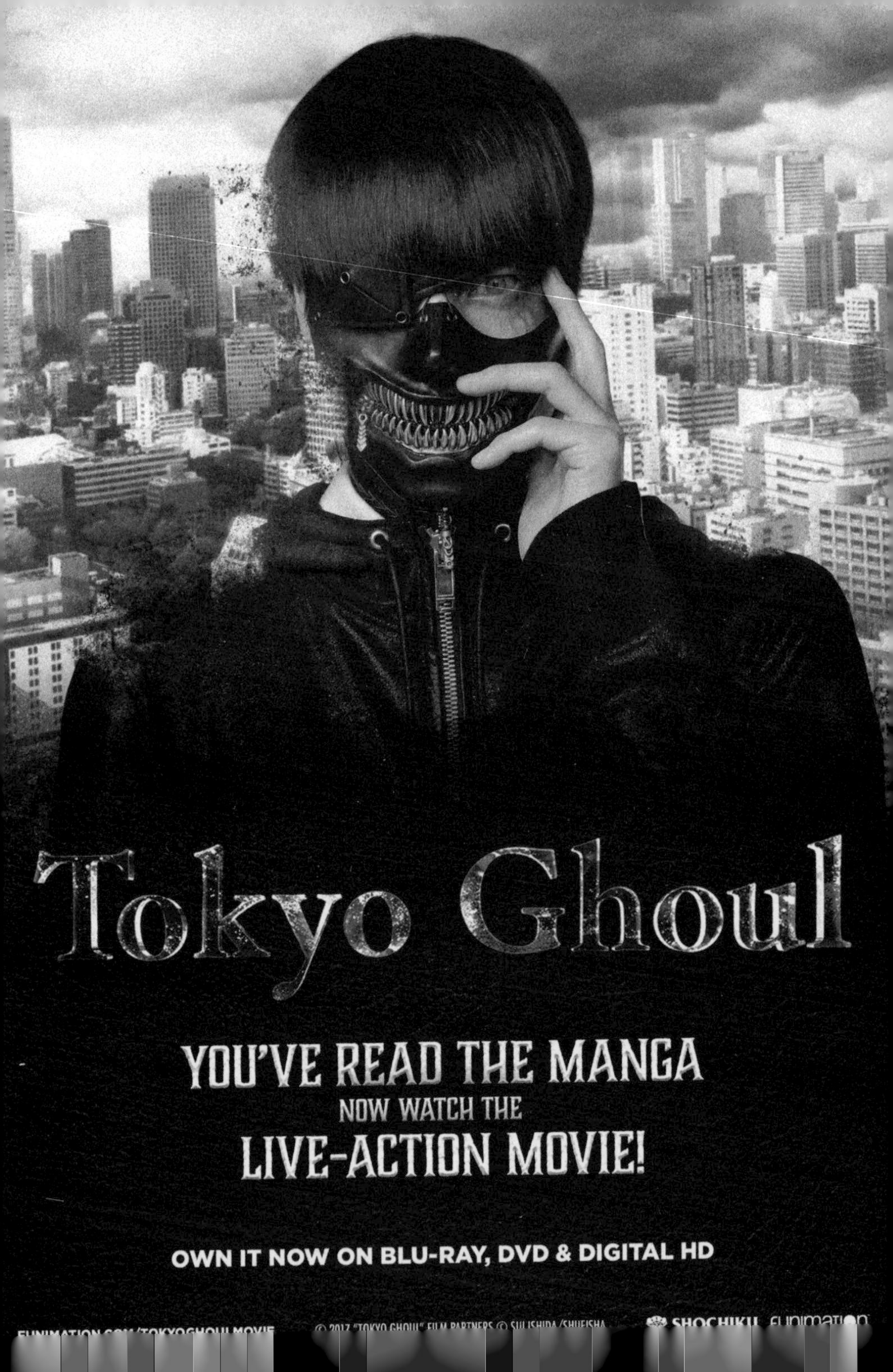
Tokyo Ghoul
YOU'VE READ THE MANGA
NOW WATCH THE
LIVE-ACTION MOVIE!
OWN IT NOW ON BLU-RAY, DVD & DIGITAL HD
FUNIMATION.COM/TOKYOGHOULMOVIE
© 2017 "TOKYO GHOUL" FILM PARTNERS © SUI ISHIDA/SHUEISHA
SHOCHIKU
funimation

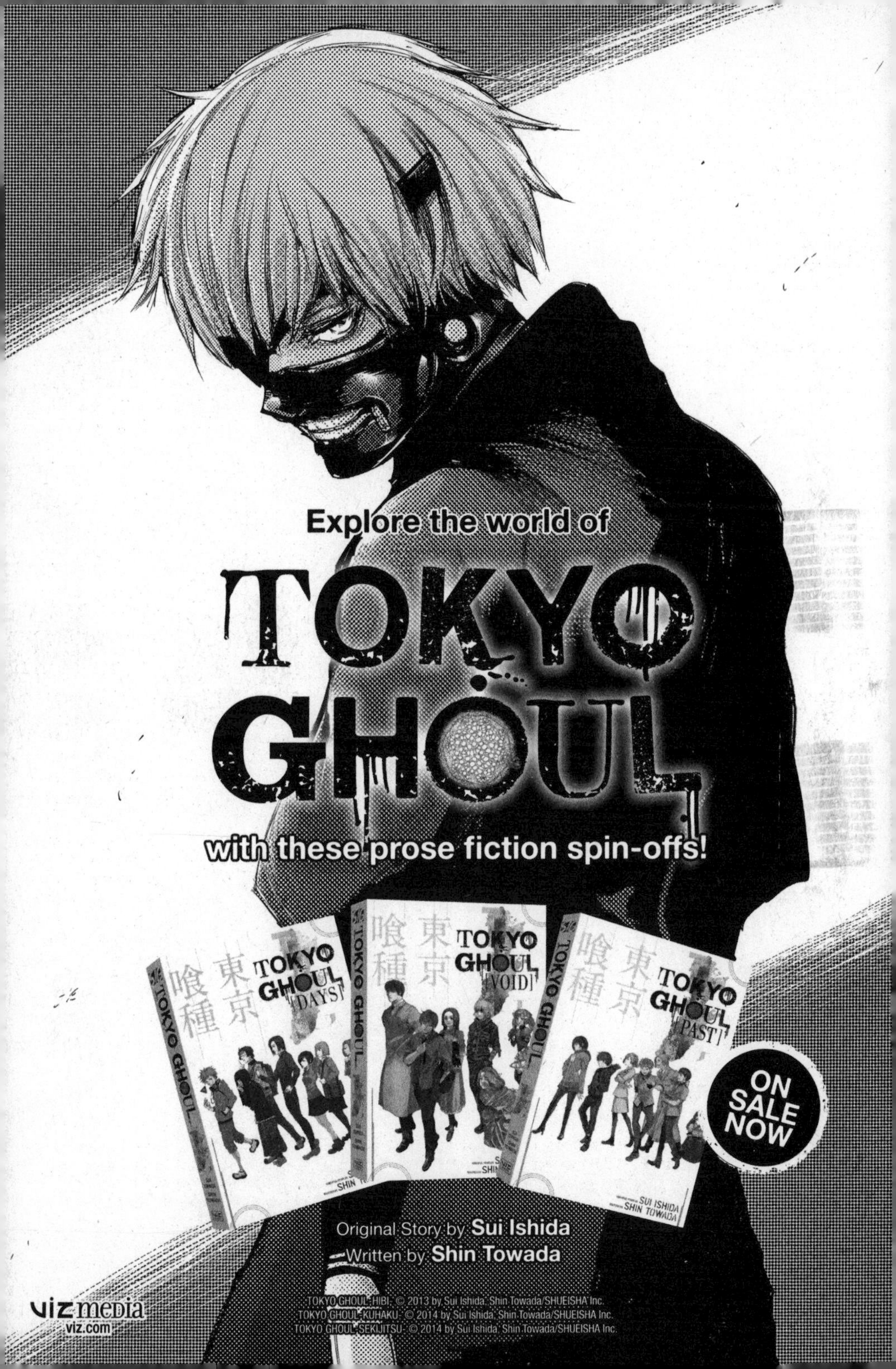
Explore the world of
TOKYO GHOUL
with these prose fiction spin-offs!
TOKYO GHOUL [DAYS]
TOKYO GHOUL [VOID]
TOKYO GHOUL [PAST]
ON SALE NOW
Original Story by Sui Ishida
Written by Shin Towada
viz media
viz.com
TOKYO GHOUL -HIBI- © 2013 by Sui Ishida, Shin Towada/SHUEISHA Inc.
TOKYO GHOUL -KUHAKU- © 2014 by Sui Ishida, Shin Towada/SHUEISHA Inc.
TOKYO GHOUL -SEKIJITSU- © 2014 by Sui Ishida, Shin Towada/SHUEISHA Inc.

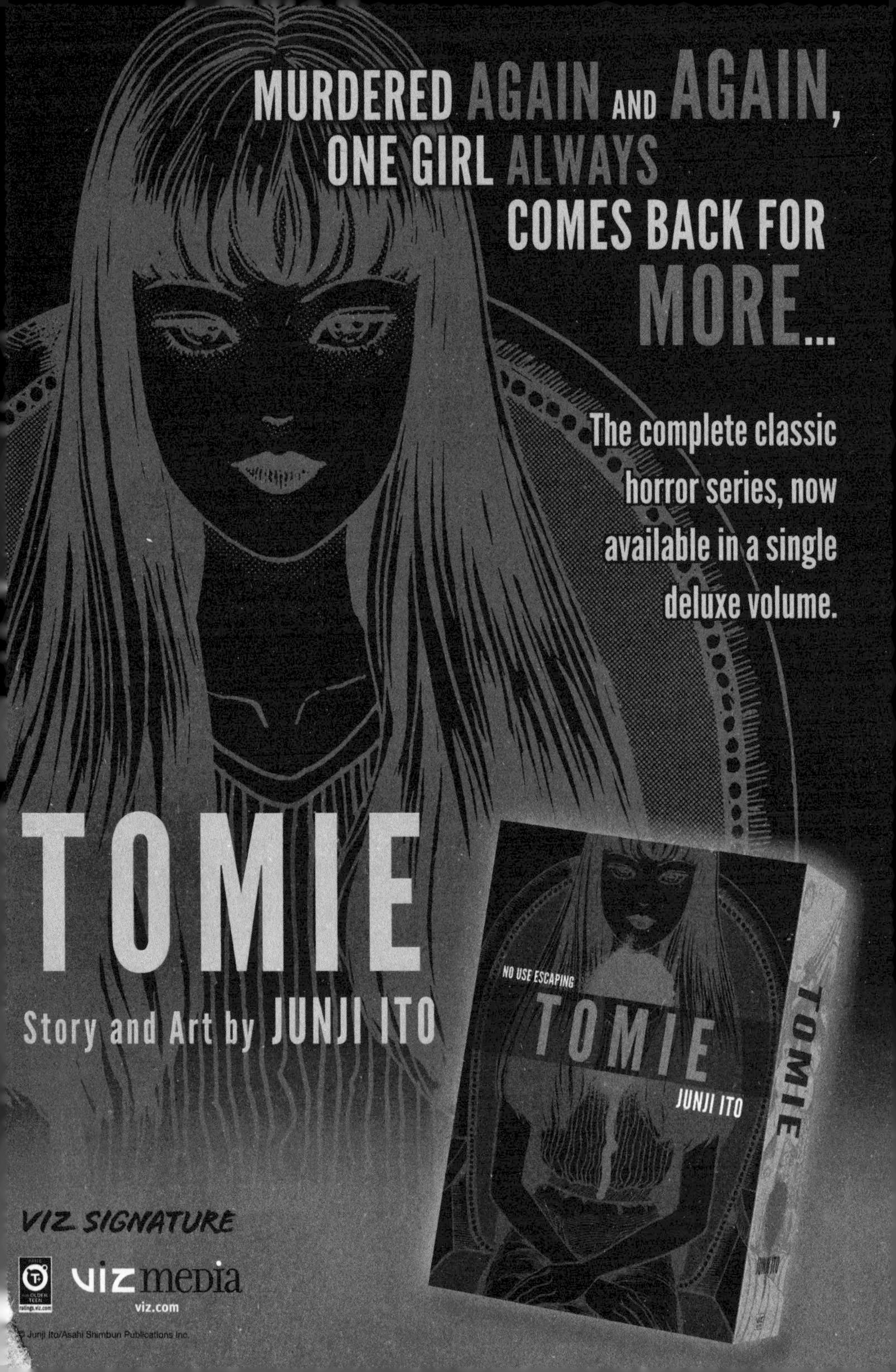
MURDERED AGAIN AND AGAIN,
ONE GIRL ALWAYS
COMES BACK FOR
MORE...
The complete classic horror series, now available in a single deluxe volume.
TOMIE
Story and Art by JUNJI ITO
NO USE ESCAPING
TOMIE
JUNJI ITO
TOMIE
VIZ SIGNATURE
VIZ media
viz.com
© Junji Ito/Asahi Shimbun Publications Inc.

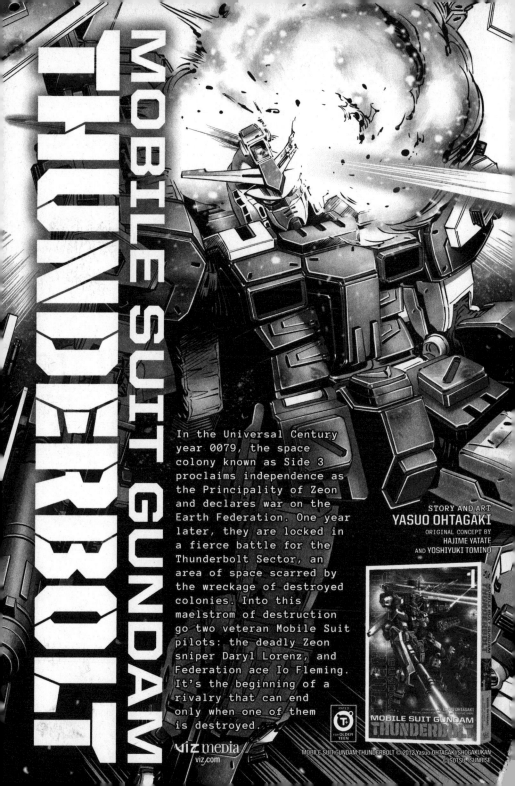

MOBILE SUIT GUNDAM THUNDERBOLT

In the Universal Century year 0079, the space colony known as Side 3 proclaims independence as the Principality of Zeon and declares war on the Earth Federation. One year later, they are locked in a fierce battle for the Thunderbolt Sector, an area of space scarred by the wreckage of destroyed colonies. Into this maelstrom of destruction go two veteran Mobile Suit pilots: the deadly Zeon sniper Daryl Lorenz, and Federation ace Io Fleming. It's the beginning of a rivalry that can end only when one of them is destroyed.

STORY AND ART
YASUO OHTAGAKI

ORIGINAL CONCEPT BY
HAJIME YATATE
AND YOSHIYUKI TOMINO

MOBILE SUIT GUNDAM
THUNDERBOLT

viz media
viz.com

TOKYO GHOUL:re

This is the last page.
TOKYO GHOUL:re reads right to left.